REGULATORY FRAMEWORK IN INDIA
LAW AND POLICY

About the Author

Dr. Sapna Chadah is currently working as Assistant Professor in Constitutional & Administrative Law at the Indian Institute of Public Administration, New Delhi. She holds her Masters in Law (LL.M) from University of Delhi and Ph.D. from Jamia Millia Islamia, New Delhi. Her major areas of interest include Constitutional Law, Administrative Law, Consumer Protection Law and Policy, Environmental Management, Laws in Urban Management, Regulation of Service Sectors and Privatization. She was associated with a number of research studies in the area of consumer protection and consumer welfare. She has also been associated with Consultancy Project on "Promoting Involvement of Research Institutions/ Universities/Colleges in Consumer Protection and Consumer Welfare" sponsored by Department of Consumer Affairs. She has nine books, four monographs to her credit and published more than 30 papers in journals of repute.

REGULATORY FRAMEWORK IN INDIA

Law and Policy

Sapna Chadah

CONCEPT PUBLISHING COMPANY PVT. LTD.
NEW DELHI - 110 059

ISBN-13: 978-93-86682-07-9

First Published 2017

Published and Printed by

Concept
Since 1974

Concept Publishing Company Pvt. Ltd.
A/15-16, Commercial Block, Mohan Garden
New Delhi-110059 (India)
T: 25351460, 25351794
E: publishing@conceptpub.com, W: www.conceptpub.com

Cataloging in Publication Data--Courtesy: D.K. Agencies (P) Ltd. <docinfo@dkagencies.com>

Chadah, Sapna, author.
Regulatory framework in India : law and policy / Sapna Chadah.
pages cm
Includes bibliographical references and index.
ISBN 9789386682079

1. Insurance law--India. 2. Industrial laws and legislation--India. 3. Industrial laws and legislation. I. Title.

KNS931.C43 2017 DDC 346.54086 23

PREFACE AND ACKNOWLEDGEMENTS

'Regulation' refers to obligation imposed by public law designed to induce individuals and firms to outcomes which they would voluntarily reach. Regulation is largely enforced by public officials and compliance is aided by the threat or imposition of some sanction. As such regulation covers a vast array of state controls over industrial and commercial activities. Regulation is a necessary part of any civilized society. We need a basic framework of reasonable and fair rules and laws to protect all of us, whether as consumers or as citizens — even as companies. But when regulation simply becomes red tapism, we all suffer.

It is, however, in the context of privatization and liberalization that regulation has assumed a new role. Not only does it play a more central role, but it also obtains a wider and expanded base. The process of privatization or significant private sector participation in public domain involves a reinventing of Government's role from that of a producer to regulator. Control, in the form of regulation, aims at the protection of customers and the promotion of competition. Regulation, therefore, becomes the new "border" between Government and the industry.

The development paradigm in the early twentieth century emphasized on market failures, discontinuities, irreversibilities leading to excessive social inequality; and stressed on the need for the state to create adequate physical infrastructure, institutional and social conditions for development. This entailed implementing large scale public investment programmes, planning and policies aimed at social sectors' modernization such as education, health, social protection and housing policies to name a few. The period of 1970s was, however, a period of skepticism and alleged regulatory failure. Nationalized industries were perceived to be inefficient, much protective regulation was considered to be rigid, poorly targeted and inadequately enforced. The lack of sustained growth was held to be largely due to all pervasive state interference in the market process both internationally through trade protection and nationally through over-regulation of goods, capital and labour markets and extended state-ownership of national productive assets. Deficiencies in infrastructure quantity and quality imposed a heavy penalty in terms of growth and welfare. Private participation in infrastructure and restructuring was thus driven by the high costs and poor performance of state-owned utilities.

The free-market mania of the 1980s and 1990s further challenged the existing notions of how utilities should be owned, organized, and regulated. It was argued that regulation had outlived its value, and that the market should determine prices. Privatization and liberalization were recognized as the critical components of economic growth and reform. This raised a host of questions relating to creation of new institutions, structures and processes and what regulatory arrangements were appropriate. What followed subsequently was often called "deregulation and re-regulation", a period of transformation of regulatory forms and arrangements. It was also suggested that the traditional "command and control" form of regulation was inappropriate in certain contexts and was gradually to be replaced by forms of "co-regulation", industry contributing to some degree to the formulation of standards, self-certification and enforcement.

Thus, there was a change in the development strategy from state-led to market-oriented. A new concept of the 'regulatory state' now emerged against the more conventional categories of 'welfare' or 'provider' state. Recognizing infrastructure's importance, many countries have implemented far-reaching reforms over the past two decades — restructuring, encouraging private participation, and establishing new approaches to regulation. There has been a significant transformation in the style of natural monopoly regulation policies away from the previous almost exclusive reliance on public ownership. Once public ownership was hailed as a "reform", but now privatization has become a "reform". "Reform" today means deregulation, competition and privatization. There has been a radical shift in the focus of state intervention and a re-evaluation of the State's role even as a provider of core public services.

The withdrawal of governments from the role of producing and delivering services, and their assumption of the dual roles of enabling and regulating, are major changes in the way societies today provide for their needs. Governments enable private delivery of services through financing, subsidizing, promoting and contracting. They regulate by setting policy, legal frameworks and standards of operation. These new tasks are more difficult and complex than governments had before. New organizational structures have to be built and new skills imparted to carry out new functions, and new attitudes developed to displace a culture of risk avoidance and secrecy. There is a growing realization that privatization is not the end of Government participation but rather a new beginning; it is the process of rebalancing the role of the State to face the challenges of change. This should not be seen as an exit from governance; it calls for more governance and better quality governance. Success depends on creating institutional reforms and designing from scratch regulatory mechanisms for privatized utilities that provides a credible commitment to safeguarding the interests of both investors and customers.

The Government's deregulation initiative aims to ensure that legislation is limited to what is really necessary. Fewer, better and simpler regulations are all part of the Government's strategy to improve the competitiveness in the markets and to ensure individual's choice. The benefits of this will be balanced regulation which is economically and effectively enforced, raises standards and opens up markets while providing necessary protection for the public. However, not all regulations are on the decline. It was an irony of the privatization programme that deregulation brought with it so much new regulations in areas, such as environmental protection, public health and safety standards. What occurred was in fact an increase in the state's control through a move from production to regulation. This was the process through which the '*regulatory state*' was born. Coupled with this deregulation process is the development of new regulatory regimes, or re-regulation, which is aimed at facilitating competition and setting the new environment for the industry by emulating market mechanisms within the confines of accepted policy. The re-regulation process necessitates the reallocation of responsibility for regulatory governance and supervision of regulation, usually from the national service provider to the regulator. This reallocation process includes the complete separation of the previous regulatory functions and the operational functions of the national service providers.

Today, countries are moving towards "new style of regulation" which involves creation of separate regulatory entities with some degree of independent decision-making authority, whether final or advisory, over the traditional regulatory tasks. The world in which regulators operate continues to change, both with the pressure on business of a more competitive world, and the changing regulations that need to be enforced. As a society, we have increased expectations that regulations can and will protect consumers, businesses, workers and the environment, coupled with an increasing need to keep our businesses efficient and flexible to face new competitive challenges. Our regulatory system has the pivotal role in resolving the regular conflict between prosperity and protection. For this the regulator must be able to balance the interests of the operator, the users, and the Government without succumbing to pressures by one or more of these parties. To perform the functions effectively the regulators must possess sophisticated technical skills and capabilities. Further, the independence must be reconciled with measures to ensure that the regulator is accountable for its actions.

The book deals with legal and policy issues underpinning the development and strengthening of the regulatory and institutional framework for better governance. Main thrust of book is to study and analyze the changes introduced under the impact of liberalization, privatization and globalization on the system and sub-systems of governance from the perspective of economy, efficiency, effectiveness, ethics and equity. The main object of the book is to study the kind of new set of regulations and regulatory mechanisms which are emerging under the deregulation initiatives and their impact on various stakeholders from the perspective of administrative law.

I am thankful to my supervisor Late Prof. T.H. Khan, Professor of Law and Former Dean, Faculty of Law, Jamia Millia Islamia, New Delhi and co-supervisor Prof. S.S. Singh, Director, National Law Institute University, Bhopal, Madhya Pradesh for their constant encouragement and valuable guidance that enabled me to complete the work. They not only encouraged me for the work, but also consistently guided me in giving proper shape to the present work.

I am extremely thankful to the cooperation extended by the administrative staff of libraries of Jamia Millia Islamia, New Delhi; Indian Institute of Public Administration, New Delhi; Indian Law Institute, New Delhi; Faculty of Law, University of Delhi; and American Centre Library, New Delhi; for access to the documents and material without which it would have been difficult to complete the present work. I am also indebted to all those learned authors and jurists whose thoughts, information and treaties, I have consulted and utilized in the present work. I am really grateful to Mrs. Sunita Gulati, Deputy Librarian, IIPA and other staff of IIPA Library for procuring books and material for the present work and helping me in preparing the bibliography.

I am extremely thankful and grateful to the Research and Consultancy Unit of Insurance Regulatory and Development Authority at Hyderabad, especially Dr. D.V.S. Sastry, DG (R&D) who had taken a lot of interest and pain in providing valuable information on the working of the Insurance Regulatory and Development Authority.

I am thankful to Prof. Suresh Misra, Chair Professor (Consumer Affairs), Shri R.C. Mangla, Consultant and my other colleagues at the Indian Institute of Public Administration for their constant help and encouragement to complete the work.

I feel extremely dedicated to my parents, Shri S.K. Chadah and Dr. (Mrs.) Santosh Chadah, who have always encouraged me in all my pursuits. I would like to acknowledge their help, support and encouragement throughout the work. It is, but their patience and sacrifice without which I could not have completed the book.

My thanks are also due to Ms. Hema Rautela and Ms. Deepa Bisht, computer operators, for their secretarial assistance.

New Delhi **Sapna Chadah**

CONTENTS

LIST OF CASES

LIST OF ABBREVIATIONS

AAA	Agricultural Adjustment Administration
AAI	Airports Authority of India
ACUS	Administrative Conference of the United States
ADB	Asian Development Bank
AERA	Airports Economic Regulatory Authority
AIR	All India Reporter
APA	Administrative Procedure Act, 1946
APEC	Asia-Pacific Economic Cooperation
APM	Administered Price Mechanism
ASCI	Advertisement Standard Council of India
ASDA	Alternative Service Delivery Approaches
ASEAN	Association of Southeast Asian Nations
AT&T	American Telephone and Telegraph Company
BBC	British Broadcasting Corporation
BIFR	Bureau of Industrial Finance and Restructuring
BIS	Bureau of Indian Standards
BoT	Board of Trustees
BOT	Build-Operate-Transfer
BR	British Rail
BT	British Telecom
BTO	Build-Transfer-Operate
CAB	Civil Aeronautical Board
CAC	Central Advisory Committee
CC	Competition Commission
CCC	Civilian Conservation Corps
CCI	Competition Commission of India
CEGB	Central Electricity Generating Board
CERC	Central Electricity Regulatory Commission
CII	Chartered Institute of Insurance
CMAPP	Common Minimum Action Plan for Power
CPC	Civil Procedure Code
CPJ	Consumer Protection Judgments
CWA	Civil Works Administration
DG	Director General
DGES	Director General for Electricity Supply

DGGS	Director General of Gas Supply
DGT	Director General of Telecommunications
DoT	Department of Transport
DTI	Department of Trade and Industry
EPA	Environment Protection Agency
ERC	Electricity Regulatory Commission
ESI	Employee's State Insurance
EU	European Union
FCC	Federal Communication Commission
FDI	Foreign Direct Investment
FERA	Federal Emergency Relief Administration
FMC	Forward Markets Commission
FOCs	Freight-Operating Companies
FOIR	Forum of Indian Regulators
FSA	Farm Security Administration
FSA	Financial Services Authority
FSSAI	Food Safety and Standards Authority of India
FTC	Federal Trade Commission
GATT	General Agreement on Tariffs and Trade
GIC	General Insurance Corporation
GoI	Government of India
GRA	Grievance Redressal Authority
IAIS	International Association of Insurance Supervisors
IBA	Independent Broadcasting Authority
IBA	Insurance Broker Association of India
IBNR	Incurred But Not Reported
ICC	Interstate Commerce Commission
IIISLA	Indian Institute of Insurance Surveyors and Loss Assessors
IIRM	Institute of Insurance and Risk Management
IMF	International Monetary Fund
IMRO	Investment Management Regulatory Organization
INPRS	International Network of Pension Regulators and Supervisors
IRDA	Insurance Regulatory and Development Authority
KB	King's Bench
KYC	Know Your Customer
LATAs	Local Access and Transport Areas
LECs	Local Exchange Carriers
LIC	Life Insurance Corporation
LPG	Liberalization, Privatization and Globalization
MCA	Motor Carrier Act
MMC	Monopolies and Mergers Commission
MoF	Ministry of Finance

MPT	Major Port Trusts
MRTP	Monopolies and Restrictive Trade Practices
MRTPC	Monopolies and Restrictive Trade Practices Commission
MSR	Multi-sector Regulator
NAV	Net Asset Value
NCDRC	National Consumer Disputes Redressal Commission
NC	National Commission
NEDO	National Economic Development Office
NEP	National Electricity Policy
NGC	National Grid Company
NIRA	National Industrial Recovery Act
NLB	National Labour Board
NLRA	National Labour Relations Act
NLRB	National Labour Relations Board
NPM	New Public Management
NPR	National Performance Review
NRA	National Rivers Authorities
NRA	National Recovery Administration
NRAs	National Regulatory Agencies
NTP	National Telecom Policy
OCC	Oil Coordination Council
OECD	Organization for Economic Cooperation and Development
OFCOM	Office of Communications
OFFER	Office of Electricity Regulation
OFGAS	Officer of Gas Supply
OFGEM	Office for Gas and Electricity Markets
OFT	Office of Fair Trading
OFTEL	Office of Telecommunications
OFWAT	Office of Water Services
OIRA	Office of Information and Regulatory Affairs
OMB	Office of Management and Budget
OPRAF	Office of Rail Passenger Franchising
ORR	Office of the Rail Regulator
OSHA	Occupational Safety and Health Administration
PFDRA	Pension Fund Regulatory and Development Authority
PIA	Personal Investment Authority
PNGRB	Petroleum and Natural Gas Regulatory Board
PPP	Public Private Partnership
PTT	Post, Telegraph and Telecommunications Utilities
PWA	Public Works Administration
QCI	Quality Council of India
RA	Resettlement Administration

RARG	Regulatory Analysis Review Group
RBI	Reserve Bank of India
RBOCs	Regional Bell Operating Companies
REA	Rural Electrification Administration
RECs	Regional Electricity Companies
RFA	Regulatory Flexibility Analysis
ROSCOs	Rolling Stock Companies
RPC	Rail Passengers Council
RROs	Regulatory Reform Orders
RT	Railtrack
SAFIR	South Asia Forum for Infrastructure Regulation
SAT	Securities Appellate Tribunal
SBA	Small Business Administration
SBREFA	Small Business Regulatory Enforcement Fairness Act
SC	Supreme Court
SCC	Supreme Court Cases
SEBI	Securities and Exchange Board of India
SEBs	State Electricity Boards
SERC	State Electricity Regulatory Commission
SFA	Securities and Futures Authority
SME	Small and Medium-scale Enterprises
SRA	Strategic Rail Authority
SROs	Self-Regulating Organizations
SSRs	Single-Sector Regulators
TAC	Tariff Advisory Committee
TAMP	Tariff Authority for Major Ports
TDSAT	Telecom Disputes Settlement and Appellate Tribunal
TELRIC	Total Element Long-Run Incremental Cost
THC	Terminal Handling Charges
TOCs	Train-Operating Companies
TPA	Third Party Administrator
TRAI	Telecom Regulatory Authority of India
TVA	Tennessee Valley Authority
UGC	University Grants Commission
UK	United Kingdom
ULIP	Unit Linked Insurance Plan
UNCTAD	United Nations Conference on Trade and Development
UNDP	United Nations Development Programme
USA	United States of America
USHA	United States Housing Authority
WB	World Bank
WPA	Works Progress Administration

1

INTRODUCTION

1.1. Background

The elected legislatures enshrine state policy in the laws they pass. The implementation of these laws by the executive requires formulation of rules and regulations etc. to take care of all the contingencies that law has to deal with from time-to-time. Neither the law nor the rules and regulations framed thereunder can take care of all the contingencies and situations. Hence, the regulator is always provided with discretionary power to frame regulations to deal with matters ranging from very major to very minor depending on the domain of the law. The system of implementation as a part of the Government department is called as old style regulation. When the whole or part of the implementation is transferred to an "independent regulatory agency" we have new style of regulation. In such a transfer, the rule-making powers enjoyed earlier by the old-style regulator must be transferred to the newly-formed independent regulator. To the extent the law is loosely drafted and leaves flexibility in implementation, the new-style regulator must be able to set out the necessary rules and regulations. However, the executive could also transfer merely the execution without the rule-making powers. In that event, the very need for such a new agency must be questioned.

Since, 1980s deregulation and contracting out of governmental functions, services and responsibilities have reverberated around the world under the impact and influence of liberalization, privatization and globalization (LPG). The shift of power from the public to the private sector has profound implications for public law. Countries have gone further in the direction of a customer/contractor structure, with diminishing core Ministries and a large amount of privatization, creation of executive agencies and contracting with the private sector under the influence of the market ideology. But privatization and liberalization has not resulted in complete withdrawal of the state from the market; the

State has merely reformed. To the reformation it has assumed a more overt regulatory role *vis-à-vis* economic power. There has been a shift in the perceived role of government from acting as the principal vehicle for socio-economic development to guiding and facilitating that development. Accordingly, while policy formulation remains one of the main functions of government, the role of the government in implementing policy decisions is changing. It has been observed that economic liberalization brings with it an increased requirement for regulatory activity. What we see is not that total retreat of the State, but rather the substitution of one form of involvement by the State in the economy for another. It is, therefore, performing the functions of supervision and monitoring, as the process of deregulation, required to be regulated with more care and caution.

With privatization and liberalization an array of regulatory agencies have spawned which carry with them rule-making and rate-making powers, grievance redressal powers in addition to their general powers of promoting competition and efficiency. Access to justice and resolution of grievances is beginning to be seen as an inherent feature of regulation. The countries like U.K. and New Zealand or for that purpose the member countries of European Union, are beginning to witness participation in standard setting. To the Indian context the increased role played by the Consumer Courts in the area of improving the quality and standards of goods and services may be seen in this perspective. Access to justice has become far more closely involved with regulatory activity. However, the experience in other countries reveals that the privatization programme has not served to minimize the role of the State and to augment the private sector. On the other hand, it has effected a confusion of public-private, has produced more comprehensive regulatory activity by public authorities and has introduced access to justice as an inherent part of that regulation.

1.2. Reasons for Emergence of Regulations

Process of industrial and economic changes is primarily responsible for the emergence of regulations. Scientific and technological advancements have further increased the rate of industrialization and urbanization of the population. The forces of industrialization and urbanization club together set in motion a chain of trends and events. For example, improvement in transport system, air, land and water helped to create regional and national markets and the population became increasingly mobile. Industrial centres became centres of attraction for discontented rural population. This phenomenon resulted in the increase of migration. The steady stream of immigrants provided a source of cheap labour for industries and traders. During the period of 1870s and 1880s dissatisfied groups such as farmers, small businessmen and working class people had started unionization to demand lowering of working hours and increase in their wages. Protests and demands had also organized demanding Government's intervention for protection of rural interests. The agitations had also started to protect the interests of working class people from abusive and discriminatory practices followed by the industry and trade. In USA such prolonged protest resulted into the enactment of the Interstate Commerce Act, 1887, which established the first Independent National Commission for the regulation of economic affairs.[1]

Regulation is largely a product of the clash of organized private economic interests seeking to utilize governmental powers for enhancement of private interests. It is a subject matter of study in the fields of political science, economics and law. Each of these areas clarifies important aspects of the subject matter. It may, however, be added that the purpose of regulation is to prescribe, promote and prohibit certain actions of producers of goods and providers of services. The literature on economics has traditionally been devoted on regulation of specific industries or group of industries. Theoretical developments in this regard assess the incentive and welfare elements of alternative policy instruments. The focus of law literature has been on enforcement of market rules and administrative procedure. The political science literature considered political and administrative dimensions of policy formulation and implementation. The study of regulation in economics prior to 1970 has emphasized pricing problems encountered in the utility industries — electricity, communication, transportation and finance. Much attention has been given to pricing with increasing returns to scale technology. Discussion has also centred on section of prices to assure the utility of a particular rate of return on its capital investment and on the related problem of maintaining incentives for cost minimization. With the growth of regulations, administrative law has grown and developed tremendously in quantity, quality and relative significance, in the twentieth century. It has become more articulate and definitive as a system in mature democracies like U.K. and U.S.A. and has assumed a more recognizable form in that century. As a result, it has come to be identified as a branch of public law by itself, distinct and separate from constitutional law, a fit subject matter of independent study and investigation in its own right.[2]

The rapid growth of administrative law during the period of 1920-1980 can partly be attributed to the critical international and internal situation leading to a sense of insecurity. This compelled the government to acquire vast powers for the defence of the country, particularly in an emergency, to provide for economic regulation and to maintain law and order within the country. Increased powers of government departments after First World War in England and New Deal Legislations during economic depression in U.S.A. are often cited as chief reasons for fast growth of administrative law. For example, in India, the Maintenance of Internal Security Act, 1971, confers vast discretionary powers on the administration to interfere with the personal freedom of the people. But, mainly, the growth of administrative law is to be attributed to a change of philosophy as to the role and function of the state. The ruling political gospel of the nineteenth century was *laissez faire*, which manifested itself in the theories of individualism, individual enterprise, and self-help.[3] The philosophy envisaged minimum government control, maximum free enterprise and contractual freedom. The state was characterized as the "law and order" state and its role was conceived to be negative as its interest extended primarily to defending the country from external aggression, maintaining law and order within the country, dispensing justice to its subjects and collecting a few taxes to finance these activities. It was an era of free enterprise and minimum governmental responsibility and functions. The management of social and economic life was not regarded as government responsibility.

It may, however, be mentioned that the *laissez faire* doctrine resulted in human misery. It came to be realized that the bargaining position of every person was not equal and uncontrolled contractual freedom led to exploitation of the weaker by the stronger, e.g. of the labour by the management in industries. On the one hand, slums, unhealthy and dangerous conditions of work, child labour, widespread poverty, and exploitation of masses, and on the other hand, concentration of wealth in a few hands, became the order of the day. It came to be pleaded that the state should take interest in ameliorating the conditions of the poor. This gave rise to the political dogma of "collectivism" which favoured state intervention in and social control and regulation of, individual enterprise.[4] The state started acting in the interest of social justice and assumed a "positive" role. In course of time, out of the dogma of collectivism emerged the concept of the "social welfare state", or "benevolent state", which promotes socio-economic welfare of the people.[5]

This trend may be illustrated very forcefully by reference to the position in India. Before 1947, India was a police state. The ruling foreign power was primarily interested in strengthening its own domination. The administrative machinery was used mainly with that object in view and the civil service came to be designated as the "steel frame". The state did not concern itself much with the welfare of the people. However, with the advent of Independence, the position in India underwent a great change. A conscious effort began to be made to transform the country into a welfare state. The philosophy of welfare state has been expressly ingrained in the Constitution of India. The Constitution aims at establishing a sovereign, democratic, socialist, secular republic in India so as to secure to all its citizens, *inter alia*, social, economic and political justice. The state is put under an obligation to strive to secure a social order in which social, economic and political justice[6] shall inform all the institutions of national life.[7] The state is required to direct its policy towards securing that the citizens have equal rights to an adequate means of livelihood; that the ownership and control of the material resources of the community are so distributed as best to subserve the common good; that there is no concentration of wealth and means of production to the common detriment; and that there is equal pay for equal work.[8] The state is obligated to provide for education and assistance in old age, in unemployment and in other contingencies.[9] The state is to provide for free and compulsory education for children up to the age of fourteen years.[10] Further, in interpretation of the law and the Constitution, the judiciary does at times take note of the ideals of a social welfare state even though some of the ideals may not be expressly incorporated in the Constitution.[11]

The emergence of the social welfare concept has affected the democracies very profoundly. It has led to state activism. There has occurred a phenomenal increase in the area of state operation. The state has taken over a number of functions, which were previously left to private enterprise and pervaded every aspect of human life. It started running buses, railways and postal services. It engaged in planning of social and economic life of the community with a view to raise the living standards of the people and reduces concentration of wealth. It improves slums, plans urban and rural life, looks after health, morals and education of the people. It started generating electricity, works mines and operates key and important industries. It acts as an active instrument of socio-economic policy, regulates individual life and freedom to a large extent, provides many benefits to its citizens[12] and imposes social control and regulation over private enterprise. The functions of a social welfare state may broadly be placed into five categories, *viz*. the state as protector, provider, entrepreneur, economic controller and arbiter.[13] The ideal of a social welfare state is sought to be translated into practice through state planning of economic resources and social control of private enterprise with a view to create a socialistic pattern of society. It involves improving the economic condition of the people keeping in view the demands of social justice and all resources of the community are organized and husbanded with that end in view. A large number of government enterprises have thus come to be started and some key industries, financial institutions and transport services have been nationalized. Increasing provision is being made by the state for social services such as education, housing and health and the state is required to arrange for foodstuffs for the people. A rigorous system of state control and regulation of private enterprise has thus been created.[14] The state also plays a major role in promoting socio-economic welfare of labour by regulating the employer-employee relationship and by other means.[15]

This state activism has led to one inevitable result. In its quest to improve physical, moral and economic welfare of the people, the state has assumed more and more powers. The state activism has led to largest extension in depth and range of functions and powers mainly at the level of executive-*cum*-administrative organ. We have come to live in an administrative age; administrative organ has become predominant and state emerged as "administrative state". Administration became the all-pervading feature of life. The truth is that the administration had acquired an immense accession of power and has come to discharge functions which are varied and multifarious in scope, nature and ambit. In the words of Robson, the hegemony of the executive is now an accomplished fact. The administration impinges more and more on the individual. It had assumed a tremendous capacity to affect the rights and liberties of the people in all spheres of their life.[16]

Political preference of last two decades, for whatever the reasons, emphasize private sector autonomy and non-governmental or market solutions to the problems and difficulties of all descriptions. To be more precise, since 1980s, major changes occurred in the world politics. In support of these changes conservatives have argued that Government have grown too fat and must be reduced. In opposition, however, liberals have contended that the conservatives' campaign for efficiency through market prescriptions is really intended to do away with the welfare state, its institutions and policies. Government employees' unions, on the other hand, have sensed, in economic globalization arguments, an effort to eliminate their jobs.[17] Claims and counter-claims apart, the fact is that the influence of market is growing and growing fast. Australia, New Zealand and United Kingdom have gone further in the direction of a customer/contractor structure, with diminishing core Ministries and throwing open a large number of areas to market forces to transact heretofore governmental business.[18] These changes are having impact, on our country too since July 1991 with the "economic liberalization". The impact of market ideology on government are broadly described as the new way of governance, government by the market,[19] reinventing government,[20] new public management,[21] sharing power,[22] slimming of state,[23] the hollowing out of the state,[24] really reinventing government,[25] downsizing, right sizing etc. This has lead to the emergence of new phase in administration/governance characterized as the phase of deregulation and re-regulation of socio-economic activities in the developed and developing societies. The change introduced in 1980s is also described as Liberalization, Privatization and Globalization (LPG).

Main thrust of the changes introduced under the impact of liberalization, privatization and globalization on the system and sub-systems of governance has been seen from the perspective of economy, efficiency, effectiveness, ethics and equity.[26] These concerns of change in reform process with varying degree of emphasis, are being promoted by a number of International Organizations, *viz.* IMF, World Bank, GATT, OECD countries, UNDP, ADB etc. to be internalized by the member states of the United Nations. In view of these changes, *the main object of the proposed study is — to study the new set of regulations in the insurance sector and its impact on the stakeholders.*

1.3. Regulation: Conceptual Consideration

The term 'regulation' is a dynamic process, having no accepted or straightforward definition. On one hand it connotes specific legal mechanisms to control deficiencies or exploitation by producers or service providers and on the other extreme it is a regime that controls the economy or a particular type of capitalism (free market, neo-liberal capitalism etc.). The term has multiple interpretations influenced by the country of origin and level of aggregation (firm, industry, economy or international). In Europe, regulation typically refers to whole realm of legislation, governance, and social control, whereas in the United States regulation has a more specific meaning, namely sustained and focused control exercised by public agency over activities that are generally regarded as desirable to society. Moreover, in Europe, policy-makers are traditionally skeptical of the efficiency of market mechanisms in recurrent crisis situations. Under such conditions nationalization was preferred to regulation. Another difference is that while in both continents the principal purpose of regulation has been to protect and promote the public 'interest', in the United States there is preference for specialist, independent agencies that are bestowed with regulatory powers. In Europe, and even more so in developing countries, regulatory power typically resides with the relevant state department or government ministry.[27]

The term 'regulation' has been defined differently among policy researchers for different purposes. Regulation is a subject, which calls for a multidisciplinary approach. It has stimulated interest in a number of disciplines like law, economics, political science, sociology, history, psychology, geography, management and public administration. Regulation may be restrictive in nature, restricting and preventing occurrence of undesirable activities or have an enabling or facilitative effect.

Regulation is spoken of as if an identifiable and discrete mode of governmental activity.[28] Selznick's notion of regulation is sustained and focused control exercised by a public agency over the activities that are valued by a community.[29] According to the Latin root, the word '*regula*' means a rule. The *Oxford English Dictionary* defines '*regulate*' as "to control or direct by means of rules and restrictions". In *Black Law Dictionary*, 'regulation' is defined as the act of regulating; a rule or order prescribed for management of Government; a regulating principle; a precept, rule or order prescribed by superior or competent authority relating to action of those under its control. In Corpus *Juris Secundum*,[30] it has been provided that the power to regulate carries with it full power over thing subject to regulation and, in the absence of restrictive words, the power must be regarded as plenary or in the interest of public. It has been held to contemplate or employ the continued existence of the subject matter. In *Craise on Statute Law*, it is stated that if the legislation enables something to be done, it gives power at the same time "by necessary implication, to do everything, which is indispensable for the purpose of carrying out the purposes in view". Thus, the legislation sets out the objectives it seeks to achieve and lays down the responsibilities, authorities and penalties and the regulator has to formulate the rules, principles etc. in order to carry them out.

The legislative power is the power to lay down the law for people in general whereas administrative power is the power to implement the law to achieve its propose. However, the administration also now laying down the law for larger number of people and the power is as much legislative. Measured by volume, more legislation is produced by the executive government than by the legislatures. Parliament is obligated to delegate very extensive law-making power over matters of details and to content itself with providing framework of more or less permanent statutes. Law making power is then vested in local authorities, utility regulators, professional bodies and various other authorities authorized by Parliament to make regulations. Parliament does not follow any particular policy in choosing the forms of delegated legislation, and there is wide range of variety and nomenclature. An Act may empower an authority to make regulation, rules or bye-laws, to make orders or to give directions. The term 'regulation' refers to various instruments by which Governments impose requirements on enterprises and citizens. It, thus, embraces laws, formal and informal orders, administrative guidance and subordinate rules issued by all levels of government, as well as rules issued by non-governmental or professional self-regulatory bodies to which Governments have delegated regulatory powers.[31] Thus, the use of the term 'regulation' is not confined only to the delegated legislation produced either by the administration or by public sector undertakings. Today, it is evident that the use of the term 'regulation' is available in context of legislative enactments as well as subordinate legislation. A case has been taken by our Constitution to dispel the doubt in this regard under Article 13(3)(a) which defines Law as *'law' includes any ordinance, order, bye-law, rule, regulation, notification, custom or usage having in the territory of India the force of law.*

In *K. Ramanathan* vs. *State of T.N.*[32] it was held that the word 'regulation' cannot have any rigid or inflexible meaning as to exclude 'prohibition'. The word 'regulate' is difficult to define as having any precise meaning. It is a word of broad import, having a broad meaning, and is very comprehensive in scope. There is a diversity of opinion as to its meaning and its application to a particular state of facts, some courts giving to the term a somewhat restricted, and others giving to it a liberal construction. In *St. Johns Teachers Training Institute* vs. *Regional Director*[33] it was held that a 'Regulation' is a rule or order prescribed by a superior for the management of some business and implies a rule of general course of action. Rules and regulations are all comprised in delegated legislation. It was held in *Air India Statutory Corporation* vs. *United Labour Union*[34] "The legislature passes laws within the overall Constitutional framework. These laws are state policy. Its implementation is by the executive. The person(s) implementing the laws are regulators who are regulating the implementation. A regulator must convert the legislation into rules, regulations, and procedures that make it possible to achieve the intentions of the legislation. Legislation can lay down general directions or it can be very detailed. In whichever manner the legislation may be drafted, every implementing bureaucrat exercises varying degrees of discretionary authority as he interprets the law."

In *U.P. Power Corporation Ltd.* vs. *National Thermal Power Corp. Ltd.*,[35] it was held that the power to regulate implies power to prescribe and enforce all such proper and reasonable rules and regulations as may be deemed necessary to conduct the business in a proper and orderly manner. It also includes the authority to prescribe the reasonable rules, regulations or conditions subject to which the business may be permitted or may be conducted. In *Hotel & Restaurant Assn.* vs. *Star India (P) Ltd.*,[36] in regard to the role of TRAI as a regulator, the Court held, the role of a regulator may be varied. A regulation may provide for cost, supply of service on non-discriminatory basis, the mode and manner of supply making provision for fair competition providing for a level playing field, protection of consumers' interest, prevention of monopoly. The services to be provided for through cable operators are also recognized. While making the regulations, several factors are, thus required to be taken into account. The interest of one of the players in the field would not be taken into consideration throwing the interest of others to the wind.

Meier defined regulation as "any attempt by the government to control the behaviour of citizens, corporations, or sub-governments".[37] In their study of Government regulations, Organization for Economic Cooperation and Development (OECD) researchers also used a short definition as "the diverse set of instruments by which Governments set requirements on enterprises and citizens".[38] On the other hand, Baldwin, Scott and Hood explained regulation in three senses:[39]

1. **Specific Set of Commands** — Where regulation involves promulgation of binding set of rules to be applied by a body devoted for that purpose.
2. **Deliberate State Interventions** — Herein the regulation is used in a much broader sense, covering all state actions designed to influence industrial or social behaviour. This would include within its ambit besides the command based regime, the other mode of influences like economic incentives in form of taxes

or subsidies, contractual powers, deployment of resources, franchises supply of information, etc.

3. **All Forms of Social Control or Influences** — Wherein all mechanisms affecting the behaviour are regulatory whether these are state driven or from other sources like market. In this kind of usage the regulatory effect need not be deliberate and designed and may be merely incidental to other objectives.

1.3.1. *Regulation in Political Science*

The political science literature stresses the political and administrative context of regulatory decision-making. Political input into the regulatory process occurs through lobbying and legislative decision-making, which establishes and monitors activities of regulatory authorities. Further, public negotiations occur in the implementation of regulatory policy. Regulation as defined by Mitnick is the public administrative policing of a private activity with respect to a rule prescribed in public interest.[40] It may, however, be mentioned that Mitnick concept of public interest is sufficiently general to encompass both welfare maximization and capture theories of regulation. For Mitnick government regulators act as agents with consumers or interest groups as their principal. He stresses that justification of regulation by public interest arguments is often rhetorical, the object being to give the appearance of a consensus to legislative, administrative and judicial decision making, even when special favours are being granted. Formulation and implementation of policy is an important aspect of regulation receiving considerable attention in political science. The implementation process as summed up by Ripley and Franklin "Bargaining — at the heart of American politics — occurs during implementation".[41] They emphasize that the government rarely involves command and control. Rather interest groups participate at each level of policy formulation, supervision and implementation. They divide regulatory policies "as competitive and protective". The former refer to allocation of franchises or the right to serve by a government agency; the latter "are designed to protect the public by setting the conditions under which various private activities can occur". Meier defines regulation as "any attempt by the government to control the behaviour of citizens, corporations or sub-governments", and lists price regulation, franchising, standard setting, direct allocation of resources, provision of subsidies and promotion of fair competition.[42] He emphasizes a multi-disciplinary approach that includes economics, law, history and political science. He states "above all, however, regulation is a political process involving political actors seeking political ends." The political science literature can make an important contribution to legal analysis of regulation through its emphasis on policy implementation.

1.3.2. *Regulation in Economics*

The classic text of Kahn, a major comprehensive work observes "the essence of regulation is the explicit replacement of competition with governmental orders as the principal institutional device for assuring good performance". He defines public utility regulation by the actions of regulators, "direct governmental prescription of major aspects of their structure and economic performance . . . control of entry price fixing, prescription of quality and conditions of service and the imposition of an obligation to serve all applicants under reasonable conditions. . .". Kahn's definition is based on the regulatory experience in public utility industries and does not generalize easily to encompass extensions of regulation to such areas as environmental pollution and workplace safety.[43]

Shephered and Wilcox[44] state, "Regulation is what regulators do". Their regulation text divides "public policies towards business" into antitrust, regulation and public enterprise. They concentrate on utilities in the energy sector, communication, transportation and urban services. The emphasis is on the policy-makers and their interaction with the regulated firms. The broadest definition of regulation is supplied by Stigler.[45] "As a rule, regulation is acquired by the industry and is designed and operated primarily for its benefit". Regulation for Stigler is the use of "power to coerce" by the state. Thus, regulation can take utmost any form to achieve the desired aim of an industry, which is ultimately to increase its profitability. He 'identifies' four principal kinds of regulations that are demanded by industry and supplied by the state: direct subsides of money, control of new entry, policies that promote complementary goods and discourage substitutes and control of prices. He, however, expanded his definition further to cover "the entire interface of public-private relations", including not only "such old fashioned fields as public utilities and antitrust policy", but also "public interventions in the resource market", "money raising and disbursement", "public interventions in the production, sale or purchase of goods and services", as well as legal institutions".[46]

In USA, since the founding of the Environmental Protection Agency (EPA) in 1970, emphasis in regulation has shifted in part to regulation of environmental quality, product safety and workplace safety. A change is observed in regulation texts that begin to emphasize "new wave" or "social regulation" applied across industries.[47] These new areas of interest have significantly broadened the theoretical background in regulation to include welfare economics, public finance, and decision-making under uncertainty.

In the context of the United States, the characteristics of the growth of business regulations have been set forth by Farnsot and Gordon. They observed that the growth of regulation "has not been the product of any farsighted plan or design or the result of any thoroughly worked out rational or theory. Step-by-step, whether in state or nation, it has represented a series of empirical adjustments to felt abuses. It has been initiated by particular groups to deal with specific evils as they arose, rather than inspired by any general philosophy of governmental control. It would be appropriate to mention here that groups demanding governmental regulation of certain industrial and trade practices turned first to local governments. And only in case of failure of local governments, demands for regulation were shifted to the states and then to the national government. To a considerable extent, national regulation has been symptomatic of the inability of the state and local governments to meet the demands of politically effective groups for public regulation of industry and trade. Although the New Deal did expand significantly the scope of public regulation but it did not originate the movement to regulate economic life. It may, however, be mentioned that the regulation by Commission has turned to be a unique American experience, but the fact of the matter is that governmental control of economic affairs in one form or another has been a universal trend.

1.3.3. *Regulation in Law*

A study of regulation is based on an elaboration of the characteristics and consequences of alternative forms of government intervention in markets. Government regulation of economic activities involves both general rules of market behaviour and specific actions to achieve short-term policy objectives. Hayek observes that the opposition to government intervention voiced by Adam Smith or John Stuart Mill applied particularly to the "exercise of the coercive power of government which was not regular enforcement of the general law and which was designed to achieve some specific purpose".[48] Regulation involves study of both general market rules and discretionary policy actions.

Markets are a social convention. Law regulates exchanges in the markets. Rules of exchange generally derive from established customs and standard practices and from the common law. Government regulation of the markets provides an additional and at times complementary set of rules that prohibit or promote the range of available transactions. The dependence of orderly market transactions on legal rules is some times taken for granted by economists. A main theme in Hayek's "Law, Legislation and Liberty" is that "the rules of just conduct which the lawyer studies serve a kind of order of the character of which the lawyer is largely ignorant and that this order is studied chiefly by the economist who in turn similarly ignorant of the character of the rules of conduct on which the order that he studies rests".[49] Therefore, the study of regulated markets must begin with study of market rules. By studying the institutional framework within which markets operate, we may better describe the efforts of particular regulatory regimes. One of the crucial issues in regulation is identification of the means of enforcing general rules and specific restrictions. Such and the other related problems have been addressed in the law and economics literature. An important question is whether rules should be enforced through public or private efforts. The common law of contracts, tort and property is generally privately enforced and criminal laws are mostly enforced publically. Antitrust, however, represents an interesting mix of public and private enforcement. The present day emphasis is not public or private but public and private in partnership. The emergence of the concepts like public-private partnership and public-private cooperation is the testimony of this fact. It may, however, be further added that the development of concepts like public property, public contract and public tort have drastically changed the earlier thinking that these are exclusively matters for private law regulation.

Regulatory agencies rely on private complaints or reports of wrong doing on obtaining information about violations of product quality standards or work place safety rules. Private provision of information to regulatory authorities, therefore, represents a combination of private and public enforcement efforts. There is a growing literature on public *versus* private law enforcement. The study on utility and reliability of public and private enforcement systems reveals that even if public enforcement has a cost disadvantage it may be socially preferable. One may like to mention here the emergence of Consumer Protection Law and institutions in India in the interest of consumer rights protection and promotion. Regulation of quality of goods and services, *inter alia*, is subject to this branch of law.

A significant influence on the economic study of regulation stems from the branch of administrative law concerned with regulation of industry. The law literature and related case law history are essential for understanding the legal framework and evolution of economic regulations. A broad definition of regulation in law literature is that economic regulation "explicitly substitutes the judgment of regulators for that of the business or the market place".[50] They distinguished direct regulation, which is primarily prescriptive, from legal restrictions, which are proscriptive, noting that "government regulation of industry is but one of many types of legal control on the use of private economic power". The study of regulation in law focuses primarily on regulatory policies that apply to utilities, particularly rate making, quality of service and entry restriction. Classical regulations may be of different kinds depending on the purpose for which they have been evolved. As Breyer categorizes six kinds of regulations such as cost of service rate making, price regulation allocation under a public interest standard's, standards setting, historically based allocation and individualized screening.[51] Breyer[52] also considered alternatives to classical regulations. These include legal institutions, such as antitrust laws and tort liability rules, taxes, such as effluent charges in environment regulations, and allocation of scarce resources through permits and licences. He also identifies bargaining between interest groups as an alternative to classical regulations. It may, however, be mentioned that Daniel F. Spulber (1989) disagrees with Breyer on the ground that bargaining between interest groups is a pervasive feature of existing regulatory procedures and institutions.

As it is mentioned earlier that regulation is a subject matter of study in the disciplines of political science, economics and law. In this regard the understanding about regulation from the perspective of political science, economics and law are briefly presented to clarify the concept of regulation. It may, however, be emphasized that the purpose of present study is not so much from the perspective of political science and economics but mainly from the law perspective and that too of administrative law.

1.4. Rationales for Government Regulations

The researchers have noticed that governments may regulate for different motives, such as influence by the economically powerful, developed as a means for political election, or the combination of both.[53] Baldwin and Cave suggested that governments regulate to address the following issues and concerns:[54]

(i) **Monopolies and Natural Monopolies** (e.g. utilities) — Monopoly describes the position in which one seller produces for the entire industry or market. Where monopoly occurs, the market 'fails' because competition is deficient. The effects of monopoly are reduced output, higher prices, and transfer of income from consumers to producers. Natural monopoly occurs where it is less costly to society to have production carried out by one firm than by many. Restoration of competition by use of competition law is not, however, an appropriate response since competition may be socially costly and thus regulation of prices, quality and output as well as access may be called for. However, not all aspects of a supply process may be naturally monopolistic like transmission of electricity. The task of government and regulators is to identify those parts of a process that are naturally monopolistic and thus can be regulated while other aspects are left to the influence of competitive forces.

(ii) **Externalities** (e.g. pollution of a river by a factory) — Generally, the price of a product does not reflect the true cost to the society of producing that good and excessive consumption accordingly results like a manufacturer might keep costs to consumers down by dumping pollutants arising from the manufacturing process into a river. Thus, the price of goods will not represent the true costs that production imposes on society if clean up costs are left out of account. The rationale for regulation is to eliminate this waste and to protect society or third parties suffering from externalities by compelling the internalization of spillover costs on 'polluter pays' principles.

(iii) **Information Inadequacies** (e.g. food, drug and drink labelling) — Competitive markets can function properly only if consumers are sufficiently well informed to evaluate competing products. Regulation, by making information more extensively accessible, accurate and affordable, may protect the consumers against information inadequacies and the consequences thereof and may encourage the operation of healthy, competitive markets.

(iv) **Continuity and Availability of Services** (e.g. transport service to remote region) — In some circumstances the market may not provide the socially desired levels of continuity and availability of service. Regulation may be justified in order to produce socially desirable results even through the cross-subsidizations affected may be criticized as inefficient and unfair.

(v) **Anti-competitive Behaviour and Predatory Pricing** (e.g. below-cost pricing) — Markets may be deficient not merely because competition is lacking; they may produce undesirable effects because firms behave in a manner not conducive to healthy competition like predatory pricing. The aim for the regulators is to sustain competition and protect consumers from the ill-effects of market domination by outlawing predatory and other forms of anti-competitive behaviour.

(vi) **Public Goods and Moral Hazards** (e.g. defense, security, and health services) — Regulations are required to share costs where benefits of activity are shared, but free-rider problems exist.

(vii) **Unequal Bargaining Power** (e.g. health and safety at work) — For efficient or fair allocation of resources in a market, one precondition is equal bargaining power. If the bargaining power is unequal, regulation may be justified in order to protect certain interests.

(viii) **Scarcity and Rationing** — Regulatory mechanism may be justified in order to allocate certain commodities when these are in short supply.

(ix) **Distributional Justice and Social Policy** (e.g. victim protection and prevent discrimination) — Regulation may be used to distribute according to public interest and prevent undesirable behaviour or results.

(x) **Rationalization and Coordination** — The firms in a industry may be too small and geographically dispersed to bring themselves to produce efficiently. Enterprises may, moreover, have developed different and incompatible modes of production. In these circumstances regulation may be justified as a means of rationalizing production processes (perhaps standardizing equipment in order to create effective networks) and in order to coordinate the market. In centralized regulation, information can be more efficiently communicated through public channels and economies of scale can be achieved by having one public agency responsible for upholding standards.

(xi) **Planning** — Regulation may be required in order to protect the interests of future generations and coordinate altruistic intentions (e.g. quality of environment). As many people may be prepared to give up some of their assets for altruistic proposes only if they can be assured that a large numbers of others will do the same.

1.5. Characteristics of a 'Good' Regulation

According to Baldwin and Cave[55] regulatory regimes and actions can be assessed by making judgements about the merits of legitimating claims under five heads which are supported by legislative authority; accountability of the action; fairness, accessibility and openness of the action; expertise of the regulator and efficiency of the regime.

(i) **Legislative Mandate** — Where the regulatory action is authorized by the elected legislature, it deserves public support as the regulators have been able to fulfil the legislative mandate. However, the Parliament's intention may be vague making it difficult to state in precise terms what it should involve. Most regulatory statutes give regulators broad discretions and implementing the mandate thus involves interpretation. Moreover, such statutes often set out objectives that exist at mutual tension. Achieving certain objectives may necessarily involve trading off performance in relation to other stated objectives. The regulatory statutes often give the regulators large discretions. Legislators deliberately avoid setting out precise objectives to give the regulators freedom to cope with the problems as they arise in the future.

(ii) **Accountability** — A regulatory body claims support of public because they are properly accountable to, and controlled by, democratic institutions. However, the controversy attending this criterion is the selection of individuals and bodies that provide accountability. If the Parliament or other elected institution is not the body holding the regulator accountable then the arrangement may be criticized as unrepresentative and competence of those institutions in specialist areas may also be called into question. Issues may also arise regarding appropriate degree of accountability, resources that should be properly devoted to accountability, and acceptability of any trade-off between accountability and the effective pursuit of regulatory objectives.

(iii) **Due Process** — The basis of due process claim is that public support is merited because the regulator uses procedures that are fair, accessible, and open. Attention is also paid to the level of participation that regulatory decisions and policy processes allow to the public, to consumers and other affected parties. The underlying rationale of such a claim is that proper democratic influence over regulation is ensured by due process being observed and that this influence has a legitimating effect. The criterion is, however, limited as further guiding principles are required in order to explain who should be allowed to participate and in what manner. Trade off once again has to be made between openness or accessibility and efficiency. Disputes may also arise concerning the appropriate mode of participation.

(iv) **Expertise** — Certain regulatory functions may require the exercise of expert judgement. In these circumstances the regulator may claim support on the basis of his expertise and the nature of task at hand. "Trust to my expertise" is the essence of such a claim because a judgement has to be made on the basis of a number of factors and variables and specialized knowledge, skills and experience have to be applied. However, in this test the public is poorly positioned to evaluate expertise and it is difficult for the expert to explain reasoning or judgement to the lay person. A natural distrust by lay person of those who lay claim to expertise also serves to undermine demands of support from specialists. This may be particularly where experts refuse to give full reasons for their actions, deny access to decision-making processes, or pursue narrow and arcane modes of analysis. Conflict between experts again affect their credibility and undermine public confidence. Public may see experts as self-interested or captured. Public is skeptical of neutrality of regulatory decisions where certain parties gain advantages.

(v) **Efficiency** — A regulator may claim support on the basis of acting efficiently and may make two kinds of claim. The first claim for support is on the basis that the legislative mandate is being implemented efficiently, at least possible level of inputs or costs and there is productive efficiency. This claim is, however, afflicted with all the problems in relation of legislative mandate. Second version of efficiency claim urges support on basis that the regulation leads to results that are efficient, as judged by criteria set down with a degree of independence from the mandate. Reference here is made to the regulatory regimes allocative efficiency and its dynamic efficiency. These claims, however, present difficulties because efficiency is not a value independent of distributional considerations and efficiency itself provides no answers on distributional considerations or in defining regulatory mandate. The pursuit of efficiency may conflict with legislative statements or distributional matters and accordingly, the appropriateness of efficiency claims may be especially questionable in those spheres of regulation where distributive concerns are central.

The five claims are all fraught with difficulties but collectively they constitute a set of benchmarks for assessing regulatory regimes. These are the rationales that are employed and have currency in real-life debates on regulation and its reform. Arguments in support or against regulators that do not fall under these five headings will be deemed to be irrelevant by most members of the public. Judging the extent to which regulation is legitimate is not to offer a sociological assessment of the actual support that regulator enjoys; it is rather, to offer an assessment of the legitimacy that a regulator deserves.

1.6. Types and Strategies of Regulation

Regulation can pursue different types of objectives. Economic regulation, social regulation and administrative regulation are among the three main categories of government intervention which may have a bearing on the market. Economic regulation focuses on the direct government intervention in corporations and market decisions, such as pricing, competition, market entry or exit. The development of the regulatory state has been related to this type of regulation since the 1930s. The purpose of economic regulation is to improve the efficiency of market operation.

Social regulation is related to government protection of citizen and social values, such as health, safety, housing, labour contracts, working conditions, and environment and consumer protection. This type of regulation was developed in the 1960s and has been expanded since 1970s. Social regulation aims at promoting new values and addressing concerns and problems resulting from the modern industrial society. Social regulation policies have grown faster than many other government activities and have affected the operation of more businesses or citizens than the impact of economic regulation.

The third type of regulation is administrative regulation, which have to do with government formalities and paperwork. The development of administrative regulation is related to the increasing complexity of public programme operation and the continuing requirements of financial and legal accountability. Businesses and citizens have complained loudly about the increasing burden of article work (red type) in such activities as filling out forms, asking for permission, reporting information, notifying the agency, and record keeping of the operation. Different regulations may require different strategies of operation. Baldwin and Cave[56] provided a good summary of regulatory instruments designed for different approaches or applications. They are:

1. the command and control approach, which was used in the areas of public health and public safety concerns;
2. the self-regulation approach, which was emphasized in some mature businesses or industries with developed associations and rules of operation (e.g. the insurance industry);
3. the incentives approach, which was designed to promote the flexibility of regulation requirements by offering differential taxes for different products (e.g. leaded and unleaded petrol);
4. the market-harnessing controls, which were developed to assure some competitions in selected markets, including for example, competition laws in the airline industry, franchising in rail, television and radio businesses, contracting if local authority refuse services, and tradable permits for the purpose of sulphur dioxide emissions);
5. the mandatory disclosure approach, which was required in certain businesses, such as in the food, drug, and drink sectors;
6. the rights and liabilities laws, which covered such areas as rules of tort law, right to clean water; and
7. the requirement of public compensation and social insurance, which was operated in the workplace safety system.

1.7. Independent Regulation or 'New Style' Regulation

The nature of regulatory powers or functions that traditional administrators enjoy involves drafting of clear and concrete rules and regulations concerning the subject and implementing or enforcing them. It thus involves only legislative and administrative powers. It does not confer judicial powers. However, opposed to the old-style regulation, the independent regulatory commissions which came into existence in mid-1990s wield regulatory powers with legislative, executive and judicial jurisdiction and are termed as quasi-judicial authorities. Thus, contrary to the basic principle of separation of powers in governmental functioning, a commission assumes the task of an administrator, a judge and a legislator.

Independent regulation has been practiced in US longer than anywhere else. This concept of government has its origin and beginning in the US. But, it has been successfully used in UK for electricity and gas sectors and has further extended itself to many other countries. An important justification used for creation of independent regulatory agencies is that they enable complex matters to be considered without discrimination between parties. A variety of disciplines have to interact for reaching a conclusion. The task is, therefore, delegated to a group of experts, who concentrate on such matters to the exclusion of others. The need for expertise sometimes accompanies the requirement for rule-making, decision-making or adjudicative functions that may be inappropriate for government department or a court. Because of their expertise and narrow focus, these new agencies may bring in economy, speed in decision-making, quick adaptation to changing conditions, and freedom from technicality and procedural complexity.

Independence lies both in relation to the individual and institution. In case of the individual, it would rest on an objective, open and fair selection process; in the terms of appointment being similarly done so as to ensure that the best people are appointed; in ensuring that the terms of office are specified; and that the members of regulatory body cannot be removed without an overwhelming cause. At institutional level, independence can be ensured by financial independence. The funding of the body must be independent of government or legislative vote. The regulatory body should be able to prepare its budget, authorize its expenses, decide on the type of staff it needs and recruit them, and use consultants as and when required. Taking these characteristic of independent regulatory bodies into account, the idea of such bodies is still evolving and yet to take its roots in India. Every new legislation creating a regulatory body brings more restraints on the body instead of ensuring higher degree of independence.

1.8. Review of Literature

Kessides, Ioannis N. (2004), *Reforming Infrastructure: Privatization, Regulation and Competition*, World Bank and Oxford University Press, Washington, D.C. Kessides describes effective regulatory systems as necessary but not sufficient for improved sector performance. He compares policy strategies applied to different sectors in regions of the world, noting how characteristics of these network industries affect the feasibility of liberalization and private participation. There are a number of checklists that identify best practice in terms of the design of regulatory agencies. Infrastructure is crucial for generating growth, alleviating poverty, and increasing international competitiveness. For much of the Twentieth century and in most countries, the network utilities that delivered infrastructure services such as electricity, natural gas, telecommunications, railroads, and water supply were vertically and horizontally integrated state monopolies. This approach often resulted in extremely weak services, especially in developing and transition economies, and particularly for poor people. Common problems included low productivity, high costs, bad quality, insufficient revenue, and shortfalls in investment. Recognizing infrastructure's importance, many countries over the past two decades have implemented far-reaching infrastructure reforms-restructuring, privatizing, and establishing new approaches to regulation. Reforming Infrastructure identifies the challenges involved in this massive policy redirection within the historical, economic, and institutional context of developing and transition economies. It also assesses the outcomes of these policy changes, as well as their distributional consequences, especially for poor households and other disadvantaged groups. And, drawing on a range of international experiences and empirical studies, it recommends directions for future reforms and research to improve infrastructure performance, identifying pricing policies that strike a balance between economic efficiency and social equity, suggesting rules governing access to bottleneck infrastructure facilities, and proposing ways to increase poor people's access to these crucial services.

Brown, Ashley C., Jon Stern, Bernard Tenenbaum, and Define Gencer (2006), *Handbook for Evaluating Infrastructure Regulatory Systems*, World Bank, Washington, D.C. Provides templates (and supporting principles) for evaluating regulatory processes and performance. It goes beyond the "how" of regulation to consider regulatory substance, the "what" of regulation. The formal elements (laws, institutions and procedures) provide clues as to how an agency is likely to respond to sector developments, but the decisions of regulators represent the "output" of agencies. The resulting incentives have significant impacts on sector performance. The handbook identifies three meta-principles that can be used for evaluating regulatory process: credibility, legitimacy, and transparency. A key indicator for social and economic impacts would be sector efficiency. If policy can create positive-sum games, then it is easier to get buy-in from stakeholders for reform initiatives. Greater efficiency in the sector means that more resources can be devoted to poverty alleviation without creating new fiscal burdens. While more politicians have run on platforms of fairness than efficiency, the latter deserves to be highlighted when evaluating regulatory performance.

S.K. Sarkar, Kaushik Deb (Edited) (2001), *Regulation in Infrastructure Services: Progress and the Way Forward*, TERI. This book is primarily based on the papers presented at the *National Conference on Regulation in Infrastructure Services: Progress and the Way Forward* held in November 2000. The book provides useful knowledge and insights on regulation, a subject that is of growing importance in India, in the light of reforms in the infrastructure sectors of the economy worldwide. The book provides a judicious mix of experiences from other parts of the world and an analysis of challenges that exist in India. Until recently, infrastructure services were produced and provided by natural monopolies. The experiences in many countries have shown that a competitive market can deliver these services in an effective manner. Independent regulation, a new form of governance in infrastructure sectors, which evolved during the last few decades in the US, UK, and Latin America, is being rapidly pursued in the South Asian region. In the region, the barriers and challenges to such a regulation are many, especially where natural monopoly service providers are owned by the Government and where there is no long history of good governance. Along with Sri Lanka, India took the lead in adopting independent regulation in its infrastructure sectors in the mid-1990s. Electricity regulators, the telecom regulator, and the port regulator in India have started functioning since then. This book outlines the progress of independent regulation in India, identifies constraints in the process, brings out issues for consideration by policy-makers, and suggests recommendations for better governance in infrastructure sectors. It incorporates experiences on the subject not only from the region, but also from other countries such as the Brazil, the UK, and the US.

S.K. Sarkar, Leena Srivastava (Edited) (2002), *Reforms in the Infrastructure Sectors Next Steps*, TERI. The book contains various papers discussed and examined in depth by various experts in the field of infrastructure sectors at the conference on *Reforms in Infrastructure Sectors: Next Steps organized by TERI* in November 2001. Liberalization of the Indian economy requires disinvestment of the public sector and moving public sector companies and assets towards private sector ownership and control. While in most sectors of the economy the existence of competitive forces would generally ensure that consumer welfare increases with efficiency. However, concerns do arise in the case of some infrastructure sectors where natural monopolies, unregulated, would extract excessive rents from consumers. It is largely in these sectors, therefore, that a strong need has to be met for setting up independent regulatory systems, which would protect consumer interests while at the same time allowing producers a fair rate of return on capital employed. The book thus traces the need for independent regulation in the South Asian context in infrastructure sectors such as electricity, telecommunications, ports, water, and gas. It also examines the constraints faced during the new style of governance for provisioning of infrastructure services and brings out concrete issues for consideration by policy-makers, independent regulators, and various stakeholders. It further looks at various contentious issues such as selection of regulators, issues on policy directions, regulatory procedures, regulatory accountability, issues relating to interaction with civil society and other sectoral regulators.

An assessment of regulatory performance has been made by examining the issues relating to tariff determination by the regulators in telecom and electricity sectors, reviewing the institutional and relationship issues among various regulators and regulatory institutions and focusing critically on regulatory processes. It traces the current practices being adopted by different regulatory agencies, highlights best practices on the subject, and raises a few issues that must be resolved on an urgent basis. It has been recognized that developing competitive markets would require a market structure that facilitates competition. It is very important in the Indian context, where incumbent monopolies, all publicly owned, have considerable market share. The need for restricting public monopolies with the ultimate objective of introducing competition in the market has been recognized. Certain issues regarding restructuring of public monopolies in the electricity, the telecom, and the oil and gas sectors have been highlighted and various constraints given the sectoral complexities and political compulsions have been brought out.

S. Sundar, M.P. Ram Mohan, Satnam Singh Kalra (Edited) (2005), ***Regulatory Law in Practice — Compendium of Orders in Electricity and Telecom Sectors,*** **TERI.** Law Reporters report all judicial decisions, and they are extensively used by the legal fraternity and the judiciary itself. There is, however, no compilation of regulatory decisions and orders. The book is a compendium of orders in electricity and telecom sectors. The publication contains summary orders and judgements of electricity and telecom regulators in India, Pakistan, and Sri Lanka between 1998 and 2003. By giving an overview of both the electricity and telecom sectors, the compendium presents succinct summaries of the decisions of regulators and courts in SAFIR countries. Divided into two parts, one dealing with electricity regulation and the other with telecom regulation, the compendium systematically compiles orders, regulations, and judgements issued by regulators in SAFIR (South Asia Forum for Infrastructure Regulation) countries.

Anjali Garg, Manisha Kabra and Rakesh Kacker (2003), *Regulatory Reforms in India — Effectiveness, Efficiency, and Impacts*, TERI. This publication draws upon the findings of the study titled "Regulatory Reforms in India: Effectiveness, Efficiency and Impacts" conducted by TERI as part of the Government of India/United Nations Development Programme, Economic Reforms Programme. This book comprises three sections — Regulatory Impact Assessment of the Power Sector; Regulatory Impact Assessment of the Telecom Sector; and Assessment of a Multi-sector Regulator. The book analyses the complexities in bringing about regulatory reforms, the creation of regulatory institutions and the nexus between appropriate policies and effective regulation. This publication focuses on the impact of the reforms in the power and telecom sectors that led to the introduction of independent regulation in the 1990s. This publication attempts to answer the question of whether regulatory reforms have yielded the desired results. Apart from this, a more detailed analysis of the concept of a multi-sector regulator has been made. The multi-sector regulator concept has been discussed from the perspective of making regulation more effective. This is necessary because in the future as more sectors, both at the centre and in the states, come under regulation, there would be a need to understand the circumstances under which a multi-sector regulator would enhance the effectiveness of the regulatory process.

Marver H. Bernstein (1955), *Regulating Business by Independent Commission*, Princeton University Press, New Jersey. The work evaluates the independent regulatory commissions as instruments of governmental regulation of business. It examines the environment in which they have developed and matured as well as the objectives and ideas of their promoters. The rise and decline of commissions have been analyzed in light of major developments in the institutional process of government and the adjustments made by regulated industries in the regulatory process. The study examines the charge that regulation by commission encourages a showing of favouratism to the regulated groups, a narrow view of the public interest, an unrealistic concept of the democratic political process and maintenance of localism and particularism in Congress. The work appraises the independent regulatory commission in terms of its capacity to develop political responsibility, act in the public interest, generate administrative vitality and initiative, and maintain independence from regulated groups. It focuses attention on the relations of commissions to Congress and the Presidency. It analyses the factors of expertness and continuity of policy in commission operation. It outlines the problems facing commissions in developing public support for and compliance with their programmes.

M.N. Srinivasan (2002), *Principles of Insurance Law*, 7th Edn., Wadhwa and Company, Nagpur. The book is a comprehensive and thorough compilation of the Constitutional and legal aspects of the different kinds of insurance cover available in India. It deals with all aspects of insurance law in detail with the help of statutory provisions and case laws. Statutory part basically deals with the regulation and functioning of the insurance companies. It is a study of principles which governs the various types of insurances prevalent in the society like life, marine, fire etc. it. The book compiles and analyses the whole gamete of statutory provisions on insurance, namely the Insurance Act, 1938, the Life Insurance Corporation Act, 1956, the General Insurance Business (Nationalization) Act, 1982, the Marine Insurance Act, 1963 and the Motor Vehicles Act, 1988, the Indian Contract Act, 1872, and other laws governing various aspects involved in insurance. A thorough analysis of the new Act Insurance Regulatory and Development Authority Act, 1999 is also provided in the book. The Act has established the regulatory body in the form of Insurance Regulatory and Development Authority for the overall regulation of the insurance sector after liberalization of the sector and has brought amendments to other legislations dealing with insurance. The book thus provides a holistic view of the regulation of the insurance sector.

Robert Baldwin and Martin Cave (1999), *Understanding Regulation —Theory, Strategy, and Practice*, Oxford University Press. The book discusses certain central issues of regulation from a number of disciplinary perspectives. The book looks at the perspective of regulation from the point of view of the business, political science, sociology, social administration, and other disciplines. The fundamental strategies, institutions, and explanations of regulations are reviewed and the means of identifying the 'good' regulation are provided. Individual chapters have been devoted to topics like self-regulation, the regulation of risks, the cost-benefit testing of regulation, the importance of enforcement, and the challenges of regulating within Europe. The second part of the book considers a series of issues of particular concern in modern utilities regulation. Questions of accountability and procedure are also examined and issues of recent public debate on regulatory reforms are reviewed.

***Universal's Insurance Laws* (2005), Universal Law Publishing Co. Pvt. Ltd.** The book is compendium of Acts, Rules, and Regulations in the Insurance Sector. The book compiles all the laws in the life and general insurance and other ancillary laws. Various regulations framed by IRDA have also been brought out. At appropriate places comments have been provided giving explanation to the provisions of the laws.

***Taxmann's Insurance Law Manual* (2009), Taxmann Allied Services (P.) Ltd.** The book provides a collection of various regulations, circulars and notifications issued by Insurance Regulatory and Development Authority along with the text of Insurance Regulatory and Development Authority Act, 1999.

***190th Report on the Revision of the Insurance Act, 1938 and the Insurance Regulatory and Development Authority Act, 1999*, Law Commission of India, June 2004.** The Report is outcome of the study undertook by the Law Commission of India of examining the Insurance Act, 1938 and Insurance Regulatory and Development Authority Act, 1999 at the instance of the Insurance Regulatory and Development Authority. It contains the recommendations made by the Commission for revision of the Acts and for consequential amendments thereto.

***Malhotra Committee Report*, Ministry of Finance, Government of India, January 1994.** In the backdrop of new industrial policy, the Government of India set-up in 1993 a high-powered committee headed by Mr. R.N. Malhotra to examine the structure of the insurance industry, to assess its strength and weaknesses in terms of the objective of providing high quality services to the public and serving as an effective instrument for mobilization of financial resources for development, to review the then existing structure of regulation and supervision of insurance sector and to suggest reforms for strengthening and modernizing regulatory system in tune with the changing economic environment. The Malhotra Committee submitted its report in 1994 which made some major recommendations for the insurance sector. The key recommendations of the Committee included the privatization of the insurance sector by permitting the entry of private players to enter the business of life and general insurance and the establishment of an Insurance Regulatory Authority.

1.9. Objectives

Objectives of the study are:

- To provide brief narration of evolution of regulation, deregulation and re-regulation in international and national perspective;
- To analyze the growth of regulation in public utility sector with special reference to insurance sector;
- To present the provisions of Insurance Regulatory and Development Authority Act;
- To study the working of the Insurance Regulatory and Development Authority (IRDA) in relation to its stakeholders; and
- To suggest appropriate changes, if necessary, in relation to institutional and operational levels to make it more effective and efficient.

1.10. Research Questions

- Whether regulating Insurance Sector has affected the socio-political, economic and administrative dynamics of our society?
- Whether deregulation in Insurance Sector increased the efficiency and effectiveness?
- Whether Regulatory Authority in the Insurance Sector has succeeded in bringing transparency, accountability, fairness and satisfaction to stakeholders?
- Whether deregulation and privatization have affected in any way the operational domain of Administrative Law?

1.11. Methodology

The methodology adopted was investigative as well as analytical involving the analysis of the data collected through questionnaire and discussions. The study was completed with the help of both secondary and primary data. The data from secondary sources was collected from published materials, such as, books, reports, articles in reputed journals, news clippings etc. The views of the stakeholders dealing with the Insurance Regulatory and Development Authority and its officials were gathered through structured and unstructured questionnaires. The views/ opinions generated through the questionnaire formed the primary source of data. The collected data and information were analyzed and tabulated.

Some of the cases on the specific applications of the provisions of the insurance regulations were specifically analyzed in the light of the responses of the parties. The responses of the higher judiciary on the decisions of the regulatory authority were focused with a view to highlight judicial response to its decisions/orders.

1.12. Chapterization

Chapter 1 — Introduction. The Chapter provides in brief the emergence of regulation in its historical process and its meaning from political science, economics and law perspective. The chapter also focuses on the main thrust of the study, its objectives, methodology followed and the highlights the coverage of other chapters of the study. In addition, the chapter also tries to clarify the concept of the regulation and provides briefly the review of existing literature available in this area.

Chapter 2 — Growth of Regulations — A Historical Perspective. This chapter provides brief history of regulatory movement from international perspective. It may be clarified that the study is not a comparative study either on the evolution of regulations in different countries or on its impact on the economy. However, the chapter certainly flags on the reasons for its introduction, changes in its structure and enforcement designs. Broadly, the growth of regulations has been traced in two phases. Phase I gives an account of its growth from early age up to Second World War and phase II captures the development for the period 1945-1980.

Chapter 3 — Regulations in the Age of Liberalization, Privatization and Globalization — An Overview. The Chapter deals with the growth of regulations often referred as Deregulation and Re-regulation under the impact of Liberalization, Privatization and Globalization broadly based on the principle of free market economy or Public Choice Theory. The growth and effect of regulations has been analyzed from Administrative Law Perspective in particular and also from governance point of view in general in this chapter.

Chapter 4 — Regulations in the Insurance Sector — An Analysis of Indian Legal Framework. This chapter focuses on the legislative framework as existing at present after the enactment of Insurance Regulatory and Development Authority Act, 1999. The review of the provisions of the IRDA Act, 1999 by the Law Commission of India also forms part of this chapter.

Chapter 5 — Working of the Insurance Regulatory and Development Authority. The working of Insurance Regulatory and

Development Authority of India forms the subject matter of the study under this chapter. In addition, analysis of views and opinions of various stakeholders on the working has been presented as a part of this chapter.

Chapter 6 — Conclusions and Suggestions. The major conclusions and suggestions emerging from the study and having policy, legislative and administrative implications for future changes have been highlighted in this chapter.

NOTES

1. See generally Marver H. Bernstein (1955), *Regulating Business by Independent Commission*, Princeton University Press, pp. 16-18.
2. See generally Daniel F. Spulber (1989), *Regulation and Markets*, Massachusetts Institute of Technology, pp. 22-23.
3. Dicey (1962), *Law and Public Opinion in England*, pp. 126-10; Jethro Brown (1971), *The Underlying Principles of Modern Legislation*, pp. 156-280.
4. Dicey, *ibid.* pp. 212-302.
5. Robson (1951), *Justice and Administrative Law*, Steven & Sons, London, p. 33.
6. *Constitution of India*, Preamble.
7. *Ibid.*, Article 38.
8. *Ibid.*, Article 39.
9. *Ibid.*, Article 41.
10. *Ibid.*, the Constitution (Eighty-Sixth Amendment) Act, 2002 inserted a new Article 21A — Right to Education:
    "21A. The State shall provide free and compulsory education to all children of the age of six to fourteen years in such manner as the State may, by law, determine.
    "Substitution of new Article for Article 45 — For Article 45 of the Constitution, the following Article shall be substituted, namely —
    Provision for early childhood care and education to children below the age of six years.
    "45. The State shall endeavour to provide early childhood care and education for all children until they complete the age of six years.
    Amendment of Article 51A — In Article 51A of the Constitution, after clause (J), the following clause shall be added, namely —
    "(k) who is a parent or guardian to provide opportunities for education to his child or, as the case may be, ward between the age of six and fourteen years."
    Eight year after the Constitution was amended to make right to education a Fundamental Right, an enabling legislation was passed by the Parliament in 2009. The Act known as **Right of Children to Free and Compulsory Education Act, 2009** would provide free and compulsory education for all children in 6-14 age group.
11. *R.J. Kapoor* vs. *State of Punjab*, A.I.R. 1955 S.C. 549, 533, and also in *Saghir Ahmad* vs. *State of U.P.*, A.I.R. 1954 S.C. 728, 741; *Crown Aluminium Works* vs. *Workmen*, A.I.R. 1958 S.C. 30.
12. Charles A. Reich, *"Individual Rights and Social Welfare: The Emerging Legal Issues", 74 Yale L.J.* 1245 (1965). Also, *"The New Property", 73 Yale L.J.* 733

(1964). Reich states in the New Property: "One of the most important developments in the United States during the past decade has been the emergence of government as a major source of wealth. Government is a gigantic syphon. It draws in revenue and power, and pours forth wealth: money, benefits, services, contracts franchises and licences. Government has always had this function. But while in early times it was minor, today's distribution of largesse is on a vast, imperial scale". *Ibid.*, p. 733.

13. See Friedmann (1971), *The State and the Rule of Law in a Mixed Economy*, Stevens & Sons, London, p. 3.
14. To name a few statutes in the area: the Industries (Development and Regulation) Act, 1951; the Essential Commodities Act, 1955; the Foreign Exchange Regulation Act, 1973; the Imports and Exports (Control) Act, 1947; the Companies Act, 1956; various statutes for regulating specific commodities, e.g. the Tea Act, 1953, the Coffee Act, 1942, the Rubber Act, 1947, the Coir Industry Act, 1953, the Cardamom Act, 1965, and the Tobacco Act, 1975. A Monopolies Commission has been established to regulate monopolies and restrictive trade practices. See M. Menon and N.G. Mysore (1970), *Law Relating to Government Control over Private Enterprise*, Eastern Book Company, Delhi.
15. Some of the important enactments in this area are: the Industrial Disputes Act, 1947; the Employees' State Insurance Act, 1948; the Factories Act, 1948; the Minimum Wages Act, 1948; the Payment of Bonus Act, 1965; the Payment of Wages Act, 1936; and the Workmen's Compensation Act, 1923.
16. Robson (1951), *Justice and Administrative Law*, Stevens & Sons, London, p. 34. See also Ramaswami (1959), "Rule of Law and a Planned Society", *I.J.I.L.I.*, p. 31.
17. Donal F. Kettl, *Sharing Power — Public Governance and Private Market*, Washington, DC: Brooking Institute, p. 157.
18. *The Changing Role of Government; Administrative Structure and Reforms*, Proceedings of a Commonwealth Roundtable, Sydney, Australia, 24-28, 1992, p. 20.
19. Peter Self (1993), *Government by the Market*? London, U.S. Westview Press; see also R.A.W. Rhodes (1994), "The Hollowing Out of the State: The Changing Nature of the Public Service in Britain", *The Political Quarterly*, Vol. 65, No. 2, April-June, pp. 138-54.
20. David Osborne and Ted Gaebler (1992), *Reinventing Government: How the Entrepreneurial Spirit the Public Sector from School House to State House*, City Hall to Pentagon Reading, MA, Addison-Wesley; see also Ronal C. Moe (1994), "The Reinventing Government Exercise: Misinterpreting the Problem, Misjudging the Consequences", *Public Administration Review*, Vol. 54, No. 2, March-April, pp. 111-22.
21. *The Changing Role of Government: Administrative Structure and Reforms* (1992), Proceedings of a Commonwealth Roundtable, Sydney, Australia, February 24-28, p. 20; See also Norman Lewis (1994), "Reviewing Change in Government, New Public Management and Next Steps", *Public Law*, Spring, pp. 105-13.
22. Donal F. Kettle, *op. cit.*
23. Peter Self, *op. cit.*
24. Rhodes R.A.W. (1994), "The Hollowing Out of the State: The Changing Nature of Public Service in Britain", *The Political Quarterly*, Vol. 65, No. 2, April-June, pp. 138-54.

25. Drueker, Peter F. (1995), "Really Reinventing Government", *SPAN*, December, p. 11.
26. S.S. Singh and Suresh Misra (1994), "Public Law Issues in Privatization Process", *Indian Journal of Public Administration*, Vol. XL, No. 2, pp. 396-410.
27. O.P. Agarwal and S.P. Paul (2001), "Framework for Independent Regulation in India: An Overview", in S.K. Sarkar and Kaushik Deb (ed.), *Regulation in Infrastructure Services: Progress and Way Forward*, TERI; p. 3. See also Turnbull P. (1999), *Regulation or Re-regulation of Transport?* Discussion Paper, Geneva: International Labour Organization.
28. R. Baldwin, C. Scott and C. Hood (1998), *A Reader on Regulation*, Oxford, Ch. 1; R. Baldwin, Martin Cave (1999), *Understanding Regulation Theory, Strategy and Practice*, Oxford, Ch. 1, p. 1.
29. P. Selznick (1985), "Focusing Organizational Research on Regulation" in R. Noll (ed.), *Regulatory Policy and Social Sciences*, Berkeley Calif, p. 363.
30. Corpus, *Juris Secundum*, Vol. 76, p. 611.
31. *United Nations Conference on Trade and Development, Model Law: the Relationship between a Competition And Regulatory Bodies, including Sectoral Regulators*, TD/B/COM. 2/CPL/23 including Corr. 118, June 2001.
32. (1985) 2 SCC 116, p. 130.
33. NCTE (2003) 3 SCC 321.
34. Supreme Court Proceedings; MANU/SC/0163/1997.
35. (2009) 6 SCC 235 at p. 253 see also *State of U.P.* vs. *Maharaja Dharmander Prasad Singh* (1989) Supp (1) SCC 684 at p. 688.
36. (2006) 13 SCC 753 at pp. 772-73.
37. Meier, K. J. (1985), *Regulation: Politics, Bureaucracy, and Economy*, St. Martin's Press: New York, p. 1.
38. Organization for Economic Cooperation and Development (OECD) (1999), *Regulatory Reform in the United States*; OECD: Paris, p. 16.
39. Baldwin, R., Scott, C. and Hood, C. (1998), *A Reader on Regulation*, Oxford University Press, New York, Chapter 1, p. 2.
40. Mitnick, B.M. (1980), *The Political Economy of Regulation*, New York: Colombia University Press, p. 7.
41. Ripley, R. and G. Franklin (1986), *Policy Implementation and Bureaucracy*, 2nd Ed., Chicago: Dorsey Press, p. 1.
42. Meier, K.J. (1985), *Regulation: Politics, Bureaucracy and Economy*, New York: St. Martins Press, p. 1.
43. Kahn, A.E. (1970), *The Economics of Regulation: Principles and Institutions*, 1, New York: Wiley, pp. 2-3.
44. Shepherd, W.G. and C. Wilcox (1979), *Public Policies Toward Business*, 6th ed., Homewood, IL: Irwin, p. 267.
45. Stigler, G.J. (1971), "The Theory of Economic Regulation", *Bell Journal of Economics*, 2 Spring, pp. 3-21, p. 3.
46. Stigler, G.J. (1981), "Comments on Joskow and Noll", in G. Fromm (ed.), *Studies in Public Regulation*, Cambridge, MA: MIT Press, pp. 73-77, p. 73.
47. MacAvoy, P.W. (1979), *The Regulated Industries and The Economy*, New York: Morton, referred in Daniel F. Pulber (1989), *Regulation and Markets*, Massachusetts Institute of Technology, p. 25.
48. Hayek, F.A. (1960), *The Constitution of Liberty*, Chicago: University of Chicago Press, pp. 220-21.
49. Hayek, F.A. (1973), *Law, Legislation and Liberty, Vol. 1: Rules and Order*, Chicago: University of Chicago Press, p. 4.

50. Gellhorn, E. and R.J. Pierce Jr. (1982), *Regulated Industries*, St. Paul: West Publishing Co., pp. 7-8.
51. Breyer, S. (1982), *Regulation and Its Reform*, Cambridge, MA: Harvard University Press, referred in Daniel F. Spulber (1989), *Regulation and Markets*, Massachusetts Institute of Technology, p. 29.
52. Breyer, S. (1982), *Regulation and Its Reform*, Cambridge, MA: Harvard University Press, Chapter 8, referred in Daniel F. Spulber (1989), *Regulation and Markets*, Massachusetts Institute of Technology, p. 29.
53. Breyer, S. (2002), *Regulation and Its Reform*, Reprinted Ed.; Harvard University Press: Cambridge, MA; Ogus, A. (2005), *Regulation: Legal Form and Economic Theory*, Hart Publishing: Oxford.
54. Baldwin, R. and M. Cave (1999), *Understanding Regulation: Theory, Strategy, and Practice*, Oxford University Press: New York, p. 17.
55. *Ibid.*, pp. 76-84.
56. *Ibid.*, pp. 34-62.

2

GROWTH OF REGULATIONS
A Historical Perspective

2.1. Introduction

It is well accepted fact that regulations are law in the sense of delegated legislation.[1] They may be substantive as well as procedural. Their objective, however, is to give effect to the policy enshrined in the legislation. The growth of regulation is neither new nor linked with the modern state only. Its existence and growth to a large extent depends on the need of the society and the approach of the state. This may emerge as a command of the sovereign or as a part of the socio-political and economic planning or as a social engineering either for reconstruction of society or to ensure social inclusiveness and entitlements. The task undertaken under this chapter is to present evolution of regulation, internationally with special emphasis on USA and UK and nationally in general; to highlight various theories which often influence the process of regulation making; and finally, to analyze its implication on the role and structure of governing institutions. The discussion in this chapter will finally lead to the emergence of various kinds of states, *viz. Laissez faire* State, Welfare State, Administrative State and Contracting State. While discussing the growth of regulations the emergence of regulatory commissions, boards and authorities is also flagged.

2.2. Development of Regulations — Theoretical Considerations

A number of approaches can be adopted to explain the development of regulations. These approaches may be descriptive and provide an account of regulatory developments or may be prescriptive offering a view on how regulation should be organized. Christopher Hood[2] sees four main ways of explaining policy on regulatory developments, which are as follows:

1. where stress is placed on the force of new ideas that upset the *status quo* in someway;
2. where emphasis rests on the pressures of interests that act in pursuit of developments that suit their own purpose;
3. where changes in habitat and new conditions, make the old policies obsolete like technological developments and economic changes are the driving forces for policy revision; and
4. where policies are said to destroy themselves because of internal problems.

The first three approaches out of the four focus on the 'external' influences on the policy regime whereas the last one looks at the internally generated factors. The description of changes in regulation may not fall completely and neatly like mathematical divisions into above categories and there may be overlapping and combinations.

There exist various theories to explain regulatory origin and development.[3] It would be optimistic to suggest that such theories can be synthesized so that reliable predictions can be made about all or most regulatory processes. Different theories exist at different levels of generality and have varying applications and uses as explanatory tools. Most theories of regulatory origin can be seen as types of interest theory, though the force that can be exerted by the ideas arguments in a number of accounts. Among interest theories a broad distinction can be drawn between 'public', 'group', and 'private' versions. A brief account of these theories has been brought out in the following paragraphs.

2.2.1. *Public Interest Theory*

Public interest theories centre on the idea that the institution and development of regulations is in pursuit of public related objectives. Thus, the purpose of regulation is to achieve certain publicly desired outcomes as opposed to any group, sector or individual self-interest, in circumstances where the markets would fail to yield these.

A number of theoretical, practical and political problems surround this public interest view. First and foremost the conception of the public interest may be hard to identify. Instead many contend that the regulation generally takes place amidst clashing images of public interest. Another problem stems from the doubt regarding disinterestedness, expertise and efficiency of the regulators. It has been argued that the regulators may be corrupted by the opportunities of personal profit and driven by personal interests.[4] It would be apt perhaps to mention observations by former Prime Minister regarding regulating the regulators. The questions are being raised as to who will regulate the regulators and also on the extent of autonomy of the regulatory authorities.[5] Doubts are also being cast on the competence of the regulators to yield public interest because of lack of attractiveness in rewards and career structure and lack of emphasis on training needs and discipline. Further, it is argued that the public interest theory understates the degree to which economic and political power influence regulation. It is argued that regulatory policies and institutions often become subject to the influence of the powerful regulated parties or politicians or sectors of consumers. Thus, regulation serves the interests of these parties or sectors rather than the wider public interest.[6] Even the theorists who concede to the fact that the regulatory regimes are established in pursuit of public interest objectives, the public interest vision may only be persuasive in the earliest stages of the life cycle of regulatory affairs.[7] As regards the results, the public interest theory is attacked as the regulations often fail to deliver public interest outcomes.

2.2.2. *Interest Group Theory*

This theory regards regulations as the product of relationships between different groups and between such groups and the state. Proponents of this theory do not regard regulatory behaviour as imbued with public spiritedness, but as a competition for power. The role of regulations is perceived to be promotion of the interest on the principle of win-win situation for all the players. Bernstein points out that the role of the regulators is to carry out mission that the legislators have negotiated between the interest groups, consumers, businesses, and other affected parties-missions that affect compromises, but are seen by the participants, nevertheless to be endeavours in pursuit of public interest.[8] Such accounts (Group Public Interest Approaches) bridge public interest and group interest approaches and offer explanations of public interest that takes on board competitions between different versions of that interest.

Versions of interest group theories range from open ended pluralism to corporatism. Pluralists see competing groups as struggling for power and elections. If coalition groups win elections, they use their power to shape regulatory regimes.[9] In contrast, corporatists emphasize that successful groups enter into partnership with the state and produce regulatory regime that exclude non-participating interests. Leigh Hancher and Michael Moran substitute the concept of 'regulatory space' within which a legitimate interplay of interests occurs.[10]

2.2.3. *Private Interest Theory*

This approach stresses that the regulatory developments are driven by private interests and not by public or group interests. Some economic theories, however, hover between group and private interest. From the historical viewpoint, Gabriel Kolko (1977) put forward the controversial thesis that US regulation originated in self-interested demands by business groups for government action to stabilize market shares, prices and profits rather than in public-spirited campaigns to curb these interests. In other words, regulation was not diverted or captured from an original high purpose. It never served the interests of consumers or other vulnerable social groups in the first place, for one simple reason — it was never intended to.[11] The economic approach is thus consistent with the public choice theories[12] that stress the extent to which governmental behaviour can be understood by viewing all actors as rational individual maximizers of their own welfare. Organizations and bureaucracies thus fall to be analyzed with reference to the competing preferences of the individuals involved. The system thus is to be analyzed with reference to the competing interests and preferences of individuals involved. Emphasis is thus on the tendency of the stakeholders to circumvent official regulatory goals and substitute ends that are self-serving and to act in pursuit of such goals.

In the 'Chicago theory' all the actors in the process are self-interested. Politicians pursue self-interest by aiming to win votes for re-election to public office, since public office will give them power to reward themselves and their followers. In pursuit to votes, politicians 'sell' legislative protection to the interest groups most likely to benefit their electoral cause. In a regulatory context, this activity typically implies setting rates above costs for user of a service, and using the 'rents' thus, obtained to benefit other groups, such as producers and powerful users. The politicians sell regulatory policy to the highest interest group bidder able to sway votes either directly or through campaign contributions. Interest groups are also self-interested with aim to bribe or threaten politicians into using legislative power to transfer wealth to themselves at the expense of other groups.[13] This economic approach assumed that all parties involved in regulation are income maximizers, all parties are well informed and learn from experience and also that regulation is costless hence, overall efficiency will not be affected by levels of regulation. However, this, theory can be attacked in at least three ways. First, the assumption that self-interest leads politicians to value re-election above all else is questionable. Such an identity need not always hold.

The regulatory behaviour might well be shaped not by re-election considerations alone, but also by those of bettering the prospects for future private sector career. Second, even if politicians do value re-election above all else they need to provide for the downside risk of not being re-elected, as an insurance against defeat. This consideration would imply a bias in regulatory policy in office conditioned by the aim of possible 'post politics' employment in the regulated sector. Third, self-interest might have other implications than the standard capture model implies. Even quite narrow and 'economistic' idea of self-interest might lead regulators to pay attention to factors other than their bank balances, prospects for future employment or legislative power. Self-interest in preserving their own lives or way of life would presumably also play a part.

Private interest theory has, however, been questioned on a number of fronts. It is difficult to explain the nature and origins of preferences. Parties may lack determinate preferences on political or regulatory issues and individuals may act altruistically and public-spiritedly in certain important respects. They may identify with legislative, group, agency or bureaucratic objectives and may behave in different ways according to the roles they adopt like consumers of services, career strategists or professional designers of regulatory policies. Further, the regulators may be prevented from acting in rational, self-serving ways by lack of information, expertise or commitment. Public choice theories, moreover, ignore or underrate such important motives as ideologies, policy goals, emotional identifications, personality limits, prejudices and moral stances.[14] Further, there are many problems for private interest theories arising out of experience. For instance, why was there a strong deregulation movement in the 1970s if concentrated business interests were in control of regulatory developments? One explanation might be that ideas, rather than pure interests played a crucial role in moves to deregulate.

2.2.4. *Force of Ideas Explanations*

In this context ideas are taken to refer to intellectual conceptions, which express how and why government ought to control business. Deregulatory movement during the Reagan and Thatcher administration prompted some commentators to argue that certain changes in regulation did not stem so much from pressing private interests as from force of ideas. Ideas might be distorted by the political considerations, but they provide the essential basis of assumed social realities whereby political leaders explain and justify their policies to the public, backed by a media which keeps the range of 'realistic' options within narrow limits.[15] Economics often explains the development of public policy in rather unworldly terms as reflecting the march of economic ideas rather than the weight of interests.[16] Martha Derthick and Paul Quirk offered a controversial explanation of deregulation in USA as a case of 'the politics of ideas' rather than 'the politics of interest'.[17] In similar vein Kenneth Minogue[18] argues that modern liberal democracies are 'loquocentric societies'. By that he means societies in which arguments and ideas if deployed persuasively enough can prompt people to act in ways which do not closely fit their own narrow interests and indeed may go against them. Giandomenico Majone[19] similarly argues that policy change depends heavily on the persuasive deployment of ideas by policy advocates rather than by an inexorable logic of interests.

How might 'ideas' turn policy around? One possibility is that public policy follows the ideas of social science (particularly economics) and that theoretical break through and 'crucial experiments' can put it into reverse. Indeed, within economics, the story of policy change can often be told in terms of a series of key journal papers which altered received opinion. As in the case of deregulation, economists had developed new concepts in the 1960s and 1970s about what made markets 'contestable' and how government regulation could be captured by regulatee. These ideas undermined the traditional justification for a particular style of regulation, built on ideas about what made monopoly 'natural' and how regulation worked. The new ideas seemed to be the driving force of the deregulatory movement. By little more than their own intellectual vigour in offering new interpretations of the regulatory world, these new ideas appeared to carry the day over the 'vested interest', all the producer lobby groups which supported the regulatory *status quo* and 'owned' the relevant regulatory bureaucracies. Others, however, stress the role of packaging than the contents in explaining how economy policy ideas become persuasive. To Donald McCloskey[20] persuasiveness in economics is not explained by 'crucial experiments', but rather by economists' success in deploying age-old rhetorical skills to make essentially contestable arguments seem persuasive, and hence close the debate. In rhetoric, success in argument does not lie in systematic examination of cases (hard data) of formal logic, but in how successfully disbelief can be suspended by making an argument fit a particular social context as a key fits a lock. We should not look for convincing 'crucial experiments' to explain why a particular policy argument triumphed.[21]

However, this argument has difficulty in explaining why certain ideas take root, how ideas can be separated conceptually from interests or in accounting for patchiness of deregulation. It may also be mentioned that the idea in a given situation may be backed by a number of considerations, *viz.* social, political, economic, behavioural etc.

2.2.5. *Institutional Theories*

Institutionalist theories centre on the notion that institutional structure and arrangement, as well as social processes significantly shape regulation. Individual actors are seen as influenced by rules as well as organizational and social settings rather than pure rational choice maximizers and have preferences that are influenced by institutional procedures, principles, expectations and norms that are encountered in cultural and historical frameworks. Thus as per the theory role of institutional arrangements and rules in shaping regulation is much more than public interest or private interests. However, one of the key problems with the institutional theory is how to balance institutional explanations with others in accounting for regulatory changes.

2.3. Growth of Regulations in the United States of America

The history of growth and development of regulations in USA is basically influenced by the practical and theoretical problems persisting during the period. In the period extending from the founding of the republic to 1928, it was realized that powerful administrative agencies were essential and the main attention was on ensuring that the administrative activities took place within an administrative justice system governed by the rule of law. "The Golden Age of Administrative Tribunals" included within its ambit the New Deal, Second World War with its monumental administrative operations and the post-war period, which, witnessed the enactment of the Administrative Procedure Act, 1946, the basic statute governing the operation of administrative law process whether administrative rule-making or administrative adjudication.

During the New Deal years theoretical discussions gave way to practical problems prevailing at that time. Concern for the rule of law was disposed of as procedural protections against arbitrary administrative activities were developed and buttressed by increased judicial review of agency activity. During the period from 1950 to 1969, it was realized that procedural regularity, general requirement of some kind of due process and availability of judicial review had failed to resolve some very basic problems of law and administration. During the period that began at the end of Johnson administration, the literature on administrative law and court rulings experienced a marked change, which was also reflected in popular responses to the energy crisis and other events of 1970s. This period was marked by attempts to respond to some of the problems of the administrative justice system with varying degrees of success. The period including the Carter administration and after can be described as counter bureaucracy challenge and attack on administrative law. The efforts during this period have been primarily directed towards dismantling programmes and organizations rather than fixing problems and blaming administrative law and administrative justice process for public sector problems.

In the latter part of the Nineteenth century development of public regulations of business in America was a reaction to industrialization, urbanization and economic changes that drastically altered the shape of the American society. There was heavy immigration of rural population to the cities and new industrial areas. A national railroad system helped to create regional and national markets and the population became increasingly mobile. These migrated rural populations provided cheap source of labour to factories and traders. However, in 1870s and 1880s workmen, farmers, small businessmen were not satisfied with their share in the profits of industrial development and these dissatisfied groups organized to protect and promote their interests. New labour organizations attempted to unionize the workmen to lower the working hours and to enhance wages. Discontent caused by the decline in the agricultural prices from 1870 to1896, resulted in establishment of farmers' organizations to protect their interests. The small businessmen and farmers joined hands to demand governmental action to outlaw the discriminatory abuses practiced by the railroads. When the state railroad legislation proved to be inadequate, these groups of farmers and small businessmen dependent on railroads to carry goods to the markets approached the national government for help. This prolonged agitation for public protection resulted in passing of Interstate Commerce Act in 1887, which established the Interstate Commerce Commission, the first National Commission for regulation of economic affairs.

Characteristics of the Growth of Regulation of Business in United States

Following are some of the salient features of the regulatory developments in the United States of America:[22]

- It has not been product of any farsighted plan or design or the result of any thoroughly worked out theory. It represented a series of adjustments to the felt abuses. It has been initiated by particular groups to deal with specific evils as they arose rather than inspired by any general philosophy of the governmental control.
- The groups demanding regulations first approached the local governments. When it became clear that these governments could not provide satisfactory public protection against the economic abuses, the demands for regulation were shifted to the state and then national government. Thus, the national regulations were result of the inability of the state and the local governments to meet the insistent demands of politically effective groups for public regulation of business.
- Although the New Deal did expand significantly the scope of the public regulation, but it did not originate the movement to regulate the economic life.
- The expansion of governmental regulations of the economy in United States has been accompanied by similar developments in other industrialized countries. The governmental control of the economic affairs in one form or the other has been universal trend in modern times. However, the regulation by the commission has tended to be a unique American experience.
- Regulation is largely a product of clash of organized private economic interests seeking to utilize governmental powers for enhancement of private interests.

The history of national regulation of business in USA up to 1980 can be divided conveniently into following chronological periods:

1. *1789-1887:* Initial experiments in regulation of business by the State governments.
2. *1887-1906:* Agrarian reforms and the Inter-state Commerce Commission (ICC).
3. *1906-1917:* Era of progressive reform movement leading to establishment of the Federal Trade Commission in 1914.
4. *1920-1929:* Post-war period, wherein after normalcy, the original Federal Power Commission in 1920 and the Federal Radio Commission in 1927 were established.
5. *1930s:* The period of depression and economic recovery and establishment of Securities and Exchange Commission, the

Federal Communications Commission, the National Labour Relations Board, the U.S. Maritime Civil Aeronautics Board.

6. *1940s:* Mobilization for war and defence.
7. *1950-1969:* New Deal to New Federalism.
8. *1969-1976:* Administrative Justice in the Modern Context.

2.3.1. *State Regulation of Business (1789-1887)*

The governmental control of the economic life originated before the civil war. The years during which America functioned under the Articles of Confederation were administrative disasters partly because of lack of effective structure of public administration. In 1789, the new government established under Constitution took over and established complete administrative machinery. By 1790 there was a feudal regulatory statute "for protecting seamen against unseaworthy ships". Under the statute judicial action was primary means of enforcement until a substantial administrative structure was established to deal with the problem in mid-nineteenth century. In 1797 and 1798 New York established a pair of statutes to regulate "noxious trade" that were believed to be dangerous to health, with enforcement responsibility vested in the Commissioner of Health, the Mayor and a judicial tribunal.[23] Thus, a number of major federal trade agencies had their beginning to statutes enacted prior to the close of civil war.

During the period from 1790-1860 the attempts of the State Governments to promote and regulate their economies demonstrate that the state and economic life were closely and intimately related. The objectives of the economic policy cherished by the State Governments at that time ramified into every phase of the business activity and were constant preoccupations of politicians and entrepreneurs. The government assumed the job of shaping decisively the contours of the economic life.

The efforts of the state to promote, guide and regulate the economic activities subsided after beginning of the civil war. The mobilization of the nation for war and accompanying administrative nightmares led to transformation of the public administration. There were difficulties with respect to communication, transportation and management of resources. One of the major results of Civil War was increased industrialization, particularly, the dramatic growth of the railroads. The industrial revolution brought not only new technology, but also led to destruction of the insular agricultural community, the burgeoning growth of urban areas and increasingly complex, interrelated and machine-oriented economy.

The social, economic and political upheavals in the post-war period led to the populist and progressive reform movements. After the Civil War the major regulatory development was the start of Granger Movement to fight the political battles of the discontented farmers. The movement opposed the railroads, denounced monopoly in general, deplored the existence of middleman and advocated cheap money and easy credit to relieve economic distress. As a result of the Granger Movement some state legislatures enacted laws prohibiting abusive railroad practices and establishing maximum rates for freight and discriminatory passenger transportation. Thus, Granger movement succeeded in several states in establishing a commission which had powers to fix maximum rates for railroads, prevent discriminatory short-haul clauses, maintain competition on the railroads and outlaw free passes to public officials. What was more significant was that the movement supported the agitation for national regulation of railroad rates.

Though during the period both before and after 1860, the post-Civil War era, there was close association of the government and economic life, still except for the temporary success of the Granger Legislation, the economic affairs were nurtured on the myths of *laissez faire*. The view that persisted during the era was that the government and business lived in two separate spheres and would co-exist in peace and prosperity so long as government made no attempt to usurp the functions of private business.

2.3.2. *Establishment of Interstate Commerce Commission (1887-1906)*

The establishment of the Independent Regulatory Commission was the product of post-Civil War industrial development. National Railroad Legislation, Interstate Commerce Act of 1887 was the first significant effort of the national government to regulate economic affairs. Federal railroad regulation began with the passage of the Interstate Commerce Act, 1887. The Act required that the carrier rates be just and reasonable, prohibited personal discrimination between shippers and established the Interstate Commerce Commission (ICC) as the enforcement agency. By 1906, amendments to the original legislation had given the ICC the power to prescribe maximum limits for rates if current rates were found to be unreasonable. However, the ICC could not set the actual rate or a minimum rate.

The advocates of the national railroad legislation did not feel that they were violating the principles of *laissez faire*. The national regulation of railroad was supported by economic groups that were individualistic in outlook than the large corporations that opposed the commission idea. One of the objectives of the Act was elimination of monopolistic abuses. The Interstate Commerce Commission was welcomed by agrarian and middle class groups as protector of individual private interest. However, the economic groups that turned pragmatically to the government for protection still maintained the general view that government should interfere as little as possible with the economic affairs. These groups were guided by short-term considerations and were only interested in using governmental power to promote their private economic interests. They still believed in the doctrine of limited government that did not conflict with their efforts to bend the use of public power to promote private interests.

The Act of 1887 was the culmination of twenty-year struggle for legislation. The Act placed the Commission in the Department of the Interior and gave the Secretary of the Interior power of general supervision over the housekeeping activities of the Commission, its budget and supplies and the appointment and compensation of its employees. The annual report of the Commission was also transmitted by the Secretary of the Interior to the Congress. Finally in 1889, Congress abolished the Secretary's powers of supervision and control with a view to make the Commission completely independent.

During the nineteenth century the character of economic regulation shifted gradually from legislative and judicial control to administrative control. At first it was essentially legislative which was enforced through judicial process. State legislatures enacted general and special laws defining legal position of railroads. *Ad hoc* committees also from time to time investigated railroad operations and proposed new legislation to protect community and shippers from discriminatory practices of railroad. The enforcement of these laws was dependent upon courts. After the Fourteenth Amendment became effective, the courts used the "commerce" and the "due process" clauses of the Constitution to invalidate the efforts of the state to regulate the economy and promote public welfare. As a result there was disenchantment and frustration among the agrarian and protest groups against the courts and bar. The courts were accused of extraordinary delays, lack of sympathy with regulatory objectives and lack of specialized knowledge required to deal with complex economic problems. The court procedures were proving to be slow, time consuming and costly. The courts lacked independent means of investigation and depended on parties to the proceeding to prove the case. Because of all these the judicial process was regarded as deficient for the purposes of regulation. Distrust of the judiciary played an important role in transferring responsibilities to an administrative agency. As the courts proved their inability to deal with complex economic relationship in railroad management, attention was diverted to devising an administrative mechanism, which was more flexible than the legislature and more competent than the judiciary in handling the complex economic issues. However, judiciary maintained pivotal position in the determination of regulatory policies by reviewing administrative decisions. The courts succeeded both before and after creation of the ICC in maintaining key position in determining the regulatory policy. Further the Commission continued to follow the judicial pattern of procedure.

Amongst the administrative bodies, the old executive departments were regarded as unsuitable for regulatory administration. When the commission was established at the national level no such comparable activity was being carried out by any executive department. The Civil Service System, which was established only four years before the creation of the ICC, was in the nascent stage and lacked merit and expertise. Thus, the executive department did not offer the creative environment required for regulation of the industry. Therefore, a need was felt for a new type of administrative agency for new type of problem. The nature of the railroad regulation was sufficiently different and technical from the ordinary work of the administrative agencies requiring degree of specialization, expertise and technical know-how. It was regarded that the commission would develop higher degree of expertise and the capacity to handle difficult and technical regulatory problems. It was argued that the commission would be able to give continuous attention to the problems of regulation, would be free from the political influences and would act more expeditiously and have more comprehensive grasp over the problem than the courts. Because of all these reasons the co-option of commission appeared more promising than the executive departments.

Although administrative regulation was devised in part to overcome the disadvantages of the legislative and judicial process, ICC failed to develop techniques required for administrating novel, experimental and complex regulatory policies. It regarded itself as tribunal for adjudicating disputes between private parties, rather than an aggressive promoter of the public interest in railroad transportation. It was believed that judicial approaches would aid the commission in establishing itself in controversial area of regulatory policy and the courts would look favourably to the commission decision. The members of the commission preferred the known virtues of the judicial modes to the untried advantages of administrative procedure. The decisions of the commission were challenged in the court by railroad, which held up the activities of the commission. The novelty and controversial character of administrative regulation and strong opposition from the railroads forced the commission to adopt a conservative and cautious approach.

The first national commission, the Interstate Commerce Commission was developed in a period of dilemma when the political majority demanded reforms, but did not know how to translate its demands into regulatory policy and administrative operations. Congress passed on to the commission the burden of resolving policy issues that it could not resolve itself. Further, a hostile environment was generated against commission because of the unsympathetic attitude of the courts, opposition of railroads and prevailing conservatism with respect to the expanding governmental powers. The Commission's survival in such an environment was defined in terms of a slow evolution of regulatory policy within the framework of judicialized operation. To adjust to the political antagonism commission emphasized on virtues like expertise, impartiality and passive administration.

In America, prior to 1890, there was no prohibition, by way of legislation, on monopolies. It was thought that big business represented a proud and fruitful achievement of the American people. However, the attractive picture of big business could not last long. The rise of modern giant corporation came to be regarded as mainly responsible for concentration of economic power. The concentration of economic power in American industries manifested in the form of trusts and cartels in the first half of the nineteenth century as a result of which many individual enterprises dominated various areas of the American economy. With a view to curtail such practices, several states passed antitrust laws, but their efforts were abortive because of the limitations of their territorial jurisdiction.[24] In addition to these state laws, monopoly was tried to be controlled in America through the application of the English common law doctrine which declared all monopolies and contracts in restraints of trade to be against the law.[25] The failure of the law to meet the desired goal resulted in the increase of monopoly and restrictive trade practices in the industrial combinations and big business, which created distrust against them in the nation. It was in these circumstances that the Federal Government set forth its footsteps in this direction by passing the Sherman Act in 1890. The Sherman Antitrust Act of 1890 marked the beginning of the federal antitrust legislation in the United States. The Sherman Act was designed to prohibit agreements to fix prices, allocation of the markets and boycotts or otherwise restrain trade through combinations or conspiracies and to prevent 'monopolization' of industries. The Act dealt both with the monopoly and the restraints of trade by declaring them to be unlawful and punishable. Thus, the United States was the first country to pass a specific legislation to control monopolies by the end of the nineteenth century. The legislation was later supplemented by two major statutes of 1914 — the Federal Trade Commission Act and the Clayton Act.

2.3.3. *The Progressive Reform Movement (1906-1917)*

This period of development of independent regulatory commission was characterized as the period of Progressive reform. The middle class, urban citizens who were shocked by the corruption and fraud prevailing in American politics at the turn of century were part of this reform movement. Thus, during this period the struggle was against corruption and privilege and for a decent standard for all. The progressives regarded politics as essentially evil and venal. They offered three techniques for purifying the political process. The first was the reform of the electoral process by tinkering with machinery of vesting. The second was to make the government more efficient and economical through use of principles of second management and business methods. An emerging social conscience was needed, which required that the society through government had an obligation to deal with social problems that developed as the nation grew and industrialization increased. The progressives argued that someone must deal with the problems that the marketplace was unable to solve. The third technique was to escape from politics by allocating the major governmental responsibilities to regulatory commissions. These commissions would be kept out of politics and would be free to make decisions on the basis of the expert knowledge and impartial judgement. The progressives strongly believed that the regulation would overcome privilege, restore decency and protect the industry from its own avarice and self-destruction provided the experts in administrative agencies could remain free from partisan political considerations. What emerged from the movement was new faith in professionalism and expertise. The growth of professions was seen as a promising means of applying newly discovered scientific and technological knowledge to social and economic problems.

During this period the modern commission movement was given a new impetus. It was marked by establishment of the State Public Utility Commissions of New York and Wisconsin in 1907 and the Federal Trade Commission in 1914. The market manipulations by large corporations, monopolies and holding companies were instrumental in creation of Federal Trade Commission in 1914.

Various weaknesses in the Sherman Act, 1890 and in the economic sophistication of the federal judiciary led to the passage in 1914 of the Clayton Act and the Federal Trade Commission Act. The main provisions of the Clayton Act related to price discrimination, tying clauses and exclusive dealing contracts, inter-corporate stocking, inter-locking directorates and certain kinds of exemptions from the anti-trust laws. The Federal Trade Commission Act established the Federal Trade Commission, an independent commission whose primary purpose was to initiate and administratively adjudicate certain kind antitrust cases. Each of these Acts made unlawful several kinds of business practices including a variety of vertical business relations as well as "unfair" business practices that firms might use to eliminate actual or potential rivals. The Clayton Act and the FTC Act also gave government some authority to block mergers between firms that would tend to create a monopoly. In the decades that followed, new antitrust legislations had taken the form of amendments to the original legislations like FTC Act was amended from time to time by various statutes for example the Wheeler-Lea Act, 1938 and Anti-Merger Act, 1950. These amendments were designed to close loopholes that arose because of unanticipated judicial interpretation of these Acts or because businesses developed new modes of behaviour not anticipated when the legislations were enacted.

The greatest mistake of the progressives was that the economic regulation by government can be made non-political and corruption can be avoided by taking regulation of economic affairs out of politics. The control of business is essentially a political issue and it cannot be completely relegated to any commission independent of close control by the policy formulating agencies of the government. The analysis of contemporary problems by the progressives was sound, but the cures suggested by them were naive and simple minded. Most of them believed that the key to effective regulation lay in the creation of a commission that would act on behalf of the public interest, but remain aloof from and untouched by the regulated groups.

The principal preoccupations of the movement were purification of political life and achievement of a higher measure of social justice for the Americans. It regarded the government as the primary instrument of social reform provided the power was in the hands of honest men.

2.3.4. *Postwar Normalcy (1920-1929)*

From 1917 to 1920, the mobilization of economy for First World War eclipsed the activities of commission. The activities of the FTC and the ICC were for all practical purposes abandoned and the U.S. Railroad Administration assumed control of all rail transportation. The period was of industrial expansion on grand scale and was unfriendly and hostile to efforts of extension of regulation of economic affairs and maintenance of ongoing programmes of regulation. The twenties was a period of tremendous growth in corporate wealth, of application of new technologies of mass production to rich natural resources and of great expansion of trade and service industries. During this period businessmen acquired prestige and status in the American community at large.

The decade of twenties contributed very little to restore the vitality of commissions. In 1920, Congress passed the Transportation Act, the furthest reaching federal regulatory statute. The 1920 Act gave the Interstate Commerce Commission even greater authority in this area, empowering the agency to set minimum and even exact rates. This Act unveiled a far broader conception of federal regulatory power. The provisions in the Act relating to pooling, consolidation, extension and termination of services created a framework for restructuring of the industry under the regulatory guidance and supervision, to make the railroad service more efficient. No previous federal regulatory legislation rested on so bold an assertion of market failure.

However, the 1920 Act was seriously defective as a regulatory mechanism for planning a reconstituted transportation network was lacking. The ICC was required to do little more than its earlier function of police ratemaking. The agency failed to establish a consolidation plan and refused to develop its strategies on market sharing service curtailment and extension questions. Instead, it followed a path of least resistance, generally acquiescing in the unsystematic efforts of various railroads to merge, combine sources or alter patterns of service.

The authority of the ICC was expanded under the Transportation Act, 1920, but it did very little to utilize its expanded new powers. The Federal Trade Commission was reduced to an investigative body and was unable to contribute to the development of law dealing with unfair trade practices. The Federal Water Power Act of 1920 established Water Power Commission, weak *ex-officio* body with some authority to license waterpower developments by private interests on public lands and to fix interstate power rates and regulate the security issues of interstate power companies. Till 1928, the Water Power Commission did not have adequate funds and depended on staff borrowed from other agencies. It was only in 1930 that it was recognized as independent commission. The most interesting development of twenties was creation of Federal Radio Commission, 1927. When in 1926 and 1927 the court declared invalid the attempts of the secretary of commerce to regulate radio broadcasting through issuance of licences, utter chaos developed in the field, as a result demands were raised by the radio industry to develop some form of public regulation to restore order. This led to creation of Federal Radio Commission, 1927, which was succeeded by Federal Communication Commission, 1934.

In historical perspective, the New Deal appears as distinct break from the past. The regulatory initiatives of the Populist and Progressive eras were largely discrete and limited measures, aimed mainly at particularized fields of activity in which vigorous competition led to sharp market practices. Pre-New Deal regulatory initiatives rested on the assumption that minor government policing could ensure a smoothly functioning market. But the Depression put to rest this constrained view of national power. Even the more traditional regulatory aspects of the New Deal conceived of governmental activity as a permanent bulwark against deep-rooted structural shortcomings in the market economy.

2.3.5. *Depression Decade — Emergence of Regulatory Commissions*

At the beginning of the 1930s the American people suffered the most disastrous economic collapse in their history. The economic crisis had begun and was connected mainly with the agrarians. This had occurred in American economic life as a result of the unplanned and uncontrolled actions of economic groups in pursuit of private interests. City people, industrialists, bankers and even workers were not much concerned with farmers' woes. Except in agriculture, a great boom had been going on in other sectors of economy. A peculiarity of this boom was that prices had not gone up. In fact, non-farm commodity prices had been remarkably stable from 1920 to 1928. The industrialists had exploited this fact by talking about "profitless prosperity". But actually it had not been profitless. As a result of the many technical advances during the war, efficiency was greater and costs were coming down. Profits, in spite of stable prices, were going up and up. However, successful continuation of large scale industry requires that purchasing power amongst the consumers must be sufficient to carry off the volume produced. In order to maintain the purchasing power of the consumers it is necessary that the consumers' income and the total prices attached to the goods and services for sale must be roughly equal, which requires that the prices must come down as costs come down otherwise, the increasing profits goes into increase production. In the long run outcome is warehouses filled with goods for which there was no demand leading to crisis. This was the basic problem in 1929 which led to economic crisis.

By 1929, productive power had far outrun purchasing power. The farmers had first been priced out of the market then other consumers had followed and all the time vast increases in plant were being made. Also vast speculations were taking place with the ever-growing surpluses of business. Suddenly, it was seen that the huge debts contracted at the inflated levels of speculation could not be paid. All creditors tried to force payment of debts to them at once, leading to panic and crisis.

It was within the context of this overriding issue that there occurred the outburst of political leadership and legislation, of socio-economic experimentation and change that is called the New Deal. Perhaps the New Deal might be defined as bewildered idealism, leftish in objectives, rightish in methods, misunderstood by liberals, misused by conservatives, mistrusted by businessmen, but still relied upon reluctantly by indebted farmers, doubtfully by organized labour, helplessly by the unemployed, and hopefully by bewildered idealists.[26] The flood of laws, government action, and social planning after 1932 did several basic things: it established the precedent of continuous governmental responsibility for the well-being of the economy, it instituted broad social welfare programme, and it worked major shifts in national political allegiances. Never before in American history had so much new legislation, and legislation of such importance, been passed in so short a time. Never before, save in wartime had the activities of government such profound and of far-reaching consequences for the way of life of the American people.

Upon the basis of experience in the great depression, organized labour, farm, and consumer groups had turned to government for assistance in improving their income and economic security. The satisfaction of these demands has made for a new and revolutionary conception of government. In the historical development of the United States, the governmental policy was primarily an admixture of measures which provided (1) equality of opportunity for the common man (such as the public school system and the Homestead Act of 1862) and

(2) generous favours for those who knew how to help themselves (tariff privileges, favourable corporation, legislation and ownership of the richest natural resources of the nation. With the advent to the "New Deal" in 1933 and subsequently called the "Fair Deal", however, the purpose of government was shaped and directed to that of guaranteeing economic safety and "fair shares" of income for all.[27] The means employed by Congress in fulfilling its duty of guaranteeing security and welfare for all consisted of (1) placing certain restrictions, curbs, limits and controls upon the economically strong and wealthy groups and (2) providing financial assistance and social services for the general public to economic well-being.

What is commonly called the First New Deal included attempts to restore America's economic vitality and reform her stricken economic institutions, and efforts for relief and reform which were directed more toward people than toward institutions. Rauch's discussion of the development of the First New Deal interprets it as a desirable, democratic programme of recovery, relief, and reform, made necessary by the accumulated evils of a business dominated economy. He argues that the measures for social relief and reform were more significant than the ones for economic recovery; that the major issues of the First New Deal were the attempt of big business to control the National Recovery Administration and the relationship of the Roosevelt administration to the rising demands of labour; and that the unreasonable resistance of the business community helped to bring on the more important and more permanent achievement of the Second New Deal. Thus, for Rauch the major force in the early New Deal was the interplay of various interest groups, and the central theme of those years was the Roosevelt administration's growing responsiveness to the aspirations of the most needy of those interest: labour, farmers, small businessmen.[28]

From 1935 to 1938 a second wave of legislation — a Second New Deal appeared, concentrating not so much on the recovery and rehabilitation of the economic structure as on further attempts at social relief and reform. The New Deal has attempted to do something about limping economy by regulation. The purpose has been twofold — to try to get it more into balance and so to stimulate activity and to do justice to underpaid farmers and workers by giving them a larger share of what is produced.

Immediately after the banking emergency, in order to put through a group of basic recovery measures with unemployment and farm reliefs as basic objectives a number of laws were enacted. Before the legislative mills had ceased to grind at the end of the famous "hundred days" a large number of important laws had been passed. A brief narration of such important laws is provided in next paras.

The Agricultural Adjustment Act which was passed as an administrative measure and signed on May 12, 1933 was an omnibus which gave the farmers of the country their three main demands of the preceding half-century and longer: protection against the ruinous effect on prices of their surplus crops, inflated currency with which to pay their debts, and cheap credit. No law had promised the farmers so much since the Homestead Act of 1862. One of the main efforts of the Agricultural Adjustment Administration had been to increase the prices received by farmers, first by the domestic allotment plan and when that was declared unconstitutional, indirectly by soil-conservation payments and other crop-limitation policies.

Unemployment relief was the second immediate objective of the administration. On March 21, 1933 the President sent a message to Congress asking for three types of legislation. Two of the requests were quickly met by establishment of the Civilian Conservation Corps (CCC), which provided 2,50,000 unemployed young men with little more than subsistence wages as workers in the national forests, and the Federal Emergency Relief Administration which made grants to the states for direct relief. The third request was met in Title II of the National Industrial Recovery Act passed in June. This Title established the Public Works Administration (PWA) and was a simple expansion of the President Hoover's policy of providing employment by the construction of public buildings, roads, and other traditional federal works.

The National Industrial Recovery Act (NIRA) was passed by large majority and signed on June 16, 1933. It was the most important and far reaching legislation ever enacted by the American Congress. Its goal was assurance of a reasonable profit to industry and living wages for labour. The New Deal's basic labour policy was established in the famous Section 7A of the NIRA. The National Recovery Administration (NRA) created under the terms of NIRA was the keystone of the New Deal programme launched by Roosevelt. By Section 7A, the New Deal morally committed itself to intervene in the industrial struggle to restrain open-shop employers, to make the workers' right to organize a reality. Under Section 7A labour was promised the inclusion in industrial codes of unspecified minimum wages and maximum hours rules, and was guaranteed the right of collective bargaining with employers through representatives freely chosen by employees. For businessmen, limitation of production and exemption of codes from the antitrust laws were provided. The question of the degree of governmental control in the drawing up of codes was left to a tug-of-war between the trade associations which were given the right to formulate them, and the government which could reject them and promulgate codes on its own motion. Violators of code agreements could be prosecuted before the federal courts and punished. The President was left free to establish whatever administrative agencies he deemed necessary. The Bill was considered by the President to be a deliberate step away from the philosophy of "equalitarianism and *laissez faire*". Ideally, the system envisaged would consist of separate institutions of self-government for both labour and industry, with the government requiring them to cooperate and preventing either one from injuring the other or the public. The whole law was later declared unconstitutional.[29]

The Tennessee Valley Authority Act passed on May 18, 1933 was a victory for those who, without discussing socialist theory, insisted that the government own and operate for the benefit of the people hydroelectric plants on the great waterways of the nation in order to prevent private corporations from exploiting these vast resources for private gains. The setting-up of great public power projects under the TVA Act with encouragement for public or cooperative distribution and the work of the Rural Electrification Administration (REA), resulted in reduced rates and wider distribution of electricity.

The Securities Act of May 27, 1933 originated in the conviction of liberals over many years that a federal "blue-sky" law was needed to protect the public from fraud and misrepresentation in the issuance, manipulation, and sale of stocks and other securities. The depression had thrown glaring light on the unscrupulous purposes behind many securities issues, the devious methods by which insiders rigged the stock market and the deceptions practiced by high-pressure salesmen who gulled the small investor. Correction of these abuses was a part of the democratic platform. Confusion of counsel separated regulation of securities issues and sales from the allied problem of stock-exchange regulation, postponed action on the latter until 1934. The main provisions of the Securities Bill were that new issues of securities be registered with the Federal Trade Commission along with a statement of the financial position of the company and that the same information be given to all purchasers of the issue.

Among the other more prominent types of economic regulation under the New Deal has been that administered by the Securities and

Exchange Commission established in 1934 with the adoption of Securities Exchange Act, 1934. This has registered the issuance of securities and exercised a certain amount of control over stock-exchange practices. It was probably a little more difficult now than before for the innocent investor of speculator to be cheated, but hardly more difficult for him to lose his money.

The Glass-Steagall Banking Act of June 16, 1933 established three reforms which most bankers as well as liberals had come to believe were necessary to prevent repetition of the abuses which had aggravated the boom, the depression and the banking crisis. Investment banking was separated from commercial banking so that affiliates could no longer be used by bankers for speculation with their depositors' money. The Federal Deposit Insurance Corporation was established to afford a government guaranty of bank deposits under $5,000. The Federal Reserve Board was given powers over interest rates and other factors, which would enable it to prevent excessive speculation with borrowed money.

The TVA Act, the Securities Act, and the Banking Act were all sustained by the Supreme Court, while the chief recovery laws, AAA and NIRA, were invalidated. The NRA and AAA did not bring the immediate benefits that labour, industry, and agriculture expected.

The second front on which the President attacked the threatened collapse was unemployment relief. Unemployment relief has brought the New Deal more intimately into the lives of Americans than any other of its activities. The NRA campaign to expand employment and production was failing. The President had been doubtful from the beginning that the PWA would put an appreciable number of the unemployed to work, because of the restriction on it that only the conventional types of public construction and repair projects might be undertaken. Relief rolls began to rise again with the business reaction. The prospect of another winter of increasing unemployment determined the President to act.

With the objectives that the federal government should provide work relief for employable rather than merely funds for direct relief to be administered by the states, that minimum wage rates higher than relief payments should be paid for labour, and that the skills of the unemployed should be used and developed, a first step towards realization was taken on November 8, when the President announced the creation of the Civil Works Administration (CWA). The essential pattern of the New Deal's relief programme was fixed by the old Civilian Works Administration, formed in December 1933. The idea was to preserve both the technical skill and the morale of the jobless by supplying them with the same sort of jobs they had in private industry. Funds were allocated from FERA and PWA appropriations supplemented by local governments. Wages were paid which represented a great increase in the purchasing power of the unemployed as compared with relief payments. The administrative machinery was entirely federal.

The CWA was followed by the FERA and then by the WPA. The WPA was established in January 1935. It had given jobs and sustenance to a minimum of 14,00,000 and a maximum of 33,00,000 persons in five years. Its work projects added immeasurably to the national wealth in some regions the school, health and recreation facilities. It had fairly revolutionized communal life.

The third action taken to support recovery was the adjustment of NRA regulations to improve the position of small business and labour. On October 22, 1933 businessmen in small towns were exempted from observing the Blanket Code, price increases by manufacturers were made subject to investigation and machinery for handling complaints against business practices was established. On December 16, 1933 the National Labour Board's (NLB) powers were increased as a result of "several flagrant cases of defiance of the Board by large employers of labour". The Board had been established to preserve industrial peace by "passing" on disputes arising under Section 7A. Now, its powers were defined to include mediation, conciliation, and arbitration. These alterations in NRA's powers were the first official recognition that NRA was not providing equal benefits for all groups rather big business was turning it to its own purposes at the expense of small business, labour, and consumers.

The year 1934 was one of transition from the First to the Second New Deal. The year ended with striking approval at the polls of the administration's course and with momentous decisions which launched major policies of the Second New Deal in 1935.

The chief controversy and one of the most fruitful changes in administrative policy during the transition from the First to the Second New Deal concerned NRA. There were charges that NRA fostered monopoly. The administration from time to time in 1934 took action designed to breakdown these monopolistic tendencies. On January 20 the President issued an Executive Order:

> To provide a practical and rapid way of making effective those provisions of the National Industrial Recovery Act that were designed to prevent persons, under the guise of purported sanctions contained

> in codes . . . from engaging in monopolistic practices or practices tending to eliminate, oppress or discriminate against small enterprises.[30]

Complainants against monopoly were empowered to appeal their cases from the code authorities to the Federal Trade Commission or the Department of Justice. In August 1934 many more categories of small business were exempted from all code provisions except those guaranteeing collective bargaining and forbidding child labour. In September President ordered creation of a new National Industrial Recovery Board consisting of five officials. On October 22, 1934 the new board announced that code provisions to limit production would no longer be enforced.

The monopolistic features of the NRA were being whittled away by the end of 1934. The chief reason was the refusal of business to enter into the cooperative spirit on which the experiment was predicated, to share the benefits of recovery with other groups, or to observe in good faith the provisions of Section 7A in return for its own privileges. Business had won official recognition for its own trade associations and their programme, but it had refused to grant similar recognition to independent labour unions and their programme.

In the 1934 session of Congress, Senator Wagner first proposed a permanent, independent agency to safeguard the right of collective bargaining. On March 1, 1934, Senator Wagner introduced in the Senate the Labour Disputes Bill to prohibit "unfair labour practices" by employers, among which the following were enumerated: the initiation and financing of company unions, interference with employees' free choice of their representatives and refusal to recognize or bargain with employees' representatives. It also called for the creation of a permanent labour board with power to impose penalties in order to enforce the provisions of the law, mediate disputes, and conduct elections to determine employees' representatives. As the President disapproved the Bill, Senate Wagner accordingly permitted his bill to be modified to remove most of the restrictions on domination by employers of the company. Congress enacted the National Labor Relations Act (NLRA) in 1935 to protect the rights of employees and employers, to encourage collective bargaining, and to curtail certain private sector labour and management practices, which can harm the general welfare of workers, businesses and the U.S. economy. The Old National Labour Board was abolished and the new National Labour Relations Board was established.

The NLRB was greeted by a vicious, concentrated attack from industry under the leadership of the National Association of Manufacturers. A brief was published by fifty-eight Liberty League lawyers — some of the most distinguished members of the American Bar — declaring the NLRB clearly unconstitutional and inferentially inviting employers to defy it. More than one hundred injunction suits were sought in the federal courts, The NLRB was paralyzed during the first eighteen months of its existence; it was no more than a shadowy corpse. This was also the period of fierce battles in the House over the Wages-and-Hours Bill, devised to carry out another purpose of the NRA by prohibiting competition at the expense of the workers.

In April 1937, the Supreme Court upheld the constitutionality of the NLRB in a five-to-four decision delivered by Chief Justice Hughes. For the first time, the NLRB was able to discharge the duties entrusted to it. One of the most significant happenings of the last eight years has been its success in winning the confidence of the rank and file of workers. In 1938, industrial disputes reduced by one-half. The period of the NLRB's existence has witnessed enormous increases in union membership and collective bargaining.

A far reaching programme of social security was also initiated in 1934. The Railway Retirement Act of June 27 provided pensions for railroad workers after thirty years of service or at an age of sixty-five, the cost to be borne one-third by themselves and two-third by the companies. On June 29, 1934 the President appointed the Committee on Economic Security to prepare plans for a universal programme of unemployment and old-age pension insurance and health and child welfare benefits.

Government regulations of business were extended to several new areas during 1934. The Securities and Exchange Act of June 6 established Securities and Exchange Commission and charged it with the enforcement of the Securities Act of 1933 and with prevention of excessive speculation, marginal trading and manipulation of prices by stock-exchange operators. The Communications Act of June 19 created the Federal Communications Commission to exercise controls over telegraph, cable and radio corporations. After revelations of fraud in letting of air mail contracts which occurred under the Hoover administration and a disastrous attempt to fly the mails by the army, the Air Mail Act of June 12 was passed to return mail flying to private companies under rigid controls calculated to prevent further fraud, kidnapping and other crimes.

The New Deal's programme of agricultural relief falls into two parts. The first comprised measures to rescue the farmers who still managed to retain land ownership, by no matter how small a margin. The second included measures for the relief of the nearly three million tenant and sharecropper families, those who had lost their access to the soil. For the first group, the owner-operators, the New Deal was sought chiefly to reduce the burdensomeness of mortgage debt.

The other half of the New Deal's programme for agricultural relief that for tenants and sharecroppers had its start with the fierce 1934 drought. By the end of that summer, the FERA's division of Rural Rehabilitation was the sole support of 30,00,000 persons. The next year, 1935, the Resettlement Administration, headed by Under-Secretary of Agriculture Rexford G. Tungwell, was created to care for all rural relief. This relief took multitudinous forms. The RA's chief planning zeal, however, was aimed at creating rural cooperatives and collectives, where farm families would raise their crops in fellowship. The RA also undertook the construction of four suburban towns, intended to be models of twentieth-century planning.

After the 1936 election, and Mr. Tungwell's resignation, this part of the New Deal's rural relief programme changed markedly. One reason for the shift was the bitter, uninformed criticism of share-croppers' collectives that had arisen in the South. The New Dealers gave assurances that this programme would be abruptly halted. At the same time, the RA's name was altered to the Farm Security Administration.

To underscore its disapproval of the RAs policies, Congress in the Bankhead Farm Tenancy Act instructed the FSA to work towards precisely the opposite ideal, that of setting up tenants and sharecroppers as ruggedly independent farm owners.

The greatest part of the FSA's activity, however, had centred on its so-called rehabilitation loans. One of the most spectacular successes of the whole New Deal had been the Rural Electrification Administration, which has lent funds to local governments and private groups for the construction of electric-power lines. The REAs competition has compelled private utilities to increase their rural facilities.

Agricultural relief has been nowhere nearly adequate to rescue a stricken farm population, but it has done something and without it conditions would have been infinitely worse.

In 1938 Congress passed a number of New Deal measures that carried out earlier policies. The most ambitious attempt made by the government to regulate wages and hours was the passage and administration of the Fair Labour Standards Act. The Act abolished child labour and provided a ceiling on hours and a floor under wages, at least for most of the workers engaged in businesses that were classified as "interstate commerce".

During the New Deal the Congress passed the Emergency Transportation Act of 1933, the Motor Carrier Act of 1935 (MCA) and the Transportation Act of 1940, which together established a legislative basis for regulating virtually all transport modes. The Motor Carrier Act of 1935 (MCA) brought interstate motor carriage under the regulatory authority of the ICC. The Motor Carrier Act established categories of carriers; it gave the ICC the authority to regulate entry into trucking by requiring common and contract carriers to obtain operating licences from the ICC. It also gave the ICC the authority to set maximum and minimum rates for common carriers and minimum rates for contract carriers. Trucking firms wishing to change their rates had to file them in advance with ICC to allow competitors the opportunity to protest and the majority of protested rates were withdrawn. ICC regulation not only helped to cartelize the existing licenced operators, but also erected insurmountable barriers to new entry. To operate legally, all trucking firms had to receive an operating licence from the ICC. The potential entrants had to make a compelling case that permitting their entry was in public interest and that the existing service was inadequate, which was almost impossible to do. In addition, under ICC regulations, permission for entry could be denied if existing carriers made a case that entry would harm them financially or that they themselves would offer the proposed service. Further, if the licence was granted to an operator, it was for a specific route or a specific commodity.

The U.S. Civil Aeronautical Act of 1938 established the Civil Aeronautical Board (CAB) and gave the CAB the authority to regulate interstate airline fares, to regulate entry into interstate airline transport sector and to provide subsidies to promote the industry. Need to regulate the airline was felt as air transport was an infant industry and further it had obvious military application and there was also a link between private air transport and U.S. Postal System. The CAB's regulatory authority was not limited to assisting in the development of air transport. The other statutory goals of CAB regulation were slightly vague and in some cases contradictory. These were encouraging competition, ensuring that carrier provide adequate and sufficient service at reasonable prices, avoiding 'unjust' price discrimination and promoting 'sound economic conditions' in the industry.

Achievements of New Deal

Roosevelt administration will be remembered chiefly for its vast engineering achievements: the Tennessee Valley Authority, Boulder Dam, Grand Coulee, Bonneville and Fort Peck. The primary purposes of these huge structures were to produce hydro-electric power in great volume at low cost, which was not only valuable in itself, but offered a useful yardstick for the prices asked by private companies for the same thing, to afford flood control and irrigation, to checkmate soil erosion through proper agricultural methods, to facilitate river navigation, bring fresh supplies of water to cities and to manufacture nitrates for fertilizer. Civilian Conservation Corps (CCC) boys had built many dams and irrigation ditches. The Agricultural Adjustment Administration had for several years been paying farmers something to leave part of their land idle and to follow other methods of saving the soil.

Depressions are bad enough on old people, but they are far harder on the young. The depression turned vagrant army of boys and girls who had nowhere to go, but nowhere to stay either, into irreclaimable derelicts. The New Deal did a heroic, unrecorded and unrecognized job in remedying many of these evils. The CCC has taken a total of about 20,00,000 young men, unemployed and without resources, and put them to work on the land, 30,00,000 at time, in service that must not be less than six months or more than two years. They had done very extensive job for the country in the way of reforestation, soil conservation, irrigation, fire-fighting and eliminating fire hazards, destruction of insects, pests and aboreal diseases and road and trail building.

There was the National Youth Administration, one of its important activities was helping boys and girls to stay in high school or college when their family resources made this impossible. Hundreds of thousands worked ten or twenty hours a month at 30 or 40 cents an hour and that sum spells to them the difference between an education completed and an education destroyed by the economic storm. Their tasks were set and supervised by the institutions where they worked, and were on good and useful project without much botheration. Many thousands of other young people were aided outside school in workshops where they were given useful employment and whenever possible were taught trades and occupations in which they could subsequently earn their livelihood.

As regards the problems of housing and home financing were concerned the Roosevelt administration has been the first to make real attempt to ameliorate these conditions. First through the Public Works Administration and later through the United States Housing Authority, some of the worst slums in the United States were destroyed and their inhabitants, or an equivalent number of very poor, were moved into new buildings. The USHA has loaned to the communities about $60,00,00,000. This money was used by the local communities who got it, to construct about 1,34,000 dwelling units in which half a million people lived. A small additional fee was charged for water, gas, electricity and heat. As a rule, family income could not be more than five times the rent. The New Deal, even in its second term, had clearly done far more for the general welfare of the country and its citizens than any administration in the previous history of the nation. Perhaps its most important achievement was the National Labour Relations Act, the result of which was to inhibit employers' opposition to union organization and true collective bargaining, so that trade union membership was more than doubled.

During the 1930s there was significant change in the place of the independent regulatory commissions in the government and its role. During this period there was demand for governmental activity to provide relief from the effects of great depression and need for recovery of economy. This shifted the priority towards the emergency and recovery activities of new emergency agencies and old executive departments. However, the interest in the independent commissions did not decline due to a number of reasons. Firstly, the country was aroused by the stock exchange scandals in 1931-32, and followed closely senate investigation of stock exchange practices. The stock market crash in 1929 causing sudden loss to the general public as well as market manipulators showed that the market system required some policing to ensure that the competition was indeed fair and open. The Roosevelt administration moved on two fronts. Firstly, it sought to stabilize the market place through several types of legislative programmes including bank regulation, market regulation, agricultural incentives and controls, codes of competition developed by members of business community under provisions of the National Industrial Recovery Act and related policies. Secondly, his administration moved on to the social welfare front with employment generating programmes and other techniques to provide more social security to the individuals. As a result the focus was on the establishment of Securities and Exchange Commission, Federal Communication Commission, the U.S. Maritime Commission, the National Labour Relations Board and the Civil Aeronautics Board etc. to regulate the economy and also to ensure proper implementation of social security measures.

Secondly, many influential senators and representatives supported the commission as a device for counteracting the trend towards concentration of powers in executive branch under a strong President. To Congress the commission remained a bulwark against presidential domination. Thirdly, there was a campaign spearheaded by American Bar Association to surround the regulatory process with procedures and rules to protect private practices from any possibility of unfair or arbitrary action by the commissions. The attention of Congress, the courts and law schools were focused on the growth of administrative discretion and the problems of judicial review and procedural due process growing out of tremendous expansion of the economic activities of the national governments.

In May 1933, Special Committee on Administrative Law was created by the Executive Committee of the American Bar Association to deal with the problem of administration explosion. The overriding purpose for the creation of the committee was the fear of burgeoning administrative powers without clear constraints on that power sufficient to ensure responsiveness and responsibility of those in administrative positions. It was recognized that one of the reasons for the increase in administrative tribunals was dissatisfaction with orthodox judicial proceedings and legislative actions and need for continuity and expertness in administration. The committee began a study of the administrative process to be used as a basis regularizing administrative procedure and clarifying standards for judicial review of agency decisions. For the next several years, the reforms in administrative justice system were slow. With change in the politico-economic climate during the second New Deal pressure for change increased. The Brownlow Commission criticized the agencies as a "headless fourth branch of government".[31] Roosevelt rejected that assessment and directed Attorney General to appoint a study commission to perform a complete analysis of the administrative justice system and provide recommendations. As a result, the Attorney General's Committee on Administrative Procedure was created in February 1939.

Though the commission was widely acknowledged to be uniquely suited to the task of adjudicating regulatory controversy, some attacked it as being unfit for this task unless its activities were safeguarded at every point by laws prescribed rules of fair procedure and judicial review. Administrative Absolutism was the term employed to characterize the alleged deficiencies of the independent commission and other agencies exercising regulatory powers. Those who criticized the commission as arbitrary and unfair simultaneously maintained the orthodox position that the impartiality, expert staff and non-political character of the commission equipped them well for the task of economic regulation and adjudication. During the 1930s there was an increased interest in improving coordination in the administration of governmental activities generally and in the coordination of the regulatory activities of the commissions and national economic policy.

During the depression decade, the regulatory commissions, especially the new ones, were relied upon for minor patrol duties to prevent American business from destroying itself. But the economic problems facing the country at that time went far beyond the limited scope of economic regulation. The National Recovery Administration (NRA) replaced the anti-monopoly programmes of the FTC and the Department of Justice until 1937 and the public works and other programmes designed to stimulate recovery took precedence. Thus, the 1930s apparently taught the United States to intervene everywhere through independent regulatory commissions.

Judicial Response to New Deal Legislations

During 1935 and 1936 the court had declared no less than four major items of Federal Legislation unconstitutional, including both the National Industrial Recovery Act, 1933 and the Agricultural Adjustment Act. The Supreme Court by using its powers of judicial review, as argued by the President Roosevelt, was threatening the entire basis of the New Deal and making it impossible for his government to carry through its programme. The judicial opponents of the New Deal were men imbued with the principles of *laissez faire*. In the case of *Home Building and Loan Association* vs. *Blaisdell*,[32] the right of the State of Minnesota to pass a law aiding householders unable to pay their mortgages was upheld by the court. The four Justices Butler, McReynold, Sutherland and VanDevanter inflexible devotees of *laissez faire* did not agree in their dissenting opinion. The New York State Bar Association was likewise convinced that interference by the government with the judiciary was subverting traditional values. They underlined that "there are certain fundamental social and economic laws which are beyond the power, and certain governmental principles which are beyond the right of official control, and any attempt to interfere with their operation inevitably ends in confusion, if not disaster".[33]

The most spectacular blow against the New Deal was, of course, the invalidation of the National Industrial Recovery Act on 27 May, 1935.

Chief Justice Hughes said that "the Constitution established a national government with powers deemed adequate as they have proved to be both in war and peace, but these powers of the national government are limited by the Constitutional grants. Those who act under these grants are not at liberty to transcend the imposed limits because they believe that more or different power is necessary". Extraordinary conditions do not create or enlarge Constitutional power.[34] Several Justices on the court, Brandeis, Stone and Cardozo, however, consistently, Hughes and Roberts intermittently believed that both the Federal administration and the State Government have a positive obligation to act to minimize the consequences of the depression. In the dissenting opinion of Brandeis in the case of *New State Ice Company* vs. *Liebmann*,[35] it was observed:

> "The people of the United States are now confronted with an emergency more serious than war. Misery is widespread, in a time, not of scarcity, but of over abundance. The long continued depression has brought unprecedented unemployment, a catastrophic fall in commodity prices and a volume of economic losses which threatens our financial institutions. . . . But rightly or wrongly, many persons think that one of the major contributing causes has been unbridled competition. Increasingly doubt is expressed whether it is economically wise, or morally right, that men should be permitted to add to the producing facilities of an industry which is already suffering from overcapacity. Many insist there must be some form of economic control. There are plans for pro-ration. There are many proposals for stabilization. . . . To stay experimentation in thing social and economic is a great responsibility. Denial of the right to experiment may be fraught with serious consequences to the nation. It is one of the happy incidents of the federal system that a single courageous state may, if its citizens choose, serve as a laboratory, and try novel social and economic experiments without risk to the rest of the country. This court has the power to prevent an experiment. . . . But, in the exercise of this high power, we must be able on our guard, lest we erect our prejudices in the legal principles. If we would be guided by the light of the reason, we must let our minds be bold".[36]

Panama Refining Co. vs. *Ryans*[37] is a case based on Section 9 of the Industrial Recovery Act, 1933. Section 9 authorized the President to prohibit the transportation in inter-State and foreign commerce, petroleum and the products thereof produced or withdrawn from storage in excess of any State law or valid regulation. The President authorized the Secretary of the Interior to exercise all powers under Section 9. Regulation V provided that every purchaser and shipper should submit the details of the purchase and sale of petroleum. Panama Refinery Company challenged Section 9 of the Industrial Recovery Act, 1933 as unconstitutional delegation of legislative powers. The Act laid down that the policy of the law is "to encourage national industrial recovery" and "to foster fair competition". The US Supreme Court held the Act as unconstitutional on the ground that the adequacy of prescribed limits of delegation of legislative power is not satisfied by laying down a vague standard for administrative action. Chief Justice Hughes observed that an executive order must, in order to satisfy the constitutional requirement, show the existence of particular circumstances and conditions under which the making of such an order has been authorized by the Congress.

In *Schechter Poultry Corporation* vs. *United States*,[38] the corporation which was engaged in live poultry operations challenged the constitutionality of Section 3 of the National Industrial Recovery Act on the ground of unconstitutional delegation of legislative power. Section 3 of the Act authorized the President to approve "Codes of Fair Conduct" laying down the standard of fair competition for a particular trade or industry. The Act made violation of the Code punishable. Chief Justice Hughes held Section 3 as unconstitutional on the ground that it supplies no standard besides the statement of the general aims of rehabilitation, correction and expansion described in Section 1. Therefore, in the opinion of the court it was a case of virtual abdication of legislative powers by the Congress which violates the principle of *delegatus non-protest delegare*.

Since, the decision in the following case, the balance has tilted in the other direction, perhaps because of social and economic imperatives. Thus, pragmatic considerations have prevailed over theoretical objections. Hence, the court has allowed a wide margin to the Congress in laying down a valid standard. If the delegation is of a regulatory nature, the court has upheld constitutionality of the delegation of legislative power even in the absence of any specified standard. Therefore, in *Lichter* vs. *U.S.*[39] the Supreme Court held the delegation valid observing that the statutory term "excessive profits" was sufficient expression of legislative policy and standards to render it constitutional. In this case the Reorganization Act, 1942 had empowered Administrative officers to determine whether the prices were excessive and to recover profits, which they determined to be excessive.

2.3.6. *1940s' Administrative Reforms*

The critics of administrative law as it existed during this period made two major arguments against the administrative agencies. The first was that the power of administrative agencies to make rules having the force of law was unconstitutional operated on unconstitutional delegations of legislative power. The people delegated the power to the legislature to make laws and that power may not be delegated to an administrative agency as per the legal maxim '*delegatus non potest delegare*'. Secondly, in addition of being abuse of legislative power, such grant of authority to the agency would also violate separation of powers. There was combination of functions since the agencies formulated rules, enforced those rules and also adjudicated disputes arising from enforcement of rules. Criticism hit a high point with condemnation by the Brownlow Commission of the administrative agencies as "headless fourth branch".[40] Landis, a New Dealer and member of the Securities and Exchange Commission, however, defending the administrative processes and the commissions argued that the administrative power grew in part because of the deficiencies of the judiciary and the legislature. To meet the practicalities of the situation, agencies were created whose functions embraced the three aspects of the government. He argued that efficient and effective responses to "problems of administering the peoples business" could only be achieved by experts with an ongoing interest in particular policy areas. These expert administrators must have some discretion to accomplish their tasks.[41] Responding to the argument against delegation of authority, he asserted that there are tasks that the government must perform. Once the legislators identify a matter that requires government action, one of the two factors may result in broad grant of discretion to administrators to deal with the problem. First, the matter may be very complex for the legislators to understand the specific problems involved in administering a policy. Second, competing interests within legislature may agree that some kind of policy and administering mechanism is necessary, but may not be able to achieve consensus on details. In such situation, the legislature instead of doing nothing, settles on a general statute vesting considerable discretion of fill in the details in the agency involved. Landis was satisfied that the existing checks were sufficient to prevent administrative arbitrariness. Their discretion within the narrow range of activity is limited by statutes and is subject to judicial review.

The next major defence of the administrative agencies came with the publication of Report of the Attorney General Committee in 1941.[42]

The report noted several important aspects of law and administration worth consideration. First, the committee recognized a central dilemma of administrative law. There is a basic conflict between those who demand complete standardization of procedures as in the judicial system and those who argue for more flexibility enabling the administrators to use their expertise in the changing administrative environment to accomplish the purposes for which these agencies were created. Second, the committee emphasized that most cases that arise in administrative law are disposed of informally rather than by formal procedures. The informality of procedure being the "lifeblood of the administrative process". Third, the administrative disputes involve more than two parties. Since, most of the decisions are not made in public proceedings, it is difficult to ensure that all interests are adequately protected. Both procedural regularity and judicial review are better devices to ensure protection for individual participants in a dispute than they are controls to ensure that agencies are sufficiently vigorous in administrative policy. Ultimately, the committee sought refuge from administrative arbitrariness in procedural regularity, due process and judicial review.

The Report of the Attorney General's Committee on Administrative Procedure suggested that administrative system could be usefully and adequately dealt with by a statutory formulation of administrative procedure which would (1) regularize policy-making by providing orderly rule-making procedures that allowed public participation; (2) ensure minimum due process protection where agencies adjudicate disputes (including guaranteed independence for administrative adjudicators); and (3) provide guidance for the conduct of judicial review adequate to ensure, that administrative law decisions would be integrated with the larger body of law.[43] These suggestions were enacted into law called as the McCarren Summers Bill, more commonly known as the Administrative Procedure Act, 1946. This law which resulted out of the recommendations of the committee was the only source of law that specifically applied to most areas of administrative decision-making by most agencies of the Federal government.

Salient Features of the Administrative Procedure Act, 1946

The Administrative Procedure Act, 1946, (APA) is largely a congressional affirmation of scheme worked out by the executive branch's New Deal lawyers. They formulated a modified and softened version of the pre-War vision of Pound and the American Bar Association and filled it into the New Deal Plan. The framers of the APA emphasized the idea that most matters of administrative law, as it was understood in 1940s when the Act was enacted, could be classified as quasi-legislative or quasi-judicial. It was around this dichotomy that the Act was enacted.

The Federal Administrative Procedure Act distinguishes between two types of decision processes — rule-making and adjudication. The courts have generally permitted agencies, subject to legislative direction, to choose which type to use for a particular decision. Each type is further divided into a formal and informal mode. Formal adjudication employs a quasi-judicial process in which an agency order is issued after a court type hearing and is based on a trial-type record. Formal rule-making employs a similar process in order to produce a rule of future effect designed to implement, interpret or prescribe law or policy. Informal rule-making employs a quasi-legislative process in which the agency publishes notice of a proposed rule of future effect and invites public comment on the rule by all interested parties, after which the agency publishes a revised usually final rule that becomes effective shortly thereafter. Procedures for informal adjudication, a residual category that includes most agency decisions and actions, are not specified by the APA. In general, judicial review is more stringent for formal than informal proceedings and for question of law.

Section 551 of the Act provides the definition of 'agency' as "each authority of the Government of the United States whether or not it is within or subject to review by another agency". However, ambiguities regarding the ambit of section led to its amendment in 1974. The new Section 552(3) indicates that the definition of 'agency' includes any executive department or military department, Government controlled corporation or other establishment in the executive branch of the Government (including the Executive Officer of the President), or any other regulatory agency.

Another major point of concern was the processes or types of actions taken by agencies that are to be covered. In particular, the framers of the APA wanted to clarify to a limited extent at least, the difference between quasi-legislative/rule-making and quasi-judicial activities/adjudication. The definitions of rule-making and adjudication were simply stated in terms of processes for making rules and orders.[44] However, there are a variety of administrative activities like rate-making and licensing that are neither rule-making nor adjudication. The convention that resulted defined rate-making within the rule definition and set special descriptive terms for licensing under Section 551(9), but treated it as a species of adjudication.

Section 551(4) of the APA defines 'rule' as:

> . . . the whole or part of agency statement in general or particular applicability and future effect designed to implement, interpret or prescribe law or policy or describing the organization, procedure or practice requirement of an agency and includes the approval or prescription for the future of rates, wages corporate or financial structures or reorganization thereof, prices, facilities, appliances, services or allowances thereof or of valuations, costs, or accounting or practices bearing on any of the foregoing.

The definition describes what is rule, the types of rules noted in the APA and includes rate-setting, rule-making as "includes" within the preview of rules. The rule-making includes within its ambit the process of formulating, amending or repealing a rule.

Agencies make different kind of regulations, each of which carries different requirements for making rule and varying degrees of legal force. The three types come from the APA referred as:

- *Substantive or legislative rules* — that rules that are described in Section 551(4) as rules that "implement . . . or prescribe law or policy". These rules are legally binding and can be enforced in court.
- *Procedural rules* — These rules are statements issued by agencies that present the agency's understanding of the meaning of the language in its regulations or the statute it administers.

Since the APA, enabling legislation has been enacted, executive branch policies and various court decisions have recognized, essentially three types of processes through which substantive administrative regulations are made:

(i) *Informal rule-making* — referred to as "notice and comment" procedure, governed by Section 553 of the APA.

(ii) *Formal rule-making* — as it involves a formal hearing. This is governed by Sections 556 and 557 of the APA.

(iii) *Hybrid rule-making* — as the term implies the procedure is a compromise between the formal and informal processes and is governed by the agency's enabling Act and in the case of executive branch agencies, by executive orders.

Section 553 of the APA describes the basic processes an agency must perform to make a rule. The procedure is provided to ensure that the rule-making is based on proper legal authority; it is within powers granted by the legislature; that there is some opportunity in one form or another for public participation in the process; that the rule is properly and clearly stated by the agency and is promulgated in a manner that will afford interested people a fair opportunity to know what the rule will require and to have some advance warning when the rule will be implemented. This rule-making section, however, exempts certain activities which are:

- Military or foreign affairs [Section 553(a)(1)];
- A matter relating to agency management or personnel or to public property, loans, grants, benefits or contracts [Section 553(a)(2)];
- Activities such as internal agency reorganizations and the like [Section 553(b) (A)]; and
- Cases where there are emergency circumstances of a special nature that require some deviation from the normal requirements of rule-making [Section 553(b) (B)].

Adjudication — Section 554 lays down the minimum procedure required to be followed during administrative adjudication. It is necessary that the cases adjudicated by the government are afforded the basic due process requirements of notice, an opportunity to be heard in some form and a decision by an impartial decision-maker. The Section in fact lays down emphasis on the observance of the requirements of the Principles of Natural Justice during the course of performance of the adjudicatory functions of agencies.

Judicial review of agency decisions — Section 701 through Section 706 prescribes the scope and method of judicial review of agency proceedings. They provide a structure of judicial review of agency actions, a judicial check against any kind of arbitrary action or abuse of discretion.

At the end, APA seems to achieve the purpose of democratization of executive power by way of ensuring participation of interest group in agencies' rule-making and adjudication to enhance acceptability of its functions.

2.3.7 *New Deal to the New Federalism (1950-1969)*

The years from early post-Second World War demobilization through the decades of the 1950s and the turbulent 1960s were years of important development in law and administration.[45] They were years of testing the

Administrative Procedure Act approach to problems facing administrators in a complex administrative environment and those facing individuals and groups attempting to deal with those administrators. In his history of the years 1945 to 1960, Eric Goldman wrote:[46]

> Beneath everything, two critically important questions were pressing to be answered. One of the questions concerned affairs inside the United States: would America continue through extensions of the welfare state and welfare capitalism and through a variety of other techniques, the economic and social revolution which had marked the previous decades. The other question concerned foreign affairs: would the United States keep moving along the path marked out in the early Truman Years, a path suggested by the words "containment" and "coexistence" and one which represented a sharp departure from deep-seated American traditions?

Congress with a unanimous vote for the Lodge-Brown Act in July 1947, created the President's Commission on Organization of the Executive Branch of Government, more popularly known as the Hoover Commission. The President called the Commission to study the Federal administrative set-up. The Commission's report, delivered in February 1949, called for a more streamlined administration organized to be more responsive to presidential direction. The report concluded: "Administrative justice today unfortunately is not characterized by economy, simplicity, and dispatch. It remains, however, a necessity in our complex economic system.[47] The Commission recommended an administrative conference for further study.

By 1953, when President Eisenhower took office, there had been a number of calls for a conference on administrative law problems. As a result, questions of law and administration were included in the second Hoover Commission Report, the result of the Commission's work from 1953-1955.[48] The Commission established the Task Force on Legal Services and Procedures staffed by leading legal scholars, several of whom had served on the Attorney General's Committee and had been instrumental in the enactment of the APA.

After examining nearly a decade of operation under the Administrative Procedure Act, the task force concluded that the administrative justice system was not operating satisfactorily. The task force examined the effectiveness of legal procedures under the Administrative Procedure Act enacted by Congress in 1946. It found that the statute had not always been implemented and followed by agencies in the executive branch to the extent intended by Congress and concluded that substantial amendments should be made to the Act to strengthen it as the charter of due process of law in administration.[49]

The Task Force began with the premise that efficiency in administration requires efficient and effective legal practices with regard to relationships between one agency and another and between the agency and the citizens served by that agency. *The goal was efficiency effectiveness, and fundamental fairness in administrative justice* (Emphasis supplied). The report specifically rejected the conventional wisdom among administrator that wide discretion permits flexibility in administration, which in turn yields efficiency. On the contrary discretionary authority may result in inefficiency:

> Positive limitations should be imposed by statute upon the exercise of administrative powers, authority, or discretion, to the end that statutes are faithfully executed, the rights of the parties are fully protected, and the administration of matters committed to agency action is prompt, fair and efficient.[50]

The task force also lamented the *ad hoc* manner in which agencies were established. Lack of planning and coordination had led to conflicts among federal agencies and between federal and state agencies. Even where no jurisdictional controversies arose, agency's authority was vague because of the lack of standards in many of the statutes that created the agencies.[51] The group saw the need for long-range congressional action to correct deficiencies in the administrative justice system, but urged self-help by administrators as the first step in the needed reform. Most urgent was the need for administrators to define the means by which their agencies planned to exercise their authority. The Administrative Procedure Act was constructed on the theory that agencies promulgate future policies through rule-making or quasi-legislative procedures, and apply existing policies to current problems using quasi-judicial adjudicatory procedures. In practice, the Task Force found, agencies were not carefully articulating policy through rule-making, but were loosely using adjudications to make policy and to resolve contemporary disputes. This common law-development approach to administration might be less of a problem if the role of *stare decisis*, or the binding effect of precedent, was followed as rigorously in administration as it was in the judiciary, but the Task Force found that agencies often took advantage of the less strenuous concept of precedent often applied to agencies.

In sum, agencies should use rule-making as much as possible to guide the public and should avoid policy-making through adjudications.[52] Where agencies do adjudicate, they have a burden to ensure prompt action primarily because the expense of protracted administrative proceedings may effectively deny due process and fundamental fairness to the person before the agency. The Task Force urged that more be done to ensure that persons appearing before agencies be made more aware of their options and the nature of the process they are confronting.[53] Further the Judicial controls over administrative action should be expanded and strengthened.[54]

The second Hoover Committee Report was highly critical of the administrative justice system and issued 74 separate recommendations for change. Among these was a call for a major administrative conference. Congress was not generally receptive to the recommendations of the second Hoover Commission, and those advanced by the Task Force on Legal Services and Procedures fared no better than the rest.

In the late 1950s there was a dramatic shift in importance in administration from regulatory administration to social service delivery. Development of health, safety, and other social services had begun earlier at the local level with the Progressive era providing a particular impetus for urban reform. But social service problems during the Depression and the two wars that followed were national in scope and required national assistance. Suburban housing development became important. New parts of the country felt growing pains as returning veterans relocated families to the West Coast and other places they had seen during their service days. Veterans housing, health, and educational benefits created administrative problems that were complex and numerous. By the late 1950s the baby boom came to school, and the need for capital expenditures for schools, costs of training teachers, and attempts to ensure some uniformity in education practices added to the strain on public administration. During this period the Social Security Administration also began to experience an increase in its workload with the enactment of the Social Security Disability Programme and increases in other programmes.

John F. Kennedy assumed office with the best intentions of examining and responding to problems of law and administration, as indicated first by his call for a major study with specific recommendations and later by his appointment of an administrative conference. Unfortunately, attention was again diverted by events abroad. Kennedy's international relations skills were tested by the Soviet Union. The world went to the brink of nuclear war in Cuban missile crisis. Besides this Kennedy's administration had to face a number of other important issues which included intensification of civil rights efforts, the Bay of Pigs fiasco, and growing involvement in the conflict in South-East Asia. President Kennedy asked Landis, who was a member of Task Force of the Second Hoover Commission, to prepare a report on the state of administrative justice and make recommendations on the administrative justice system. Landis in the *Report on Regulatory Agencies to the President-Elect* recognized the need for the agencies, the complexity of their work environment, and the stakes involved in the cases and policies with which they deal. If administrative law procedures have been developed to save time and money, they had failed. Even with the entire complex procedures, Landis was not satisfied that agency decisions were characterized by fundamental fairness. In addition to political interference or unethical *ex parte* contacts with agency decision-makers, he saw an increasing tendency towards institutional decision-making. The Johnson years saw dramatic increases in administrative activity in particular the "War on Poverty" was waged in part by use of grants and contracts that increased the complexity of intergovernmental relations.

2.3.8. *Administrative Justice in the Modern Context (1969-1976)*

The Nixon administration pronounced the Great Society a failure and substituted for it the New Federalism, which purported to return decision-making in social programmes and other policy areas to states and local governments. The dismantling of the Great Society meant transfer of essential services to other levels of government, and with this came revenue sharing and other complex grant programmes. While the President's men were engaged in elimination of some agencies, Congress and the administration itself were responding to new demands for regulation in consumer product safety, occupational health and safety, and environmental quality with the establishment of new agencies. The Environmental Protection Agency created during the Nixon administration, but it was based not upon a statute pressed by Congress, but by a presidential reorganization plan developed at the White House.

The 1970s witnessed attempts to ameliorate problems noted in earliest years. Executive experiments included reorganization of agencies, attempts to reduce interagency conflicts through the use of interagency working groups, limited derequisition initiatives, civil service reform, and proposals to deal with privacy and freedom-of-information problems. Congress was extremely active during the 1970s with efforts to come to grips with administrative problems. Ironically, one of the methods used by Congress was its own counter bureaucracy — administrative offices designed to prepare research and monitor activities of other administrative agencies on behalf of Congress. Some of the statutes enacted in the 1970s reacted to earlier criticisms about vague and open-ended wording in laws that left administrators free to roam in a given policy area. Ribicoff Committee's *Study on Federal Regulation* figured prominently in regulatory reform efforts, well before the deregulation movement of the late 1970s and 1980s. Congress also had the benefit of recommendations from the Administrative Conference of the United States (ACUS), a prestigious body of experts from several areas of scholarship and practical experience in administration.

The courts were also part of this period of experimentation, although different courts approached the subject differently. On the basis of the criticisms of the earlier period and the experiences of the courts with agencies, some judges were less willing to grant wide deference with only cursory review of administrative decisions. Judges at all levels became more willing than before to send opinions or rules back to agencies (the term is to remand them) for clarification and for a demonstration that the procedures of the APA had been followed in letter and spirit.

In 1969 Kenneth Culp Davis published his *Discretionary Justice: A Preliminary Inquiry*[55] and a related article, "*A New Approach to Delegation*".[56] A longstanding supporter of conventionally defined administrative law, he had arrived at the conclusion that much remained to be done before it could be said that the administrative justice system was functioning properly. Davis made a strong case that discretion is widespread and open to abuse. The dangers of abuse were exacerbated, by the lack of public proceedings and by the burdens placed on those who attempt to get judicial review of agency actions. Davis, confident that the discretion could be controlled, structured, and limited with relative ease in the benefit of the citizen and society.

2.4. Growth of Regulations in the United Kingdom

The British approach to legal regulation has a long history and has evolved gradually on a case by case basis. From the late fifteenth century onwards there were commissioners created by statute for special purposes, such as commissioner of sewers, empowered to make land drainage schemes, build sea-walls and levy rates and there were commissioners of customs created by the royal prerogative. In the

Tudor period the justices were given many new statutory powers which they exercised in their quarter sessions along with their judicial powers. They controlled the upkeep of roads and bridges, the licensing of alehouses, the poor law, the building of goals, the levying of rates etc. The reign of the country justices did not close until 1888. But long before that there had been a proliferation of statutory authorities such as Poor Law Commissioners (1834), Highway Boards, Board of Health, Burial Boards and so forth, creating a dense governmental jungle. Remnants of the justices' power can still be seen in their representation on police authorities and in their liquor licensing functions.

Government in the days before the industrial revolution in this country was traditionally a matter of protecting the realm against the King's enemies, and of maintaining internal order, the latter being achieved somewhat inadequately by the minimum possible number of officials and administrative agencies; local government was almost exclusively in the control of the local justices of the peace. On occasion, however, a particular problem would arise demanding the setting-up of some kind of special administrative machinery. The Council of the North and the Council of Wales were the answer of the early Tudors to the menaces from across the borders of their kingdom; and when the drainage of Romney Marsh, the Fens and of other areas became a necessity, a semi-military organization was abandoned in favour of purely civilian Commissioners of Sewers.[57] These Commissioners had several features in common with the modern public corporations, in that they were established by statute for the purpose of carrying out a limited range of functions and a particular administrative task, and, moreover, in order to carry out that task, they were given considerable independence of the Central Government. They were controlled primarily (like their contemporaries, the justices of the peace) through and by the superior courts of law, especially the Court of King's Bench, and they were themselves regarded rather as courts of law than as public corporations or local authorities in any modern sense. Indeed, at that time, the idea of corporate personality had not been developed, and a Tudor lawyer would have seen no point in ascribing personality to a commission of private gentlemen subject to control by the prerogative writs of certiorari, mandamus and prohibition.

Nevertheless, the germ of the idea that a special administrative task needed a special administrative authority to carry it out. With the development of more sophisticated juristic concepts, the *ad hoc* authority was created, having a separate corporate personality. Many such authorities were brought into being in the nineteenth century under various Private Acts of Parliament, such as the Improvement Commissioners, the Paving Commissioners, the Boards of Health and the Poor Law Boards (and later the School Boards), established for many urban areas. Those survivors from Victorian days, the Mersey Docks and Harbour Board and the Metropolitan Water Board, like the *ad hoc* authorities, were nearer to the modern corporations than were the earlier Commissioners. All these various bodies, however, were entrusted with statutory functions to be exercisable only over a defined, comparatively restricted local area.[58]

Historically, the regulation and scrutiny of industry in Britain developed from the nineteenth century. Legal powers were first granted through Private Acts of Parliament in return for statutory responsibilities assumed by the industries — the railways and the electricity companies are two good examples. Also relevant is the experience of early Poor Law Commission in 1834 which struck a balance between Central and Local Government. This early form of government regulation permitted commissioners to determine the qualification and duties of local poor law guardians and they, in turn, appointed paid officers to administer relief, subject to the Poor Law Commission. The establishment of Boards, which acted in a quasi-ministerial manner combined administrative decision-making and had both non-political and semi-independent status. A number of examples such as railways and the factories inspectorate illustrate the experiment of placing certain activities beyond the direct reach of political intervention. Eventually, these activities succumbed to ministerial control, but attempts at combining or isolating ministerial intervention with regulation were made. In the example of the railways, the Railways Department in the Board of Trade in 1840 was a Department Board in 1844, a Commission in 1846 before absorption into the Board of Trade in 1851.

A wide variety of powers were enjoyed by such regulators; invariably, a statutory framework would set the general shape and scope of the individual Board of Inspectorate. Additionally codes of practice, circulars, directions, rules, regulations were all included as part of that legal framework. Occasionally, a feature of regulation involved enforcement procedures through adjudication processes which invariably might involve a fine or criminal sanction. For example, the early factory inspectorate under the Factories Act, 1934, had the status of a Magistrate with corresponding legal powers. One of the characteristics of the nineteenth century was a remarkable degree of detail and openness in the reports published by the various boards, departments and agencies. This characteristic gradually diminished as the nationalization process took place in the post-Second World War period which was characterized by secrecy and lack of information on the actual performance of each industry.

Whereas the characteristic nineteenth century statute was public, national and obligatory, in the eighteenth century, much legislation, particularly in the social and economic sphere was private, local and facultative, setting-up local agencies, such as turnpike, paving, enclosure, or improvement commissioners where such things appeared to be desired by preponderant local interests.[59] It was practice for many measures originating under Private Bill procedure to be declared Public Acts to relieve the promoters of the heavy fees which would otherwise have been required.[60] Maitland took the statutes of 1786 and concluded that "fully half of the public Acts are of a petty local character".[61] A decade later, the picture was much the same. One hundred and eighty public Acts received the Royal Assent in the session of 1796-97. In all there were seventy-seven Acts of a "petty local character". But 1796-97 was a period of war, and the total was swollen by twenty-eight Acts, relating to defence.[62] Many of the private Acts of 1796 had still more the character of privilegia, as they related to particular individuals and places.[63] Maitland .called the eighteenth century the century of privilegia.[64]

The cumulative effect of private Act was enormous. Vast changes in such fields as highway administration and local government resulted from them. The turning point in their decline was the 1830s. "What was revolutionary about the Reform Act of 1832 and the Municipal Corporation Act of 1835 was that they proceeded by public Bill. . . . The interesting thing about the Reform Act is that it was a Public General Act, that it did not follow the procedure of piecemeal reform, . . . It ushered in a spate of highly important Public General Acts, the destruction of the old machinery of local government being the most radical of them all".[65]

Soon after the Reform Act of 1832 Parliament began to legislate with remarkable vigour to overhaul the whole law of the country. But about the same time it gave-up the attempt to govern the country, and began to lay down general rules about these matters and entrust their working partly to officials, to secretaries of state, to boards or commissioners, who for this purpose were endowed with new statutory powers, partly to the law courts.[66] As the nineteenth century wore on,

Private Bill legislation declined in importance, relatively to Public General Acts. With the exception of divorce, which became a matter for the courts in 1857, the decline was accompanied by an increase of administrative responsibilities in corresponding fields. An Act of 1844 delegated to the Secretary of State the power to issue certificates of naturalization, and this procedure administered by the Home Office, superseded naturalization of Acts.

Statutory Commissions were created to deal with enclosures, change of tenure (e.g. substitution of freehold for copyhold) and commutation of titles. The Home Secretary took the responsibility from 1834 onwards of introducing an annual Turnpike Acts (Continuation) Bill, which reduced the need for road commissioners to promote separate Bills of their own. In the field of local government, Public General Acts starting with the Poor Law (Amendment) Act of 1834 and the Municipal Corporations Act of 1835 became the standard mode of procedure, in place of old method whereby bodies of improvement commissioners for particular towns, each with its special powers, were set-up by private Acts.[67] However, the local authorities continued to seek special powers. Here the introduction of the Provincial Order made it often possible for them to secure the powers they needed from Central administration rather than from Parliament.

In one field, railways, Private Bill procedure remained of prime importance. But there was a great difference in the attitude of government, as compared with its attitude towards the road, navigation and canal Bills of the eighteenth century. "The expansion of railways brought more clearly than ever before into the consciousness of Parliament the conception that in private legislation there was an aspect of public, as well as one of private, interest, to which no government could be indifferent".[68] From the 1840s onwards, the promoters of private Bills "were frequently in communication with the Chairman of Ways and Means, or the Chairman of the Lord's Committees".[69] Public General Acts too delegated to Ministers powers to authorize companies to proceed by certificate, instead of by private Acts in certain cases.[70]

The notion that government needed administrative machinery to enforce the law, outside certain fields such as the collection of the revenue, was foreign to the thought of eighteenth century Britain. In the traditional view, law enforced itself through such agencies as common informers, grand juries and interested parties. "The eighteenth century notion of *ubi jus ibi remedia* in practice made the enforcement to the law depend on suits brought, for the most part, at the instance of private individuals: a cumbersome, intermittent and costly process".[71]

There was not even a police force. The Gordon Riots of 1780 had put the problem on the agenda. The radical movements of the revolutionary and Napoleonic periods, coupled with such symptoms of industrial unrest as Luddism, kept the ruling class in a continual mood of insecurity. The obvious solution would have been administrative — the creation of a police force.[72] Yet in fact, as Dicey pointed out, "the revolutionary movements of 1795 and 1815-20 were combated, not by departmental action, but by Parliamentary legislation. The suspension of the Habeas Corpus Act, the passing of the Libel Act, and of the "six Acts" of 1819, was severely coercive measure; but they contain no evidence of any attempt to give a Continental Character to administration. In so far as individual liberty was destroyed, it was destroyed by and in pursuance of Acts of Parliament'.[73] The turning point here was setting-up of the metropolitan police in 1829, followed by the requirement in the Municipal Corporations Act of 1835 that Boroughs should provide themselves with police forces.

In the field of prison reforms, the first general Prison Act was passed in 1791. However, it was not so such for want of good laws, as from their non-execution, that the state of prison was so bad.[74] The 1824 Act went further. It was "the first attempt ever made to formulate a national policy for prisons, provided for classification of prisoners, hard work for convicts, and regular reports to Home Office on committals and prison discipline. Parliament having established no machinery to administer it, saw the Act go largely unenforced".[75] More than half a century of experience had proved beyond doubt the futility of passing elaborate statutes without administrative machinery for enforcing their provisions, before the lesson at last bore fruit in the Act of 1835.[76]

A similar pattern was seen in the field of mental health. There had been an Act for Regulating Private Madhouses, but "the provisions for enforcing the regulations contained in this Act were so ineffectual that it remained almost a dead letter".[77] The 1828 Madhouse Act on the other hand, created administrative machinery within the metropolitan area at least, in the form of paid inspectors and led to considerable improvement. In 1842 the system was extended throughout the country, for a trial period of three years. The report of the inspectors on this experiment led to its becoming permanent in 1845.[78]

In the sphere of railways, the Liverpool and Manchester Railway Act, 1826, provided for reduction in the company's charges if it paid a dividend in excess of ten per cent. But, it was never operative because no procedure was laid down for enforcing it. The turning point in the public regulation of railways was the Act of 1840, which delegated powers to the Board of Trade and authorized the appointment of inspectors.[79]

Around the year 1830 a profound change was occurring in the public mind as to the relation between the law and administration. It has been said that "a statute — book crammed with lovely things is pointless without the means to carry them into practice. Indeed, it is a sign of a softening of the brain to tolerate such a state of affairs".[80] All the British legislators in the period 1770-1830 or thereabout were addlepated. However, the fact was accepted that legal change would often imply administrative machinery for the purpose of enforcement, which was previously been rejected. *The Times* made this point clear in comparing the two Factory Bills that came before Parliament in 1833, one a, private member Bill and other, a government measure. Neither was new in principle there were five Factory Acts on the statute book already, all largely ineffective for want of enforcement machinery. There were a number of differences between the two Bills; for example in the age of children to be protected and in the hours they could work. However, the most important distinction which contained the seed of mighty change in domestic policy was the executive machinery. The Private Member's Bill was nearly destitute of executory machinery, on the contrary, the Ministerial Act, provided important class of new officers called "inspectors", who shall have the authority of magistrates for enforcing its executions.[81]

The period of 1830s was the beginning of novel relationship between Central and local authorities, and between both sets of authorities and the people, Central Government replacing a loose local administration, the paid professional superseding the unpaid amateur, delegation of legislative powers, the possibility of appeal from administrative decision, strictness of judicial interpretation, the well-intentioned bureaucrat's outpacing of public opinion and so on. The contrast with the immediate past was striking. In the years 1819 and 1820, there was plenty of talk of "regulation" in Acts of Parliament, but they were regulations actually contained in the Acts, not regulations to be made by some other authority. Thus, in the factory and workshop legislation a century ago the ages of employees in cotton mills were specified; the hours of work were fixed; there was definite time for breakfast and a definite time for dinner. There was no margin for elasticity; nothing was left to be arranged by departmental order.[82]

By 1854 there were already sixteen Central Government Inspectors.[83] The period of 1865-1900 had been called "the period of collectivism"[84] because of the outburst of regulatory legislation and the tendency to entrust more and more power to the state. In 1888 Maitland wrote:[85] "we are becoming a much governed nation, governed by all manners of councils and boards and local, high and low, exercising the powers which have been committed to them by modern statutes."

In England by 1914 there were abundant signs of the profound change in the conception of Government which was to mark the twentieth century. The state school-teacher, the national insurance officer,. the labour exchange, the sanitary and factory inspector, the tax collector were among the outward and visible signs of this change. The modern administrative state was already taking shape, reflecting the feeling that it was the duty of Government to provide remedies for social and economic evils of many kinds. The advent of the welfare state might be dated from the National Insurance Act, 1911 though the Education Act, 1902, the Old Age Pensions Act, 1908, and the Housing and Town Planning Act, 1909, also have claims for consideration. But, before that period Parliament had imposed controls and regulations by statutes such as the Factories Acts, the Public Health Acts and the railway legislation.

2.4.2. *Nationalization of Industry after Second World War*

The period since the Second World War recognized the need for the administrative state and to devise more efficient machinery. The Ministerial department was replacing the older commissions and boards. The doctrine of Ministerial responsibility was crystallizing, with its correlative principle of civil service anonymity and detachment from politics. Thus, were laid the foundations of the vast and powerful bureaucracy which is the principal instrument of administration today. Scarcely less striking has been the expansion of the sphere of local government, extending to education, town and country planning and a great many other services and controls.

The urge towards nationalization of many public undertakings recognized and implemented by the socialist government that came into power at the end of the Second World War, made development of some new form of administrative machinery essential. The modern form of public corporation was adopted to administer the newly "nationalized industries", and also to play its part in managing some of the agencies of the "Welfare State" (in particular the hospitals), which formed the other part of the Government's "reconstruction" programme. The new agencies were, therefore, given separate corporate existence and limited functions, but responsibility for those functions extended over the whole country, or over a wide area thereof, much greater than that which could conveniently be administered by a single all purpose local authority. The public corporation was a compromise between nationalization and private enterprise; the institution was essentially an instrument devised for administering some particular enterprise in the public interest. The other outstanding feature of the public corporation was its independence — legally virtually complete of the Central Government, while carrying on an enterprise of national importance. In some cases the idea of a commercial enterprise was to the fore, for example in the case of the gas and electricity corporations; in the case of other corporations such as the Countryside Commission, the emphasis was on regulation, but even here the idea of public enterprise was not totally absent, the purpose of the corporation being to further "national parks" and the proper use of the countryside.[86]

The model adopted in England for nationalization after Second World War in 1945 was public corporation at arm's length from government. However, the use of Public Corporation from 1945 was not the first use of this type of institution in British Government. Notable earlier examples included the Central Electricity Board in 1926 and the British Broadcasting Corporation in 1927. It was clear that because of the nature both of the industries themselves and of the view of the post-War Government, extensive regulation of their activities would have to take place after nationalization. The major nationalization measures were the Bank of England Act, 1946; Coal Industry Nationalization Act, 1946; the Civil Aviation Act, 1946; the Transport Act, 1946; and the Electricity Act, 1947; the Gas Act, 1948; and the Iron and Steel Act, 1949. The statutes were to a large extent modelled on that nationalizing the coal industry. The importance of these statutes is not merely historical as the later nationalization measures in the 1970s retained many of the important features of the first generation legislation.

The corporations managing the great public utilities were taken into public ownership and control for the most part during the years immediately succeeding the Second World War, and they are sometimes referred to as "the nationalized industries". The group, therefore, includes:

(i) *Electricity* — The Central Electricity Generating Board, the Central Electricity Council and the twelve Area Electricity Boards established under the Electricity Act, 1947 and 1957.

(ii) *Gas* — The former Gas Council and the Area Gas Boards, then replaced by the British Gas Corporation created under the Gas Act, 1948, as amended by the Gas Act, 1972.

(iii) *Coal* — The National Coal Board created under the Coal Act, 1938; the Coal Industry (Nationalization) Act, 1946; and Coal Industry Act, 1949.

(iv) *Steel* — The British Steel Corporation established under the Iron and Steel Act, 1975.

(v) *Surface Transport* — On the nationalization of the railways in 1947, the Transport Act of that year established the British Transport Commission and six subordinate executives, all of which were public corporations, but which could act only as agents for and on the instructions of the British Transport Commission. The Transport Act, 1962, made drastic alterations in this organization. The British Transport Commission was dissolved, its assets and responsibilities being divided between four Boards, the British Railways Board, the London Transport Board, the British Transport Docks Board, and the British Waterways Board. The Transport Act, 1968, also established the National Freight Corporation and the Freight Integration Council (the latter not having corporate status). The Council have the duty of integrating the work of the railways, the Docks Board, the Waterways Board, the Freight Corporation, the National Bus Company, the Scottish Group, under the general directions of the Secretary of State for the Environment, and the Post Office (under the general directions of the Minister for Posts and Telecommunications).

(vi) *Broadcasting and Communications* — The Independent Broadcasting Authority (I.B.A.), and the British Broadcasting Corporation (B.B.C.) are not really of equal status, as the I.B.A. was originally established as the Independent Television Authority by the Television Act, 1954, and is legally independent of but subject to general directions from the Minister of Posts and Telecommunications. The B.B.C. was established by charter in 1927, the charter being renewable periodically (at ten years interval), and a licence to broadcast programmes is reserved to the Minister enabling him to give instructions prohibiting the Corporation from broadcasting specified matter. The Post Office was established as a public corporation by the Post Office Act, 1969, and given the responsibility of providing postal and telecommunications services, and also a "giro" system; the National Savings Bank was, by the same Act, made the responsibility of the Treasury.

(vii) *Atomic Energy* — The Atomic Energy Authority created under the Atomic Energy Authority Act, 1954.

(viii) *Air Transport* — The Civil Aviation Authority (responsible for the regulation and licensing of civil aircraft), the British Airways Board (responsible for providing air transport services) established under the Civil Aviation Act, 1971, and also the British Airports Authority created under the Airports Authority Act, 1965, responsible for management of aerodromes at Heathrow, Gatwick, Stansted and Prest-wick.

The functions carried on by the particular corporations were really commercial businesses, and because of the nature of the work undertaken, the managing body resembled the board of directors of a public company. These enterprises were usually, but a monopoly, and therefore, the corporations were expected to conduct its affairs in the public interest, and not exclusively for profit, as in private industry.

The model adopted was such as to suggest that the boards should be autonomous as regards day-to-day administration, but the Ministers should have some power to determine matters of policy and engage in general economic control. To enable such control provisions were made in the statute for certain types of powers. First, the Minister had the power to appoint the Chairman and Members of the boards which included the power of dismissal in certain circumstances. Secondly, the Minister was empowered to issue general directions to the board. Thirdly, the boards needed the approval of the Minister for programme of reorganization and development involving substantial outlay on capital and less importantly in relation to training and research. In addition there were further ministerial powers over finance usually exercised with Treasury approval.

However, the extensive government intervention was unavoidable because of the commitment to economic planning, reluctance to dispense with the extensive economic controls of wartime and the expectations raised by nationalization. The issuing formal directions, however, was regarded as last resort rather than a standard form of control to be adopted where relations between the board and minister were on the verge of breakdown. No general directions were issued by Labour government of 1945-51.[87] The use of *ad hoc* informal intervention rather than of formal controls served both to confuse and reduce accountability and to prevent the industries themselves from achieving a clear idea of their role. The Government did not provide clear objectives yet short-term intervention prevented the industries from properly developing these for themselves.

The arrangement that existed in 1940s provided for four types of arrangements for monitoring apart from monitoring by the minister. The first was the existence of consumer councils or consultative committees representing consumers, established to perform a varying range of consultative and grievance-resolving functions. However, the consumer machinery was weak, lacking in independence and seen as a part of the protective machinery of boards and ministers rather than as an independent watchdog for the public. The second potential mean of monitoring the industries was through Parliament. However, the Parliamentary Questions had concentrated on local problems of management rather than issues of policy or overall efficiency; the result again was the worst of both worlds, as the boards were not left free on matters of detailed administration yet there was no general and regular scrutiny of policy-making or efficiency. The third means of monitoring the industries was through audit, both financial and as regards efficiency. Finally, some degree of measurement and publicity could have been provided by the need to justify pricing decisions to the outside body. However, only such body to be set-up was Transport Tribunal, a descendant of the highly complex system of regulation of railway companies before nationalization. It was not a success and in 1953 the Conservative Government severely limited the powers of the tribunal as a part of plans to give greater commercial freedom to nationalized industries. Effective outside scrutiny of pricing was not to be developed until the entry on the scene of the Prices and Income Board in 1967. Thus, the machinery for "measurement and publicity" was weak and limited.

The major problem with public corporation which had their origin on nationalization in the late 1940s was that the implications of the model adopted for nationalization were never thought through. There was "the intellectual void at the heart of Labour's proposal for nationalization".[88] Most importantly, the respective roles of ministers and boards were never clarified so the control of the industries as part of general policy was conducted by back-door methods with an accompanying blurring of responsibility. No proper attempt was made to set out the tasks of the boards or to provide the means of monitoring their attainment. These problems arose largely from the belief that the change of ownership would remove the profit motive, which itself would resolve the major political problems of industrial policy.

The idea was that the 'public interest' alone would be an adequate guide for the boards. This neglected the central issue that a shift from private to public ownership does nothing in itself to solve problems of control or direction of the enterprise and that the task of defining the 'public interest', or rather of weighing competing interest, is a difficult matter of political values. Thus, the concern with the private law issue of ownership disguised the importance of the public law issues of constitutional and institutional design. Moreover, the machinery for monitoring the boards' actions and for creating a flow of information on which accountability could be based was highly deficient. By 1951 it was clear that there would be major problems as regards the overall role of the industries in the economy, their policy-making and their accountability.

2.4.3. *The White Papers of 1961 and 1967*

The major conclusions of the White Paper, 1961 were as follows.[89] Firstly, the duty to break even was to be applied over a period of five years. Secondly, and most importantly, financial targets were to be agreed with each industry specifying a particular rate of return on capital or level of self-financing. Commercially unprofitable activities were to be taken account of in setting the targets. Scrutiny of investment plans by Government would be clarified. The existing informal consultation with ministers on pricing would continue and if the minister modified the board's proposals the latter could require a written statement of his views and could propose an adjustment in the financial target. The White Paper proposed a model of the industries as commercial concerns with social responsibilities imposed from outside which prevailed. However, the final paragraph adopted an explicit compromise on this issue, stating that the industries had wider obligations than commercial concerns in the private sector, and a balance was to be struck between these obligations and commercial interests. The central element in government control was to be the financial target, and such targets were soon set for most of the industries, normally specifying a rate of return on net assets. They were not very successful. Little guidance was given on how to achieve them and they were inadequately related to overall economic policy and indeed conflicted with sectoral policies such as fuel policy.

In 1967 a further White Paper appeared. The 1967 paper marked a much fuller acceptance of the principle that the industries should be run as commercial concerns and also stressed the need to ensure the optimum allocation of resources throughout the economy as a whole. Although there were inevitable elements of compromise, the overall thrust was clear. Rather than control by financial targets set for each industry, control would be through general criteria of rational economic decision-making designed to shape performance to be as close as possible to that allegedly shaped by the disciplines of the private sector. It would certainly be a mistake to dismiss the White Paper as having no effect in practice, but as an attempt to rationalize decisions about the industries it was little applied and unsuccessful. The attempt to develop general economic and financial criteria as a basis for decisions on pricing and investment was a failure, and the result was continuing confusion about the respective responsibilities of government and the industries.

Some developments of the early 1970s suggested that the corporate planning process would become of central importance as the location of government influence. In 1970 Sir Henry Benson, advising on information flows between the industries and sponsor departments, had made recommendations centring on long-term corporate plans, five-year investment programmes and short-term progress reports. These recommendations were partially implemented. The Select Committee, reporting on capital investment procedures, noted a move towards the corporate plan as the core for relations with government and recommended the extension of corporate planning throughout the nationalized sector. There was also some development in statutes passed during this period to reflect greater ministerial involvement. Thus, several pieces of legislation included provisions for the minister to set a financial target for the industry, after consulting the board[90] and in certain cases the boards were obliged to act on lines settled from time to time with the approval of the minister in preparing their corporate plans.[91]

2.4.4. *The National Economic Development Office Study of 1976*

The move towards corporate planning might suggest that the way was being prepared for the establishment of new machinery for the continuing development of objectives and policy with participation by Government and other interested groups. The proposal for such machinery came in the report from the National Economic Development Office (NEDO) in 1976.[92]

The analysis of existing relations between Government and the industries was both convincing and devastating. The Office found that the arm's length relationship had failed. There was little debate between the industries and government and an unwillingness to listen to each other's case. The report said that the relationship was one of mutual mistrust and of confusion as to their respective responsibilities. Short-term monitoring of the industries was inadequate; there was no effective system for measuring performance or for assessing managerial competence. The 1967 criteria were simplistic and had not been implemented; and in any case the Office considered the analogy with the private sector, on which they had been based, to be false. It was the view of the Office that any successful guidelines would have to be tailored to the requirements of individual industries. Extensive short-term government intervention had been accompanied by confusion as to goals and an absence of long-term policies; no systematic framework for the agreement of long-term objectives and strategy existed and there was no assurance of continuity when decisions were reached. Overall, successive governments had failed to recognize that "in any large industrial organization . . . some assurance of stable objectives and policies is a precondition of efficiency". The lack of these not only made it impossible for the industries to plan with confidence, but the ambiguities of responsibility led to an absence of accountability.

The study proposed solutions which were essentially participative. Interest groups were to be involved in the evolution of strategic plans for the industries. This should be a "combined operation" and in it government and the industries would work more closely together. In other areas management should have greater freedom to take decisions and should be held accountable for them. The real importance of the proposals lay in the institution in which the 'combined operation' would take place — the Policy Council. Such a council would be established for each industry to agree corporate aims and objectives and the strategic policies needed to achieve them, to endorse corporate plans, to establish performance criteria and to monitor performance against the pre-determined policies and criteria. Separate from the Policy Council, though appointed by it, would be an Executive Corporation Board to manage the industry within the framework agreed by the Council. Government was not to intervene directly at executive level; rather its influence was to be exercised through the Policy Council, normally through the government representation on it. In extreme circumstances where such persuasion was not adequate there should be statutory power to issue a published general or specific direction to the Council.

The Policy Council's membership was to include senior civil servants from sponsoring departments and the Treasury, representatives of the trade unions involved in the industry and executive management. In some circumstances major suppliers were also to be represented. The representation of interest groups in this way led to the danger that relations could fall into a sort of cosy corporatism, without reference to outside interests. It was, therefore, suggested that independent members should also be appointed to prevent problems being swept under the carpet, to bring outside experience and to reduce the risk of long-term domination of the Council by particular interest groups.

The proposals in the NEDO study represented the first major and worked-out attempt to recognize problems of participation, accountability and continuity of expectations. In 1978 a new White Paper was published, largely in response to the Study.

2.4.5. *The 1978 White Paper*

It was accepted that there had been failure by Government to exercise control publicly and according to well-defined rules rather than by interfering in management. It was also accepted that government should be concerned with strategic and major issues rather than day-to-day management.[93] However, the Policy Council idea was firmly rejected; the industries were opposed to it and in practice the Government would not be prepared to delegate its powers to the Council on matters of major political and public importance. The Government did express support for the greater involvement of interest groups in policy formulation by the industries and for wider discussion of corporate plans. The plans were to be given a central place in relations between the industries and government and it was envisaged that they would provide a systematic framework for reaching agreement on long-term objectives and strategies.

In some cases civil servants were to be appointed to the boards, as had already happened in the case of the British National Oil Corporation, and Ministers were to be given a new general power to issue specific directions to the boards. It was claimed that this would clarify responsibility through indicating publicly that government had intervened and would be accompanied by estimates from the Minister and the industry of the extra cost which would be incurred through implementing the direction. It was not, however, to be an exclusive means of government intervention and there would continue to be many issues on which informal agreements would be reached.

There were further proposals on financial and economic control. New financial targets were to be set and published after discussions with each industry, and where prices were not directly market-determined, they were to be determined by the targets. On the need for non-financial tests of performance, the Government proposed that performance indicators would be published in the Annual Reports of the industries, covering such matters as service standards. The precise content of these indicators and the nature of monitoring arrangements were, however, not made clear in the White Paper.

The 1978 White Paper explained that estimates of external finance through loans, public dividend, capital and grants would continue to be agreed with the industries in advance and used as a cash limit for each year, thus, supplementing the longer-term financial target. In comparison with the report to which it responded, the White Paper was a weak and uninspiring document. The most important elements in it documented developments that had already occurred.

Thus, the attempts to improve matters by the development of criteria for rational economic and financial decisions failed because of theoretical and practical weaknesses and because of the larger political pressures on government. The sole attempt to develop new institutional arrangements in the National Economic Development Office Report remained unimplemented and the final White Paper of 1978 did little to provide new ideas apart from indicating the increased role of corporate planning.

In the period covered, governments of both parties were of a fairly interventionist disposition as regards the economy. From 1979, of course, the election of a radical Conservative Government with quite different ideas on the industries from its predecessors changed the scene dramatically. In 1979 a government with far greater apparent commitment to the ideology of free enterprise and liberalism was elected.

2.5. Growth of Regulations in India

2.5.1. *Regulations in British India*

Till the end of the British rule in India, the government was concerned with the most primary duties only, and the functions of a welfare state were not discharged. The government was mainly pre-occupied with the law and order problems and did not perform even such functions as would have been performed by a state wedded to the *laissez faire* philosophy. Till 1918, the British India Government was primarily concerned with the collection of revenue and maintenance of law and order. During this period, administrative power was given to the executive officials for the purpose of protecting public health, morality and public safety. However, increasing and rapid strides in the fields of communication and transport in the West, resulted in the need for the control of administrative agencies through regulatory bodies and tribunals like the Interstate Commerce Commission in USA and Railways and Canal Commission in England. Finally, the two world wars brought in a plethora of administrative agencies exercising control over almost every aspect of individual life. A brief account of the growth of administrative process during the British rule may be given as follows:[94]

I. *1834 to 1939*

A. ***Public Safety:*** The Sarai Act, 1867 required registration of sarais with the District Magistrate, who could refuse to register a sarai if the owner failed to produce a character certificate. The Arms Act, 1878, prohibited the manufacture or trade and keeping of arms without a licence. The Indian Explosives Act, 1884, empowered the Government to regulate or prohibit by licensing all aspects of trade and traffic in explosives. The Indian Boilers Act, 1923, regulated the use of boilers and banned their use without permission. A hierarchy of officers with regular appeals from one to another was created under the Act. Thus, from an order of the Inspector, appeal lay to the Chief Inspector and a further appeal to the higher Appellate Authority. The courts were barred from reviewing the orders of these administrative bodies. These Acts thus, prohibited the carrying on of an activity without a licence or permission of the administrative authority.

B. ***Health:*** The Acts like the Opium Act, 1878, the Epidemic Diseases Act, 1897, the Dangerous Drugs Act, 1930, and the Medical Council Act, 1933, sought to protect public health.

C. ***Morality:*** Among the Acts which sought to protect public morality were the Dramatic Performance Act, 1876, which authorized the local government to prohibit a dramatic performance in a particular area and the Cinematograph Act, 1918, which provided for the licensing of cinema and the exhibition of only such films as had been certified by the prescribed authority.

D. ***Transport:*** The State regulation of road transport started as early as in 1861 with the passing of the Stage Carriage Act. The Stage Carriage Act, 1861, which prohibited the plying of stage carriages without a licence indicates the beginning of administrative licensing. The Bombay Port Trust Act, 1879 established the first public corporation as an agency for administering the social and economic functions of the State. The Indian Motor Vehicles Act, 1914, provided for the licensing of drivers and registration of vehicles. It made elaborate provisions for issuing permits to private operators to ply their vehicles. Discretion was given to the licensing authorities to limit the number of permits. The other Acts providing for the regulation of carriage business during the British Period were Indian Railways Act, 1890; Indian Merchant Shipping Act, 1923; Railway Rates Advisory Commission, 1926; and Motor Vehicle Act, 1939.

E. ***Labour:*** Under the provision of the Employees and Workmen Disputes Act, 1860, a Magistrate could decide a trade and wage disputes of workmen employed in construction, railway and canal and public works departments. Until the Workmen's Compensation Act was enacted in 1923, no law for the regulation of labour-management relations existed. The real intention behind this legislation was to impose burden on Indian manufacturers so as to make it difficult for them to compete with their English counterparts. However, it paved way for further legislation providing protection to industrial workers. The Workmen's Compensation Act, 1923, provided for the appointment of a Commissioner to adjudicate disputes relating to workmen's compensation and barred the jurisdiction of the ordinary courts. A further attempt, albeit a half-hearted one, to regulate industrial relations by providing machinery for third-party settlement of industrial disputes was made in 1929 when the Industrial Trade Disputes Act was enacted. It provided for reference to a court of inquiry, of disputes by the Government. Its major defect was that it did not make compulsory the acceptance by the parties of the recommendations contained in the report of the court. The Industrial Disputes Act, 1947, is a much more effective legislation for that purpose. The Act provides for an industrial tribunal whose decisions were binding on the parties. Other beneficial legislations which sought to regulate trade and industry in the interest of the workers were the Indian Mines Act, 1923, the Factories Act, 1934, and the Payment of Wages Act, 1936.

F. ***Economic Regulation:*** In the field of economic regulation, governments all-over the world used tariffs as the main device to give protection to indigenous industries. The British Government, however, followed the policy of free trade, which caused harm to the indigenous industries. Some very elementary type of economic regulation was started when the Indian Companies Act was first enacted in 1850. This Act, however, was intended merely to provide the limited liability of the shareholders. The idea of controlling or regulating a company in public interest had not then developed. More direct state regulation was undertaken by the Cotton Transport Control Act, 1923, which sought to maintain the quality and reputation of the long staple cotton grown in certain areas; the Indian Tea Control Act, 1933, which provided for administrative control over tea exports and cultivation; and the Reserve Bank of India Act, 1934, which created the Reserve Bank of India to regulate the issue of bank-notes and to supervise over the scheduled banks with a view to securing monetary stability in the country and generally to operate for currency and credit system of the country to its advantage. Various laws were enacted during colonial rule to claim state sovereignty and regulate the consumptions of natural resources like land, water, forests, minerals etc.

II. *Second World War and Thereafter (1939 to 1947)*

The outbreak of the Second World War gave rise to legislation which granted unprecedented amount of power to the executive. The Defence of India Act, 1939, empowered the Central Government to make such rules as appear to it to be necessary or expedient for securing the defence of British India, the public safety, the maintenance of public order or the efficient prosecution of war or for maintaining supplies and services essential to the life of the community. This gave very wide powers to the executive to interfere with the life, liberty and property of the citizen. A number of orders were issued under this Act providing for the control of prices, supply and distribution of various commodities, production, consumption and supply of raw materials etc. A characteristic feature of a large number of such control orders, which introduced a system of licensing, was that they authorized the respective licensing authorities to issue general or special directions to the licensees. This was a very broad power and neither the Act nor the rules or orders laid down any restrictions thereupon.

The emergency legislation enacted during the war significantly increased the powers and functions of the State. These powers did not vanish after the war ended. The condition of scarcity, which had necessitated economic control, had not only continued, but was accentuated after the end of the war. Many provisions of the Defence of India Rules were, therefore, continued after the end of the war under

Acts such as the Essential Supplies (Temporary Powers) Act, 1946, and the Import and Export Control Act, 1947.

2.5.2. *Regulations in Independent India*

To ameliorate the socio-economic condition of the people, India after Independence resorted to economic planning in a big way to achieve ultimately the goal of a "socialist pattern of society". When India became Independent, the philosophy of welfare state was made the creed of the Constitution of India. The Preamble of the Constitution aims at establishing a sovereign, socialist, secular, democratic, republic, so as to secure to all its citizens, social, economic and political justice, liberty of thought, expression, belief, faith and worship, equality of status and opportunity and to promote among them fraternity, assuring dignity of the individual and unity of the nation.

Accordingly, the Governments in India embarked upon policies designed to accelerate the rate of economic growth, speed-up industrialization, expand public sector, and to build up a large and growing cooperative sector. Though an increasing role was envisaged for the state in this process, the private sector was not completely barred. It continued to have an opportunity to function, develop and expand. India has consciously adopted the philosophy of mixed economy where the Government-owned enterprises and private enterprises co-exist side-by-side. For successful implementation of such an economic pattern, however, it became inevitable to impose certain restraints and disciplines on private economic activity. The respective areas of operation of the private and the public sectors were required to be demarcated. This was the objective sought to be achieved by the Industrial Policy Resolution of the Government of India, firstly, of 6 April, 1948, and then of 30 April, 1956. Thereunder, industries were grouped into three categories, having regard to the role which the state would play in their promotion and management. Industries like railways, air transport, arms, ammunition, atomic energy, power, iron and steel, coal, heavy electrical and mechanical machinery, basic minerals and petroleum, aircraft and ship building; *inter alia*, fell in the first category and their development was the exclusive responsibility of the State. Industries like road and sea transport, coke, alloy steels, machine, tools, aluminium, fertilizers, basic and intermediate chemicals, antibiotics and synthetic rubber etc. fell in the second category and constituted the mixed sector where both public and private enterprises would meet. All other industries were put in the third category and their future development was left mainly, though not exclusively, to private enterprise.

After Independence under the ideology of welfare state, a phenomenal growth of the public sector took place both by setting-up new Government undertakings and nationalizing several existing private enterprises. On the other hand, private enterprise also made rapid strides and innumerable new lines of production and manufacture were developed. However, private enterprise was not given a complete freedom of action even in the area allotted to it. A number of considerations and factors had dictated its regulation, policing and control by government, e.g. it has to fit into the broad framework of socio-economic policies; plan priorities have to be observed in the matter of industrialization; expansion of public enterprise, co-operative sector as well as of small scale industries; undue concentration of economic power in a few hands and private monopolies should be avoided so as to lessen disparities in income and wealth; new enterprises should be encouraged so as to distribute wealth and income; regional economic imbalances in the country should be lessened; the interests of the consumers of manufactured goods and producers of raw materials need to be safeguarded; it is necessary to ensure that interests are not jeopardized. Consequently, a whole mechanism of state regulation of private business, trade and industry became a leading tenet of the economic planning.

A. *Regulation — the Constitutional Perspective*

The Constitution of India in Articles 38, 39, 42, 43, 46 and 47 provides that state shall strive to secure a social order for the promotion of welfare of the people, it shall direct its policies in such a way that operation of economic system does not result in the concentration of wealth and means of production to the common detriment, it shall make provision for securing just and humane conditions of work and for maternity relief; it should endeavour to build an economic organization or to make suitable legislation to ensure a decent standard of life to all the workers who constitute the bulk of the consumers; it should promote educational and economic interests of Scheduled Castes, Scheduled Tribes and other weaker sections and it shall also raise the level of nutrition and standard of living and to improve public health. Although these are not justiciable, but are the cardinal principles and laudable objectives which the Union and State Governments are required to translate into action in due course of time to improve the quality of life of the workers as consumers.

Under Part III of the Constitution of India dealing with Fundamental Rights, Article 19 guarantees certain freedoms to all citizens. Article 19(1)(g) of the Constitution guarantees that all citizens have the right to practice any profession, or to carry on any occupation, trade or business. The freedom is, however, not uncontrolled. The clause (6) of the Article authorizes legislation which (i) imposes reasonable restrictions on this right in the interests of the general public; (ii) prescribes professional or technical qualifications necessary for carrying on any trade or business; and (iii) enables the state to carry on any trade or business to the exclusion of private citizens, wholly or partly.

Part XIII of the Constitution of India is concerned with Trade, Commerce and Intercourse in India in six Articles. Part XIII purports to provide for free trade throughout India and to specify the restrictions upon the freedom which are constitutionally permissible. Article 301 enacts the general rule that the trade, commerce and intercourse throughout the territory of India shall be free. The object of this Article is to break down the border barriers between the States and to create one unit with a view to encouraging trade and commerce in the country. However, the freedom of trade and commerce in Article 301 is not absolute and is to be read subject to the exceptions provided in Articles 302-305.

Article 302 gives Parliament power to make laws imposing such restrictions on the freedom guaranteed by Article 301 "as may be required in the public interest". Article 303 is in two clauses. The first denies both Parliament and the State Legislatures power to make laws "by virtue of any entry relating to trade and commerce" which provide for the giving of preference to one state over another or which discriminate between states. The second clause is a proviso to the first and, so far as the Parliament is concerned, removes the prohibition of preference and discrimination if the law made by Parliament declares that the preference or discrimination is necessary so that a situation arising from scarcity of goods in any part of India may be dealt with.

Article 304 is also in two clauses, so far as its substantive parts are concerned, and each clause operates as a proviso to Articles 301 and 303. The first clause authorizes the states, notwithstanding Articles 301 and 303, to impose taxes on goods imported from other states provided that such taxes are imposed on similar goods produced in the taxing state and that there is no discrimination between the two classes of goods — local and imported. The second authorizes the states to impose "such reasonable restrictions on the freedom of trade, commerce or intercourse with or within that state as may be required in the public interest." And to that second clause there is a procedural proviso requiring Bills and amendments for the purpose of that clause to receive the "previous sanction of the President" before being introduced or moved in the State Legislatures. Article 305 saves from the operation of Articles 301 and 303, unless the President orders otherwise, all laws which were made before the commencement of the Constitution and also all laws which relate to (and so far in they relate to) "the carrying on by the state, or by an undertaking owned or controlled by the state, of any trade, business, industry or otherwise". Article 307 authorizes Parliament to establish an authority for carrying out the purposes of Articles 301, 302, 303 and 304. No action has yet been taken under this provision.

B. *Other Regulatory Measures after Independence*

After Independence a mass of economic development and regulatory legislations were placed on the Indian Statute Book for the purpose of regulating trade, established a number of regulatory agencies and imposed a number of restrictions and regulations for the purpose. Some of which are as follows:

The Imports and Exports (Control) Act, 1947, provides a legal mechanism for regulating imports to, and exports from, the country. The Act, passed in 1947, is intended to control the imports and exports of various specified commodities in the interest of public, economy and with a view to conserve foreign exchange. The restrictions on imports and exports were originally introduced under the Defence of India Rules as a temporary measure to meet the emergency situation arising out of the last War. The Act initially was to be in force for a limited period of three years. However, its life has been extended from time-to-time. Besides the Imports and Exports Control Act, there are provisions in other legislations regulating the import-export trade of certain specified commodities, such as the Foreign Exchange Regulation Act, 1947, (Section 8), the Customs Act, 1962, (Section 11), the Coffee Act, 1942, the Tea Act, 1953, the Coir Industry Act, 1953 etc.

Under the Act, the Central Government has assumed the powers to prohibit, restrict or otherwise control the import and export of various commodities. The power given to the Government under the section is very wide and any conceivable commodity can be controlled under it. The regulation of export and import under the Act is operated by Chief Controller, Imports and Exports, through the mechanism of licensing. In exercise of the power given to it under Section 3(1), the Central

Government has promulgated the Imports (Control) Order, 1955, and the Exports (Control) Order, 1962, consisting of rules regarding the conditions and procedure for the grant of licences for the importation and exportation of scheduled goods. Contraventions of the provisions of the Act and Orders thereunder entails not only the cancellation or suspension of the licence, but also for prosecution under Section 5 of the Act which provides for imprisonment which may extend to one year, or fine, or both.

The Foreign Exchange Regulation Act, 1947, designed to conserve the foreign exchange of the country, empowers the Central Government and the Reserve Bank of India to control and regulate all dealings and transactions in foreign exchange and securities. Under Section 3 of the Act, the Reserve Bank is empowered to issue licences to deal in foreign exchange and to lay down the conditions under which licences may be granted. Such licensees are called "authorized dealers in foreign exchange." The Act affects in general all those transactions having international monetary implications. Under various sections of the Act [Sections 20(c), 25 and 27] the Central Government and the Reserve Bank are authorized to make rules, to issue notifications and to give directions for the purpose of the Act. The Act, together with such rules, notifications and, directions, constitutes the law of exchange control in India. Section 4 prohibits transactions in foreign exchange except as permitted by the section and any transaction contrary thereto is made punishable under Section 23(1) of the Act. For the purpose of enforcing the provisions of the Act a Director of Enforcement is appointed by the Central Government.

The issue of shares and debentures to the public by a company seeking to raise capital is controlled by the Capital Issues (Control) Act, 1947. The objective was the fostering of a rational and healthy growth of the corporate sector by ensuring, *inter alia*, that investment does not go into channels which are wasteful and not in accordance with the objectives of the Plan; that companies have capital structure which are sound and conducive to the public interest and that there is no undue congestion of offers for public subscription during any part of the year. Regulation of balanced investment in all sectors of the economy in accordance with the priorities laid down in the Five Year Plans was the primary object of Capital Issues (Control) Act as well as of the Industries (Development and Regulation) Act. While the former looks after the financial structure of Joint Stock Companies in terms of national needs and interests of the investing public, the latter enactment controls the licensing of industries in accordance with Plan targets.

The Control is administered by the Ministry of Finance (Department of Economic Affairs) through the Controller of Capital Issues, who is especially appointed for the purpose and who is invested with the powers conferred upon the Central Government under Sections 3, 4, and 6(2) of the Act. In terms of Section 11 of the Act, Government constitutes an Advisory Committee, whose advice it obtains from time-to-time, in formulating guiding principles for the administration of the control.

The Central Government's consent to the issue of capital within the country is necessary in all cases where the company is or would be in the banking or in the insurance field. Where the company is or would be in the industrial or trading field, consent is necessary if the nominal value of the securities (including premium) etc. to be issued within the country during a period of 12 months is more than ₹ 25 lakh. If any person intends to make a public offer of sale of any securities held by him: (a) in a private company, or (b) in a company which had previously been issued a consent order containing a condition that the shares of that company should be privately subscribed, the consent of the Central Government is required by that person for making such a public offer of sale. Since, the Act also applies to a company within the meaning of Section 591 of the Companies Act, 1956, the Central Government may, on application, accord recognition to an issue of capital made or to be made outside India by a company not incorporated in India, but having an established place of business in India.

There are exemptions granted by Government in regard to loans from banks purely for purposes of working capital etc. There are also a few other exemptions which are embodied in the Capital Issues (Exemption) Order, 1966, as modified by the Order of 1969. Capital Issues Control played vital part in developing our economy and helped to build-up, through the Capital Issues Control Advisory Committee set-up by the Central Government, a healthy and sound set of financial principles for the corporate sector. It has not allowed the exploitation of ordinary investor by regulating share prices, bonus issues, takeover and merger rates, share valuation cases etc.

The Drugs (Control) Act was passed in 1950 which provided for the control of the sale, supply and distribution of drugs. This Act briefly provided for fixing of maximum prices and maximum quantities which may be held or sold, general limitation on quantity which may be possessed at any one time, duty to declare possession of excess stocks, marking of prices and exhibiting list of prices and stocks, and obligation to state price separately on composite offer. The Act further provides prohibition or regulation of the disposal of drugs, offences by corporations, power of search and seizure etc.

The Industries (Development and Regulation) Act, 1951, introduced a legal framework for industrial licensing, and conferred certain supervisory powers on the Government as regards certain types of industrial undertakings. This enactment controlled the industrial activities of the country with a view to give effect to the industrial policies of the Central Government. The control over the scheduled industries ("Scheduled Industry" consists of industries in the First Schedule) is exercised through (1) registration of existing industrial undertakings;[95] (2) licensing of new industrial undertakings;[96] (3) licensing the manufacture or production of new articles;[97] (4) licensing of industries in special cases;[98] (5) the institution of investigation into the affairs of industrial undertakings;[99] (6) the issuing of appropriate directions after investigation;[100] (7) the assumption of management and control of an industrial undertaking in certain cases;[101] and (8) the control of supply, distribution, price etc. of certain articles in such industries.[102] Thus, the Industries (Development and Regulation) Act, 1951, provided for the development and regulation of certain industries. Under section 18-G of the Act, the Central Government is empowered to regulate or prohibit any class of commercial or financial transaction of articles which is considered to be detrimental to public interest.

The Indian Standards Institution (Certification Marks) Act, 1952, provides for the standardization and marking of goods which is a prerequisite to the establishment of a healthy trade and to compare favourably with the established makes of foreign products. The Indian Standards Institution (now BIS) is performing the following functions: to prepare and promote the general adoption of standards on national and international basis; to promote standardization, quality control and simplification in industry; to provide for registration of standardization marks applicable to products, commodities etc. and to provide or arrange facilities for the examination and testing of commodities etc. The Act has been amended in 1961 and 1976 to make it more effective in order to achieve its objectives. The Indian Standards Institution (now BIS) prescribes specifications for most of the commodities and manufactured articles which figure in India's export trade with foreign countries and also in the home markets.

The Drugs and Magic Remedies (Objectionable Advertisements) Act, 1954, regulates the area of objectionable advertisement. The Act in brief provides for prohibition of advertisement of certain drugs for treatment of certain diseases and disorders. It further imposes curb on misleading advertisements relating to drugs, magic remedies for treatment and regulation of certain advertisements of goods of which import and export have been prohibited. There is also provision for punishment for those guilty of contravention of the law.

Keeping in view the hazards to national health and safety from the menace of adulteration, the Prevention of Food Adulteration Act, 1954, was enacted. To make the machinery, provided under the Act, more effective to curb the increasing tendencies in adulteration, it was amended in 1964. The amendment provided that for the proper enforcement of the provisions of the Act the Central Government should also have power to appoint food inspectors. Under the Act the power to appoint inspectors vested in the State Governments except at major ports, airports, customs stations and Railway Stations. The common practice followed by a State Government is to appoint the inspectors of local authorities as food inspectors. In brief all the measures provided in the original Act and its subsequent amendments are designed for the prevention of adulteration in food to ensure safety and health to the consuming public at large in the country. The Act provides, broadly to protect the interest of the consumer, a Central Committee for Food Standards, Central Food Laboratory, prohibition of import of certain articles of food, law on sea customs, powers of customs officers, prohibition of manufacture and sale of certain articles of food. The Act further contemplates for the machinery of analysis of food which bears the ample testimony to the consciousness on the part of the Central and State Government to protect the interest of consumers in the area of foodstuffs.

The Essential Commodities Act, 1955, constituted a legal framework for exercise of power to control prices, supply, distribution, movement, storage etc. of a number of commodities, designated as "essential commodities". The dominant object and intendment of the Act is to secure availability and equitable distribution of essential commodities at fair prices in the interests of general public. The Central Government has declared several commodities as "essential commodities" and several All India Control Orders have been issued under the Act from time-to-time. The object of the legislation is to provide, in the interest of the general public, for the control of the production, supply and distribution of any trade and commerce in certain commodities. The classes of commodities that are deemed to be essential commodities are enumerated in Section 2(a). It further provides that the Central Government may, by a notified order, declare any other commodity as essential commodity for the purpose of this Act, provided it is a commodity with respect to which Parliament has power to make law by virtue of Entry 33 in List III of the Seventh Schedule to the Constitution.

Section 3 of the Act gives powers to the Central Government to pass orders under the Act if it is necessary or expedient to do so for maintaining or increasing supplies of any essential commodity or for securing their equitable distribution and availability at fair prices. The power of the Central Government to issue orders under section 3 may be delegated to such officer or authority subordinate to Central Government, to State Government or to any officer or authority subordinate to it.[103] Such orders may contain directions to any State Government or its officers as to the exercise of the delegated power.[104] Sections 7 to 10 provide penalties for contravention of any order made under section 3 and for making false statements or furnishing false information. A large number of orders relating to various commodities have been promulgated from time-to-time by the Central Government in exercise of its powers under section 3 of the Act conferring enormous discretionary power on administrative officers.

The Act of 1955 was amended in 1964, 1966, 1967, 1971, 1974, 1976, 1981 and again in 1984. The unamended Act of 1955 provides for imposition of duties on the State Governments and power to direct them for discharge of any duty or for the exercise of any powers contained in the Act. It further contemplates confiscation of foodgrains, and others, cognizance of offences and power to try summarily all the amendments to the Act provide for the quick and effective trail of offences committed by traders and middlemen, forfeiture of packages, vehicles, animals involved in the contravention of orders issued under the Act. The amendment of 1967 provides for the confiscation of all essential commodities instead of foodgrains, edible oils or edible oilseeds if they contravene the provision of section 3 of the Act of 1955. The 1967 amendment further deals with offence which have been made cognizable and bailable and increase of maximum punishment for three years to five years. It also prohibits a person to carry on any business in the commodity in which he has been convicted and that period is not less than six months as may be specified by the court.

The Indian Companies Act, 1956, confers a vast reservoir of supervisory and regulatory powers on the Government with a view to making the corporate sector conform to the new socio-economic policies of the country and to protect the shareholders' interests against misuse of power by the company management. Under the Act the Central

Government assumed wide and far-reaching powers to control corporate management and administration at different stages. The Act set-up an administrative agency called the Company Law Board, to administer the regulatory provisions in the Act. The Act embodies provisions as to keep proper books of accounts giving a true and fair picture of the company's affairs and financial transactions. The Act confers certain statutory powers on the shareholders to regulate company's affairs. These powers enabled the shareholders to intervene in the conduct of corporate management and to get themselves posted with the financial position of the company.

The Mines and Minerals (Regulation and Development) Act, 1957, seeks to promote a planned mineral development of the country. The Trade and Merchandise Marks Act, 1958, provided for the registration, better protection of trade marks and for the preventions of the use of fraudulent marks on merchandise. The Act of 1958 provides enhanced punishment for offences relating to trade and merchandise marks particularly drugs and food on grounds of public interest and public health. The Act of 1958, has consolidated the Trade Marks Act, 1940, and Indian Merchandise Marks Act, 1889, and provided a comprehensive law in tune with consumer protection relating to registration and better protection of trade marks in the country. It further provides assignability of registered and unregistered trade marks, proposed use of trade mark by company to be formed and removal from register and imposition of limitations on ground of non-use. The Act further provides rectification, alteration of trade marks and correction of the registration and certification of trade marks. It also deals with specially textile goods and procedure for penalty for various offences.

The Monopolies and Restrictive Trade Practices Act, 1969, was enacted with the objective to provide that operation of economic system does not result in the concentration of economic power to the common detriment. It also provides for controlling the monopolies, and prohibition of monopolistic and restrictive trade practices. The object is to keep watch over the behaviour of all monopolies and monopolistic and restrictive trade practices and interfere only when they are prejudicial to public interest. The Act has established as administrative paraphernalia for the purpose; the Monopolies and Restrictive Trade Practices Commission has been created and Government has also acquired significant powers *vis-à-vis* private enterprise.

This enactment was a positive step towards consumer protection. Monopolistic trade practice simply provides the possession of economic power in order to control and determine prices of the commodities at the discretion of the manufacturers and exclude competition which is against the interest of consumers at large. The monopolistic trade includes possession of technological superiority, ownership of patent rights, absorption of competition through amalgamation on merger or take over or adoption of other dubious means to make the competition business difficult to operate.

Keeping in view the dangers of monopoly and monopolistic tendencies and need for curb on unfair trade practices for safeguarding the interest of consuming masses, the Act 1969, has been amended by the Monopolies and Restrictive Trade Practices (Amendment) Act, 1984. The amended Act provides measures for unfair trade practices which are the new concepts inducted for the protection of consumers. The MRTP (Amendment) Act, in Sections from 36A to 36E in Part B of the Chapter V provide for the substantive law as well as the procedural law.

The MRTP Act creates two authorities. There is the Director-General of Investigation and Registration who is appointed by the Government of India. He has several functions under the Act, *viz.* to investigate into complaints of monopolistic, restrictive or unfair trade practices, register restrictive trade agreements, make application to the Commission to undertake investigation into restrictive or unfair trade practices. Then there is the Monopolies and Restrictive Trade Practices Commission, appointed by the Central Government. A person who is, or has been, or is qualified to be, a Supreme Court or a High Court Judge is appointed as the Chairman. Other members of the Commission are persons possessing knowledge or experience of dealing with problems relating to economics, law, commerce, accountancy, public affairs or administration. Thus, the Commission is not purely a legalistic body; it has several other disciplines represented in its membership. The Commission has investigatory, advisory and adjudicatory functions. The Central Government may refer to the Commission any matter relating to the concentration of economic power or monopolistic trade practice for investigation and report. The power to make final orders in these matters vests with the Central Government.[105] The Commission can enquire into any restrictive or unfair trade practice on receiving a complaint from any trade or consumers' association, or a consumer, upon a reference made to it by the Central Government or a State Government, or upon an application of the Director-General, or *suo motu* in respect of any restrictive/unfair trade practice. As regards prevention of concentration of economic power, as stated above, the

Commission has no power to undertake a *suo motu* enquiry; it becomes active only when a reference is made to it by the Government, and the power to make final orders in this area vests with the Government. In case of a monopolistic trade practice, the Commission can initiate a *suo motu* enquiry without any reference being made by the government, but the Commission is to send its report to the Central Government which alone can make a final order.

The criminal law of the country does protect the consumer in some degree or so. In this regard Section 153 of the Code of Criminal Procedure, 1973, empowers a station-house officer of a police station without warrant to enter any place within the limits of such station for the purpose of inspecting or searching for any weights or measures or instruments for weighing, used or kept and whenever there is reason to believe that in such place weights, measures or instruments for weighing are false. In that eventuality it specially authorizes an officer-in-charge of police station to seize the same in larger public good and forward the information of such seizure to a Magistrate having jurisdiction.

The Cigarettes (Regulation of Production, Supply and Distribution) Act, 1975 regulates trade and commerce, production, supply and distribution of cigarettes. The Standards of Weights and Measures Act, 1976 provides for the establishment of standards of weights and measures on metric system, regulation of inter-state trade or commerce in weights, measures and other goods which are sold or distributed, penalties for the use of non-standard weights or measures and an Indian Institute of Legal Metrology for training inspectors and other persons.

The Prevention of Black Marketing and Maintenance of Supplies of Essential Commodities Act, 1980 was enacted with the objectives of the Act are to deal effectively with malpractices such as black marketing, profiteering and unjustified rise in prices of essential commodities by providing for the preventive detention of person likely to indulge in such practices. Although the Essential Commodities Act, 1955, does provide comprehensively for the regulation of production, prices and trade and commerce in commodities declared essential under the Act and although the penal provisions in the Act of 1955 have been made time-to-time more stringent even then it was not found adequate to deal with the situation existing in the country. Hence the Act of 1980 came into force to protect the interest of vast consuming public in the country.

The Essential Commodities (Special Provisions) Act, 1981 is another important Central legislation in which the provisions of the Essential Commodities Act, 1955 by way of amendments for a period of five years, have been made more stringent. The Act of 1981 provides for summary trials by courts specially constituted for the purpose of dealing effectively and curbing hoarding, black marketing and profiteering in the essential commodities and also the evil of vicious inflationary prices. It also aims at ensuring availability of essential commodities at fair prices. Under section 12A of the Act of 1981, the State Government is empowered for the purpose of providing speedy trail for the offences to constitute as many 'Special Courts' as may be necessary for area or areas as may be specified in the notification.

The Narcotic Drugs and Psychotropic Substances Act, 1985, has consolidated and amended the law relating to narcotic drugs and made stringent provisions for the control and regulation of operations relating to narcotic drugs and psychotropic substances and other related matters.

There are numerous other statutes passed by the Central and the State Governments to control and regulate various aspects of trade and commerce. Some of which have not been examined here are the Banking Companies Act, 1949; the Customs Act, 1962; the Mines and Minerals (Development and Regulation) Act, 1958; the Gold Control Act, 1968; the Forward Contracts (Regulation) Act, 1952; the Securities Contract (Regulation) Act, 1956; the Commission of Enquiry Act, 1952; the Income Tax Act, 1961; the Reserve Bank Act, 1934; the Banking Companies (Acquisition and Transfer of Undertakings) Act, 1969. The momentum towards enactment of economic legislation has by no means exhausted itself. As new and new problems come to the surface, new and new laws can be expected. It may also be worthwhile to note that the Government control of private enterprise is not all 'control' merely. Government has undertaken several development and promotional activities as well in relation to relation to private economic activity. The word 'control' has, therefore, a broad significance insofar as it includes not only the specific regulation of business, but also intervention of government in economic affairs through aids, subsidies, loans, ownership and other controls designed to influence the economy.

2.6. Regulations and State

2.6.1. *Laissez Faire State*

Laissez faire literally means, "allow to do". As a social policy it means letting people alone to do what they want. Government abstention from interference in actions of individuals, especially in commerce; general non-interference or indifference. *Laissez faire* was a synonym for strict free market economics during the early and mid-nineteenth century. In economic policy *laissez faire* capitalism amounts to capitalism in which all property is privately owned and owners are absolutely free to do anything with their property, including industrial property. Thus, *laissez faire* is an economic doctrine that government should not interfere in the economic or social regulation of society unless absolutely necessary. *Laissez faire* assumes that competitive system of free markets is the best means of allocating scarce resources between alternative users. Government intervention in the market place to regulate economic activity is seen as illegitimate and inefficient. In *laissez faire*, state would consist only of a police power and courts to protect citizens from enemies within the state, the armed forces for enemies from outside and a small efficient government to pass laws.

'*Laissez faire*' doctrine implied that the government should leave the private sector alone, and it should not attempt to regulate or control private enterprises. Unfettered competition was expected to serve the best interest of the society. However, many social thinkers of that time, like Karl Marx, were not persuaded by profit motive. To the people the evil of society could be attributed to the private ownership of capital and profit motive and argued for a greater role for the state in controlling the means of production. The ideological differences between "capitalism and socialism" had thus begun.

In the nineteenth century capitalist society, it was of considerable importance that the new middle-class entrepreneurs should be able to engage in commerce and manufacture untrammelled by government control or social obligations. On the one hand they needed freedom to introduce new methods of manufacture, and the freedom of trade to exploit the advantages that these new methods gave them. On the other hand they wanted to be able to treat labour like any other factor of production, both in moulding their employees into a tractable labour force and in exploiting a buyers' market, without having to concern themselves with the welfare of that labour force.

As per the *laissez faire* approach, the governmental powers and functions should be limited to protection of life and property and maintenance of certain essential services, i.e. least government is the best. The commissions while operating in the environment hostile to the expansion of governmental services and activities defined their goals in a very limited term and were hesitant in disturbing the traditional ways of doing business. A much-restrained approach was followed by these commissions in developing their policies and programmes.

The crisis in the economic system between the two world wars brought about profound changes in the political system and popular demands for state intervention in favour of unemployment benefits, pensions for the aged, low-cost housing, legislation regulating the work sphere etc. challenging the *laissez faire* ideology.

2.6.2. *Welfare State*

A government which seeks to provide every citizen with minimum guarantees for material welfare-medical care, education, employment, housing and pensions — has come to be called by its supporters the "welfare state" and by its critics, the "Santa Claus state" and the "transfer-payment state". The basic idea underlying the welfare state is the view that each individual is a human being and, as such is entitled to a fair share of welfare, even though he does not have the necessary financial resources to secure it. Slogans expressing this idea are "fair share for all", "welfare for all", and "a good life for all".[106] The Italian legal writer, del Vecchio, declares that out of consideration for social continuity and the development of human personality, the classical formulas "To each according to his meri" and "To each according to her work" must be modified in favour of "To each according to his needs".[107]

The core idea of the welfare state is that of a state providing for citizens who are not able to cover basic needs. Basic needs are defined within a cultural context and vary from a daily ration of rice to universal economic security measured in relation to a national income. The set of welfare institutions constructed to meet basic needs is one of several operational definitions of a welfare state. The role of the state can be either that of organizing, guaranteeing or acknowledging these institutions. As the concept of basic needs expands, the welfare institutions grow more comprehensive and diversified, and the role of the welfare state merges with the role of the state.

In the post-War British society, the term "the Welfare State" reflects the new emphasis on state responsibility for social welfare and ignores the elements of social organization that show continuity with the past. Penelope Hall epitomized this approach when she wrote:[108]

> The distinguishing characteristic of the Welfare State is the assumption by the community, acting through the State, of responsibility for providing the means whereby all its members can reach minimum standards of health, economic security and civilized living, and can share according to their capacity in its social and cultural heritage.

Slack[109] has examined a number of approaches to the definition and assessment of "the Welfare State". By some, and particularly by its supporters, the Welfare State is seen as the culmination of a long process to right the errors and injustices of nineteenth century *laissez faire* capitalism. To others it is an attempt to modify "the normal play of economic forces in a market economy",[110] a phrase which implies an acceptance of the nineteenth-century concept of economic forces whose operation is somehow 'more normal' if it takes place independently of human, and, in particular, government decisions about social objectives.

Piet Thoenes[111] puts this into perspective by defining the Welfare State as "a form of society characterized by a system of democratic government sponsored welfare, placed on a new footing and offering a guarantee of collective social care to its citizens, concurrently with the maintenance of a capitalist system of production". This definition includes aspects of our social system which show continuity as well as contrast with the nineteenth century, notably democratic control and capitalism. Thoenes still accepts the term the Welfare State, but the definition suggests that "welfare capitalism" might be a more accurate designation for this form of society, or even, if it was not so cumbrous, "democratic welfare capitalism", as Marshall has suggested.[112]

The welfare state has served as the major peace formula of advanced capitalist democracies for the period following the Second World War. The peace formula consists of first, in the explicit obligation of the state apparatus to provide assistance and support (either in money or in kind) to those citizens who suffer from specific needs and risks which are characteristic of the market society; such assistance is provided as a matter of legal claims granted to the citizens. Second, the Welfare State is based on the recognition of the formal role of labour unions both in collective bargaining and the formation of public policy. Both of these structural components of the Welfare State are considered to limit and mitigate class conflict, to balance the asymmetrical power relation of labour and capital, and thus to overcome the condition of disruptive struggle and contradictions that was the most prominent feature of pre-Welfare State, or liberal, capitalism. The Welfare State has been celebrated throughout the post-War period as the political solution to societal contradictions. The accomplishments which were won under conditions of war and in post-War periods were regularly maintained and added to them were the innovations that could be introduced in periods of prosperity and growth. The Welfare State came to be seen not so much as a burden imposed upon the economy, but as a built-in economic and political stabilizer which could help to regenerate the forces of economic growth and prevent the economy from spiraling downward into deep recessions.[113]

Most of the authors see the welfare state as a way of bridging conflicts of interest, between classes, different distributional systems, market forces and human needs, majority and marginal groups, and between interests of specific kinds. More generally, the welfare state is seen as setting the limits to the degree of social distance which a society can accept without conflict emerging. At the same time the welfare state serves as a frame for bridging all these conflicts and a legitimation of the political and economic arrangements and institutions which represent these interests.[114]

The conception of the welfare state has no precise meaning. The phrase is sometimes used to describe any state that 'concerns' itself in any manner with problems other than those of the maintenance of law and order. There is undeniably a wide field for non-coercive activities of government and a clear need for financing them by taxation. Indeed, no government in modern times has ever confined itself to the "individualist minimum". All modern governments have made provision for the indigent, unfortunate and disabled and have concerned themselves with questions of health and dissemination of knowledge. There is no reason why the volume of these pure service activities should not increase with the general growth of wealth. There is little reason why the government should not also play some role, or even take the initiative, in such areas as social insurance and education, or temporarily subsidize certain experimental development.

A welfare state is a state in which organized power is deliberately used (through politics and administration) in an effort to modify the play of market forces in at least three directions-first, by guaranteeing individuals and families a minimum income irrespective of the market value of their work or their property; second, by narrowing the extent of insecurity by enabling individuals and families to meet certain "social contingencies" (for example, sickness, old age and unemployment) which lead otherwise to individual and family crises; and third, by ensuring that all citizens without distinction of status or class are offered the best standards available in relation to a certain agreed range of social services.[115]

It is the conception of "market forces" that sets the problems of the welfare and welfare state within the context of the age of modern political economy. An attempt has been made, and is still being made, to create and maintain a self-regulating system of markets, including markets in the fictitious commodities, land, money and labour.

The conception of "Social Contingencies" is strongly influenced by the experience of industrialism. Unemployment as a social contingency, is a product of industrial societies and it is the unemployment mere than any other social contingency which has determined the shape and timing of modern welfare legislation The existence of chronic unemployment has been a powerful spur from the nineteenth century onwards leading organized labour groups to pass from concentration on "sectional interests" to the consideration of "social rights" of workers as a class, to philanthropic businessmen wishing to empower the 'efficiency' and strengthen the social justice of the business system and to politicians and governments anxious to avoid the dangerous political consequences of unemployment. The memories of chronic unemployment in the inter-war years and discovery of new techniques of controlling it reinforced welfare state policies in many countries after the Second World War.

Often the philosophies of welfare and interests sustaining them have been inimical to the suggestion that the state itself should intervene. The possibility of using governmental power has been related in each country to the balance of economic and social forces; intimates of the people functions and of the available resources of the state; effective techniques of influence and control, resting on knowledge; and not least; the prevalence or absence of the conviction that societies can be shaped by conscious polices designed to eliminate 'abuses' which in earlier generations had been accepted as 'inevitable' features of the human condition. The question why the state rather than some other agency becomes that main instrument of welfare involves a detailed examination of wide range of historical circumstances.

Though the position that the state should have nothing to do with matters not related to the maintenance of law and order may seem logical so long as we think of the state solely as a coercive apparatus, we must recognize that, as a service agency, it may assist without harm in the achievement of desirable aims which perhaps could not be achieved otherwise. The reason why many of the new welfare activities of government are a threat to freedom, then, is that, though they are presented as mere service activities, they really constitute an exercise of the coercive powers of government and rest on its claiming exclusive rights in certain fields.

The welfare state, for this term does not designate a definite system. What goes under that name is a conglomerate of so many diverse and even contradictory elements that, while some of them may make a free society more attractive, others are incompatible with it or may at least constitute potential threats to its existence.

Some of the aims of the welfare state can be realized without detriment to individual liberty, though not necessarily by the methods which seem the most obvious and are, therefore, most popular; that others can be similarly achieved to a certain extent, though only at a cost much greater than people imagine or would be willing to be, or only slowly and gradually as wealth increases; and that, finally, there are others — and they are those particularly dear to the hearts of the socialists — that cannot be realized in a society that wants to preserve personal freedom.

Main ambition that inspires the welfare state: the desire to use the powers of Government to ensure a more even or more just distribution of goods. Insofar as this means that the coercive powers of Government are to be used to ensure that particular people get particular things, it requires a kind of discrimination between, and an unequal treatment of, different people, which is irreconcilable with a free society. This is the kind of welfare state that aims at "social justice" and becomes "primarily a re-distributor of income". It is bound to lead back to socialism and its coercive and essentially arbitrary methods.

In many fields persuasive arguments based on considerations of efficiency and economy can be advanced in favour of the state's taking sole charge of a particular service; but when the state does so, the result is usually not only that those advantages soon prove illusory, but that the character of the services becomes entirely different from that which they would have had if they had been provided by competing agencies. If, instead of administering limited resources put under its control for a specific service, Government uses its coercive powers to ensure that men are given what some expert thinks they need.

It is sheer illusion to think that when certain needs of the citizen have become the exclusive convert of a single bureaucratic machine, democratic control of that machine can then effectively guard the liberty of the citizen. So, far as the preservation of personal liberty is concerned, the division of labour between a legislature which merely says that this or that should be done and an administrative apparatus which is given exclusive power to carry out these instructions is the most dangerous arrangement possible.

It would, scarcely, be an exaggeration to say that the greatest danger to liberty today comes from the men who are most needed and most powerful in modern government, namely, the efficient expert administrators exclusively concerned with what they regard as the public good.

2.6.3. *Crisis of Welfare State*

Since, the welfare state has grown out of the many conflicting interests, it has also co-opted and integrated them into its system. In the process the welfare state has become an extremely complex organization of programmes, legislations and ideologies, the internal logic of which is at best difficult to discern, and at worst directly counteractive to the idea of a welfare states. This complexity has become a distinct feature of the welfare states. It only adds to the complexity in relation to the many interest groups involved in the welfare scene and the rapid social changes confronting most countries.

Since 1970s, the sociologists, political scientists, historians, philosophers and economists have turned their attention in the direction of research on the welfare state. The attention is clearly related to the 'crisis' of the welfare state — whether the phenomenon is seen as a crisis of, a crisis in, or a crisis by the welfare state; or a crisis located in capitalism, i.e. construction of the state or the national/international economy spilling over into the welfare state. The welfare state is under attack. It is accused of creating a crisis, through high social expenditures which undermine and twist the national economy, through the level of unemployment benefits which is seen to contribute to unemployment and distortion of the labour market, and through its ideology which is considered contradictory to important social goals. The welfare state is also accused of being in crisis because of lack of financing, rigid organization, poor delivery of services, unsolved problems and never ending needs for expansion.

Growth of social welfare functions of government raises the question of how far the Government should go in providing for material well-being of its citizens. If the Government provides care "from the womb to the tomb", some persons ask, will not individual initiatives, ambitions and resourcefulness be dulled? If the government increasingly offers public assistance, people will accept the crutch and lean on the government the rest of their lives. "Too much government" it is said, "means little men". It is only by struggle, adversity, and victory many believe, that man gains self-reliance, self-confidence and stature. Further, problem created by the social objective of welfare for all is the effect of heavy taxation, required to finance it, upon the initiative of individuals engaged in productive activity. In our economy, financial gain is the strongest and most effective incentive for getting people to work hard, assume risks, and undertake responsibility. If private initiative and enterprise are overburdened by taxation, it is said government will sooner or later be required to assume ownership and control over an increased sector of the economy.[116]

In many capitalist societies from the mid 1970s the welfare state has become the object of doubts, fundamental critique, and political conflict. It appears that the most widely accepted device of political problem-solving has itself become problematic, and that, at any rate, the unquestioning confidence in the welfare state and its future expansion has rapidly vanished. It is exactly its multi-functional character, its ability to serve many conflicting ends and strategies simultaneously, which made the political arrangement of the welfare state so attractive to a broad alliance of heterogeneous forces. But it is equally true that the very diversity of the forces that inaugurated and supported the welfare state could not be accommodated for ever within the institutional framework which came increasingly under attack. The machinery of class compromise has itself become the object of class conflict.

Faced with this complexity and a range of problems for which there are no precedents, it seems that governments are turning to the past for solutions when pushed to make decisions on the welfare state. The disturbing uncertainty of future challenges is met with the security of former time, although the old solutions hardly seem to solve the problems. The very market forces that the welfare state was developed to curb, are called upon again in order to meet the 'crisis'. State intervention which developed as a guarantee for equal access to welfare provisions is to be reduced, private organizations and the family are again seen as the most adequate units for extending welfare, while self-help groups are being encouraged. Centralized responsibility for social programmes is being returned to the local communities, now under the label of democratic reforms, and hard-won universalistic measures are being questioned. Redistributional systems in favour of the less privileged are slackened. High unemployment rates are now defined as tolerable and even necessary for a healthy national economy, while unemployment compensations are decreasing.[117]

Altogether, these 'solutions' have swept over the world, regardless of the size and content of the problems they are intended to solve. In all the countries these kinds of solutions have increased strongly during the last few years. The demands for the solutions have been set forward independent of the degree of development of the welfare states or the colour of the political party in power. They have also been forwarded independent of whether economic difficulties have penetrated the national economies or only touched upon the fringes, whether state intervention and bureaucratic responsibility are extensive or limited, and whether national unemployment rates are unusually high or moderate. There is little doubt that the sum of solutions offered is detrimental to the welfare state and, if carried forward with sufficient strength and intensity may be fatal, or, can throw the welfare state into a real crisis which will strip it of its present content and functions. These forces set into motion have been called "recapitalization of capitalism", and are the same antagonistic forces which had initially to be overcome in order to develop a welfare state.[118]

The sharp economic recession of the mid-1970s has given rise to an intellectually and politically powerful *renaissance* of *neo-laissez faire* and monetarist economic doctrines. These doctrines amount to a fundamental critique to the welfare state that is seen to be the illness of what it pretends to be the cure rather than effectively harmonizing the conflicts of a market society, it exacerbates them and prevents the forces of social peace and progress (namely, the forces of the market-place) from functioning properly and beneficially. This is said to be so for two major reasons. First, the welfare state apparatus imposes a burden of taxation and regulation upon capital which amounts to a disincentive to investment. Second, the welfare state grants claims, entitlements and collective power positions to workers and unions which amount to a disincentive to work, or at least to work as hard and productively as they would be forced to under the reign of unfettered market forces. Taken together, these two effects lead into a dynamic of declining growth and increased expectation, of economic "demand overload" (known as inflation) as well as political demand overload ('ungovernability'), which can be satisfied less and less by the available output.[119]

The socialist critique[120] of the welfare state is on three points. The welfare state is said to be ineffective and inefficient, repressive and conditioning a false ('ideological') understanding of social and political reality within the working class. In sum, it is a device to stabilize, rather than a step in the transformation of, capitalist society.

One aspect of the ineffectiveness of welfare state has been that it has done little or nothing to alter the income distribution between the two principal classes of labour and capital. A further aspect of its ineffectiveness is that the welfare state does not eliminate the causes of individual contingencies and needs (such as work-related diseases, the disorganization of cities by the capitalist real estate market, the obsolescence of skills, unemployment, etc.), but compensates for (parts of) the consequences of such events (by the provision of health services and health insurance, housing subsidies, training and re-training facilities, unemployment, benefits and the like). The kind of social intervention most typical of the welfare state is always 'too late', and hence its *ex post facto* measures are more costly and less effective than a more 'causal' type of intervention would allow them to be. Further in the welfare state there is constant threat to which social policies and social services are exposed due to the fiscal crisis of the state. The bureaucratic and professional form through which the welfare state dispenses its services in increasingly seen to be a source of its own inefficiency. Bureaucracies absorb more resources and provide less services than other democratic and decentralized structures of social policy could.

The critique of the repressiveness of the welfare state relates to social control aspect. Such repressiveness is indicated by the fact that, in order to qualify for the benefits and services of the welfare state, the client must not only prove his or her 'need', but must also be a deserving client — a client, that is, who complies with the dominant economic, political, and cultural standards and norms of the society. The heavier the needs, the stricter these requirements tend to be defined. The welfare state can be looked upon as an exchange transaction in which material benefits for the needy are traded for their submissive recognition of the 'moral order' of the society which generates such need. A third major aspect of the socialist critique of the welfare state is to demonstrate its political-ideological control function. The welfare state is seen not only as the source of benefits and services, but, at the same time, as the source of false conceptions about historical reality which have damaging effects for working-class consciousness, organization and struggle.

The liberal-conservative and the socialist critics exhibit somewhat surprising parallels on three points. First, contrary to the ideological consensus that flourished in some of the most advanced welfare states throughout the 1950s and 1960s, nowhere is the welfare state believed any longer to be the promising and permanently valid answer to the problems of the socio-political order of advanced capitalist economies. Critics in both camps have become more vociferous and fundamental in their negative appraisal of welfare state arrangements. Second, neither of the two approaches to the welfare state could and would be prepared, in the best interest of its respective clientele, to abandon the welfare state, as it performs essential and indispensable functions both for the social and economic well-being of the working class. Third, the welfare state remains a theoretically, though in reality firmly entrenched, fact of the social order of advanced capitalist societies. In short, it appears that the welfare state, while being contested both from the Right and the Left, will not be easily replaced by a conservative or progressive alternative.[121]

Nonetheless changes are occurring in every welfare state and these changes now seem to be moving in the same direction. If allowed to continue they can profoundly alter the profile and functions of the welfare state. Two main trends are visible, namely the changes in redistributive patterns and change in the role of the state. In all the countries, whether they are well-developed welfare states or not, the redistributional patterns are changing to the detriment of the most disadvantaged and marginal groups. They are losing out both in relative and absolute terms. In the area of social policy-making it can be safely said that in both developed and developing welfare states progress has come to a halt. Few new programmes are being introduced, and established programmes are being assessed with an eye to greater efficiency and cost-cutting. However, major programmes do not seem to be abandoned, although incremental changes erode the principles upon which they are built. The welfare bureaucracies are no exceptions and much criticism is directed towards the quality of service delivery. The welfare state has become so complex that large parts of it are left outside political mechanisms of control.

The second trend which can alter the profile and functions of the welfare state is the changing role of the government. Part of the ideology of the welfare state is based on the idea of government responsibility for social programmes, because government is seen — rightly or wrongly — as a guarantor of justice, a defender of the weaker groups in society, a controller of quality of service, an independent judge in conflicts, and a reliable source of funding. Underneath lies the assumption that there is a need for a dominant public sector to counteract the impact of a dominant private market sector which is crucial in creating wealth as well as poverty. There is little doubt, however, that much of the future argument about the welfare state will be over the muddled issue of state intervention. The call for 'privatization' of public welfare services has been made worldwide, and again, it makes little difference whether the country has a well- or poorly-developed welfare state, or even the extent to which the state presently intervenes. The solution offered is still less state intervention, regardless of the problems being faced. These trends coincide with, and in some cases are reactions to, the short-comings of the welfare state in proving adequate services. The development of these trends is also part of the process, where capitalistic market forces are able to exploit the antagonism towards the welfare state, created through their own crisis.[122]

2.6.4. *Emergence of Administrative State and Contracting State*

Administrative State

The development of administrative state can be divided very roughly into four periods; an early stage culminating in the progressive-era regulatory agencies and administrative reforms; the New Deal watershed; the post-New Deal period including the consolidation of the administrative state and its vast expansion in the social regulation initiatives beginning in the mid-1960s on the name of welfarism; and the deregulation movement beginning in the mid-1970s and accelerating in the Reagan and Thatcher years. This is not to say of course that administrative power did not raise important issues of constitutional legitimacy, judicial control and effective governance before the establishment of the first federal regulatory agencies in 1880s. In the sixteenth century, the Tudors created an extensive, notoriously oppressive system of regulation in England, one that led to the first great landmark decision legitimating judicial review of agencies, *Dr. Bonham's case.*[123] In the United States, the decision establishing the principle of judicial review for constitutionality, *Marbury* vs. *Madison*[124] also involved a suit against an agency official, here the Secretary of State. Between 1816 and the Civil War, as James Q. Wilson[125] points out, the executive branch grew nearly eightfold, although almost all of this growth was confined to the Post Office where bureaucratic discretion, was not a great problem. However, exercise of discretion is a major complaint about agency today.

The excerpt from Stephen Skowronek[126] sounds the dominant themes of administrative development in United States from the close of reconstruction through 1920. His detailed study emphasized that the long process of reforming the civil service, the army and business regulation show how the embryonic national state of "courts and parties" gave way after protracted political struggles — first to "patch work" reforms that proved wholly inadequate by 1900, and then to a genuine reconstitution of the administrative apparatus under presidents Roosevelt, Taft, and Wilson. The Rabin[127] excerpt picks up the story in 1920, carrying it to the mid-1980s and the deregulation movement. He traces the gradual legitimation of the administrative state by congress and (after 1937) the courts, the different visions of regulatory power that agencies initiated at various times, and the complex interactions between the courts, agencies, and Congress beginning in the 1960s. He concludes by noting the remarkable continuity of controversy, now spanning more than a century, over the appropriately scope and mechanisms of federal regulatory authority.

The administrative state is now inevitable because of the ever-lengthening agenda of complex public policy problems and the institutional limitations of legislatures. The broad delegations of power to these agencies — making the workplace "reasonably safe" (Occupational Safety and Health Act, 1985); assist the disabled who cannot engage in "substantial gainful activity" [Social Security Act, (Disability Insurance), Workers Compensation Act (Gradation of Disability)]; award licenses and allocate scares resources in accordance with the "public interest, convenience and necessity" (Federal Communication Act and various Inter-state Commerce Commissions) and similar formulas create administrative discretion far more sweeping in scope and pervasiveness than the familiar and inherent Ministerial discretion for the executive. As if to codify sweeping discretion many statutes include a catch all delegation of substantive rule making authority to the agency instructing the administrator to make any rules "necessary" or "appropriate" to accomplish the purposes of the statute. As the bureaucracy's role has grown, so have the risk and benefits associated with official action. The stakes involved in judicial intervention to check malfeasance and misfeasance have also grown, so that familiar way, discordant with judicial activism and the powerful social role of judiciary is only a derivative problem, the real one being awesome agency power.

Contracting State

A key and continuing issue in government reform is the option of utilizing the private sector in producing services. Governments have long used the private sector. However, the use of private operators in supplying services was very restricted. Their role was limited to providing a few in-house functions and a very limited number of direct services. Spurred by the emergence of "reinventing", the acceleration of privatization efforts began in the mid-1980s with the growth of privatization in many service categories. The greater utilization of the private sector continued throughout the 1990s. Utilization of the private sector in producing services is an important element in the movement towards reforming Government. Most people today believe that some amount of state intervention is must to alleviate the worst social problems, but no one knows what is the extent of it. This confusion has given rise to the concept of 'mixed economy' where government undertakes some economic activities while the rest are left to private firms. In addition, the Government also undertakes the obligation to alter the behaviours of the private sector through a variety of rules, regulations, taxes and subsidies. However, the problem of defining appropriate boundaries between government and private activities still persists and remains to be the most important political, philosophical, and economic debate.

The privatization movement set in motion by Reagan Administration in the 80s in the United States started a global trend of restoring the free enterprise spirit. In Britain, the Thatcher Government privatized some of its huge Government Corporations including British Gas, British Telecom and British Airways. Privatization was also witnessed in other

European countries like Germany, France, Italy etc. Following the trend, India also began to privatize and liberalize its economy in 1990s after 40 years of socialistic pattern of society and welfare state. China, ASEAN countries like Philippines, Singapore, Indonesia, Thailand and Malaysia and newly constituted independent states of Soviet Union are no exception to the global trend and are embarking on privatization programmes. Privatization has become the most influential concept in later part of Twentieth century.

Privatization could contextually means measures taken to initiate a more commercial (private) approach into activities, undertaken by the public sector. Privatization, "any process aimed at shifting functioning and responsibilities, in whole or in part, from the Government to the private sector".[128] Privatization in broad terms encompasses involvement of greater market forces to ensure higher competition and reduce the role of the state in economic sphere and thus bring in greater private involvement into government activities. Thus, privatization can be defined as "any measure resulting in transfer of ownership and/or control over assets or activities from the public to private sector".[129] Privatization as liberalization programme envisages a larger role for private sector wherein key infrastructure areas (including power, telecom, roads, posts, etc.) are open for private sector participation. Further, the entry of private sector is also permitted in the financial sector including banks, financial institutions and service and insurance sector. Thus, all entails streamlining and simplification of rules, procedures, reduction in bureaucratic and political interferences and intervention to allow professionalism and to grant greater autonomy to management.

The movement after 1990s is from controlled economy to a liberalized one. In controlled economy the government uses licences, permits, quotas and other such regulations as control tools, whereas in liberalized economy 'deregulation' is the only regulation, which creates an environment that encourages fair-play in efforts to eliminate price restrictions, to reduce or eliminate domestic and international barriers to the entry of new firms, to remove barriers for free flow of trade and resulted in debureaucratization of the services. However, deregulation has its own costs towards economic welfare and there is need to focus on regulation as a potential way of limiting the market failures associated with imperfect competition. That is why the deregulated utility services like telecommunication, transport, electricity, railways etc. are subject to diverse regulating measures.

Privatization could take various forms. As a result of privatization and liberalization of the economy, alternative service delivery approaches have experienced a marked increase in use since the middle of this century. The most complete form of privatization, load shedding, occurs where the government simply disassociates itself from providing the service and turns financing and production entirely over to the private sector. A modified form of load shedding involves franchising, i.e. a special privilege granted to a private operator. The service is turned over to the private sector, but the government chooses the private operator or operators. The government also may exercise some operational control over the franchisee such as setting quality standards for effluent discharges in the case of waste treatment plants. There are at least two variants of franchising: design-build-transfer-operate (BTO) and design-build-operate-transfer (BOT). In the BTO case, in which the private operator designs, constructs, and transfers ownership upon completion to the government, but operates the facility. BOT is a more complete form of privatization since the private sector.may continue to own the facility, often subject to government regulation, on a long-term basis. After a number of years, however, the private firm may transfer ownership to the public sector.

A mixed technique of service provision/production is that of a public-private partnership. Under this relationship, the Government fashions a contractual arrangement with its private sector partners. Infrastructure projects illustrate this approach such as in the BTO model where each partner has carefully defined responsibilities. Also, a government agency may work with a private social service organization to address a particular social problem. The oldest and most common Alternative Service Delivery Approaches (ASDA) is service contracting wherein governments seek outside agents to fulfil the needs of a project, yet continue to maintain the ultimate responsibility for, or "ownership" of the service provision. Rather than employing some form of load shedding, most governments have preferred contracting as the method to shift operations to the private sector. In this model, the government entity retains ownership and overall control, but employs the private vendor to actually render the service. Except for activities involving infrastructure or voucher/subsidy systems, contracting out is the way practically all privatization is now being implemented. Everything from in-house support services to direct taxpayer services falls under the contracting out umbrella. When used correctly, contracting arrangements may enhance efficiency by promoting competition among service providers and encourage governments to provide services in times of increasing demands and shrinking resources. The introduction of competitors into a previously monopolistic realm may also result in new innovations in service delivery. Osborne and Gaebler have indicated that service contracting releases government employees from the burden of some projects and allows them to redirect their efforts and time on other, needed endeavours — especially in times of limited government capacities, such as seasonal, part-time, or emergency-related work. Like other ASDAs, contracting seeks to promote innovation by allowing outside agents to suggest changes in service provision and provide flexibility in determining what services will be delivered, who will deliver them, and how they will be provided. Finally, service contracting may also enhance the quality of work performed. It may allow governments to be more efficient in the allocation of resources when dealing with economies of scale issues.[130]

These anticipated benefits do not come without costs. One of the risks associated with contracting includes reduced government control over the service area or the cost of the project. Because the government is no longer the direct or sole provider of the good or service, many new variables are introduced to the day-to-day operations. For example, each time a new service contract is created, new actors, rules, and regulations are introduced — in addition to the many of the existing regulations. These compounding factors create the potential for fragmentation and confusion — as well as cost overruns.[131] To complicate matters, once a city or county decides to enter into a service contract with an outside agent, most do not have routine methods for systematically evaluating the work. This may ultimately lead to poor quality work. Still other problems relate to resistance from unions, citizens, or employee-based groups.

Since, the mid-1980s the combination of fiscal constraints on governments and the growing popularity of the "smaller government" philosophy weakened opposition to privatization and encouraged the use of the privatizing option. In the face of the twin forces of budget pressure and the unpopularity of service cuts, public decision-makers became more sympathetic towards experimenting with privatization initiatives. Another force for greater use of the private sector was the "anti-big government" point of view of some voting groups. However, there is strong feeling that privatization of public assets has resulted into large scale discrimination and rent-seeking tendencies in the developing countries. It may not provide satisfactory services to the citizens. Moreover, efficiency is not the function of ownership, it relates to the efficacy of management. However sometimes privatization is considered politically easier and soft option. Due to diverse range of economic and political systems, it may not be possible to adopt a generalized approach. There is a dominant view that where government is a major or secondary provider of goods and services, where the public sector has to compete with the private sector, a level playing field should be established. To establish level playing field traditional public administration system should be replaced by NPM. One of the facets of this is regulation of the public utilities by independent regulatory commissions/authorities. The World Bank is also encouraging the client countries to establish independent regulators. The reason for this is largely the failure of the traditional department based, non independent regulators. Thus, privatization since early 1990s has been associated with the consensus that private investment would not be possible unless it is backed by a 'de-politicized' independent regulator. Thus, the most critical task for the developing and transition economies is to design and implement stable and effective regulation for all those activities where both public and private sectors are the operators and providers of socio-economic goods and services. There is need for regulation that provides credible commitment to safeguard the interests of both investors and customers. Regulatory procedures must be predictable, accountable and transparent.

NOTES

1. Article 13(3)(a) of the Indian Constitution reads:
   "law" includes any ordinance, order, bye-law, rule, regulation, notification, custom or usage having in the territory of India the force of law; See also *St. Johns Teachers' Training Institute* vs. *Regional Director*, NCTE (2003) 3SCC 321.
2. C. Hood (1994), *Explaining Economic Reversals*, Open University Press, Buckingham, p. 4.
3. R. Baldwin and M. Cave (1999), *Understanding Regulation — Theory, Strategy, and Practice*, Oxford University Press, pp. 19-33; C. Hood (1994), *Explaining Economic Reversals*, Open University Press, Buckingham, pp. 5-16, 20-32.
4. Mitnick, B. (1980), *Political Economy of Regulation*, New York, p. 94.
5. "Address of the Prime Minister in Chief Ministers Conference on the Working of Electricity Regulatory Authority", *The Hindustan Times*, dated 29.05.2007, p. 1.
6. E.S. Redford (1952), *Administration of National Economic Control*, London, pp. 251-52.
7. M.H. Bernstein (1955), *Regulatory Business by Independent Commission*, Princeton University Press, New York, pp. 74-100.
8. *Ibid.*, p. 76.
9. P. Self (1985), *Political Theories of Modern Government*, Allen & Unwin, London, pp. 79-107.
10. L. Hancher and M. Moran (ed.) (1989), *Capitalism, Culture and Regulation*, Oxford, ref. in R. Baldwin and Martin Cave (1999), *Understanding Regulation — Theory, Strategy and Practice*, Oxford, p. 21.

11. G. Kolko (1994), *The Triumph of Conservatism*, New York; 1977 referred in Christopher Hood (1994), *Explaining Economic Policy Reversals*, Open University Press, Buckingham, p. 23.
12. Public Choice Theory which emphasizes the force of private interests, and preferences in governmental decisions are in stark contrast to public interest, A. Ogus (1994), *Regulation: Legal Form and Economic Theory*, Oxford, pp. 58-71.
13. Christopher Hood (1994), *Explaining Economic Policy Reversals*, Open University Press, Buckingham, p. 23.
14. P. Self (1993), *Government by the Market?*, Westview Press, Basingstoke, p. 46.
15. *Ibid.*, p. xii.
16. Rhoads, S. (1985), *The Economist's View of the World*, Cambridge University Press, Cambridge, p. 214.
17. Derthick and Quirk (1985), *The Politics of Deregulation*, Washington, quoted in Christopher Hood (1994), *Explaining Economic Policy Reversals*, Open University Press, Buckingham, p. 5.
18. Minogue, K. (1986), "Loquocentric Society and Its Critics" in *Government and Opposition*, 21, pp. 338-61 at p. 342.
19. Majore, G. (1989), *Evidence, Argument and Persuasion in the Policy Process*, New Haven, CT, Yale University Press; quoted in Christopher Hood (1994), *Explaining Economic Policy Reversals*, Open University Press, Buckingham, p. 5.
20. McCloskey, D.N. (1985), *The Rhetoric of Economics*, Madison, WI, Wisconsin University, p. 31.
21. Christopher Hood (1994), *Explaining Economic Policy Reversals*, Open University Press, Buckingham, pp. 5-6.
22. Merle Fainsod and Lincoln Gordan (1948), *Government and the American Economy*, rev. ed., W.W. Norton & Co., Inc., New York, pp. 3-80 and 221-236.
23. Ernst Freund (1928), *Administrative Powers over Persons and Property: A Comparative Survey*, University of Chicago Press, Chicago, p. 145.
24. J.E. Richardson (1962), "The Control of Monopolies and Restrictive Trade Practices in the United States of America, Canada and the United Kingdom", 35, *A.L.J.*, pp. 332, 333.
25. Thomas J. Anderson (1958), *Our Competitive System and Public Policy*, pp. 381-84.
26. In 1938 the editors of *Times* invited their readers to define New Deal. This was one of the reply. See Morton Keller, (ed.) (1963), *The New Deal: What was It?*, Holt, Rinehart and Winston, New York, p. 6.
27. Vernon A. Mund (1960), *Government and Business*, 3rd Edn., Harper and Brothers, New York, pp. 30-31.
28. Basil Rauch (1994), *The History of the New Deal*, New York as quoted in Morton Keller (ed.) (1963), *The New Deal: What was It?*, Holt, Rinehart and Winston, New York, p. 2. c.f. Robinson's view of the developments of 1933 and 1934 is different indeed. The development of the New Deal was not, as Rauch saw it, a response to national conditions and popular demands so much as it was the work of administration officials influenced by alien and socialistic ideas who without any popular mandate sought to recast American society. Edgar E. Robinson (1955), *The Roosevelt Leadership*, New York as quoted in Morton Keller (ed.) (1963), *The New Deal: What was It?*, Holt, Rinehart and Winston, New York, p. 3.

29. *Infra* page 77, Judicial Response to New Deal Legislations.
30. Basil Rauch (1963), "The First New Deal", in Morton Keller (ed.), *The New Deal: What was it?*, American Problem Studies, Holt, Rinchart & Winston Inc., p. 30.
31. *Brownlow Commission Report of the President's Committee on Administrative Management*, Washington, DC, Government Printing Office, 1937.
32. (1934) q. in John Major (1968), *The New Deal*, Longman, Green & Co. Ltd., pp. 103-04.
33. R.H. Jackson (1941), *The Struggle for Judicial Supremacy*, Knopf, New York, p. 79 and E.S. Corwin (1934), *The Twilight of the Supreme Court*, Yale University Press, p. 213.
34. H.S. Commager (ed.) (1963), *Documents of American History*, 7th edn., Appleton-Century-Crofts, New York, Vol. II, pp. 279-80, 282, 283.
35. (1932) q. in John Major (1968), *The New Deal*, Longman, Green & Co. Ltd., pp. 107-08.
36. H.S. Commager, *op. cit.*, pp. 231-32.
37. 293 US 388 (1935).
38. 295 US 495 (1935).
39. 334 US 742 (1947).
40. Brownlow Commission (1937), *Report of the President's Committee on Administrative Management*, Washington D.C.
41. James M. Landis (1938), *The Administrative Process*, New Heaven, CT, Yale University Press, pp. 2, 24.
42. *U.S. Senate Report of the Attorney General Committee on Administrative Procedure, Administrative Procedure in Government Agencies*, Sen, Dec. No.8, 77th Congress, 1st Sess. 1941.
43. *Ibid.*
44. APA sections 551(5) & (7).
45. Phillip J. Cooper (2000), *Public Law and Public Administration*, 3rd Edn , F.E. Peacock Publishers, pp. 97-105.
46. Eric Goldman (1960), *The Crucial Decade and After: America, 1945-1960*, New York: Vintage Books, p. vi.
47. Commission on Organization of the Executive Branch of Government (1949), *The Hoover Commission Report on the Organization of the Executive Branch of Government*, McGraw-Hill, Inc., New York, p. 436.
48. For details see Neil MacNeil and Harold W. Metz (1956), *The Hoover Commission Report, 1953-1955: What it Means to You as Citizens and Taxpayers*, MacMillan, New York.
49. U.S. House of Representatives, Task Force on Legal Services and Procedure, *Report on Legal Services and Procedure*, Prepared by Commission on Organization of the Executive Branch, House Doc. No. 1128, 84th Cong., 1st sess. (1955), p. 2.
50. *Ibid.*, pp. 19, 30.
51. *Ibid.*, p. 22.
52. *Ibid.*, p. 24.
53. *Ibid.*, p. 19.
54. *Ibid.*, p. 28.
55. Kenneth Culp Davis (1969), *Discretionary Justice: A Preliminary Inquiry*, Baton Rouge, Louisiana State University Press.
56. Kenneth Culp Davis (1969), "A New Approach to Delegation", 36, *U. Chicago L. Rev.*, 713.

57. At first *ad hoc* Commissions were issued by virtue of the royal prerogative, them from 1427 onwards Commissioners of Sewers were established by statute, empowered to issue ordinances and to supervise their execution almost is the modern fashion Holdsworth, *History of English Law*, Vol. X, p. 196. *et seq.*
58. J.F. Garner (1979), *Administrative Law*, 5th Edn., Butterworth, London, pp. 344-45.
59. R. Pares (1953), *George III and the Politicians*, Oxford, p. 3.
60. C. Hughes (1957), *The British Statute Book*, Hutchinson University Library, London, p. 100.
61. F.W. Maitland (1908), *Constitutional History of England*, Cambridge, pp. 382-83.
62. Henry Parries (1969), *Constitutional Bureaucracy — The Development of British Central Administration since the Eighteenth Century*, George Allen & Unwin Ltd., London, p. 161.
63. *Ibid.*
64. F.W. Maitland (1908), *Constitutional History of England*, Cambridge, p. 383.
65. C. Hughes (1957), *British Statute Book*, Hutchinson University Library, London, pp. 45 & 112.
66. F.W. Maitland (1908), *Constitutional History of England*, Cambridge, pp. 383-84.
67. S. and B. Webb (1922), *Statutory Authorities for Special Purposes*, Longmans, Green & Co., London, 1922 q. in Henry Parries (1969), *Constitutional Bureaucracy — The Development of British Central Administration since the Eighteenth Century*, George Allen & Unwin Ltd., London, p. 163.
68. O.C. Williams (1948), *Historical Development of Private Bill Procedure and Standing Orders in the House of Commons*, His Majesty's Stationery Office, pp. i, 67.
69. T. Erskine May (1969), q. in Henry Parries, *Constitutional Bureaucracy — The Development of British Central Administration since the Eighteenth Century*, George Allen & Unwin Ltd., London, p. 163.
70. H. Parris (1965), *Government and the Railways in Nineteenth Century Britain*, Routledge & Kegan Paul, pp. 48-49.
71. S.E. Finer (1952), *Life and Times of Sir Edwin Chadwick*, pp. 15-16. Henry Parries (1969), *Constitutional Bureaucracy — The Development of British Central Administration since the Eighteenth Century*, George Allen & Unwin Ltd., London, p. 164.
72. Henry Parries (1969), *Constitutional Bureaucracy — The Development of British Central Administration since the Eighteenth Century*, George Allen & Unwin Ltd., London, p. 164.
73. J. Redlich and F. Hirst (1903), *Local Government in England*, MacMillan & Co., London, pp. ii, 240.
74. A. Wedderburn (1794), *Observations on the State of Prisons*, q. in Henry Parries (1969), *Constitutional Bureaucracy — The Development of British Central Administration since the Eighteenth Century*, George Allen & Unwin Ltd., London, p. 165.
75. D. Roberts (1960), *Victorian Origins of there British Welfare State*, New Haven, p. 56.
76. S. and B. Webb (1922), *English Prisons under Local Government*, Longmans, Green & Co., London, pp. 110-11.
77. K. Jones (1955), *Lunacy, Law and Conscience*, 1744-1845, pp. 37-38.
78. *Ibid.*, pp. 142, 171, 175 and 191.
79. H. Parris (1965), *Government and the Railways in Nineteenth Century Britain*, Routledge & Kegan Paul, pp. 28ff.

80. C.H. Sisson (1959), *Spirit of British Administration*, Faber & Faber Ltd., p. 139.
81. *The Times*, September 21, 1833 q, in Henry Parries (1969), *Constitutional Bureaucracy — The Development of British Central Administration since the Eighteenth Century*, George Allen & Unwin Ltd., London, p. 167.
82. Sir C. Cars (1921), *Delegated Legislation*, Cambridge, p. 49.
83. Henry Parries (1969), *Constitutional Bureaucracy — The Development of British Central Administration since the Eighteenth Century*, George Allen & Unwin Ltd., London, p. 200.
84. Dicey (1905), *Law and Opinion in England in the Nineteenth Century*, MacMillan, London, p. 64.
85. F.W. Maitland (1955), *Constitutional History of England*, Cambridge, reprint, p. 501.
86. J.F. Garner (1979), *Administrative Law*, 5th Edn., Butterworth, London, p. 345.
87. Sir Norman Chester (1970), *The Nationalization of British Industry*, 1945-51; HMSO, pp. 1036-37.
88. Morgan, K.O. (1984), *Labour in Power 1945-51*, Larendon, p 105.
89. T. Prosser (1986), *Nationalized Industries and Public Control Legal Constitutional and Political Issues*, Basil Blackwell Inc., Oxford, U.K., pp. 36-41.
90. Iron and Steel Act, 1969, Sec. 5; Civil Aviation Act, 1971, Sec. 50; Water Act, 1973, Sec. 29; Industry Act, 1975, Sec. 6; Petroleum and Submarine Pipelines Act, 1975, Sec. 5; Aircraft and Shipbuilding Industries Act, 1977, Sec. 10; British Telecommunications Act, 1981, Sections 24 and 71.
91. Railways Act, 1974, Sec. 4(2); Petroleum and Submarine Pipelines Act, 1975, Sec. 3(1); Aircraft and Shipbuilding Industries Act, 1977, Sec. 7(1). The Board of the British National Oil Corporation was also to include two civil servants [Petroleum and Submarine Pipelines Act, 1975, Sec. 1(3)(c)].
92. T. Prosser (1986), *Nationalized Industries and Public Control Legal Constitutional and Political Issues*, Basil Blackwell Inc., Oxford, U.K., pp. 41-43.
93. *Ibid.*, pp. 44-47. The White Paper in general terms accepted many of the criticism made by the NEDO, but rejected most of the practical proposals for reforms.
94. S.P. Sathe (2004), *Administrative Law*, Seventh Edition, Lexis Nexis, Butterworths, pp. 14-18 and I.P. Massey (2005), *Administrative Law*, Eastern Book Co., Lucknow, pp. 12-16.
95. Industrial (Development and Regulation) Act, 1951, Section 10.
96. *Ibid.*, Section 11.
97. *Ibid.*, Section 11-A.
98. *Ibid.*, Section 13.
99. *Ibid.*, Section 15.
100. *Ibid.*, Section 16.
101. *Ibid.*, Section 18-A.
102. *Ibid.*, Section 18-G.
103. The Essential Commodities Act, 1955, Section 5.
104. *Ibid.*, Section 4.
105. See provisions in Chapters III and IV of the MRTP Act.
106. Vernon Mund (1960), *Government and Business*, 3rd Edn, Harper & Bros. Publishers, New York, p. 8.
107. Giorgio del Vecchino (1953), *Justice*, New York, pp. 142, 147-148.
108. M. Penelope Hall (1953), *Social Services of Modern England*, 2nd Edn., Routledge & Kegan Paul, p. 303.
109. Kathleen M. Slack (1966), *Social Administration and the Citizen*, Michael Joseph, Ch. 4.

110. Mark Abrams, quoted by Slack in *ibid.*, J. Redlich and F. Hirst, *op. cit.*
111. Piet Thoenes (1966), *The Elite in the Welfare State* (ed.), J. Banks, Faber & Faber, p. 125.
112. T. Marshall (1972), "Value Problems of Welfare-Capitalism", *Journal of Social Policy*, Vol. I, p. 1, January, Marshall attributes the term 'Welfare Capitalism' to Crossman in R. H. Crossman (ed.) (1952), *New Fabian Essays*, Turnstile, pp. 6 & 25.
113. Claus Offe (1984), *Contradictions of the Welfare State*, Hutchinson & Co. Ltd., London, pp. 147-48.
114. See Titmuss Richard M. (1963), *Essays on 'The Welfare State'*, Allen & Unwin, London; Titmuss Richard M. (1968), *Commitment to Welfare State*, Allen & Unwin, London. Oyen, Else, Mishra, Ramesh (1981), *Society and Social Policy*, MacMillan, London.
115. Asa Briggs (2000), "The Welfare State in Historical Perspective" in Christopher Pierson and Francis G. Castles (ed.), *The Welfare State*, Polity Press, Cambridge, UK, p. 18.
116. Vernon Mund (1960), *Government and Business*, 3rd Edn., Harper & Bros. Publishers, New York, pp. 9-10.
117. Else Oyen (1986), "Identifying the Future of the Welfare State" in Else Oyen (ed.), *Comparing Welfare States and Their Futures*, Gower Publishing Company Ltd., England, p. 9.
118. *Ibid.*, p. 10.
119. Claus Offe (1984), *Contradictions of the Welfare State*, Hutchinson & Co. Ltd., London, p. 149.
120. *Ibid.*, pp. 154-57.
121. *Ibid.*, p. 157.
122. Else Oyen (1986), "Identifying the Future of the Welfare State" in Else Oyen (ed.), *Comparing Welfare States and Their Futures*, Gower Publishing Company Ltd., England, pp. 13-14.
123. 8 Coke Rep 107 (1610).
124. 5 U.S. (1 Cranch) 137 (1803).
125. Excepts from James Q. Wilson (1989), *Bureaucracy*, Basic Book Inc., Harper Collin Publishers; see Peter H. Schuck (1994), *Foundations of Administrative Law*, Oxford University Press, p. 32.
126. Excepts from Stephen Skowronek (1982), *Building a New American State: The Expansion of National Administrative Capacities 1877-1920*, Cambridge University Press; see Peter H. Schuck (1994), *Foundations of Administrative Law*, Oxford University Press, p. 32.
127. Excerpts from Robert Rabin (1986), *Federal Regulation in Historical Perspective*, Leland Stanford Junior University; see Peter H. Schuck (1994), *Foundations of Administrative Law*, Oxford University Press, p. 32.
128. *Privatization Lessons Learned by State and Local Governments*, GAO/GGD-97-48; US General Accounting Office, Washington, DC, 1997.
129. Pierre, Guislain (1992), *Divestiture of State Enterprise*, World Bank Technical Paper No. 186.
130. Osborne, David; Ted Gaebler (1992), *Reinventing Government: How the Entrepreneurial Spirit is Transforming the Public Sector;* Penguin Books, New York, p. 35.
131. See, Williamson, Oliver E. (1985), *The Economic Institutions of Capitalism*, The Free Press: New York; and Savas, E.S. (1977) *Alternatives for Delivery Public Services Toward Improved Performance*, Westview Press: Boulder.

3

REGULATIONS IN THE AGE OF LIBERALIZATION, PRIVATIZATION AND GLOBALIZATION
An Overview

3.1. Introduction

In European usage, the word 'regulation' is sometimes taken as a synonym for 'governance' in general.[1] In the traditional American usage regulation has a narrower usage, to mean a specific kind of policy-making designed to interfere with the way that markets would otherwise operate by making and enforcing standards or rules.[2] But regulation in both senses ultimately comes from government traditional role in providing a basis for trading, by setting standards and rules for the operation of markets. Regulation in the narrower sense can take many different detailed forms, in the way standards are set and compliance obtained. Although regulatory reform in 1980s went under the slogan of 'deregulation', regulation was massively extended in some areas, notably safety and pollution.[3] And even in areas of regulatory reform, what happened was not so much a complete withdrawal of government interest in areas such as telecommunications or aviation, but rather a change in the way the public authority was used to shape these markets. Many have pointed out that 're-regulation' would be a more accurate term.[4] It may, however, be mentioned that discussions on various regulatory authorities either in U.K. or in India mainly created under the impact of liberalization as a requirement of governmental reform process are only illustrative.

A powerful attack was launched on traditional regulation in the 1960s and 1970s from a numbers of quarters — liberal economics, consumerism, law and political science — culminating in a devastating critique of progressive-era regulation. Regulation was attacked in terms such as 'producer capture', weak enforcement by agencies, self-defeating bureaucratization and juridification, failure to balance costs of compliance against regulatory benefits, and often ineffective programme design. The conventional interpretation of deregulation as reflecting the ideological hegemony of 'small government' has to account for some notable counter trends. Regulation has intensified not fallen back in areas such as pollution, smoking, equal opportunities, finance, trade union etc. Similarly, privatization of public utilities such as telecommunication has led to a substantial extension of regulation and juridification as a substitute for government ownership.

With the move towards liberalization and privatization in most public utilities, the major policy focus is on the role of the old monopolies. In this process, the role of state owned enterprises is changing. Most have been commercialized, some are partly or fully privatized, and new entrants emerge, changing the face of competition. New regulatory institutions and traditional antitrust institutions aim to control monopoly power and facilitate entry as competition is emerging. In addition to this behavioural, often asymmetric regulation, that attempts to foster the emergence of a more competitive industry structure, governments are helping the emergence of competition also *via* structural policies. Examples are the restructuring of the industry prior to privatization and/ or the divesting of important facilities, so that they may be available to new entrants (Like the divestiture of telephone networks or related industries, for example from railroads, electricity and highway systems). But some countries have pursued structural policies that point in the opposite direction, for example concentrated the industry itself before liberalization and privatization and supported the incumbent in the restructuring process.

Privatization policies have continued to evolve since the 1980s. New regulatory agencies and legal framework to regulate the utilities have been put in place. A wide range of statutory powers, contracts, licences and conditions provide the main legal mechanisms which govern the relationship between regulator, the company and the consumers. Regulating the privatized utilities has proved to be a complex and detailed process. The result is a complex hotchpotch of legislation, regulation, rules, guidance, codes and licences, far removed from the consolidation and simplification that was hoped might result after privatization. In recent years there has been a shift in regulation with an emphasis in protecting the consumer and environmental concerns.

3.2. New Regulatory Regime in UK

The Conservative Government elected in May 1979 in many ways represented a fundamental break with the pattern of political and economic thought which had characterized other governments since the Second World War. The existence of an important nationalized sector of industry had been subject to broad support by previous governments of both parties. However, the rhetoric of the new Government was highly charged with the virtues of private enterprise and competition. As a result between 1984 and 1991, telecommunications, gas supply, water and sewerage and electricity generation, transmission, supply and distribution were privatized reversing decades of state ownership and appointing a dedicated industry regulator for each sector.

In U.K. the first stage of privatization began in the 1980s and 1990s with the adoption of a privatization strategy intended to remove Government from the business economics of the different industries. This period is concerned with the transfer of the nationalized companies into Company Act companies with as wide as possible shareholding. With privatization of the utilities in 1980s and 1990s a new regime was established which was similar in all utility services — telecommunications, gas, electricity and water. The regime was established by means of series of statutes: the Telecommunication Act, 1984; the Gas Act, 1986; the Water Act, 1989; the Water Industry Act, 1991; the Water Resources Act, 1991; the Competition and Service (Utilities) Act, 1992; the Environment Act, 1995; the Gas Act, 1995. The Public limited companies replaced the former corporations and shares were sold to private investors.

The enabling legislation had a number of features: the setting-up of individual regulators for the main utilities; the creation of licences and pricing arrangements; the development of a regulation strategy including the challenge of replacing the past ethos of "self-regulation" with greater competition; the liaison between individual regulators and the Monopolies and Mergers Commission (MMC), replaced by the Competition Commission under the Competition Act 1998, over competition policy; protection of the interests of consumers and the creation of rather weak but vocal consumer groups to represent consumers.

Traditionally, the UK did not have regulatory bodies for utility regulation. Different institutional designs were a ministry, a competition authority or a regulatory agency.[5] After assessing a variety of alternatives, the regulatory agency model was opted for, and a 'specialist look alike' to the Office of Fair Trading (OFT) was invented.[6] OFTEL was the first network and utility regulatory body in the UK. The regulatory agencies that emerged from the early legislation include the Office of Telecommunications (OFTEL), the Officer of Gas Supply (OFGAS), the Office of Electricity Regulation (OFFER), the Office of Water Services (OFWAT) and the Office of the Rail Regulator (ORR).[7]

The second stage to the regulation of the privatized utilities has come about more recently. In order to align United Kingdom Competition Policy more closely with the EU, the Competition Act, 1998, has replaced the MMC with the Competition Commission and relevant to coordinating the competition policy in the utility sector is the cross-utility panel. By the merger of OFGAS and OFFER into OFGEM under the Utilities Act, 2000, the regulators in the gas and electricity sectors have been replaced by one regulator for both the sectors. The Office of Communications Act, 2002, provides for the establishment of OFCOM replacing five regulators: Office of Telecommunications (OFTEL), the Independent Television Commission, the Broadcasting Standards Commission, the Radio Authority and Radio-Communications Agency.[8]

Unlike in the USA where regulatory commissions have been favoured, the UK set-up offices each headed by a single Director General (usually referred to as 'the regulator'). Although the regulatory offices are technically within government, the regulator is not civil servant and each has considerable discretionary powers — hence, the U.K. regulation is often called 'independent regulation'. However, the regulators do not have total independence. The regulators are appointed by and accountable for their actions to the Secretary of State (Minister) and through them ultimately to Parliament. The regulators are required to publish annual reports and accounts and are asked, on occasion, to justify their actions before Parliamentary Select Committees (notably, the Select Committee on Trade and Industry and the Select Committee on the Environment, Transport and Regions) and the Public Accounts Committee (which oversees public expenditure). Parliament does not, however, have any rights (in the absence of amending the law) to require changes in the decisions or regulatory practices, although it is to be expected that Parliamentary opinion will not be entirely ignored. The Secretaries of State do have power to direct the regulator on certain matters. These powers vary in detail from industry-to-industry, but to date there is no evidence that a minister has tried to compromise the regulator's 'independence' from detailed political control. In practice the U.K. regulators have achieved a high degree of independence from political interference which has been reinforced by the professionalism of the regulatory offices.

The main regulatory offices are the Office of Telecommunications (OFTEL) established in 1984, the Office of Gas Supply (OFGAS) established in 1986, and the Office of Electricity Regulation (OFFER) and the Office of Water Services (OFWAT) both established to 1989. There are also two regulatory offices for the newly privatized railways, the Office of the Rail Regulator and the Office of Passenger Rail Franchising. The U.K. airports are also subject to regulation by the Civil Aviation Authority. Each regulatory office is staffed by a mixture of generalists and experts (such as economists, accountants and engineers). In each sector consumer councils represent the consumer interest and report to the regulator, in general, the regulators are not intended to be representatives of specific interests. Rather, they are intended to be impartial or disinterested in arriving at decisions, subject to the objectives laid down in the legislation. The offices are financed by fees from the regulated companies which are paid into the Consolidated Fund. Most of the expenses of the offices are then met from public expenditure voted by Parliament.[9]

The powers of each of the regulatory offices are derived from the legislation which privatized the industry and established the regulation, subsequent legislative amendments and the Competition and Services (Utilities) Act, 1992. The latter placed certain obligations on companies with respect to standards of service and made provisions with respect to the powers of regulators over the companies' performance standards. The privatization legislation sets down 'primary' and 'secondary' objectives for the regulators. These objectives differ in detail from industry to industry, but the primary objectives include ensuring that all reasonable demands for the service are satisfied; and securing that the regulated companies are able to finance those services. Secondary, objectives vary reflecting the circumstances surrounding each industry, but include promoting efficiency and economy in service delivery. In practice all of the regulators have taken a keen interest in the prospects for competition.[10]

The privatization legislation does not attempt to prescribe the way in which regulators should attempt to fulfil their statutory duties. The duties are widely drawn leaving scope for regulatory discretion. The result has been some differences in approach across the regulatory offices and from the same office when the Director General (DG) has changed. In addition to the legislation, each regulated company in the U.K. has an operating licence granted by the Secretary of State or the regulator. The operating licence defines the service obligations of the company and lays down codes of practice, for example, on network — access charges and price control. However, the regulators have considerable discretionary powers while interpreting and changing the licence conditions.

In U.K. the legal recourse against a regulatory decision is limited to a 'judicial review'. The grounds of challenge include illegality, manifest error and irrationality in the decision-making process. Instead of recourse to the courts, in the U.K., regulatory reviews are undertaken by the Monopolies and Mergers Commission (MMC) and now by the Competition Commission, the U.K.'s main competition tribunal, after consultation with the government's competition office, the Office of Fair Trading. The Commission reviews decisions when a regulated company and its regulator cannot agree on an operation licence amendment, including a change in the pricing formula.

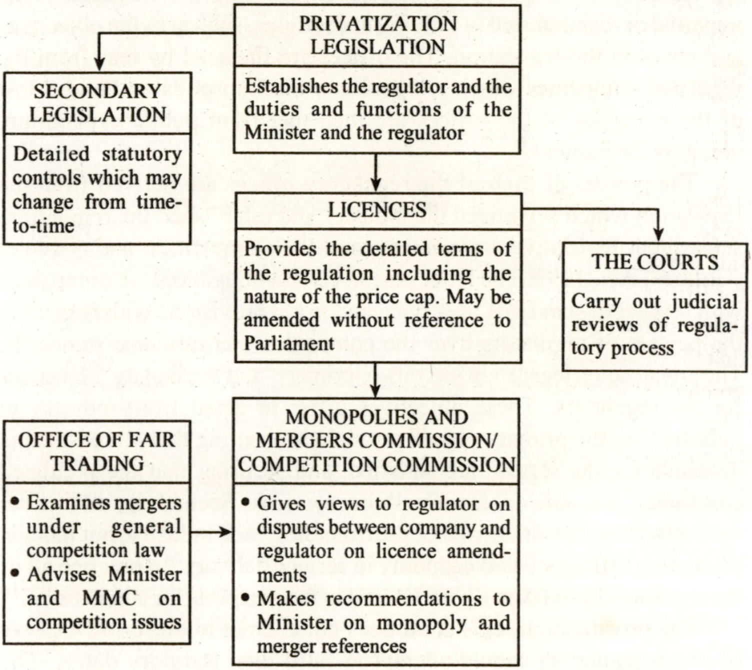

Figure 3.1: UK Regulation — The Legal Framework[11]

3.2.1. *Regulation of Telecommunication Sector*

The pre-liberalization telecommunication sector in the U.K. was dominated by the Post, Telegraph and Telecommunication utilities (PTT), in which, operative and regulative functions were linked together and were vertically integrated in the hands of a state monopoly from 1912 until 1981. The strong link between political, administrative and private actors entailed 'highly closed games' and strong state intervention.[12] The key regulatory reforms transformed the PTT into National Regulatory Agencies (NRAs) in 1984.

In 1981 the first stage, prior to privatization, took place when legislation, the British Telecommunication Act, 1981, separated telecommunications from postal services thereby establishing British Telecom as a public corporation. The separation prepared the ground for the second Telecommunications Act in 1984, which privatized BT and created an independent regulatory body, the Office of Telecommunications (OFTEL), as a non-Ministerial department within the ambit of the Department of Trade and Industry (DTI). As a uniquely British feature, a single Director General of Telecommunications (DGT) was appointed to head OFTEL. The privatization of British Telecom in 1984 and the Telecommunications Act, 1984, were the first major reforms of a public utility industry.

The 1984 Telecommunications Act created a Director-General of Telecommunications (DGT) with regulatory powers based on guidelines as to how the DGT is expected to perform his duties. The hallmark of this particular privatization was the need to find a suitable competitor for British Telecom. The characteristics of the 1984 Act are the use of an independent regulator (OFTEL) appointed by the Secretary of State, and that the operators of telecommunications systems must possess a licence granted by the Director-General of OFTEL and the Secretary of State. There is a power to refer matters to the Monopolies and Mergers Commission (MMC) (now Competition Commission) to decide if the matter referred is in the public interest. The Director-General of Fair Trading has powers to supervise and investigate any possible anti-competitive practices or abuses of market power.

Two institutions are involved with the competition authorities in the telecommunications regulatory regime: the Office of Fair Trading (OFT) and the Competition Commission (CC), [known as the Monopolies and Mergers Commission (MMC) until 2000]. Regarding the modification of licences, if OFTEL and the company involved do not reach an agreement, reference is made to the CC, which then investigates the licence conditions and takes a final decision.

The Telecommunications Act, 1984, is still in place. However, over the years OFTEL has changed its design. When OFTEL was set-up in 1984, Europe did not play a role in telecommunications. Since, the

1990s, especially since the liberalization of the whole European telecommunications market, OFTEL has had to take decisions in accordance with European legislation. Until the mid-1990s the focus of OFTEL was on infrastructure investment. With European legislation, the regulator was forced to increase competition. Additionally, policies changed when new DGTs came into office.[13]

Competition and Services (Utilities) Act, 1992

The telecommunications regulatory structure created in 1984 was weak. Additional powers have been introduced under the Competition and Services (Utilities) Act, 1992, intended to set a uniform standard of regulation for the utilities and in the case of telecommunications, gas and water, to generate greater competition. Thus, the 1992 Act introduced additional powers for the Director of Telecommunications to set standards for levels of performance, provide greater information to the Director on the working of the industry, to determine disputes between the customer and the industry, and to make provisions relating to consumer protection such as disconnection charges.

Office of Communications

The Office of Communications Act, 2002, passed on 19th March, 2002, established a body corporate to be known as the Office of Communications (OFCOM) to confer functions in relation to the regulation of communications. The various regulatory bodies covering telecommunications, television and radio were merged under the Office of Communication Act, 2002, into a single regulator OFCOM — an 'umbrella agency' combining the expertise of five previously independent institutions. The five bodies covered by OFCOM are the Office of Telecommunication (OFTEL); the Independent Television Commission; the Broadcasting Standards Commission; the Radio Authority and Radio-communications Agency. Thus, OFCOM is the regulator for the U.K. communications industries, with responsibilities across television, radio, telecommunications and wireless communications services. It also sets and enforces rules on fair competition between companies in these industries. The Office of Telecommunications Act, 2002, contains seven sections and establishes OFCOM and provides general duties set out in detail in the Communications Act, 2003. The Act also provides for the management of OFCOM and its organization and finance.

Under the Communications Act, 2003,[14] the principal duty of OFCOM, in carrying out the functions is to further the interests of citizens in relation to communications matters; and to further the interests of consumers in relevant markets, where appropriate by promoting competition. Main legal duties of OFCOM, set out in the UK Communications Act, 2003, are to ensure that:

- the UK has a wide range of electronic communications services, including high-speed information services (for example, broadband);
- a wide range of high-quality television and radio programmes are provided, appealing to a range of tastes and interests;
- television and radio services are provided by a range of different organizations;
- people who watch television and listen to the radio are protected from harmful or offensive material;
- people are protected from being treated unfairly in television and radio programmes, and from having their privacy invaded; and
- the radio spectrum (the airwaves used by everyone from taxi firms and boat owners, to mobile-phone companies and broadcasters) is used in the most effective way.

3.2.2. *Regulation of Energy Sector*

The UK was the first European country to shift its focus from "energy planning to the realm of competition administration".[15] Before liberalization, the gas and electricity sectors were primarily nationalized industries in public ownership. In the 1990s as a result of the government's decision to reduce the number of nationalized industries, first, the British Gas Corporation was sold; later companies from the electricity sector were sold to the public. To ensure the influence of the state, regulatory agencies for gas and electricity were established: OFGAS (Office for Gas Regulation) and OFFER (Office for Electricity Regulation). In 2000, the two regulators were merged in the Office for Gas and Electricity Markets (OFGEM).

(a) *Gas Sector — OFGAS*

The nationalization of the British gas industry in 1948 and its centralization in 1962 had created a single industry centralized under British Gas, a public corporation. In 1985 the Government decided to privatize British Gas giving serious consideration to the question of how competition and efficiency might be achieved. Privatization was undertaken by the Gas Act, 1986, which followed the model set by telecommunications in 1984. A regulatory structure was set-up under a Director-General of Supply (OFGAS) and an OFGAS office. No attempt was made to restructure the industry in the 1986 Act. The Gas Act, 1986, in practical effect insulated British Gas from competition. As no new competitor was created it was difficult not to see the monopoly of British Gas as virtually impregnable by any new entrant to the market. The main function of the regulator was to monitor British Gas by price cap. British Gas, as a carrier as well as provider of gas, was "a monopoly carrier and a near monopoly supplier".[16] The 1986 Act provided a complex formula for pricing supervised by the Director-General of Gas Supply (DGGS) and OFGAS.

Legal powers similar to OFTEL were provided to OFGAS to promote efficiency to gas suppliers and users. The DGGS might impose conditions upon the grant of authorization to a public gas supplier and there is a possibility of a referral to the Monopolies and Mergers Commission to specify any modification to the authorization. Compliance powers granted to the DGGS and investigative powers over conditions granted in the authorization were all part of the regulatory framework. The powers of the regulator were considerably less than the powers possessed by British Gas. For example under the 1986 Act it was impossible for the DGGS to alter the legal structure of the gas industry. British Gas was in a strong market position post-privatization with the resultant effect that the regulator (OFGAS) became a surrogate competitor in its attempts to regulate the gas industry effectively.

In the early stages of the newly privatized life of British Gas, it was apparent that a number of grounds for dissatisfaction existed. The complaints were reviewed by the MMC after OFGAS made a reference on the basis of there being a monopoly enjoyed by British Gas. The MMC upheld this view of a monopoly and concluded that greater competition was required. An additional finding was that the only effective means of remedying adverse consequences flowing from the monopoly status of British Gas was direct gas to gas competition. Inevitably the MMC findings in 1988 required a reorganization of the gas market and provided the regulator with increased powers in terms of enhancing his status and in securing compliance with his objectives. As a result in February 1990 the British Gas entered into a number of undertakings. In July 1991 the effectiveness of the remedies applied by

British Gas after the MMC Report (1985) was referred to the Office of Fair Trading (OFT) for consideration which concluded that although British Gas had complied with its undertakings, nevertheless the dominance of British Gas in the market had remained and there is need for fundamental reconsideration of the market position of British Gas.

A new Gas Act was passed which came into force on March 1, 1995. This Act gave additional powers to the regulator to allow for a more radical re-structuring of British Gas; to provide additional competition for suppliers to domestic customers and for access to the gas pipeline. This aimed to fully open the gas market to competition. Under the new structure British Gas was forced to separate into two companies. From March 1995, there was separation of Transco International from British Gas, now responsible for the production and transport of gas. While British Gas Energy has taken over the responsibility for supply, retail and service. The Act sets-up a new structure for the licensing of gas supply. Additional powers have been granted to the Director of Gas Supply under the Competition and Service (Utilities) Act, 1992. These include the powers to set standards, improve the procedures for complaints by customers and set regulations to determine disputes over the accuracy of bills.

(b) *Electricity Sector — OFFER*

Electricity privatization posed some of the most complex legal problems and the experience gained from gas and telecommunication privatizations proved to be insufficient to meet the challenge posed by electricity privatization. This was because the electricity industry was the largest of the United Kingdom's nationalized industries in terms of turnover and capital employed. The pre-liberalization electricity sector had a market structure with a network of actors involved. Under nationalization the generation, supply and transmission of electricity were integrated by the Electricity Act, 1957. The Central Electricity Generating Board (CEGB) coordinated both generation and transmission. A national grid was created with 12 Area Boards, as regional monopolies, for distribution purposes. These purposes were left to the autonomy of the boards particularly in respect of financial matters. Consumers' interests in England and Wales were represented by 13 district organizations. There were 12 Area Electricity Consultative Councils, one for each Area Board and an Electricity Consumers' Council.

The privatization strategy adopted by the Government set out six objectives to be followed, namely: the needs of customers should be considered an important part of the industry; competition is an essential guarantee of customers' interests; regulation was required to promote competition, oversee price and protect customers' interest; security and safety should be maintained; customers should be given new rights and share ownership should include those who work for the company.

The privatization of the industry was brought by the Electricity Act, 1989. The CEGB was split into three power-generating companies; for transmission a National Grid Company (NGC) was created, jointly owned by 12 Regional Electricity Companies (RECs) and replacing the area boards. The RECs were privatized, and the regional monopolies were abolished to promote competition. In 1995 the NGC, too, was privatized. The government's core goal for the Electricity Act, 1989, was to promote competition in power generation and supply and "to regulate the behaviour of the monopoly companies in the market".[17] Therefore, a Director General for Electricity Supply (DGES) and a new Office for Electricity Regulation (OFFER) were established. Because electricity supply and distribution were already separated, the regulator was, mainly concerned about ensuring open access to the grid and regulating prices.

The Electricity Act, 1989, adopted a combination of licensing, contractual and statutory powers to regulate and operate the newly created structure under the post-privatization arrangements. Wider reserve powers are given to the Secretary of State (Section 96) for preserving the security of electricity supply, the maintenance and the security of buildings or installations used for the purposes connected with the generation, transmission or supply of electricity. The Secretary of State may set the percentage of electricity required from non-fossil fuel after consultation with the Director-General of Electricity and Suppliers; such order is subject only to negative resolution in the procedure of laying the order before Parliament. The Director-General of Electricity with the consent of the Secretary of State and after consulting public electricity suppliers and affected individuals may set individual and overall standards of performance. The Director-General of Electricity is required to publish information which is expedient to provide information for customers of public electricity supplies. The wide range of statutory powers is also reinforced by licensing conditions such as the avoidance of cross-subsidization and the separation of accounts between different businesses. The 1989 Act, allows the DGES discretion to make a reference to the Monopolies and Mergers Commission (MMC) (now Competition Commission). But the Secretary of State for Energy can direct the MMC not to proceed with the reference. Once a report is prepared the Secretary of State may prohibit publication of "any matter" if it appears to him that it would be against the public or commercial interest of "any person".

The Secretary of State possesses wide powers to keep a register of information on licences, modifications and the like. By placing the Secretary of State as the electricity supply industry's licensing authority, the 1989 Act allows intervention in the work of the DGES as a regulator that challenges any sense of independence or freedom from political influence which the DGES may want to develop. While the DGES has a duty to review the "carrying on" of electricity generation, transmission and supply, the Secretary of State may give the DGES directions as to the priorities or matters which form the DGES's remit.

The Secretary of State's powers extend to the day-to-day operations of the electricity supply industry. The constitution of generating stations and the consents required may be supervised by the Secretary of State, under section 36 of the Act. The use of fuel stocks and the requirement that electricity is available from non-fossil fuel sources are all part of the wide powers possessed by the Secretary of State.

The management functions of the person operating the generating station could be directed by the Secretary of State as well as the "specified objectives" which may be given to the National Grid Company to operate the transmission system. It is clear that the legal powers contained in the 1989 Act provide the Secretary of State with the means to take over the operational management of the industry. Finally, wide emergency powers are included in Part III of the 1989 Act which provides the Secretary of State with extensive powers to give directions to the industry. The term "civil emergency" is widely defined in subjective terms in Section 96 of the 1989 Act. It includes any national disaster or other emergency which in the opinion of the Secretary of State is against the interest of national security or commercial interests. The power to give directions does not contain any requirement of laying the direction before Parliament. The 1989 Act provides the Secretary of State unparalleled powers in the history of the electricity supply industry to intervene in the day-to-day running of the industry. Electricity privatization provided more extensive regulatory powers than pervious privatizations. The few changes introduced by the Competition and Service (Utilities) Act, 1992, include standards of performance, complaints and disputes, the level of achievement of each public electricity supplier, and the power for the Director to make determinations regulating the accuracy of bills.

The Utilities Act, 2000

The Act has achieved four objectives which are as follows:

- The merger of OFGAS and OFFER into a single regulatory body OFGEM;
- To provide for a fair deal and greater consumer protection than in the past;
- To meet more widely defined social and environmental objectives; and
- To provide and implement more transparent trading arrangements.

In order to meet these new objectives, a number of changes have been introduced to the licensing regime for electricity. The Utilities Act, 2000, has also brought additional regulatory controls over electricity companies in the following areas: the powers to introduce efficiency standards of performance on both suppliers and distributors; a requirement to meet greater transparency through the disclosure of Directors' pay and remuneration in terms of meeting performance standards; a requirement on suppliers to have a certain percentage of electricity to come from renewable supply and a power to raise a cross-subsidy to meet the needs of various identifiable groups.

The Utilities Act, 2000, has also introduced a revision of the Gas Act, 1986, in favour of consumers. A specific requirement is to ensure that the disabled, or the chronically sick and those who are pensioners or live on low incomes in rural areas are given protection. The consumers' interest are to be somehow reconciled with different categories of consumers and at the same time fit within the general duties of the Regulator and the Secretary of State to promote efficiency and economy in the use of gas. The licensing schemes under the Gas Act, 1995, and the Electricity Act, 1989, are brought into alignment by the Utilities Act, 2000. The Competition Commission appears to have the final say on whether to modify licence conditions, replacing the previously held OFGAS power of referral.

3.2.3. *Regulation of Water Sector*

The privatization of water proved to be a greater problem than that of gas or telecommunications. Water privatization had to address one of the most complex legal arrangements for water services. In the case of water, 10 public water authorities and 29 private water companies comprised the water industry before privatization. The Water Act, 1989, had to address the problem of not only the new structure under privatization, but the question of merger and investment in the water industry, which also included major health and environmental issues. Privatization was carried out under the Water Act, 1989, which created a new public body, the National Rivers Authority (NRA) now subsumed under the Environment Agency under the Environment Act, 1995, with the rights and liabilities of the existing water authorities divided between NRA and the successor companies.

The Water Services Regulation Authority (OFWAT) is the economic regulator of the water and sewerage industry in England and Wales. Before 1 April, 2006 the regulatory functions rested with the Director General of Water Services. The framework for the changeover is outlined in the Water Act, 2003. It provides a similar structure to other economic regulators. Section 34 of the Act established a new corporate body to be known as the Water Services Regulation Authority and the Office of the Director General of Water Services (OFWAT) was abolished. However, the new Authority is still publicly known as OFWAT.

3.2.4. *Regulation of Rail Sector*

The rail sector was the last utility sector to be liberalized by the Conservative Government in U.K. Before the rail reform, the sector was publicly owned, with British Rail (BR) with heavy involvement of the State. British Rail was financed by the State and supervised by the Department of Transport (DoT). Following privatization, British Rail was divided into two main elements. In outline, the first element consisted of the national rail network (track, signalling, bridges, tunnels, stations and depots) and the second being the operating companies whose trains run on that network. In regulatory terms, ORR is responsible for regulating the national rail network operator (Network Rail), while the DoT looks after passenger and train related matters. The Railways Act, 1993, provided for the privatization of the rail industry in Great Britain and established what remains the core of the system of economic regulation of the industry. It has been amended by the Transport Act, 2000, the Railways and Transport Safety Act, 2003, the Railways Act, 2005, the Railways Infrastructure (Access and Management) Regulations, 2005, and the Railways (Licensing of Railway Undertakings) Regulations, 2005.

The Railways Act, 1993, initiated a rail reform with the core goal of splitting up British Rail. The separation of rail track and services led to vertical and horizontal fragmentations. The following private bodies were created:

- Railtrack (RT), constituted as a separate track authority in 1994 and privatized in 1996, is responsible for managing the infrastructure (network and stations), i.e. for train planning, signaling and supplying access to tracks and stations.
- The Rolling Stock Companies (ROSCOs) own the trains and lease them to private businesses.
- For passenger transport, 25 private train-operating companies (TOCs) were set-up.
- The TOCs are franchises, where private sector companies compete to buy the rights of operation.
- For freight and parcel business, freight — operating companies (FOCs) with specific tasks — such as regional distribution or transportation from harbours or airports were established and sold to the private sector.

To regulate this complex and fragmented system of privatized bodies, interlinked by contractual relationships, not just one regulator, like in case of other utility sectors, but two regulatory bodies were created. They have to regulate the private market, but as a second sector-specific function they also have to subsidize unprofitable passenger services. Especially, because of this second regulatory function, the regime is described as "radically different from . . . other utility regulators". This reflects the "considerable regulatory complexity" of the rail sector.[18]

The Act provided for the appointment and functions of two regulatory bodies known as a Rail Regulator and a Director of Passenger Rail Franchising. The Secretary of State shall appoint an officer to be known as "the Rail Regulator"(referred to as "the Regulator"), and an officer to be known as "the Director of Passenger Rail Franchising" (referred to as "the Franchising Director"), for the purpose of carrying out the functions assigned or transferred to the Regulator, or (as the case may be) the Franchising Director, by or under this Act. An appointment of a person to hold office as the Regulator or the Franchising Director shall be for a term not exceeding five years; but previous appointment to either of those offices shall not affect eligibility for re-appointment (or for appointment to the other of them). The Secretary of State may remove any person from office as the Regulator or the Franchising Director on the ground of incapacity or misbehaviour.[19]

The Secretary of State and the Regulator shall each have a duty to exercise the functions assigned or transferred to him in the manner which he considers best calculated —

(a) to protect the interests of users of railway services;
(b) to promote the use of the railway network in Great Britain for the carriage of passengers and goods, and the development of that railway network, to the greatest extent that he considers economically practicable;
(c) to promote efficiency and economy on the part of persons providing railway services;
(d) to promote competition in the provision of railway services;
(e) to promote measures designed to facilitate the making by passengers of journeys which involve use of the services of more than one passenger service operator;
(f) to impose on the operators of railway services the minimum restrictions which are consistent with the performance of his functions under this Part; and
(g) to enable persons providing railway services to plan the future of their businesses with a reasonable degree of assurance.[20]

The Rail Regulator was set-up as a primary regulatory body, functioning similarly to regulators such as OFTEL or OFGEM.[21] The overall task of the agency was to regulate the newly created market in the rail sector, including promoting competition and preventing the abuse of dominant position. To do so, first, the regulator grants and enforces licences to operate trains. Second, the regulator defines and monitors the access to and charges for the network. Third, the regulator supervises the contracts negotiated between TOCs and Railtrack, and monitors the performance of Railtrack.[22] The second regulator the Office of Rail Passenger Franchising (OPRAF), established as a franchise authority to negotiate and monitor the franchise contracts with the TOCs. The central characteristic of the rail sector is that it is mostly a non-profitable entity, with TOCs dependent on state subsidies. The central goal of OPRAF was to distribute public funding as subsidies and to ensure the quality of the rail service at the lowest possible cost.[23]

The Railways Act, 1993, thus took a radical stance, initiating changes that went beyond regulatory reforms in other utility sectors in the U.K. With ORR and OPRAF the reform established a unique dual regulatory regime that went "against the grain" of the general trends in other utility sectors. However, this regime had problems in successfully regulating the sector. A central concern was the imbalance between Railtrack and the TOCs. Contracts were not negotiated carefully enough. The confusion between ORR and OPRAF within the system of 'dual regulation' presented another challenge. For example, both institutions had overlapping competencies in consumer protection. There were still unsatisfactory outcomes, e.g. with train delays, underinvestment in the net and a high rate of accidents. The performance of the whole liberalized rail system was described as 'rather poor'.[24]

The Labour Government, which came to power in 1997, started an investigation of the sector and developed the regulatory regime further. First plans to renationalize the sector were stopped. Instead, with a reform of the rail law, the fundamental weaknesses of the sector were to be overcome. The most prominent proposal was to reform the regulatory regime by setting-up the Strategic Rail Authority (SRA), an institution described as a "vehicle for long-term commitment by Government to the railways".[25] The Transport Act, 2000, established the SRA as a "multi-party merger", taking over other institutions from authorities still in operation as well as individual competencies.[26] OPRAF was abolished, and the SRA took over its competencies. In contrast to the short-term oriented regulatory style of OPRAF, the SRA decided with reference to long-term perspectives. The SRA became a strategic investor, with competencies to negotiate passenger rail franchises and to enforce consumer protection. The aims of the SRA have been to secure development of the rail network and contribute to an integrated transport system. The objectives of SRA were:

- to protect the interests of consumers;
- to contribute to sustainable development;
- to promote efficiency and economy in the rail network;
- to provide the minimum necessary restrictions on rail operators;
- to enable providers of rail services to make future plans and business decisions with some degree of certainty; and
- to promote the use of the railway through ticketing.

The Transport Act, 2000, reflects a bargain between business use for profit and public service use for customers.

The Railways Act, 2005

The Railways Act, 2005, implements the changes to the governance of the rail industry in Great Britain proposed by the 2004 White Paper

"The Future of Rail" published on 15th July, 2004. Part 1 of the Act provided for the winding up of the Strategic Rail Authority (SRA) established by the Transport Act, 2000. The SRA's strategic and financial functions have been passed to the Department for Transport and in some cases, to the devolved administrations. The consumer protection powers transferred from the Rail Regulator by the Transport Act, 2000 are transferred back to the Office of Rail Regulation (which replaced the Rail Regulator under the Railways and Transport Safety Act, 2003). The Act also enables the SRA's assets, rights and liabilities to be transferred to third parties. It establishes the Office of Rail Regulation (ORR) as a combined safety and economic regulator. It provides for the transfer of health and safety regulation powers and functions under the Health and Safety at Work etc. Act, 1974, (HM Railways Inspectorate) from the Health and Safety Executive to the Office of Rail Regulation.

The Act allows the Government to take charge of setting the strategy for the railway, and to streamline the structure of the rail industry at the national level. It provides for greater local and devolved decision-making. The Rail Passengers Council (RPC) has been established as a single national body reporting to the Secretary of State and the formal federal structure of the regional committees has been dissolved. As a consequence of the other structural and organizational changes in the Act, it sets out revised procedures for operators and public sector funders to follow when they wish to discontinue all passenger services on a line or from a station or close all or part of a network or station.

The Office of Rail Regulation

The Office of Rail Regulation (ORR) was established on 5 July, 2004 under the Railways and Transport Safety Act, 2003, as a body corporate, taking over the function of the Rail Regulator which had been created by the Railways Act, 1993. ORR is an independent statutory body led by a Board. The Secretary of State for Transport makes appointments to the Board for a fixed term of up to five years and may dismiss a member on the grounds set out in paragraph 2 of Schedule 1 to the Railways and Transport Safety Act, 2003. The Board is led by a balance of non-executive and executive members, and is funded by a safety levy and licence fees from the industry. The Railways and Transport Safety Act, 2003, also introduced a railway safety levy (then payable to the Health and Safety Executive, but to be transferred to the Office of Rail Regulation under the Railways Act, 2005), created the Rail Accident Investigation Branch within the Department for Transport, reformed the British

Transport Police and amended laws relating to alcohol and drug use by shipping and aviation staff.

The Office of Rail Regulation (ORR) is the combined safety and economic regulator for the UK's rail industry. It is independent from Government and has its functions and duties set out in statute (the Railways Act, 1993, as amended, by the Railways Act, 2005). It is also the rail sector competition authority with powers concurrent with the UK's consumer and competition authority (Office of Fair Trading) and acts as an appeal body.

As the economic regulator of the railway industry, ORR's principal function is to regulate Network Rail's stewardship of the national rail network. It also licenses the operators of railway assets, approves agreements for access by operators to track, stations, and light maintenance depots, and enforces domestic competition law. As the health and safety regulator, ORR's principal function is to secure the safe operation of the railway system, and to protect both those working on the system, and members of the public, from health and safety risks arising from the railways.

The ORR's economic regulation functions (or powers) are defined and limited by statute, which also sets its objectives and duties. There is no statutory hierarchy for these and ORR's Board has the freedom to balance them in the way that they think is best calculated to promote the public interest. These economic duties do not apply to ORR's safety functions but do include, amongst others, duties to:

- promote improvements in railway safety performance;
- promote the use of the railway network in Great Britain for the carriage of passengers and goods, and the development of that railway network, to the greatest extent which it considers economically practicable;
- promote competition in the provision of railway services for the benefit of users of railway services;
- act in a manner which it considers will not render it unduly difficult for persons who are holders of network licences to finance any activities or proposed activities of theirs in relation to which ORR has functions; and
- enable persons providing railway services to plan the future of their businesses with a reasonable degree of assurance.

It is this latter duty along with the Investment Framework published by ORR that should enable private investors to have confidence that they will be able to enjoy the benefits of their investment in a fair and equitable manner. Only with this confidence, which clearly takes time to build-up, will private investment be forthcoming.

The independent ORR is also responsible for the publication of many key rail industry statistics. Such independence is essential to have credibility of the information. Since, if they are produced by one train operator, there will always be the suspicion that they may be 'adjusted' to make them look more favourable. The rail industry generally trusts ORR as a fully independent appeal body with large *ex-ante* competencies designed to solve disputes or market failures quickly.

3.2.5. *Regulation of Commerce*

The bulk of the law relating to the regulation of commerce[27] is now found in the Competition Act, 1998, which is designed to ensure that UK competition law is consistent and in line with the European Community law.[28] The Competition Commission under the Competition Act, 1998, replaced the Monopolies and Mergers Commission in 1999. The Enterprise Act, 2002, introduced a new regime for the assessment of mergers and markets in the UK. The CC's legal role is now clearly focused on competition issues, replacing a wider public interest test in the previous regime. The Enterprise Act also gives the CC remedial powers to direct companies to take certain actions to improve competition; in the previous regime its role was simply to make recommendations to Government. The Enterprise Act, 2002,[29] establishes the current control regime for mergers and inquiries into monopolies (the latter now called "market investigations").

Subject to widespread exemptions, both particular and general, agreements between undertakings (i.e. companies, partnerships, or individuals), decisions by associations of undertakings and concerted practices which affect trade within the UK and have as their object or effect the prevention, restriction or distortion of competition within the UK are prohibited (Chapter One prohibitions)[30] and void.[31] The fixing of prices, the limitation of supply, the sharing of markets (or sources of supply), discrimination against trading parties and making contracts conditional upon conditions unconnected to the subject of the contract are all prohibited.[32] These prohibitions are intended to mirror Article 81 of the Treaty of Rome.

In a similar way, the abuse of a dominant position in a market which may affect trade in the UK is also prohibited (Chapter Two prohibition).[33]

Such abuse includes, but is not limited to, the imposition of unfair prices or other trading conditions, the limitation of production, or markets, or technical developments to the detriment of the consumer as well as discrimination against trading parties and making contracts conditional upon conditions unconnected to the subject to the contract.[34] These prohibitions are intended to mirror Article 86 (now 82) of the Treaty of Rome.

The Director General of Fair Trading has power to investigate if there are reasonable grounds for suspicion that there has been an infringement of either Chapter One or Chapter Two.[35] If he concludes that there has been an infringement he may issue directions to bring the infringement to an end,[36] and he may impose penalties.[37] If a person fails without reasonable excuse to comply, the Director may apply to the court for an order requiring the default to be made good.[38] The Director may also give guidance whether particular agreements or conduct are infringements,[39] and he may take interim measures before he has completed an investigation where there would otherwise be irreparable damage to a particular person or groups.[40]

Any decision of the Director in respect of an agreement, or in respect of some person's conduct, may be appealed to the Competition Tribunal.[41] Moreover, third parties with sufficient interest may apply in writing to the Director asking that a particular decision be withdrawn or varied. If the Director rejects such an application, the applicant may appeal to the Competition Tribunal.[42] There is a further right of appeal, with leave, to the Court of Appeal on a point of law or on any penalty.[43]

The Enterprise Act, 2002, establishes a new control regime governing the approval of mergers and market investigations (previously monopoly inquiries). The broad test of 'public interest' used in the past has been replaced by much narrower test. The Office of Fair Trading may make a reference to the Competition Commission when it concludes, following a market investigation, that there are "reasonable grounds" for suspecting that a feature of a market "restricts of distorts competition".[44] And proposed mergers are assessed by a text of whether they may expect to result in "substantial lessening of competition".[45]

The Competition Commission itself decides on the appropriate action and has powers to that end.[46] Its decision, however, as well as the original decision to make a reference is subject to appeal to the Competition Appeal Tribunal[47] which, however, applies judicial review principles.[48] There is a further appeal on a point of law to the Court of Appeal.[49]

3.2.6. *Regulation of Financial Services*

The Financial Services and Markets Act, 2000, brings together the many bodies[50] that previously regulated various forms of financial services;[51] its remit extends beyond simple consumer protection. It established a Financial Services Authority[52] which has power to regulate books, building societies, insurance companies, friendly societies, Lloyd's investment and pension advisers, stockbrokers, fund managers and derivative traders. The Act specifies the FSA's regulatory objectives and the authority must "so far as reasonable possible" discharge its functions in a way that is compatible with these objectives.[53] These objectives are market confidence, public awareness, protection of consumers and reduction of financial crime.[54] The Authority is placed under a general duty to consult both practitioners in the market and consumers.[55] The Treasury has power to appoint an independent person to carry out a review of the economy efficiency and effectiveness with which the Authority uses its resources; and to appoint such a person to carry out an inquiry where events have occurred which pose or could have posed "a grave risk" to the financial system or the interests of consumers;[56] or where through the failure of the regulatory system "significant damage" has been or could have been caused to the holders of listed securities.[57]

The basic mechanism for regulation is that, subject to exemptions,[58] the permission of the Authority is required[59] before any person can undertake regulated activities[60] as an "authorized person".[61] In addition employees and office-holders of authorized persons must be approved by the Authority and comply with its requirements.[62] The Authority may impose financial penalties (without limit of amount) on authorized person who contravene any requirement imposed by or under the Act.[63] It may also withdraw permissions granted.[64] A Financial Services and Markets Tribunal is established[65] to which adverse decisions of the Authority may be referred by the party affected. The Act provides no procedural safeguards before adverse decisions other than "warning notices" which must give reasons and against which representations may be made. But the Authority must determine and publish its own procedural rules,[66] which must provide that the decision is taken by a person not directly involved in establishing the evidence, and which will doubtless be subject to judicial review. Where the Authority determines that an individual is not a fit and proper person to perform a particular function it may make a "prohibition order",[67] and such orders may be referred to the tribunal.[68] There is an appeal from the decisions of the tribunal to the Court of Appeal on a point of law.[69]

The Authority also has power to make general rules applying to the carrying on of regulated activities as appear to it to be "necessary or expedient".[70] And it may make "endorsing rules" approving the City Code on Takeovers and Mergers (issued by the Takeover Panel).[71] Rules may also be made governing price stabilization, financial promotion and money laundering.[72] Contravention of a rule does not render a transaction void[73] and does not necessarily entail disciplinary action.[74] But, unless the rules provide otherwise,[75] a private person who has suffered loss as a result of a contravention has an action for damages "subject to the defences and other incidents applying to actions for breach of statutory duty".[76] Proposed rules must be published in draft and the Authority must consider representations made to it about the draft rules.[77] The Authority may also give guidance on the operation of the Act and of the rules made under it.[78]

The Authority must establish a compensation scheme for the benefit of investors and others where authorized persons are unable to satisfy the claims against them, and there is power to impose a levy on authorized persons for the funding of the scheme.[79]

3.2.7. *Regulation of Postal Services*

Privatization policy has not always been successfully implemented by the Government even when it is desired. Since 1992, there have been plans to privatize the Post Office. The proposed sale of Parcel Force, a major part of the mail service, and the Royal Mail has been considered, proposed and rejected. Post Office Counters Ltd., a type of public-private-partnership, was created covering an agency function for many Government departments such as Transport, Social Security and the Passport Agency; it was intended to be sold but this proved impossible. Privatization has been put on hold as public opinion and support is doubtful.

The Postal Service Act, 2000, is an attempt to modernize the Post Office. It falls short of privatization but it permits market competition and unlike previous proposals maintains the Post Office as a single entity. The Post Office is formed into a limited liability company under Crown ownership. The Post Office thus now operates as an ordinary commercial company under the control of its Board of Directors. There is to be a new regulator, the Postal Service Commission, and a five-year strategic business plan. The Commission whose members are appointed by the Secretary of State has, in addition to its licensing functions, statutory duties such as to "exercise its functions in the manner which it considers is best calculated to ensure the provision of a universal postal service". The new regulator is expected to encourage competition and regulate the market in postal services. The Post Office no longer enjoys a formal statutory monopoly on the carriage of letters but subject to a range of exemptions provided under section 7 of the Act, the letters may only be carried under licence issued by the Postal Commission. The Commission has not yet licensed other operators to compete generally with the Post Office. The Secretary of State retains the power to give directions to the Commission in the interest of national security or in the interests of encouraging or maintaining the UK's interests with other countries.

The Act also takes account of the EU Directive on Common Rules for the Development of the Internal Market of Community Postal Services and the Improvement of Quality of Service. Consumers are provided with a statutory framework for the Consumer Council for Postal Services replacing the old Post Office Users' Councils. Though the Post Office is unlikely to face full-scale privatization, but through a number of economic devices it is expected to become more competitive.

3.2.8. *The Broader Regulatory Framework*

In addition to the regulatory agencies put in place post-privatization, mention should also be made of the various "quasi-governmental agencies" or non-departmental public bodies. There is a wide range and a large number of such bodies ranging from the Gaming Board, the Advisory Conciliation and Arbitration Service, Health and Safety at Work, Civil Aviation Authority, the Office of Fair Trading, the Competition Commission, to the Environment Agency. Their diversity and size is reflected in their *ad hoc* development.

Innovatory procedures and specialization gives rise to new agencies such as the Human Fertilization and Embryology Authority under the Human Fertilization and Embryology Act, 1990. Regulating professional standards of various occupations may require statutory interventions. The Osteopaths Act, 1993, establishes a new body known as the General Osteopathic Council. This Council will regulate the professional education and conduct of around 2000 persons in the U.K. in the delivery of osteopathic treatment.

3.2.9. *Legislative and Regulatory Reform Act, 2006*

U.K. Legislative and Regulatory Reform Bill which received the Royal Assent on 8 November, 2006, replacing the Regulatory Reform Act, 2001, purports to cut "red tape" by purporting to give Government Ministers new powers to "strip away" statutory regulation. Part 1 of the Act headed "Power to reform legislation", enables a Minister to make secondary legislation in the form of statutory instrument to reform legislation that is perceived to be "outdated, unnecessary or over-complicated". A similar procedure under the Regulatory Reform Act enabled a Minister to make Regulatory Reform Orders (RROs). The new Act was enacted as the earlier Regulatory Reform Act "presented a number of hurdles which inhibited the production of RROs". Furthermore, its powers were "too technical and limited" and it was considered that the procedure should be "extended to deliver non-controversial proposals for simplification".[80]

Under section 1 of the Legislative and Regulatory Reform Act, 2006, a Minister can only make an order for one of the two purposes: reforming legislation or implementing, with or without changes, recommendations made by the Law Commission, the Scottish Law Commission or the Northern Ireland Law Commission. Under section 2, an order may amend, repeal or replace any Act or secondary legislation. Section 3 provides that, before such an order can be made, the relevant Minister has to be satisfied that a legislative change is required to secure the policy objective, and that the proposed order —

- is "proportionate";
- "strikes a fair balance" between the public interest and the interest of any persons adversely affected;
- does not remove any "necessary protection"; and
- does not prevent anyone from exercising rights or freedoms that they "might reasonably expect to continue to exercise".

The Act contains express limitations on the exercise of power by the Minister under Sections 5-11. A Minister is required to consult widely before making an order under the Act and must lay a draft of a proposed order before Parliament together with a comprehensive explanatory document. The draft order may become a statutory instrument by being approved by the Parliament.

Part 2 of the Act, which is headed "Regulators", implements recommendations of a review conducted by Philip Hampton (the

Hampton Report[81]). Under section 21 of the Act, regulators must have regard to two principles while exercising particular regulatory functions. These are that regulatory activities must be carried out in a way that is "transparent, accountable, proportionate and consistent", and should be targeted only at cases in which action is needed. Section 22, enables a Minister to introduce a mandatory Code of Practice with which a regulatory agency must comply.

Part 3 of the Act which is headed "Legislation Relating to the European Communities etc.", makes provision about the legislation relating to the European Union, with a view to reducing the number of U.K. Statutory Instruments required to transpose European Union legislation into domestic U.K. Law.

Earlier there was the Deregulation and Contracting Out Act, 1994, and then Regulatory Reform Act, 2001, providing for procedures to simplify existing regulations and unnecessary rules. The Deregulation and Contracting Out Act, 1994, provides that amending orders, called deregulation orders, may be introduced to amend delegated legislation or where necessary primary legislation. This procedure is a novel way to lift the burden of unnecessary regulation from industry. Under the Deregulation and Contracting Out Act, 1994, [Section 3(3)] and the Regulatory Reform Act, 2001, [Section 6(1)] the Government is able to make Orders to amend or repeal provisions in primary legislation, which are considered to impose a burden on businesses or others, which could be reduced or removed without removing any necessary protection. The Regulatory Reform Act replaced the equivalent provisions in the Deregulation and Contracting Out Act, 1994, but allowed proceedings on Deregulation Orders which had started before the passage of that Act to continue. The main provision of the Regulatory Reform Act removed some of the barriers to wider application of the deregulation order-making power under sections 1-4 of the Deregulation and Contracting Out Act, 1994 (the 1994 Act). The new order-making power in the Act is wide enough, but not wider than necessary, to deal with regulatory reform measures which the Government wishes to achieve. In parallel with the widening of the power, the Act adds to the tests and safeguards governing its use.

3.3. Deregulation and Regulatory Reforms in USA

The reform of economic regulation in network industries in the United States began in the 1970s. Regulatory reforms in the United States have been developing since the late 1970s when policy-makers started emphasizing on deregulation and other initiatives to deal with the stagflation problem. Economic deregulation coincided with rapid increases in environmental, health, and safety regulations, and even with direct government intervention in the energy sector and in setting wages and prices. In USA deregulation became central to economic policy in the mid-1970s as evidence grew that government intervention was needlessly restricting competition and harming the performance of many sectors. This led to deregulation in many areas: financial deregulation (abolition of fixed brokers' fees) began in 1975, followed by deregulation of the railroads (1976), air cargo (1977), airlines and natural gas (1978), satellite communications (1979), trucking, railroads again, financial institutions, cable television (1980), petroleum, radio (1981) and buses and communications equipment (1982). Replacement of price and entry controls with pro-competitive regulatory regimes, backed-up by strong competition policies, continues today in many sectors.

Focusing on economic issues and concerns, policy-makers have introduced various legislations and changes to remove or reduce the regulation of prices, entry and exit activities (i.e. economic regulation activities). For example, many changes or new initiatives have been introduced in such industries as the airline (e.g. the Airline Deregulation Act of 1978), the road transport (e.g. the Motor Carrier Act of 1980), the electric power (e.g. AT&T divestiture decision in 1982, the Telecommunications Act of 1996, and various changes in state regulation), and the financial services (e.g. the Depository Institution Deregulation and Monetary Control Act of 1980, and interstate branching at state level). The natural gas deregulation was also adopted in 1978 and Carter immediately announced his intention to roll back price constraints on oil, with effective deregulation to be completed by mid-1981.

Attempts to impose quality controls on the use of delegated regulatory powers in social policy areas began in the 1970s "in reaction to the explosive growth of new regulatory programmes" of the 1960s and 1970s.[82] By the mid-1970s, over 100 federal agencies were issuing economic and social regulations in areas such as health, safety, housing, agriculture, labour contracts and working conditions, environment, trade, and consumer protection. Their output was voluminous: the Code of Federal Regulations grew from 9745 pages in 1950 to more than 1,00,000 pages by 1980 to almost 1,40,000 pages by 1995.[83]

The new social regulations affected a far broader cross-section of economic, production and consumption activities than had older-style economic regulation, and hence, they were far more visible and interactive. The administrative and economic side-effects of rapid regulatory expansion began, in the late 1960s, to command political attention. Conflict and duplication, for example, between various regulatory agencies occurred more and more frequently. Regulatory costs, both on and off-budget, escalated. The administrative on-budget costs of federal regulatory activities rose from $4 billion in 1970 to over $11 billion by 1994, while staffing of regulatory agencies rose from 70,000 to over 1,28,000 in the same period.[84]

Criticism grew of the failure of detailed regulations to keep-up with changing social, economic and technological conditions. By the 1980s, a political backlash against regulation had emerged, fuelled by the economic crisis of the time. The message was simple: "American life is burdened by too much regulation".[85] The existing control and oversight processes were not suited to regulations. New means were needed to manage the enlarged federal regulatory structure. In 1981, President Reagan made regulatory relief a top priority. Agencies were directed to "weed out and eliminate wasteful, unnecessary, intrusive regulatory standards". Late in the 1980s, competitiveness in opening global markets became key to the regulatory reform programme. In 1989, regulatory reform was linked directly to US trade policy when President Bush established the cabinet-level Council on Competitiveness, chaired by the Vice-President, to review major regulatory issues. Bush went so far as to declare a 90-day moratorium on the issuance of regulations, which was later extended. He then created Quayle Commission on Competitiveness, which provided a mechanism for those targeted by agency regulations to take political appeals directly to the White House, around the agencies and off the record. The Council was abolished by President Clinton in 1993 due to concerns about lack of transparency and bias towards business concerns.

3.3.1. *Carter Administration and After: the Deregulation Movement*

Each President since Nixon has vowed to control the costs of the expanding federal regulatory state and to carry out policies more cost-effectively, while at the same time supporting the establishment of major new regulatory programmes. The balance of federal action has shifted from "regulatory relief" under Reagan to the Clinton philosophy of "regulatory quality" based on the idea that "the American people deserve a regulatory system that works for them, not against them". Much of the debate in the United States has centred on the economic costs of providing social benefits, and the difficulty of balancing the two.

At about the time the Carter administration came to Washington, a rather significant change occurred. It was a shift that was maintained and indeed intensified from about 1977 through the Reagan years, with varying levels of intensity, through the Bush administration, and, in a particular form, through the Clinton administration. At the core of the debate and activity surrounding these changes were several key factors, including: (1) promoting of a mythology of bureaucracy; (2) a deliberate politicization of the public service; (3) the use of reform to cloak ideological challenges to the idea of a public service; (4) a dramatic deregulation movement; (5) a problematic reshaping of inter-governmental relations; (6) a shift in response by courts to administrative responsibility; (7) the effects of fiscal stress; and (8) a growing impact of globalization on domestic public administration.[86]

Presidential and congressional candidates of both parties in campaigns from 1976 through 1984 pressed a "government is the problem" theme with great success. The picture that emerged was that public administration had rapidly grown at an alarming rate (particularly during the 1970s) and the government was becoming a much greater consumer of national resource, which was the cause of the economic woes of the nation. The number of bureaucrats had grown enormously and that they were generally incompetent, inefficient, irresponsible, and unresponsive to the people. The bureaucracy was engaged in profligate spending, throwing away money that had been wrested from the taxpayers of various states and localities around the nation. The mechanisms of accountability were all but non-existent and the government, principally the bureaucracy was rife with fraud, abuse and waste of resources.[87]

The deregulation revolution began under President Ford, accelerated under President Carter and President Reagan. President Jimmy Carter made no secret of his interest in challenging the regulatory regime that operated from there. Carter led successful efforts to deregulate significant portion of airline operations, rail service and trucking. He emphasized on the need to review the laws that established the regulatory programmes. Those that needlessly restrict competition, impose rigidity, or are otherwise out of date must be revised or eliminated. The result of deregulation has been lower prices, improved customer services and choices, technological change in the previously cartelized industries and increased competitiveness and efficiency of economy as a whole. One of the first experiments in deregulation came in 1968 when Federal

Communication Commission (FCC) was allowed limited competition against the American Telephone and Telegraph Company (AT&T) in the sale of terminal equipment. The FCC continued to open up more and more telecommunication services to competition during the mid-to late-1970s. In 1980, it permitted AT&T through a separate subsidy, to market enhanced services such as its advanced communications system on an unregulated basis.

It is generally assumed that the contemporary market-oriented approaches to regulation were creatures of the 1980s or even the 1990s, but virtually all the techniques now in use were advocated by Carter. The reform programme of the Carter administration emphasized use of innovative regulatory techniques as an alternative to traditional command-and-control regulation. These techniques were generally less likely to interfere with competition. Many of these work by structuring incentives that will resolve regulatory programmes through market mechanisms. These innovative regulatory techniques move away from centralized decision-making and allow industry and consumers more freedom of choice.

President Carter went beyond support for deregulation legislation to call upon regulatory agencies to re-examine their decision-making processes, both to improve their existing operations and also to consider alternative approaches to regulation that made greater use of market oriented tools. He championed what came to be known as the Paperwork Reduction Act, intended to reduce the paperwork burden often encountered in regulatory enforcement. He created the Regulatory Analysis Review Group (RARG), made-up of representatives of regulatory agencies to consider agency efforts, and developed a Regulatory Council to contemplate innovative techniques of regulation that avoided what was increasingly referred to a traditional "command-and-control" approach. The Carter administration also used executive orders to enhance the role of the Office of Management and Budget (OMB) by authorizing the OMB to monitor proposed rule-making in order to discourage unnecessary regulation and encouraging the promulgation of cost/benefit analysis of rules.

Airlines Deregulation

The most significant transport deregulation took place during Carter Administration, when the Civil Aeronautics Board (CAB) and the Interstate Commerce Commission (ICC) began to repeal the rules that set prices, allocated markets, and restricted the entry of new competitors into the airlines, trucking and railroad industries. In the period from 1950 to 1974, most of the competitive forces were suppressed by the CAB. The CAB did not permit one single new airline to enter the market for scheduled airline service, despite receipt of almost eighty applications.[88] Even exiting airlines were almost never granted permission to serve new routes. Thus, the market discipline imposed by actual and potential entry was eliminated. In addition, its rate setting policies effectively prevented price competition. There was a regulatory misdirection in CAB's functioning as it appeared to be more concerned with protecting the existing competitors in the market rather than promoting air transport competition.

By mid-1970s it was widely apparent that airline regulation was not functioning as it should. The calls for deregulation became common and gave impetus to airline deregulation. Given CAB behaviours, for all intents and purposes, airline deregulation began in 1977 or 1978. By 1977, the CAB was relaxing restrictions of entry, and allowed the first certification of a new airline for interstate travel since the 1940s. In 1978 the Airline Deregulation Act was passed, removing most price and entry restrictions. By 1985, the CAB was totally out of business and in January 1985 the CAB was abolished. Authority for regulating airline mergers was transferred to the Department of Transportation effective from December 31, 1984 and to the Department of Justice in 1989.[89] Early assessment of airlines deregulation tended to be very positive — there was a flurry of new entrants, fares fell dramatically, more attractive service/price combinations to consumers etc. Airline deregulation was viewed so positively that it played a significant role in encouraging deregulatory legislation affecting many types of regulation governing diverse sectors of the US Economy. Today all airline entry, fare, routes structure etc. are almost completely unrestricted, although airline safety and access to airport, gates are still tightly regulated by the Federal Aviation Administration.

Railroad Deregulation

During the 1970s there was a general ideological movement towards less government intervention in the economy, a movement that was greatly strengthened by the initial success of airline deregulation in 1978. The economic and political pressures for deregulation led to passage of the Staggers Rail Act of 1980, which was intended to increase the role of competition in setting rates. The Staggers Rail Act partially, though not entirely, deregulated rail transport. The ICC continues to monitor rail traffic rates and perform rate reasonable determinations. However, under the terms of the Act, it may review the rates only if a railroad has a dominant market position and if the rate is above a certain percentage of variable costs, if the rate is below a given percentage, the ICC is not empowered to review it. Further, commodity movements whose prices are set under contract are exempt from regulation. Built-in flexibility allows rates to increase with inflation without review. The Act also made it easier for railroads to add or abandon rail lines and to buy and sell lines.

Trucking Deregulation

In case of trucking, the deregulatory pressures culminated in passage of the Motor Carrier Act, 1980, a sweeping reform measure. The Act substantially reduced licensing barriers to trucking entry, limited collective rate-making agreements, and removed many administrative restrictions on rate-setting. Route restrictions were removed, potential entrants no longer had to prove public necessity for proposed services, and permits were to be issued to qualified applicants unless there was a compelling reason not to — the latter a reversal of the previous burden of proof.

The Reagan administration took the tools provided by its predecessor and moved well beyond the policies of the Carter administration. President Reagan followed suit but his administration was even more intense in criticizing regulatory practice. In 1980, Presidential hopeful Ronald Reagan vowed to "get the government of the backs of the people". Regulatory relief, not reform, was the linchpin in his vision of a revitalized American economy.[90] Reagan envisaged a new nation in which industry and the federal government, unfettered by red tape, would be free to surge ahead in efficiency and productivity. One of the first steps of President Reagan Administration was to lift the oil price-controls and allocation quotas that had been initiated by President Nixon and were gradually being phased out by President Carter. And in the face of congressional opposition, he had been steadily whittling away at the regulatory apparatus governing the pricing and distribution of natural gas. During the Reagan Administration, the FCC has substantially deregulated television and radio broadcasting and computer related telecommunication services. It has also taken steps necessary to implement the divestiture of AT&T ordered by Federal District Judge, Herold Greene in 1982.

President Reagan wasted no time in creating the management structure that was to deliver regulatory relief. He appointed Vice-President Bush to head the "Task Force on Regulatory Relief", which was to serve as point patrol, targeting areas encumbered by excessive regulation. Regulatory review also was centralized within the Office of Information and Regulatory Affairs (OIRA), a division of the Office of Management and Budget (OMB). The most important early initiative, Executive Order 12291, was issued. It directed executive agencies, "to the extent permitted by law", to review existing and newly proposed regulation by means of a stringent cost-benefit analysis. He employed executive orders and Presidential memoranda to constrain even those agencies charged by Congress with implementation of new complex regulatory programmes such as EPA. He also directed his political appointees to trim back on regulatory activity. Thus, agencies such as the Federal Communications Commission (FCC) undertook to deregulate by administrative proceedings.

The Reagan administration also took the initiative in attempting to reform social regulation, which was a centerpiece of its agenda. The principle intended was "economic benefits of social deregulation are reduced costs of compliance for businesses and lowered costs of enforcement for government". However, the administration failed notably to achieve any fundamental change in the legislative framework of social regulation. Not one of the important pieces of social legislation was successfully altered, even though several including the Clean Air and Clean Water Acts came up for reauthorization during the administration's first year. The Reagan administration did little more than continue the deregulation of aviation, trucking, and railroads started by Jimmy Carter.

3.3.2. *Present Institutional Framework for Regulatory Reform in the United States*

Like other OECD countries, the United States has over the course of a century constructed an enormous and complex regulatory state to provide citizens a wide range of vital services and protections, ranging from accessible buildings to safe food to a cleaner environment. In addition to new laws, over 60 executive agencies in the federal government are authorized to issue subordinate regulations. Each year, they issue between 4,000 and 5,000 new regulations. More than 200 volumes of federal rules are now on the shelves.[91] The result is that federal regulations now affect virtually all individuals, businesses, state, local and tribal governments, and other organizations in virtually every aspect of their lives or operations. Regulations in the United States are based on an implicit but strong policy framework of competition principles. Problems, such as the monopoly characteristics of networks, which other countries traditionally addressed through public ownership, are addressed in the United States through less interventionist economic regulation. Problems, such as service quality and distributional issues, which other countries address through economic regulation, are usually handled in the United States through competition-neutral social regulation, other social policies, or the market supported by competition and consumer policies.

The focus of reform shifted in the 1980s from economic deregulation to fast-growing social regulation. Today, the United States is rare among OECD countries in focusing on improving the quality of social regulations (defined as meeting benefit-cost and cost-effectiveness tests, while reaching defined policy goals) and reducing paperwork burdens as the main objectives of regulatory reform.

For the Congress and the Executive, the 1990s has been an active period for regulatory reforms and a series of important improvements in performance measures, impact analysis, and congressional oversight have been launched which hold considerable promise for improving regulatory quality. The Government Performance and Results Act of 1993 required agencies to prepare strategic plans to identify a mission statement, strategic objectives, and performance measure. At the state and local level, governments have been interested in deregulating the public service through the privatization strategy, which includes such formats as contracting out (outsourcing), franchising, public private partnership, asset divestment, grants, subsidies and vouchers. The 104th Congress (1995-96) debated a raft of legislation on regulatory reform. Significant laws emerging from the debates included the Unfunded Mandates Reform Act of 1995, the Paperwork Reduction Act of 1995 and the Small Business Regulatory Enforcement Fairness Act of 1996. Unfunded Mandates Reform Act provides the first statutory basis for government-wide RIA; regulators are required to assess expected costs and benefits for most important regulations (but the benefit-cost principle is not included); the federal government must find financing if costs fall on state, local, or tribal governments. It addresses concerns from state and local officials regarding problems of inter-governmental mandates. The Act requires procedures for assessing the impacts of major federal mandates on other levels of government and on the pirated sector. Amended Paperwork Reduction Act widens OMB's authority and requires OIRA to establish government wide and agency specific paperwork reduction goals. Small Business Regulatory Enforcement Fairness Act toughens requirements to consider small business impacts of regulations. Congressional Review Act of 1997 requires regulators to send all regulations to the Congress for review; most important rules have a delay of 60 days before becoming effective. Congress may nullify all rules within 60 days. Treasury and Government Appropriations Act, 1997 requires OMB to submit to Congress estimates of total annual costs and benefits of federal regulations, and recommendations for improvements.

Finally, policy-makers have considered other approaches to social regulation, including the adoption of several market-based mechanisms (e.g. emission trading programmes for pollution reduction and the use of negotiation or consultation methods in the rule making process. In the area of administrative regulation, policy-makers have considered or implemented new ideas to reduce problems of federal bureaucracy and to increase accountability and transparency in governmental operations of regulation. For example, the Volcker Commission recommended in 1989 that the federal government deregulate personnel and compensation rules, introduced merit-based incentives for employees, and give supervisors more flexibility in management decisions. In 1993, President Clinton issues executive order on "Regulatory Planning and Review" and Vice-President Gore's National Performance Review (NPR) called for broader reforms in federal and state governments.

Role of Competition Policy in Regulatory Reform

Competition principles are woven tightly into the legal framework for regulation, and are backed-up by strong watchdog institutions. The principle aims of US competitive policy are to promote consumer welfare, protect the competitive process, and enhance economic efficiency. The United States has strong, well-established enforcement institutions, and many enforcement methods. The two enforcement agencies — the Antitrust Division of the Department of Justice and the Federal Trade Commission — are both staffed by lawyers and economists, both combine policy expertise and prosecutorial duties with political accountability (achieved in different ways), and both implement competition policy by applying general principles case by case. The parallel structure has not historically led to conflict, as the two agencies have managed to avoid duplication and forum shopping. But coordination of policies and actions imposes costs.

The level of transparency is high and enforcement decisions do not appear to depend on political influence due to institutional independence, a strong tradition of professionalism, and judicial oversight. Both agencies publicize decisions to initiate actions. Final decisions for courts or commissions are always accompanied by detailed explanations. Unnecessary delay has long been a concern about competition cases.

Judicial review provides a constant process of defining and balancing the role of competition policy institutions and regulators. The meaning of the basic competition laws is determined principally by a common-law process in which courts are the highest authorities. The courts also play important roles in interpreting the laws that establish regulatory programmes. The mediating role of the judiciary helps keep US competition policy coherent, despite multiple participants and laws. The result is a constant process of defining and balancing the roles of competition policy institutions and those responsible for economic and social regulation. Because so much US economic policy is based on competition, many different regulators and other bodies, in both federal and state governments, implement competition policy. Such wide diffusion risks weakening competition policy by increasing uncertainty and inconsistency.

Anxiety about reform and deregulation has been to some extent overcome, by the credibility of competition law enforcement. Agreements among competitors about the critical competitive dimensions of price and output can be treated as crimes, subject to felony penalties of high fines and imprisonment. The effect or reasonableness of the prices of market divisions agreed on is not relevant; such agreements are illegal *per se*. Other kinds of horizontal agreement may also be illegal, but their legality depends on the outcome of the "rule of reason" test, that is, on a review of net competitive effects. Sanctions for violation of competition law are unusually harsh, which makes it harder to apply sanctions to conduct that had been previously permitted or even required by other government regulation. High penalties encourage claims for exemption, special treatment, or even regulation as a substitute for competition enforcement. Recognizing the risk of disproportion, the agencies have brought most actions against horizontal constraints in regulatory settings as civil, not criminal, cases. Mergers are handled flexibly so that competition authorities can tailor their actions to the market structures of different sectors. Mergers and combinations, including joint ventures and open market acquisitions, are covered by the Clayton Act. Markets are defined based on data about actual and likely cross-elasticities and substitution responses. Assessment of likely effect depends critically on the long-term significance of entry. Possible entry by a firm that could exit quickly, at no cost, is treated differently than possible entry by a firm that would have to commit sunk resources. Different treatment of entry can be significant in regulatory settings. Hurdles faced by a "facilities-based" competitor could be higher than those faced by a reseller of an incumbent's basic service.

US competition agencies have been unusually active in promoting competitive, market methods and outcomes in policy and regulatory processes. Their advocacy contributed to the first major deregulation successes in airlines and natural gas and continued with trucking, communications, broadcasting, and electric power. Advocacy interventions have included: Price and rate regulations affecting long distance telephone service, liquor distribution, and marine pilotage; Entry in such contexts as allocation of airport landing and take-off privileges, certified public accounting, local multipoint telephone and video distribution services, automobile sales, and conveyancing; Output regulation such as television's prime time access rules, must-carry rules for television retransmissions by satellite and open video system, and restrictions on collision damage waivers for automobile rentals; Limitations on forms of practice, such as rules against commercial relationships by optometrists and veterinarians with non-professionals and against linkages between cemeteries and funeral establishments.

The level of advocacy activity declined in the 1990s, probably because the easier battles at the federal-level have been won. Today, the Antitrust Division concentrates advocacy almost entirely on federal agencies and departments, while the FTC addresses about half of its efforts to state and local issues. Antitrust and consumer protection policies are complementary tools for achieving the benefits of market competition, and the FTC is responsible for both policies. The general competition law is intended to ensure markets provide consumers with range of options, while the general consumer protection law is intended to ensure that the consumers can select freely and effectively from the options offered be the market. Having both responsibilities in the same organization allows closer integration of the two complementary policies.

In the US legal system, competition policy often enjoys priority over regulatory policies. Exercise of authority by another regulatory body will not usually displace competition law. If Congress wants to exempt conduct from competition law or apply special rules, it must, say so clearly. It has done so often. A surprisingly large number of special industry rules, and sectoral regulators and exemptions constrain application of the basic competition laws. Most national regulations that fixed prices, limited output, reduced quality, divided markets or constrained entry have been eliminated. Many of the remaining sector-specific agencies apply competition policies consistently with the competition agencies. In sectors, notable energy and telecommunication, regulatory programmes have co-existed with the application of general competition laws. And in those sectors, the introduction of competition principles through the regulatory process appears to be proceeding better. The courts have instructed the regulators to include competition policy in their application of regulatory statutes. Congress has also supported the move towards deregulation, and the competition agencies have encouraged these moves, offering advice and assistance. Many exemptions and special rules obviously respond to pleading by industry interest. Indeed, most of these were enacted after the beneficiaries were found liable for violating the law. One protected "special interest" is the government itself. The United States does not submit government entities involved in commercial operations to its competition law. This exemption, unusual in OECD countries, may be significant for government owned power systems, hospitals and port authorities affected by regulatory reform. Another major set of exemptions arises from the US Commitment to federalism. The "state action doctrine" exempts private anti-competitive conduct from antitrust law if the conduct is explicitly authorized by state policy. This doctrine has permitted anti-competitive state regulation of transportation, hospitals, health care and professional services and other areas. The doctrine demonstrates that national competition policy, though privileged in relationship to US national regulatory policy, may be less important than some other political values, in this case federalism.

Regulatory Reforms in the Telecommunications Industry

The United States is the world leader and has pioneered the reform of telecommunications regulation. As a result of the 1984 divestiture and the Telecommunication Act, 1996, the equipment and long distanced prices *de facto* were deregulated. There has been introduction at state-level of various alternatives to rate of return regulation like revenue sharing, price caps. Open entry in long distance and business services and data transmission and legal barriers to entry into local market have been removed. However, the local services remain regulated.

The 1984 divestiture which split AT&T into a long-distance company and seven local operating companies was a pivotal step that directly addressed underlying anti-competitive incentives, and provided a sound foundation for pro-competitive regulatory reform. The 1984 divestiture generated a market structure that is unique. Under the decree, AT&T was required to divest its local operating subsidiaries, creating seven Regional Bell Operating Companies (the RBOCs) which, subject to some exceptions, were not allowed to provide "long-distance" service. The divestiture separated long-distance services and local exchange services. It defined 164 different Local Access and Transport Areas ("LATAs"), generally smaller than states and stipulated that the RBOCs were not allowed to provide any services that crossed these lines. RBOCs were not allowed to provide information services, either. These restraints, by assuring that regulated monopolists could not compete in long distance or other competitive markets, eliminated the risk of discrimination between competing long-distance carriers and the monopolist's own long-distance service. This structure was based on the view that local exchanges had natural monopoly properties, though technological developments since 1984 have eroded those properties. It also helped to open network equipment markets and contributed, among many factors, to a dramatic decline in telecommunications switching and transmission costs. The 1984 antitrust action provides a striking example of the central role of competition policy in regulatory reform.

The most important impact of regulatory reform is its contribution to facilitating a level of innovation that has transformed the industry and had positive effects throughout the economy. The quality of telecommunications service in the US has improved, particularly for large business customers, because of technological improvements and also because telecommunication operators compete on the basis of service quality. Moreover, the number of households with telephones increased over the reform period.

The key policy challenge is introducing competition into local markets. Divestiture did not facilitate competition into local markets. Conditions of entry into local markets varied, and still vary, significantly across states. The approach to promoting local competition differs from the strategy for long-distance markets. The Telecommunications Act of 1996 attempts to strengthen earlier initiatives by making approval to enter in-region inter-LATA toll markets contingent on a demonstration that local markets are open to competition. This was meant to establish incentives for the RBOCs to open local monopolies in return for competing in long distance markets.

The dual federal-state roles can promote innovation, but also produces complexity and uncertainty in the regulatory regime. Successes in reducing barriers to entry, promoting cost-based interconnection, rate rebalancing and equal access have been most pronounced at the federal level. The 1996 Telecommunications Act provides for the pre-emption of state legislation that raises barriers to entry.

The 1996 Act provides two mechanisms for systematic review of FCC regulations. First, the Act provides for a "Biennial Regulatory Review". The FCC is required to review all regulations applicable to providers of telecommunications service in every even numbered year beginning in 1998, to determine whether the regulations are no longer in the public interest due to meaningful economic competition between providers of the service and whether regulations should be appealed or modified. The 1996 Act also provides "forbearance" procedures to eliminate regulations that are no longer necessary given the current market condition. Carriers can request initiation of the review procedure. While enactment of these provisions is an important step, they do not include an explicit recognition of the costs that regulation imposes, and important provisions of the 1996 Act are exempted. Additional benefits are possible from a more systematic review process.

Some of the key features of the 1996 Telecommunications Act are:

- **Interconnection:** Incumbent local exchange carriers (the incumbent "LECs") are required to provide interconnection to any requesting carrier at any technically feasible point. The FCC concluded that prices should be based on Total Element Long-Run Incremental Cost (TELRIC) plus a reasonable share of forward-looking joint and common costs.
- **Unbundling:** Incumbent LECs are required to provide requesting telecommunications carriers non-discriminatory access to network elements on an unbundled basis at any technically feasible point. The FCC concludes that prices should be based on TELRIC plus a reasonable share of forward looking joint and common costs.
- **Resale:** Incumbent LECs are required to offer for resale, any telecommunications service that the carrier provides at retail to subscribers. The FCC concludes that the price of resale services should be set at a discount of retail-based on the costs that the

incumbent LEC can avoid by selling at wholesale rather than retail.

- **Universal Service:** An explicit mechanism to maintain local rates at affordable rates is mandated.
- **Access Charge Reform:** To facilitate the development of an explicit mechanism for universal service, the FCC reformed the access charge rate structure.
- **Entry into Long-distance:** RBOCs are allowed to provide out-of-region inter-LATA service. A procedure is provided for under which the RBOCs are permitted to enter in-region inter-LATA when their local market are found to be sufficiently open to competition. In assessing whether the local markets are open, the FCC in directed to give "substantial weight" to the DOJ's assessment of a "competitive checklist". Once an RBOC gains approval to offer inter-LATA service, they are required to do so subject to an accounting separation for a three-year period.
- **Forbearance:** The FCC is directed to forbear from aspects of regulation that are deemed to be unnecessary.
- **Removal of State Barriers to Entry:** State regulation that raises barriers to entry into local markets is pre-empted.

3.3.3. *Managing Regulatory Quality in the United States*

A. *Ensuring Regulatory Transparency*

According to Vice-President Gore, a public forward planning system for regulations allows citizens "to be a well-informed participant in the regulatory matters that affect your life".[92] The United States has had for many years an extensive planning system for regulations under development. There are two major planning documents:

- *The Unified Agenda of Federal Regulatory and Deregulatory Actions* is published twice a year. It provides information in a common format to help the public identify which new regulations will affect them. All entries include information about the regulation's priority, its affect on SMEs and other levels of government, whether it is part of the NPR programme, an abstract and timetable for action.
- *The Regulatory Plan* is published annually as a defining statement of the Administration's regulatory and deregulatory

> policies and priorities. Entries are restricted to only the most important regulations, and contain a statement of need, a description of the alternatives considered, and description of the magnitude of risks and risk reduction expected.

The forward planning process has been a core element of the regulatory quality control system. In 1985, President Reagan ordered that federal agencies conduct, under the oversight of OIRA, an annual process of regulatory planning that would produce the *Regulatory Programme of the United States Government*, to be issued under the President's signature. The planning process was intended to improve interagency coordination, establish the President's regulatory priorities, increase the accountability of agency heads for the regulatory actions of their agencies, and improve public and Congressional understanding of the President's regulatory objectives.[93] Regulatory planning was needed because regulation was "one of the most important and costly activities of government", yet, despite the regulatory review process set-up in 1981, it was "managed far less systematically than direct government spending".[94] The 1993 Clinton executive order retained forward planning, and put more emphasis on its value for communication and consultation. The regulatory plan made it possible for the citizen "to be a well-informed participant in the regulatory matters that affect your life".

When draft regulations are proposed, the "notice and comment" process permits open and accessible consultation that allows all interested voices a chance to be heard. Public consultation is highly developed in the United States. Almost all federal regulations are developed through mandatory administrative procedures intended to ensure public consultation and openness. These "notice and comment" procedures dominate the rule-making process in Washington by establishing the channels through which multiple interest groups strive to influence the regulatory decision by developing empirical or legal arguments supporting their positions.

The Administrative Procedure Act, 1946, establishes minimum procedural requirements for rule-making. While it leaves agencies great flexibility to develop procedures, the Act requires that an agency publish a proposed rule in the Federal Register. Except for some widely used exceptions, the public must be given atleast 30 days to comment in writing and the agency must consider any comments received. The comments themselves are made public *via* the establishment of a legal rule-making "record", which contains all factual material received and potentially relied upon in the regulatory decision. When an agency publishes a final rule, it must explain the factual and logical basis for its decision, how it reached its conclusion, and how it dealt with the public comments received. Where important new material is received, there may be a need for more than one round of comments. Rules must be published not less than 30 days before becoming effective.

Written comments may be supplemented by a public hearing. Hearings tend to be formal in character, with limited opportunity for dialogue or debate among participants. Experimentation with "on-line" hearings has also commenced. A separate consultation process on paperwork requirements is established by the Paperwork Reduction Act. This process is open to all citizens, rather than being based on representative groups. Its effect is to increase the quality and legitimacy of policy by ensuring that special interests do not have undue influence.

Once a regulation is adopted, it is easily accessible to affected entities. Final regulations are indexed and published in the consolidated Code of Federal Regulations, which is also available on-line on the Internet. The Code provides a comprehensive view of the regulation in force at a given time. A "simplicity and clarity" policy was adopted in June 1998 when President Clinton instructed civil servants to write all documents "in plain language". One notable effort to improve communication of regulatory text has been the publication by some regulators of plain language "Small Business Compliance Guides" distributed by "outreach" programmes.

Improving enforcement strategies has now become a national priority. The Vice-President, through the National Performance Review, instructed agencies to shift the focus of enforcement activities away from "paperwork violations" to an emphasis on performance results and to move away from adversarial relations with regulated parties towards a more cooperative approach. Compliance assistance and enforcement issues for SMEs were also targeted in the 1996 SBREFA. The Act obliges agencies to publish compliance guides for all rules with a significant small business impact. SBREFA also establishes a complaint process whereby any SME can complain about enforcement actions to the new SBA Ombudsman or one of the 20 Small Business Regulatory Fairness Boards established across the country.

B. *Promoting Regulatory Reform and Quality within the Administration*

To manage the large and complex US regulatory system, the United States has established a series of oversight mechanisms. The reform policies are established directly by the President on the basis of his executive authority. The Vice-President is identified as the principal adviser to the President on regulatory policy, planning and review. The day-to-day centralized oversight and quality management is conducted by the Office of Management and Budget, located at the very centre of government. The OMB has a strong coordination, reviewing, and reporting role for regulatory reform.

Both the President and the Congress carry out strong regulatory oversight, the President through a Central Management Office accountable directly to him, and the Congress through a system of oversight committees organized largely along programme lines, and through investigations by its organs such as the General Accounting Office. The concerns of the two branches of government may not always coincide; a congressional committee, for example, may focus on implementation of a specific regulatory law, while the President may focus on the functioning of the regulatory system as a whole, consistency with empirical tests of benefit-cost and cost-effectiveness, and its consistency with his policies. Centralization of review authority in the Office of the President is a means of exercising oversight on broad discretionary powers delegated to unelected officials.

In the executive branch, competition between President and Congress for influence over regulatory decisions had contributed to the emergence of an unusually centralized and hierarchical regulatory oversight process. The Office of Management and Budget within the Executive Office of the President has evolved to become among the most powerful of the central oversight bodies in any OECD country. This reflects the strong constitutional powers of the President in overseeing the executive branch.

The OMB has had a strong coordination, reviewing, and reporting role on regulatory reform since the earliest days of the policy. OMB is responsible for many central management tasks of government that have been very helpful to regulatory reform. These include preparation of the President's budget, legislative review, information policy, financial management, and procurement policy. The traditional government-wide authority of OMB and its control of many levers of influence in the public administration has given it the potential for enormous authority in promoting broad-based reform.

A distinguishing characteristic of the Office of Information and Regulatory Affairs (OIRA) in OMB is its intimacy with every stage of regulatory decision-making in the agencies. President Reagan's 1981 order and subsequent orders have placed OMB firmly and unavoidably within the normal process of regulatory development. OIRA reviews the most important regulations three times: (1) at the planning stage during preparation of the annual Regulatory Plan; (2) at the proposed stage before they are published for comment in the Federal Register (the national gazette); and (3) at the final stage before publication as a finished rule. OIRA's role is to review the regulations and the impact analysis in order to identify decisions and policies that are not consistent with the President's policies, principles, and priorities; to coordinate among agencies; to discuss any inconsistencies with the regulators, and to suggest alternatives that would be consistent. OIRA is, in effect, the President's trusted intermediary in overseeing the regulatory apparatus of the federal government. In addition, OIRA has legal authority under the Paperwork Reduction Act to review and nullify any "information collection" requirement imposed on citizens, businesses, or state and local governments.

The Small Business Administration (SBA) has an increasing role, too, in reviewing assessments of small business impacts. The regulatory difficulties of Small and Medium-scale Enterprises (SMEs) have been prominent since the early days of reform. Reports have found that SMEs in the United States are disproportionately affected by regulatory costs. A vibrant SME sector would perform even better if regulatory burdens were reduced. For these reasons, an important feature of the regulatory and paperwork reduction programmes in the United States has been the focus on SMEs.

The Congress enacted the Regulatory Flexibility Act (RFA) in 1980, and sixteen years later, the Small Business Regulatory Enforcement Fairness Act of 1996 (SBREFA) to correct flaws in the RFA that had undermined its effectiveness. The Small Business Administration's (SBA) Office of Advocacy has been the main institution to monitor compliance with these laws. Both Acts increased SBA powers in the federal regulatory process.

The most significant mechanism concerns the RFA review process which requires federal agencies to analyze the anticipated effects of proposed rules on small entities unless they certify that the rules will not have a "significant economic impact on a substantial number of small entities". Agencies are also required to identify alternative regulatory approaches. This review is done through a "Regulatory Flexibility Analysis" and notification in the Federal Register. SBREFA reinforced these requirements by permitting judicial review of agency compliance with the RFA and enhanced the authority of the SBA Office of Advocacy to file amicus briefs in court involving agency violations. In practice, this provides to the aggrieved SME court awards, attorney's fees, and costs when an agency has been found to be excessive in its enforcement of federal regulations.

A second innovation introduced by SBREFA concerns the establishment of EPA and OSHA Regulatory Review Panels to review the initial Regulatory Flexibility Analysis for each draft rule. The panel process supplements the public comment requirements established by law. Each panel consists of employees from OIRA and SBA's Office of Advocacy, the regulatory agency responsible for the draft rule and representatives of affected small entities. Since the biggest problem for SMEs seems to be tax-related burdens, as is true in most countries, it is unfortunate that a Review Panel was not established for tax compliance issues.

Coordination within and between Levels of Government

The continued importance of this issue was demonstrated by the adoption in 1995 of the Unfunded Mandates Reform Act. This Act is important in a number of areas. However, from the point of view of federalist relations the key requirement is for a cost analysis of any bill that would impose costs on state, local or tribal governments. If a mandate exceeds $50 million, or if the cost analysis is not attached, a procedural point of order can be raised in either chamber of the Congress (by end 1998, no bill had been blocked through this procedure, although points of order had been raised several times in the House). The Congressional Budget Office, which scrutinizes compliance, has testified that this analytical requirement seemed to have a preventive effect in reducing regulatory costs.

C. *Adopting Explicit Standards for Regulatory Quality*

In 1993, President Clinton issued an executive order on "Regulatory Planning and Review" that aimed at "building the foundation for a regulatory system that will improve the lives of Americans without imposing undue costs and burdens". Based on earlier orders issued by President Reagan, it mandates for regulators a programme of regulatory quality standards, rational decision procedures, development of consensual rather than adversarial approaches, promotion of innovative policy instruments, and centralized oversight by the Office of Management and Budget of the most important regulations. In the Clinton executive order, the Vice-President is identified as the principal adviser to the President on regulatory policy, planning and review, OMB (part of the White House Office) as the "repository of expertise" on regulatory issues, and the head of the Office of Information and Regulatory Affairs (appointed by the President) as the coordinator of the policies. These administrative policies are backed up in some respects by laws supporting central review and impact analysis.

Clinton's 1993 executive order is the primary reference for regulatory quality standards. The order requires that agencies take a "minimalist" approach to regulation, by promulgating ". . . only such regulations as are required by law, are necessary to interpret the law or are made necessary by compelling public need, such as material failures of private markets. . . ."[95] It requires regulators to:

- identify the problem to be addressed and assess its significance.
- identify and assess alternatives to direct regulation, including economic incentives and information, and use performance standards to the extent possible if regulation is chosen.
- set priorities by considering the degree and nature of risks from different sources.
- if regulation is the best method, design it in the most cost-effective way.
- regulate only upon a reasoned determination that benefits justify costs.
- base decisions on best, reasonably obtainable information on the need for and consequences of regulation.
- avoid regulations that are inconsistent or duplicative with other regulations.
- draft regulations to be simple and easy to understand.

Under this programme, regulators themselves must show why they should regulate, and demonstrate that regulation is the most beneficial feasible approach. In principle, uncertainty and lack of information work against rather than for regulation. These and similar principles in place since 1981 represent a critical shift in US regulatory culture: they reversed the burden of proof for regulation, that is regulations not be issued unless regulators showed that benefits justified costs.

D. *Assessing Regulatory Impacts*

The United States was the first OECD country (in 1981) to adopt broad requirements for regulatory benefit-cost analysis and is still one of only a handful of countries to use a benefit-cost test. Such a test is the preferred method for considering regulatory impacts because it aims to produce public policy that meets the criterion of being "socially optimal" (i.e. maximizing welfare). The high priority placed on regulatory analysis reflects a belief that regulators are not truly accountable to the electorate unless the consequences — the social benefits and costs of their actions are known. Today, quantitative benefit-cost analyses are prepared for over 90 per cent of major social regulations, but only 18 per cent of major economic regulations (OMB, 1998). OMB provides quality control and guidance for these analyses. RIA has only recently been prepared for primary legislation as part of Congressional processes under the Unfunded Mandates Reform Act of 1995, and its value in improving the quality of primary legislation has yet to be proven. Evidence is building that RIA, when well prepared, helps increase the net social benefit of regulations. Yet weaknesses in the quality and completeness of the analysis contribute to wide variance in the quality of federal regulations. It also seems likely that the multiple assessments now required — benefit-cost analysis, small business analysis, paper-work analysis, and unfunded mandates analysis — are fragmenting efforts and reducing analytical quality overall.

E. *Towards Accountable and Results-Oriented Regulation*

During the Clinton Administration, the National Performance Review has constituted another mechanism for regulatory reform. The NPR is conducted under the responsibility of the Vice-President, strengthening political commitment to reform and accountability at the highest level. In 1993, Vice-President Al Gore launched a systemic view of institutional reform and the "culture" of the public administration under the National Performance Review (NPR). The NPR aims to "move from red tape to results to create a government that works better and costs less". Under the goal of "eliminating regulatory overkill", the Review recommended 10 regulatory reforms that are similar to best practices accepted by OECD countries, including: encourage more innovative approaches to regulation; encourage consensus-based rulemaking; streamline agency rulemaking procedures; rank risks and engage in "anticipatory" planning; provide better training and incentives for regulators.

Another tool with potentially profound impacts on regulation is the Government Performance and Results Act of 1993. This law requires government departments to prepare and submit to Congress strategic plans that identify, among other issues, a mission statement, strategic goals and objectives, strategies to achieve goals, programme evaluations, major management problems, and data capacity. Among the performance measures set out by regulators in 1999 are commitments by the Labour Department to reduce fatalities in the construction industry by 3 per cent, and by the Food and Drug Administration to assure that 40 per cent of domestic produce is grown and processed using good practices to minimize dangerous contamination. The strategic plans are supplemented by government-wide and agency-specific annual performance plans, the first of which were required in February 1998. If it works as intended, the Results Act should stimulate regulatory reform by making regulatory failures more transparent and increasing accountability to the Congress.

F. *Alternatives to Traditional Regulations*

There is a long history of efforts to expand the use of innovative instruments. In 1978, President Carter issued an order to regulators — to install what he called "common-sense management for the regulatory process" — to show that "alternative approaches have been considered and the least burdensome of the acceptable alternatives have been chosen". Similarly, in 1981, the Reagan executive order required regulators to ensure that "Among alternative approaches to any given regulatory objective, the alternative that maximizes net benefits to society should be chosen." Crucially, assessment of alternatives was to be documented through regulatory impact analysis. The Clinton executive order as well as the National Performance Review make it clear that alternatives such as market incentives are preferable to command and control regulations. A considerable amount of effort has gone into encouraging regulators to be more innovative by using three main approaches: performance standards, market incentives, and information strategies.

However, despite efforts to spur innovation, federal regulatory system lags behind in flexible and market-oriented regulatory approaches. One of the anomalies in American regulation is that positive social views towards competition have not led to a greater use of market-based approaches to problem-solving. Efforts to expand the use of innovative instruments have struggled with legalistic styles, risk-avoidance, and cumbersome procedures, combined with weak accountability for regulatory results that discourage experimentation and learning. Positive initiatives include:

- A pioneering law — the Performance Management and Results Act of 1993 — should strengthen incentives to innovate to improve programme results. The Act requires regulators to establish concrete performance measures and annual plans.

- Another good practice is to better use the states as testing grounds. A 1998 agreement gives the states greater scope to implement innovative ideas for achieving better environmental outcomes. More attention to good practices in other countries could also spur regulatory innovation.
- General rules for local air-pollution-permit trading were proposed by the EPA to speed-up use of emissions trading by the states.

At the heart of the most severe regulatory problems in the United States is the quality of primary legislation. The trend toward higher quality in delegated regulation cannot be seen in the quality of primary legislation in the Congress. Strikingly, major laws, such as the Clean Air Act, prohibit regulators from using good decision practices. Innovation and the development of more cost-effective policy approaches are often blocked by rigid legislation. Rational priority-setting is difficult like the Environment Protection Agency is hobbled by overly prescriptive statutes that pull the agency in too many directions and permit the managers too little discretion to make wise decisions.

Recent reforms such as the legal requirement that the congressional Budget Office estimate the costs of proposed legislation and "unfunded mandates" on state and local governments are positive. But, if it is to have value, the Congress will have to integrate such information in its deliberations. Current proposals to establish a new congressional agency to study costs and benefits of regulations could improve the attention of the Congress to the downstream consequences of its legislative decision.

3.4. Present Regulatory Regime in India

As discussed in the previous chapter, Indian economy has been amongst the most regulated economies. There have been endless restrictions and regulations like industrial licensing, import licensing, export assistance, size restrictions under Monopolies and Restrictive Trade Practices Act, storage restrictions under Essential Commodities Act, restrictions on interstate movement of food products and some cash crops, interstate permits for vehicle movement. At the operating level, factories have well over 30 inspectors visiting them every month. There are numerous regulations which affect individual citizen particularly the trader and the manufacturer, violation of which is subject to interpretation and punishment.

Thus, Indian experience with regulation is not new. Till recently all sectors of the economy were regulated. In the infrastructure sectors, the governments or their instrumentalities owned, operated and regulated services. The Central Government, the Central Electricity Authority, State Governments and State Electricity Boards regulated the power sectors under the authority of the Electricity (Supply) Act, 1948, and Indian Electricity Act, 1910; the Department of Telecommunications regulated the telecom sector under the Indian Wireless Telegraphic Act, 1933, and the Indian Telegraphic Act, 1885; the Central Government, State Governments, Directorate General of Shipping and Dock Labour Boards regulated the port sector under the Port Act, 1908, the Major Port Trusts Act, 1963, the Merchants Shipping Act, 1958, and the Dock Workers (Safety, Health and Welfare) Act, 1986. Then there are other regulators created under various other Acts in relation to environment, safety, labour etc. The deep rooted belief at that time was that only public sector can provide the basic infrastructure facilities. Therefore, the entry of the private sector should be strictly regulated if it cannot be altogether prevented. There was no attempt to distance the government's role as the policy-maker and protector of public interest from its role as operator or provider of services. In this form of set-up, efficiency, productivity and consumer interests were not relevant. Further, it was believed that accountability to the government and through the government to the Parliament and legislature was sufficient to ensure accountability and transparency and disclosure to public was not necessary. This form of regulation lead to unlimited discretionary power to the service provider, inefficiency, poor quality of service, lack of transparency and accountability, negligible flow of private capital, financial mismanagement, and lack of protection of consumers' interests.

Our regulatory systems have evolved as a part of government. Their scope and extent have expanded with the economy becoming more broad based and its expansion into more sectors. In the past there have also been regulators appointed outside the normal government administrative systems, like Reserve Bank of India (RBI) and Securities and Exchange Board of India (SEBI). Many years ago, Forward Markets Commission (FMC) was an independent regulator of forward markets. The Tariff Commission was an independent regulatory body which recommended tariff levels. The Company Law Board, the Bureau of Industrial Finance and Restructuring (BIFR) for sick companies, the Human Rights Commission etc. were others. Some of these were, however, abolished during the 1960s and 1970s and many were brought under the control of the government. Neither RBI nor SEBI constituted under the Resolution of the Government of India, Department of Economic Affairs dated 12th April, 1988 can be called an independent regulator. The RBI ultimately reports to the Finance Ministry and takes over all directions from the government. Till 1992 the SEBI was also not an independent regulator as the appeal against it laid before the Finance Secretary and not to the courts. Other such bodies like the Company Law Board are, in fact, part of the government mechanism. The BIFR has powers but like a government body it lacks speed. Other bodies like human rights, minorities and disinvestments commissions are without powers.

Infrastructure has been recognized as a major constraint on economic development and growth, requiring vast investments. The Government does not have such huge funds for investment. The entry of private investment — both domestic and foreign is thus inevitable and most essential in addition to public investment. The investors who would be required to bring in large funds need a regulatory environment which is independent, transparent, consistent and predictable. Such environment was not available within the constraints of Government departments. The independent regulatory mechanisms were mooted as the solution and such independent regulators were created for telecom, electricity, insurance, port sectors.

Liberalization, Privatization and Globalization (LPG) lead to reforms and liberalization of Indian economy in 1990s with service sectors like power, telecom being gradually thrown open to private investment and competition. Telecom sector was opened up in 1991 with private investment being permitted in manufacture of telephone equipment and value added services were allowed private investment in 1992. The National Telecom Policy in 1994 reiterated the government's commitment to further liberalize the sector. In power sector, guidelines of 1991 allowed private sector entry in the generation of power, followed by several initiatives to attract and facilitate private investment in power sector. Private sector participation by way of leasing port facilities was permitted in 1994 and investment for creation of new facilities in the existing ports or establishing new ports in 1996.

Unlike UK where the electricity industry restructuring and positioning of regulator was simultaneous, in India regulation of power and telecom sectors was not contemplated or provided for as a part of initial reform process. In these two sectors the regulators came much later, whereas in case of port sector the decision to set-up tariff regulatory authority was announced as part of policy statement in 1996. In the insurance sector the regulatory authority has preceded the opening of the sector. Thus, progressively there is realization in the government that reforms can not be put into force without independent regulation and for that a regulatory authority should be set-up.

3.4.1. *Regulation of Securities and Exchange Market*

Gaps in securities market regulation are worldwide phenomenon. Strong regulation is vital for market development, financial stability, and growth. Securities market regulation refers to the regulation of public issuers of securities, secondary markets, asset management products, and market intermediaries (brokers, dealers, advisers). Regulation is intended to address asymmetries of information between issuers and investors, clients and financial intermediaries (such as brokers and dealers), and between counterparties and transactions. It is also meant to ensure the smooth functioning of trading and clearing and settlement mechanisms to prevent market disruption and foster investor confidence. Securities market regulation has three core objectives: to protect investors; to ensure that markets are fair, efficient, and transparent; and to reduce systemic risk. In India the regulatory and supervisory developments in 1990s in respect of the capital markets were mainly on the basis of the recommendations of the Committee on Financial System (1991) which advocated in favour of making the Securities and Exchange Board of India (SEBI) the official market regulator. Prior to this the capital market was regulated by the Controller of Capital Issues which fixed the equity issue prices in the primary market. Transactions in the secondary market were regulated by the Securities (Contract) Regulation Act, 1956. In April 1988, the Securities and Exchange Board of India was set-up, but, without statutory powers. In 1992, the SEBI obtained statutory powers following the passage of the SEBI Act, 1992.

The Securities and Exchange Board of India Act, 1992 (the SEBI Act) has been enacted for the establishment of the Board with the object of protecting the interests of investors in securities and to promote the development and to regulate the securities market and for matters connected therewith or incidental thereto. Securities market is very dynamic and the laws governing it have to be responsive to the market needs. The SEBI Act was amended in the years 1995, 1999 and 2002 to meet the requirements of changing needs of the securities market and responding to the development in the securities market.

The Securities and Exchange Board of India Act, 1992, provides for the establishment of Securities and Exchange Board of India to regulate the securities and exchange market in India. The Central Government shall establish a Board by the name of the Securities and Exchange Board of India. The Board shall be a body corporate, having perpetual succession and a common seal, with power subject to the provisions of this Act, to acquire, hold and dispose of property, both movable and immovable, and to contract, and shall, by the said name, sue or be sued. The head office of the Board shall be at Mumbai. The Board may establish offices at other places in India.[96] The Board shall consist of (a) Chairman; (b) two members from amongst the officials of the Ministry of the Central Government dealing with Finance and administration of the Companies Act, 1956; (c) one member from amongst the officials of the Reserve Bank; (d) five other members of whom at least three shall be the whole-time members, to be appointed by the Central Government.[97] The Chairman and members referred to in clauses (a) and (d) of sub-section (1) shall be appointed by the Central Government and the members referred to in clauses (b) and (c) of that sub-section shall be nominated by the Central Government and the Reserve Bank respectively.[98] The Chairman and the other members referred to in clauses (a) and (d) of sub-section (1) shall be persons of ability, integrity and standing who have shown capacity in dealing with problems relating to securities market or have special knowledge or experience of law, finance, economics, accountancy, administration or in any other discipline which, in the opinion of the Central Government, shall be useful to the Board.[99] The term of office and other conditions of service of the Chairman and the members referred to in Clause (d) of sub-section (1) of Section 4 shall be such as may be prescribed.[100] Notwithstanding anything contained in sub-section (1), the Central Government shall have the right to terminate the services of the Chairman or a member appointed under clause (d) of sub-section (1) of Section 4, at any time before the expiry of the period prescribed under sub-section (1), by giving him notice of not less than three months in writing or three months' salary and allowances *in lieu* thereof, and the Chairman or a member, as the case may be, shall also have the right to relinquish his office, at any time before the expiry of the period prescribed under sub-section (1), by giving to the Central Government notice of not less than three months in writing.[101]

Functions of Board

Subject to the provisions of this Act, it shall be the duty of the Board to protect the interests of investors in securities and to promote the development of, and to regulate the securities market, by such measures as it thinks fit. Without prejudice to the generality of the foregoing provisions, the measures referred to therein may provide for —

(i) regulating the business in stock exchanges and any other securities markets;
(ii) registering and regulating the working of stock brokers, sub-brokers, share transfer agents, bankers to an issue, trustees of trust deeds, registrars to an issue, merchant bankers, underwriters, portfolio managers, investment advisers and such other intermediaries who may be associated with securities markets in any manner;
(iii) registering and regulating the working of the depositories, participants, custodians of securities, foreign institutional investors, credit rating agencies and such other intermediaries as the Board may, by notification, specify in this behalf;
(iv) registering and regulating the working of venture capital funds and collective investment schemes, including mutual funds;
(v) promoting and regulating self-regulatory organizations;
(vi) prohibiting fraudulent and unfair trade practices relating to securities markets;
(vii) promoting investors' education and training of intermediaries of securities markets;
(viii) prohibiting insider trading in securities;
(ix) regulating substantial acquisition of shares and take-over of companies;
(x) calling for information from, undertaking inspection, conducting inquiries and audits of the stock exchanges, mutual funds, other persons associated with the securities market inter-mediaries and self-regulatory organizations in the securities market;
(xi) calling for information and record from any bank or any other authority or board or corporation established or constituted by or under any Central, State or Provincial Act in respect of any transaction in securities which is under investigation or inquiry by the Board;
(xii) performing such functions and exercising such powers under the provisions of the Securities Contracts (Regulation) Act, 1956, as may be delegated to it by the Central Government;
(xiii) levying fees or other charges for carrying out the purposes of this section;

(xiv) conducting research for the above purposes;

(xv) calling from or furnishing to any such agencies, as may be specified by the Board, such information as may be considered necessary by it for the efficient discharge of its functions; and

(xvi) performing such other functions as may be prescribed.[102]

No order passed by the Board or the adjudicating officer under this Act shall be appealable except as provided in Section 15T or Section 20 and no Civil Court shall have jurisdiction in respect of any matter which the Board or the adjudicating officer is empowered by, or under, this Act to pass any order and no injunction shall be granted by any court or other authority in respect of any action taken or to be taken in pursuance of any order passed by the Board or the adjudicating office by, or under, this Act.[103]

Securities Appellate Tribunal — The Central Government shall, by notification, establish one or more Appellate Tribunals to be known as the Securities Appellate Tribunal to exercise the jurisdiction, powers and authority conferred on such Tribunal by or under this Act or any other law for the time being in force. The Central Government shall also specify in the notification the matters and places in relation to which the Securities Appellate Tribunal may exercise jurisdiction.[104] A Securities Appellate Tribunal shall consist of a Presiding Officer and two other Members, to be appointed, by notification, by the Central Government.[105] A person shall not be qualified for appointment as the Presiding Officer of a Securities Appellate Tribunal unless he is a sitting or retired Judge of the Supreme Court or a sitting or retired Chief Justice of a High Court. Provided that the Presiding Officer of the Securities Appellate Tribunal shall be appointed by the Central Government in consultation with the Chief Justice of India or his nominee. A person shall not be qualified for appointment as Member of a Securities Appellate Tribunal unless he is a person of ability, integrity and standing, who has shown capacity in dealing with problems relating to securities market and has qualification and experience of corporate law, securities law, finance, economics or accountancy.[106] The Presiding Officer and every other Member of a Securities Appellate Tribunal shall hold office for a term of five years from the date on which he enters upon his office and shall be eligible for re-appointment. However, no person shall hold office as the Presiding Officer of the Securities Appellate Tribunal after he has attained the age of sixty-eight years. Further, no person shall hold office as Member of the Securities Appellate Tribunal after he has attained the age of sixty-two years.[107]

Any person aggrieved, — (a) by an order of the Board made, on and after the commencement of the Securities Laws (Second Amendment) Act, 1999, under this Act, or the rules or regulations made thereunder; or (b) by an order made by an adjudicating officer under this Act, may prefer an appeal to a Securities Appellate Tribunal having jurisdiction in the matter. However, no appeal shall lie to the Securities Appellate Tribunal from an order made: (a) by the Board on and after the commencement of the Securities Laws (Second Amendment) Act, 1999; or (b) by an adjudicating officer, with the consent of the parties. Every appeal under sub-section (1) shall be filed within a period of forty-five days from the date on which a copy of the order made by the Board or the adjudicating officer, as the case may be, is received by him and it shall be in such form and be accompanied by such fee as may be prescribed. However, the Securities Appellate Tribunal may entertain an appeal after the expiry of the said period of forty-five days, if it is satisfied that there was sufficient cause for not filing it within that period.

The Securities Appellate Tribunal shall not be bound by the procedure laid down by the Code of Civil Procedure, 1908, but shall be guided by the principles of natural justice and, subject to the other provisions of this Act and of any rules, the Securities Appellate Tribunal shall have powers to regulate their own procedure including the places at which they shall have their sittings.[108] No civil court shall have jurisdiction to entertain any suit or proceeding in respect of any matter which an Adjudicating Officer appointed under this Act or a Securities Appellate Tribunal constituted under this Act is empowered by or under this Act to determine and no injunction shall be granted by any court or other authority in respect of any action taken or to be taken in pursuance of any power conferred by or under this Act.[109] Any person aggrieved by any decision or order of the Securities Appellate Tribunal may file an appeal to the Supreme Court within sixty days from the date of communication of the decision or order of the Securities Appellate Tribunal to him on any question of law arising out of such order. However, the Supreme Court may, if it is satisfied that the applicant was prevented by sufficient cause from filing the appeal within the said period, allow it to be filed within a further period not exceeding sixty days.[110]

Power to make rules and regulations — The Central Government may, by notification, make rules for carrying out the purposes of this Act.[111] The Board may, by notification, make regulations consistent with this Act and the rules made thereunder to carry out the purposes of this Act.[112]

3.4.2. *Regulation in the Telecom Sector*

The pressure on the Government to restructure the Telecom Sector resulted in the first liberalization initiative in 1984. Until then, the Indian Telecom Sector was the monopoly of the Government and was characterized by under-investment, outdated equipment, and growth that was beneath the actual potential. The Government of India set-up the Athreya Committee in 1990 for restructuring Indian Telecommunication Sector and another committee reviewed the India Telegraph Act of 1885 in 1992. Further, the Government announced in 1991 that all services, other than basic services, would be opened up to private investment in July 1992. These services, termed value-added services, included cellular mobile telephone, radio paging, e-mail, video-conferencing, data services, video text and audio text services, and voice mail.

The NTP 94 (National Telecom Policy of 1994) heralded a new era in the Indian Telecom Sector with the intention to promote the expansion and improvement of India's basic telecommunication infrastructure, particularly to the underserved rural areas. The focus of this policy was on telecommunication for all and telecommunication within the reach of all. This meant ensuring the availability of telephone on demand as early as possible. Another basic objective of the policy was to achieve universal service covering all villages as early as possible. With regard to the quality of telecom services, the policy aimed to match world standards. Provision of the "widest permissible range of services" at "reasonable prices" was also explicitly stated in this policy. Some of the main objectives of NTP 94 were not achieved. In addition, there were several other factors that necessitated a relook into the existing policy framework. New technologies, rapid growth, and the worldwide trends ushering in competition brought out the limitations of this policy as a comprehensive strategy for the sector.

In order to overcome the difficulties of NTP 94, and in view of the new developments, the government announced the NTP 99 (National Telecom Policy 1999) in March 1999. This policy made several adjustments to the telecommunication regulatory framework. The main objectives of this policy were as follows:

- availability of affordable and effective communications to the citizens to further the country's social and economic goals;

- strive to provide a balance between the provision of universal service to all uncovered areas, including the rural area, and the provision of high-level services capable of meeting the needs of the country's economy;
- encourage development of telecommunication facilities in remote, hilly, and tribal areas of the country;
- convert PCOs, wherever justified, into public tele-info centres having multi-media capability like ISDN services, remote database access, government and community information systems, etc.; and
- provide a competitive environment in both urban and rural areas offering equal opportunities and level playing field for all players in a time-bound manner.

One of the biggest impediments to the success of NTP 94 was the lack of an effective and autonomous regulatory authority, with clear lines of jurisdiction, for implementing the telecom policy. Hence, a comprehensive Bill, titled Telecom Regulatory Authority of India Bill, 1995, was prepared and TRAI came into being in 1997. TRAI was reconstituted in 2000 through an ordinance and a smaller body without judicial powers was formed. A clear distinction was made between its advisory and regulatory functions. The amendment to the TRAI Act made it mandatory for the government to seek recommendations of TRAI on issues like the need and timing of new service providers and the terms and conditions applicable to them. However, such recommendation would not be binding on the government. TRAI's orders on tariffs and the terms and conditions of interconnectivity would, however, be binding, irrespective of anything contained in licence agreements issued prior to the ordinance.

A separate dispute settlement and appellate body the Telecom Disputes Settlement and Appellate Tribunal (TDSAT) was set-up to adjudicate any dispute between a licensor and a licensee, among service providers, and between a service provider and a group of consumers. It would also hear and dispose of any appeals against the decisions of the new TRAI.

The TRAI Act, 1997, establishes Telecom Regulatory Authority of India with a view to ensuring fair competition between different service providers and protecting consumer interests.[113] The Authority is a body corporate by the above-mentioned name, having perpetual succession and a common seal, with power, subject to the provisions of the Act, to contract and to acquire, hold and dispose of both movable and immovable property, and shall by the same name sue and be sued.[114] TRAI consists of a chairperson, not less than two whole-time members, and not more than two part-time members, to be appointed by the Central Government.[115] Its head office is at New Delhi.[116] The chairperson and members are appointed from amongst persons who have special knowledge of, and professional experience in, telecommunication, industry, finance, accountancy, law, management, or consumer affairs.[117] A person in government service shall not be appointed as a member, unless such person has held the post of secretary or additional secretary in the Government of India or a State Government for a period of not less than three years.[118] Before appointing any person as chairperson or member, the Central Government shall satisfy itself, that the person does not have any such financial or other interest as is likely to affect prejudicially his functions.[119] The chairperson and other members shall hold office for a term not exceeding three years, from the date on which he enters upon office or until he attains the age of sixty-five years, whichever is earlier.[120] The chairperson shall have powers of general superintendence and direction in the conduct of affairs of the TRAI. He shall in addition to presiding over TRAI meeting exercise and discharge such powers and functions of TRAI and shall discharge such other powers and functions as may be prescribed.[121]

Notwithstanding anything contained in the Indian Telegraph Act, 1885, functions of TRAI shall be:

(a) to make recommendations, either *suo motu* or on a licensor's request, on the following matters, namely:

- (i) need and timing for introduction of new service provider;
- (ii) terms and conditions of licence to service providers;
- (iii) revocation of licence for non-compliance of terms and conditions of licence;
- (iv) measures to facilitate competition and promote efficiency in operation of telecommunication services so as to facilitate growth in such services;
- (v) technological improvement in services provided by service providers;
- (vi) type of equipment to be used by service providers after inspection of equipment used in the network;
- (vii) measures for development of telecommunication technology, and any other matter relatable to telecommunication industry, in general; and
- (viii) efficient management of available spectrum.

(b) to discharge the following functions:

(i) ensure technical compliance of terms and condition of licence;

(ii) fix terms and conditions of inter-connectivity among service providers, notwithstanding anything contained in the terms and conditions of the licence granted before commencement of the Telecom Regulatory Authority of India (Amendment) Act, 2008.

(iii) ensure technical compatibility and effective inter-connection between different service providers;

(iv) regulate arrangement amongst service providers of sharing their revenue derived from providing telecommunication services;

(v) lay down standard of quality of service to be provided by service providers, ensure quality of service, and conduct periodical surveys of such service provided by service providers, so as to protect interests of consumers of telecommunication services;

(vi) lay down and ensure time periods for providing local and long distance circuits of telecommunication between different service providers;

(vii) maintain register of inter-connect agreements and of all such other matters as may be provided in regulations;

(viii) to keep register maintained under clause (vii) open for inspection to any member of the public on payment of such fee and compliance of such other requirement, as may be provided in the regulations; and

(ix) ensure compliance of universal service obligations;

(c) to levy fees and other charges at such rates and in respect of such services, as may be determined by regulations; and

(d) to perform such other functions including such administrative and financial functions as may be entrusted to it by the Central Government or as may be necessary to carry out the provisions of this Act.

Recommendations of TRAI specified in clause (a) of this section shall not be binding upon the Central Government. The Central Government shall seek recommendations of TRAI in respect of matters specified in sub-clauses (i) and (ii) of clause (a) of this section in respect of a new licence to be issued to a service provider, and TRAI shall forward its recommendations within 60 days from the date on which that government sought recommendations. TRAI may request the Central Government to furnish such information as may be necessary for making recommendations under sub-clauses (i) and (ii) of clause (a) of this section and that government shall supply such information within seven days from the receipt of such request. The Central Government may issue a licence to a service provider, if no recommendations are received from TRAI within the period specified above or within such period as may be mutually agreed upon between the Central Government and TRAI. If the Central Government, after having considered TRAI's recommendations comes to a *prima facie* conclusion that such recommendations cannot be accepted or need modifications it shall refer the recommendations back to TRAI for its reconsideration, and TRAI may within 15 days from the date of receipt of such reference, forward to the Central Government its recommendations after considering the reference made by that government. After receipt of further recommendations, if any, the Central Government shall take a final decision.[122]

The TRAI Act, 1997, has included provisions for settlement of disputes and appeals against decisions of the TRAI.[123] Appeals in this regard lay to the High Court.[124] The TRAI (Amendment) Act, 2000, provided for establishment of an appellate tribunal called the Telecom Disputes Settlement and Appellate Tribunal (TDSAT) to:

(i) adjudicate any dispute:
   (a) between a licensor and a licensee,
   (b) between two or more service providers, and
   (c) between a service provider and a group of consumers; and

(ii) hear and dispose of appeals against any direction, decision or order of the TRAI.[125]

The Central Government or a State Government or a local authority, or any person may make an application to the appellate tribunal for adjudication of any dispute referred to above.[126] Any of the above-mentioned, if aggrieved by any direction, decision or order made by the TRAI, may prefer an appeal to the appellate tribunal.[127] An appeal must be made within thirty days from the date on which a copy of the direction or order or decision of the TRAI is received. It has to be filed in such form, verified in such manner, and to be accompanied by such fee as may be prescribed.[128] The appellate tribunal may, however, entertain an appeal after the expiry of the above period, if it is satisfied that there was sufficient cause for not filing it within that period.[129] On receipt of an application or an appeal as mentioned above, the Appellate Tribunal may, after giving the parties to the dispute or the appellant an opportunity of being heard, pass such orders thereon as it thinks fit.[130] The appellate tribunal must send a copy of every order made by it to the parties to the dispute or the appeal, as the case may be, and to the TRAI.[131] The application and the appeal must be dealt with as expeditiously as possible and the appellate tribunal must endeavour to dispose it of finally within ninety days from the date of receipt of application or appeal, as the case may be.[132] Where the tribunal cannot dispose of an application or an appeal within ninety days, it shall record reasons in writing for not disposing it of within that period.[133] The tribunal may, for the purpose of disposing of an application or appeal, call for relevant records either on its own motion or otherwise, and make such orders as it thinks fit.[134]

The appellate tribunal consists of a chairperson and not more than two members to be appointed by notification by the Central Government.[135] Selection of chairperson and members is to be made in consultation with the Chief Justice of India.[136] The chairperson and members hold office for a term not exceeding three years from the date he enters into office.[137] However, no person can continue to hold office as chairperson after the age of seventy, and no person can continue to hold office as member after attaining the age of 75 years.[138] A person shall not be appointed as chairperson or member unless he:

(i) in the case of chairperson, has been a judge of the Supreme Court or the Chief Justice of a High Court; and
(ii) in the case of a member, has held the post of secretary to the Government of India or any equivalent post in the Central Government or State Government for not less than two years, or is a person who is well-versed in the field of technology, telecommunication, industry, commerce or administration.[139]

The jurisdiction and power of the tribunal are exercised by Benches[140] that comprise chairperson and one or more members, as the chairperson may deem fit.[141] Benches sit in New Delhi and at such places as the Central Government may, in consultation with chairperson, notify.[142] Chairperson may transfer a case from one Bench to another.[143] He may, from time-to-time, by notification, make provisions as to distribution of business of the tribunal amongst Benches, and also provide for matters that may be dealt with by each Bench.[144] He may transfer any case pending before a Bench for disposal to another Bench after notice to the parties and after hearing such of them as may desire to be heard.[145] All applications pending before the TRAI immediately before the date of establishment of the appellate tribunal stood transferred to the tribunal.[146] However, all disputes pending before the TRAI before commencement of the Telecom Regulatory Authority of India (Amendment) Act, 2000, continued to be adjudicated by the TRAI in accordance with the provisions of the Act as they existed before the amendment, until the establishment of the Appellate Ttribunal.[147] All cases of disputes referred to above are transferred by the TRAI to the Tribunal on its establishment.[148] No civil court has jurisdiction to entertain any suit or proceeding in any matter, which the Appellate Tribunal is empowered by or under this Act to determine. Likewise, no injunction is to be granted by any court or other authority regarding any action taken or to be taken in pursuance of any power conferred by or under this Act.[149]

The Appellate Tribunal is not bound by the procedure laid down by the CPC, but it is guided by the principles of natural justice. Moreover, subject to other provisions of this Act, the Tribunal has powers to regulate to own procedure.[150] Notwithstanding anything contained in the CPC, an appeal against an order, which is not an interlocutory order, lies to the Supreme Court on one or more grounds specified in Section 100 of the CPC.[151] No appeal lies against the Appellate Tribunal's decision or order that had the consent of the parties.[152] Every appeal has to be made within a period of ninety days from the date of the decision or order appealed against.[153] The Supreme Court may, however, entertain an appeal after expiry of the above period, if it is satisfied that the appellant was prevented by sufficient cause from preferring appeal in time.

The Government is the policy-maker and licensor of services. It determines the extent as well as the timing of introduction of competition in the various segments of the Telecom Sector. As mentioned above, the regulator makes recommendations to the government on issues like the need and timing of introduction of new service providers as well as the terms and conditions of licences. Competition has been introduced in phases in the sector and several other steps have been taken in the course of regulatory reforms.

At the heart of the reforms process and the creation of a regulatory authority was the objective of introducing more transparency in the decision-making process. Prior to reforms and the creation of the regulator, activities like tariff setting were conducted behind closed doors. The general public was neither informed of nor involved in any decision-making activity. There was no forum for utilities or the public to express their views or to demand information that led to consequent decision. Hence, one of the important tasks that lay in front of the regulator was to induce openness in decision-making and invite public participation. TRAI has generally been following a transparent and consultative approach in its decisions, tariff review exercises, recommendations etc.

Regulatory reforms have brought about greater awareness on various issues in the sector. Besides this, the ordinary citizen has also begun expressing his/her views and informing the regulator on various issues. There is a provision whereby consumer organizations are registered with the regulator and have access to various consultation documents. This has been part of the regulator's attempt to play a role in the education of these bodies and, hence, create awareness. Moreover, in the post-reform years, access of the public to data and information has increased substantially. At the same time, service providers have also got an opportunity to be an integral party of the decision-making process. Service providers from various segments of the industry have been able to openly discuss their views on various matters and the problems likely to be faced by them. Often, the regulator has also held informal discussion with groups of service providers to discuss the problems that would be faced by them in the implementation of certain issues, leading to greater transparency of processes.

3.4.3. *Regulation of Electricity Sector*

Since the early 1990s, the power sector in India has been going through a process of reforms and restructuring. In the first phase of reforms, beginning in 1991, the focus was on the induction of private investment into power generation. In 1991, the government opened up the Indian power sector by an amendment to the Electricity (Supply) Act, 1948, thereby promoting the entry of independent power producers. The second phase of reforms began in the mid-1990s when there was widespread realization that more comprehensive reforms were required, including changes in the regulatory set-up to tackle the problems facing the sector. This paved the way for chartering a new policy and in December 1996, the Common Minimum Action Plan for Power (CMNAPP) was framed with primary agenda of setting-up regulatory commissions at the Centre and State levels. Besides, it proposed to restructure and corporatize the State Electricity Boards (SEBs), to allow them greater autonomy and permit them to operate along commercial lines. The other important agenda were the rationalization of tariffs. In 1998, the Electricity (Supply) Act, 1948, was further amended to facilitate private sector participation in power transmission services.

The reforms programme gained momentum with the enactment of the Electricity Regulatory Commissions Act, 1998. Under the provisions of this Act, the Central Government constituted the Central Electricity Regulatory Commission (CERC) to regulate the operations/businesses relating to the Central sector as well as inter-State issues. The CERC regulates the tariff of generating companies, owned or controlled by the Government of India, and any other generating company which has a composite scheme for generation and the interstate transmission of energy including tariff of the transmission utilities. A number of States followed suit in the creation of their own State Regulatory Commissions either through the enabling provision of the Central Act or their respective State Acts.

The Electricity Act, 2003, notified on June 2, 2003 and brought in force from June 10, 2003, has replaced the three existing Acts, namely the Indian Electricity Act, 1910, the Electricity (Supply) Act, 1948, and the Electricity Regulatory Commissions Act, 1998. The conceptual framework underlying the new legislation is that India's electricity sector must be opened to the competition. Thus the Electricity Act, 2003, has consolidated the laws relating to generation, transmission, distribution, trading, and use of electricity, and for generally taking measures conducive to development of electricity industry. Other purposes of the Act are promoting competition between generators, transmitters, and other players in the industry; protecting interests of consumers; supply of electricity to all areas; rationalization of electricity tariff; ensuring transparent policies regarding subsidies; promotion of efficient and environmentally benign policies; constitution of Central Electricity Authority and Regulatory Commissions; and establishment of an Appellate Tribunal.[154] The Act provides for two commissions, namely Central Electricity Regulatory Commission (CERC)[155] and State Electricity Regulatory Commission (SERC).[156] A Joint Commission may be constituted by an agreement to be entered into (i) by two or more governments of States, or agreement; and (ii) by the Central Government in respect of one or more Union Territories and one or more governments of States.[157]

The functions of the CERC and SERCs under this Act are different from those under the 1998 Act. There are three distinct roles that ERCs have to play:

1. **Core Role:** This role includes tariff regulation, monitoring quality of service, adjudication of disputes, enforcing licensing conditions, monitoring compliance, and redressing grievances.
2. **Recommendatory Role:** If approval (of licences, for example) does not come under its jurisdiction, the ERC can give its recommendations to the concerned authorities.
3. **Advisory Role:** In this role, the ERC provides to the Government, on request, information and advice on matters of importance to the sector.

Central Electricity Regulatory Commission — The Act provides that the Central Commission established under section 3 of the Electricity Regulatory Commissions Act, 1998, and functioning as such immediately before the appointed date, is to be deemed the CERC under the 2003 Act. The chairperson, members, secretary and other officers and employees thereof are deemed to have been appointed under the 2003 Act, and they continue to hold office on the same terms and conditions on which they were appointed under the 1998 Act.[158] The chairperson and other members appointed under the 1998 Act may, on the recommendations of the selection committee constituted under the Act, be allowed to opt for terms and conditions under the 2003 Act by the Central Government.[159] CERC is to be a body corporate by the name aforesaid, having perpetual succession and a common seal with power to acquire, hold and dispose of property, both movable and immovable, and to contract, and shall, by the same name, sue or be sued.[160] The head office of the CERC shall be at such place as the Central Government may, by notification, specify.[161]

CERC consists of (i) a chairperson and three members; and (ii) the chairperson of the central electricity authority, appointed under section 70 of the Act, as the *ex-officio* member.[162] The chairperson and members of CERC are appointed by a Central Government on the recommendations of a selection committee.[163] The chairperson and members are to be persons, who have adequate knowledge of, or experience in, or shown capacity in dealing with, problems relating to engineering, law, economics, commerce, finance or management. They are to be appointed in the following manner: (i) one person having qualifications and experience in engineering with specialization in generation, transmission or distribution of electricity; (ii) one person having qualifications and experience in finance; and (iii) two persons having qualifications and experience in economics, commerce, law or management. Not more than one person from a particular category shall be appointed under clause (iii).[164] Notwithstanding anything contained in the above provision, the Central Government may appoint any person as the chairperson from amongst persons who are, or have been, judges of the Supreme Court or Chief Justice of a High Court. No appointment of a judge shall be made, except after consultation with the Chief Justice of India.[165] The chairperson or any other member shall not hold any other office.[166] The chairperson shall be the chief executive of the CERC.[167] The Central Government shall constitute a selection committee for selecting members of the Appellate Tribunal and the chairperson and members of the CERC. It will consist of:

(i) member of the Planning Commission in charge of the energy sector, who will be chairperson of the committee;
(ii) secretary in-charge of the Central Government Ministry dealing with legal affairs, as member;
(iii) chairperson of Public Enterprise Selection Board, as member;
(iv) a person to be nominated by the Central Government from amongst persons holding post of chairperson or Managing Director, by whatever name called, of any public financial institution, specified in section 4-A of the Companies Act;
(v) a person to be nominated by the Central Government from amongst person holding post of Director or head of the institution, by whatever name called, of any research, technical or management institution; and
(vi) Secretary in-charge of the Central Government Ministry dealing with power who shall be the convener of the committee.[168]

This requirement is not applicable where the chairperson of the Central Commission is or has been a Supreme Court Judge or Chief Justice of a High Court.[169]

CERC shall discharge the following functions:

(i) to regulate tariff of generating companies owned or controlled by the Central Government;
(ii) to regulate tariff of generating companies other than those owned or controlled by the Central Government specified in (i), if such generating companies enter into or otherwise have a

composite scheme for generation and sale of electricity in more than one State;

(iii) to regulate the inter-state transactions of electricity;

(iv) to determine tariff for inter-state transmission of electricity;

(v) to issue licences to persons to function as transmission licensee and electricity trader with respect to their inter-state operations;

(vi) to adjudicate upon dispute involving generating companies or transmission licensee in regard to matters connected with (i) to (iv) above, and to refer any dispute for arbitration;

(vii) to levy any fees for the purpose of this Act;

(viii) to specify grid code having regard to grid standards;

(ix) to specify and enforce standards with respect to quality, continuity and reliability of service by licensees;

(x) to fix trading margin in inter-state trading of electricity, if considered necessary; and

(xi) to discharge such other functions as may be assigned under this Act.[170]

CERC shall advise the Central Government on all or any of the following matters, namely: (i) formulation of national electricity policy and tariff policy; (ii) promotion of competition, efficiency and economy in activities of electricity industry; (iii) promotion of investment in electricity industry; and (iv) any other matter referred to CERC by government.[171] CERC shall ensure transparency while exercising its powers discharging its functions.[172] In discharging its functions, CERC shall be guided by the National Electricity Policy (NEP), National Electricity Plan and Tariff Policy published under section 3 of the Act by the Central Government, in consultation with the State Governments and the Electricity Authority.[173]

Section 178 gives powers to the Central Commission to make regulations. It adds some other functions primarily in relation to the SERCs. The Central Commission may, by notification make regulations consistent with this Act and the rules generally to carry out the provisions of this Act.[174] In particular and without prejudice to the generality of the power contained in sub-section (1), such regulations may provide for all or any of the following matters, namely:

(i) rates, charges and terms and conditions in respect of intervening transmission facilities under proviso to section 36;

(ii) payment of the transmission charges and a surcharge under sub-clause (ii) of clause (d) of sub-section (2) of section 38.

(iii) reduction and elimination of surcharge and cross-subsidies under second proviso to sub-clause (ii) of clause (d) of sub-section (2) of section 38.

(iv) payment of transmission charges and a surcharge under sub-clause (ii) of clause (c) of section 40.

(v) proportion of revenues from other business to be utilized for reducing the transmission and wheeling charges under proviso to section 41.

The Central Government may establish a committee known as the Central Advisory Committee (CAC),[175] consisting of not more than thirty-one members, to represent the interests of commerce, industry, transport, agriculture, labour, consumers, non-governmental organizations, and academic and research bodies in the electricity sector.[176] The chairperson of the CERC shall be the *ex-officio* chairperson of the CAC and members of the commission, and secretary to the Government of India, in-charge of consumer affairs and public distribution shall be the *ex-officio* members of the committee.[177] The objects of the CAC are to advise CERC on (i) major questions of policy; (ii) matters relating to quality, continuity and extent of service provided by licensees; (iii) compliance by licensees with conditions and requirements of their licence; (iv) protection of consumer interest; and (v) electricity supply and overall standards of performance by utilities.[178]

Every State Government shall, within six months from the appointed date (which the Central Government may, by notification, appoint), by notification, constitute for the purpose of this Act, a commission (SERC).[179] However, State Regulatory Commission, established under the 1998 Act and functioning as such, shall be the State Commissions for the purpose of the 2003 Act, and the chairperson, members, secretary and other officers shall continue to hold office on the same terms and conditions on which they were appointed under the 1998 Act.[180] They might be allowed to opt for the terms and conditions under the 2003 Act by the concerned State Governments, if the selection committee constituted for selection of such chairperson and members recommends it.[181] SERC shall be a body corporate having permanent succession and a common seal, with power to acquire, hold, and dispose of property, both movable and immovable, and to contract and sue and be sued by the same name.[182] Head office of SERC shall be at such place as State Government may, by notification, specify.[183] SERC shall consist of not more than three members including chairperson.[184] The chairperson and members shall be appointed by State Government on the recommendation of a selection committee. The selection committee consists of:

(i) a person who has been a judge of a High Court, who shall be the chairperson of the selection committee;
(ii) the Chief Secretary of the concerned state; and
(iii) the chairperson of the Central Electricity Authority.

The recommendation of selection committee will, however, not be required, if a person who is or has been a High Court Judge is to be appointed as chairperson of SERC.[185]

Reference is to be made to the selection committee by State Government, and the selection committee is to suggest a panel of two names in the same manner as is described above in respect of the CERC.[186]

Functions of SERC are as follows:

(i) generation, supply, transmission and wheeling of electricity, wholesale, bulk or retail, as the case may be, within state, where open access has been permitted to a category of consumers, the state commission shall determine only wheeling charges, if any, for the said category of consumers;
(ii) regulate electricity purchase and procurement process of distribution licensees, including the price at which electricity shall be procured from generating companies or licensees or from other sources through agreements for purchase of power for distribution and supply of electricity;
(iii) facilitate intra-state transmissions and wheeling of electricity;
(iv) issue licences to persons seeking to act as transmission licensees, distribution licensees and electricity traders with respect to their operations within state;
(v) promote co-generation and generation of electricity from renewable sources of energy by passing suitable measures for connectivity with the grid and sale of electricity to any person, and also specify, for purchase of electricity from such sources, a percentage of the total consumption of electricity in the area of a distribution licence;
(vi) adjudicate upon disputes between licensees and generating companies, and to refer any such dispute for arbitration;
(vii) levy fee for the purpose of this Act;
(viii) specify State grid code, consistent with the grid code laid down by the CERC;

(ix) specify or enforce standard with respect to quality, continuity and reliability of service by licensees;

(x) fix trading margin in intra-state trading of electricity, if considered necessary; and

(xi) discharge such other functions as may be assigned to it under this Act.[187]

SERC may advise State Government on all or any of the following matters:

(i) promotion of competition, efficiency and economy in activities of electricity industry;

(ii) promotion of investment in electricity industry;

(iii) reorganization and restructuring of state electricity industry; and

(iv) matters concerning generation, transmission, distribution, and trading of electricity or any other matter referred to the state commission by that government.[188]

SERC shall ensure transparency while exercising its powers and discharging its functions.[189] In discharge of its functions, SERC shall be guided by the NEP, National Electricity Plan and Tariff Policy announced by the Central Government.[190] There is a State Advisory Committee similar to CAC.[191]

A Joint Commission may be constituted by an agreement between two or more State Governments or by the Central Government, in respect of one or more Union Territories, and one or more States. It shall be in force for such period and shall be subject to renewal for each further period, if any, as may be stipulated in the agreement.[192] The joint commission constituted under the 1998 Act and functioning as such immediately before the appointed day, shall be the joint commission for the purpose of the 2003 Act. Its chairperson, members, secretary, and other officers and employees shall be deemed to have been appointed as such under the 2003 Act and shall continue to hold office on the same terms and conditions on which they were appointed under the 1998 Act.[193] The joint commission shall consist of one member from each of the participating States and Union Territories and the chairperson shall be appointed from amongst the members by consensus, failing which, by rotation.[194] The joint commission shall determine tariff in respect of the participating States or Union Territories separately and independently.[195]

The chairperson or other members shall hold office for five years from the date he enters upon his office. The chairperson or member in the CERC or a SERC shall not be eligible for re-appointment in the same capacity as chairperson or member in that commission in which he had earlier held office as such. Further, no chairperson or member shall hold office as such after he has attained the age of 65 years.[196]

Under section 110 of the Electricity Act, 2003, an appellate tribunal for electricity is to be established by the Central Government to hear appeals against orders of adjudicating officers or appropriate commissions (Central, State, and joint electricity regulatory commissions) established under the Act.[197] Any person, aggrieved by an order made by an adjudicating officer or appropriate commission, may prefer an appeal to the Appellate Tribunal for electricity.[198] Every appeal is to be filed within a period of 45 days from the date on which a copy of the order made by the adjudication officer or the appropriate commission is received by the aggrieved person, and it has to be in such form, verified in such manner and accompanied by such fee, as may be prescribed.[199] The tribunal may, however, entertain an appeal after the expiry of 45 days, if it is satisfied that there was sufficient cause for not filing it within that period.[200] In receipt of an appeal, the Appellate Tribunal may, after giving the parties an opportunity of being heard, pass such orders thereon as it thinks fit, confirming, modifying or setting aside the order appealed against.[201] The appellate tribunal must send a copy of its every order to the parties to the appeal, and to the concerned adjudicating officer or the appropriate commission.[202] The appellate tribunal has to deal with an appeal as expeditiously as possible, and endeavour to dispose of it finally within 180 days from the date of receipt of the appeal.[203] Where an appeal cannot be disposed of within the above-mentioned period, the Tribunal must record its reasons for the delay in writing.[204]

The appellate tribunal consists of a chairperson and three other members.[205] The jurisdiction of the appellate tribunal may be exercised by Benches thereof.[206] A Bench may be constituted of chairperson of the tribunal and two or more members, as the chairperson deems fit.[207] Every Bench, however, must include at least one judicial member and one technical member.[208] Benches of the Appellate Tribunal ordinarily sit at Delhi and such other places as the Central Government may, in consultation with the Appellate Tribunal's chairperson, notify.[209] Chairperson may transfer a member of the Tribunal from one bench to another Bench.[210]

A person is not qualified for appointment as chairperson of the tribunal unless he has been a judge of the Supreme Court or the Chief Justice of a High Court.[211] A person is qualified to be a member if:

(i) he is, or has been, or is qualified to be a judge of a High Court; or

(ii) he is, or has been a secretary for atleast one year in a Central Government Ministry or department, dealing with economic affairs or matters of infrastructure; or

(iii) he is, or has been a person of ability and standing, having adequate knowledge or experience in dealing with matters relating to electricity generation, transmission and distribution, and regulation, or economics, commerce, law or management.[212]

Chairperson of the tribunal is appointed by the Central Government after consultation with the Chief Justice of India.[213] Members of the tribunal are appointed by the Central Government on the recommendation of a selection committee, whose composition is given in Section 78(1) of the Act.[214] Tenure of chairperson and member of the Tribunal is for three years from the date on which they enter upon their office.[215] They are eligible for reappointment for a second term of three years.[216] Chairperson or member is not to hold office after (i) in the case of chairperson, the age of 70; and (ii) in the case of member, the age of 65.[217]

The tribunal is not bound by procedure laid down by the CPC, but is guided by the principles of natural justice, and, subject to other provisions of the Act, has the power to regulate its own procedure.[218] The tribunal, while trying a suit, has the same powers as are vested in a civil court under the CPC. An order by the appellate tribunal is executable as a decree of a civil court and, for this purpose; the tribunal has all the powers of a civil court.[219] The appellate tribunal may transmit any order made by it to a civil court having local jurisdiction and that civil court has to execute the order, as if it were a decree made by that court.[220]

The chairperson of the appellate tribunal exercises general power of superintendence over appropriate commissions.[221] Decisions of the tribunal are by majority.[222] A person preferring an appeal to the appellate tribunal under this Act may either appear in person or take the assistance of a legal practitioner of his choice to present his case before the appellate tribunal.[223] The appropriate commission may authorize one or more legal practitioners or any of its officer to act as presenting officers and every person so authorized may present the case with respect to any appeal before the appellate tribunal.[224]

Any person aggrieved by any decision or order of the appellate tribunal may file, within 60 days from the date of communication of the appellate tribunal's decision or order to him, an appeal to the Supreme Court on any one or more of the grounds specified in Section 100 of the CPC.[225] The Supreme Court, may, if it is satisfied that the appellant was prevented from filing an appeal within the above-specified period by sufficient cause, allow it to be filed within a further period of 60 days.[226]

The earlier Act had no provision for coordination between the CERC and SERCs. The FOIR (Forum of Indian Regulators) was voluntarily created; all members and chairpersons of ERCs would be its members, with the possible induction of all other regulators in the future. The FOIR enabled new SERCs to get to work quickly because of experience sharing. However, the FOIR did not enable the consistency in approach between SERCs that might also have resulted. Section 166 of the new Act has the following provisions:

1. The Central Government shall constitute a Coordination Committee consisting of the chairperson of the Central Commission and members thereof, the chairperson of the Authority, representatives of the generating companies and transmission licensees engaged in inter-state transmission of electricity for smooth and coordinated development of the power system in the country.
2. The Central Government shall also constitute a forum of regulators comprising the chairperson of the Central Commission and chairpersons of the State Commission.
3. The chairperson of the Central Commission shall be the chairperson of the forum of regulators referred to in sub-section (2).

Under the Act most of the states have constituted State Electricity Regulatory Commissions. These regulatory commissions have issued a number of regulations on issues related to service rules, appointment of consultants, advisory committees, consumer's right to information, complaint handling procedure, tariff, licensing etc.

It is thus observed that in the reform process, the regulatory commissions were envisaged to function independently, bring in greater transparency and improve information availability in the sector, and involve consumers in the regulatory process. The reform process and the consequent setting-up of regulatory commissions at the state-level has indeed brought about greater transparency and openness in the decision-making processes. The consultative process followed by the regulatory commissions has provided an opportunity to all the interested parties to be heard. The public hearing process followed by the commissions has also led to greater awareness among consumers about the sector and its related issues. An important outcome of the regulatory process has also been to put the resultant pressure on utilities, as they now have to work in an environment of transparency and consumer awareness. As a result of this, in general more information and data on the performance of the utilities are now available to the stakeholders. The regulatory process has helped not only the consumers, but also the utilities to openly put forth their views. The regulatory set-up has enabled the utilities, especially those in the public sector, to present their cases independent of the government.

3.4.4. *Regulation of Competition*

The economic crisis in which the country found itself finally led to the reforms that started in 1991. In 1990s India responded to the worldwide trend of globalization by opening up its economy, removing controls and resorting to liberalization. Correspondingly, it was felt that the Indian market should be geared to face competition from within the country and outside. The MRTP Act attracted sharp criticism as it proved to be ineffective in achieving the objectives stated in the Act. The Act failed in curbing concentration of economic power or regulating the diverse monopolistic, restrictive and unfair trade practices. Further, as the focus of the MRTP Act was more on the control of monopolies and the prohibition of monopolistic and restrictive trade practices, it was felt that the MRTP Act has "become obsolete in certain respects in the light of international economic developments relating more particularly to competition law, and there is need to shift the focus from curbing monopolies to promoting competition".[227] Hence, the Government decided to enact a new law for bringing competition in the Indian market. Therefore, the Central Government, constituted a high level committee in October 1999 under the chairmanship of S.V.S. Raghavan, to go into the aspects of competition policy and the related law. The committee submitted its report in May 2000. Its recommendations formed the basis of a draft Bill, which was presented in the Parliament. After considering its report and the suggestions from trade, industry and the general public, legislature enacted a new law called the Competition Act, 2002. The Bill got President's assent in January 2003, after two and half years.

The Competition Act, 2002

The Competition Act, 2002, received assent of President of India on January 13, 2003 and was published in the Gazette of India dated January 14, 2003. Some of the sections of the Act were brought into force on March 31, 2003 and majority of the other sections on June 19, 2003. The Competition Commission of India was established on October 14, 2003, but could not be made functional. Before the Chairman could enter office, a Public Interest Litigation was filed before the Supreme Court of India on October 30, 2003. Certain provisions of the Act and rules framed thereunder were subject matter of the legal challenge on the following grounds:

(i) The Competition Commission to be headed by a bureaucrat, would replace the MRTP Commission which had all along been headed by a Judicial Member; and
(ii) Commission has adjudicatory functions which mandated that the Chairperson must be a Judicial Member.

Hon'ble Supreme Court of India delivered its judgement, on the legal issues raised, on January 20, 2005. While disposing of the writ petition, the Hon'ble Supreme Court held that if an expert body is to be created by the Union Government, it might be appropriate for the Government to consider the creation of two separate bodies, one with expertise for advisory and regulatory functions and the other for adjudicatory functions based on the doctrine of separation of powers recognized by the Constitution. Keeping in view the observations of the Hon'ble Supreme Court of India, the Act was amended by the Competition (Amendment) Act, 2007. By the amendment the Government of India introduced provisions to constitute a judicial appellate authority while leaving the expert regulatory space to the Commission. The Competition Act, 2002 as amended, provides for setting-up of the Competition Commission of India (CCI) comprising of a Chairperson and a minimum of two and maximum of six Members. In addition, it also provides for establishment of a Competition Appellate Tribunal to hear and dispose of appeals against the order of the Commission and also to adjudicate on the claims of compensation that may arise from the findings of the Commission or orders of the Appellate Tribunal.

In accordance with the provisions of the Amendment Act the Competition Commission of India and the Competition Appellate Tribunal have been established. The provisions of the Competition Act relating to anti-competitive agreements and abuse of dominant position have been brought into force, w.e.f. 20th May, 2009 and the Commission has started dealing with cases under these provisions. The MRTP Act and Commission established thereunder have been repealed on the Competition Commission and Appellate Tribunal becoming fully operational.

As per the Preamble of the Act, the Act is for achieving the following objectives:

- to prevent practices having adverse effect on competition;
- to promote and sustain competition in markets;
- to protect the interests of consumers; and
- to ensure freedom of trade carried on by other participants in markets.

To achieve the above objectives the major areas of focus under the Act are:

(i) Prohibition of anti-competitive agreements;
(ii) Prohibition of abuse of dominance;
(iii) Regulation of Combinations (Acquisitions, Mergers and Amalgamations of Certain Size); and
(iv) Competition Advocacy.

Competition Commission of India

To achieve the above objectives, the Act provides for the establishment of a Commission known as Competition Commission of India (CCI). The Central Government may, by notification, establish the CCI.[228] The Commission is a body corporate having perpetual succession and a common seal with power, subject to provisions of this Act, to acquire, hold and dispose of property, both movable and immovable, and to contract, and shall, by the said name, sue or be sued.[229] The head office of the Commission shall be at such place as the Central Government may decide from time-to-time.[230] The Commission may establish offices at other places in India.[231]

Section 8 as substituted by the Competition (Amendment) Act, 2007 provides that the Commission shall consist of a Chairperson and not less than two and not more than six other Members to be appointed by the Central Government. The Chairperson and every other Member shall be a person of ability, integrity and standing and who has special knowledge of, and such professional experience of not less than fifteen years in, international trade, economics, business, commerce, law, finance, accountancy, management, industry, public affairs or competition matters, including competition law and policy, which in the opinion of the Central Government, may be useful to the Commission. The Chairperson and other Members shall be whole-time Members. The Chairperson and other Members of the Commission shall be appointed by the Central Government from a panel of names recommended by a Selection Committee consisting of—

(a)	the Chief Justice of India or his nominee	*Chairperson*
(b)	the Secretary in the Ministry of Corporate Affairs	*Member*
(c)	the Secretary in the Ministry of Law and Justice	*Member*
(d)	two experts of repute who have special knowledge of, and professional experience in international trade, economics, business, commerce, law, finance, accountancy, management, industry, public affairs or competition matters including competition law and policy	*Members*[232]

The Chairperson and every other Member shall hold office as such for a term of five years from the date on which he enters upon his office and shall be eligible for re-appointment. However, the Chairperson or other Members shall not hold office as such after he has attained the age of sixty-five years.[233] The Chairperson and other Members shall not, for a period of two years from the date on which they cease to hold office, accept any employment in, or connected with the management or administration of, any enterprise which has been a party to a proceeding before the Commission under this Act. However, nothing contained in this section shall apply to any employment under the Central Government or a State Government or local authority or in any statutory authority or any corporation established by or under any Central, State or Provincial Act or a Government company as defined in Section 617 of the Companies Act, 1956.[234]

When the Chairperson is unable to discharge his functions owing to absence, illness or any other cause, the senior-most Member shall discharge the functions of the Chairperson until the date on which the Chairperson resumes the charge of his functions.[235] The Chairperson or any other Member may, by notice in writing under his hand addressed to the Central Government, resign his office.[236] The Central Government may, by order, remove the Chairperson or any other Member from his office, if such Chairperson or Member, as the case may be,—

(a) is, or at any time has been, adjudged as an insolvent; or
(b) has engaged at any time, during his term of office, in any paid employment; or
(c) has been convicted of an offence which, in the opinion of the Central Government, involves moral turpitude; or
(d) has acquired such financial or other interest as is likely to affect prejudicially his functions as a Member; or
(e) has so abused his position as to render his continuance in office prejudicial to the public interest; or
(f) has become physically or mentally incapable of acting as a Member.[237]

However, no Member shall be removed from his office on the ground specified in Clause (d) or Clause (e) of that sub-section unless the Supreme Court, on a reference being made to it in this behalf by the Central Government, has, on an inquiry, held by it in accordance with such procedure as may be prescribed in this behalf by the Supreme Court, reported that the Member, ought on such ground or grounds to be removed.[238]

The Chairperson shall have the powers of general superintendence, direction and control in respect of all administrative matters of the Commission. The Chairperson may delegate such of his powers relating to administrative matters of the Commission, as he may think fit, to any other Member or officer of the Commission.[239] The Commission shall meet at such times and places, and shall observe such rules and procedure in regard to the transaction of business at its meetings as may be provided by regulations.[240] The Chairperson, if for any reason, is unable to attend a meeting of the Commission, the senior-most Member present at the meeting, shall preside at the meeting.[241] All questions which come-up before any meeting of the Commission shall be decided by a majority of the Members present and voting, and in the event of an equality of votes, the Chairperson or in his absence, the Member presiding, shall have a second or/casting vote. The quorum for such meeting shall be three Members.[242] A person or an enterprise or the Director-General may either appear in person or authorize one or more chartered accountants or company secretaries or cost accountants or legal practitioners or any of his or its officers to present his or its case before the Commission.[243]

Duties and Functions of Commission

It shall be the duty of the CCI is to eliminate practices having an adverse effect on competition, to promote and sustain competition in markets, to protect interests of consumers, and to ensure freedom of trade carried on by other participants in markets in India and matters connected therewith or incidental thereto.[244] This objective is distinguished from the objective of the MRTP Commission, which was to ensure that the "operation of the economic system does not result in the concentration of economic power to the common detriment" and "to prohibit the growth of monopolies and restrictive trade practices". The difference in the objectives of the MRTP Commission and the CCI reflects the difference in the nature of state intervention. While under the MRTP Act, the Commission was concerned with preventing the growth of monopolies, in the Competition Act the Commission is concerned with ensuring free and fair competition and protecting consumer interest. The shift is from control to regulation, and also from ideology to pragmatism. This is in consonance with the new economic policy of liberalization.[245]

The Act, in Section 3(1), prohibits enterprises or associations of enterprises or persons or association of persons from entering into agreements in respect of production, supply, distribution, storage, acquisition, or control of goods or provision of services that cause or are likely to cause an appreciable adverse effect on competition within India. Clause (2) of the section makes such agreement void. Clause (3) describes what types of agreements would be presumed to have an appreciable adverse effect on competition. Clause (4) declares that any agreement amongst enterprises or persons at different stages or levels of production chain in different markets, relating to production, supply, distribution, storage, sale or price of, or trade in goods or provision of services shall be in contravention of sub-section (1) if such agreement causes or is likely to cause an appreciable adverse effect on competition in India. Such agreements include (i) tie-in arrangement, (ii) exclusive supply agreement, (iii) exclusive distribution agreement, (iv) refusal to deal, and (v) resale price maintenance. Clause (5) says that nothing herein, however, applies to copyright or patent, etc.

Section 4 forbids abuse of dominant position. What amounts to abuse of dominance has been detailed in sub-section (2) of that section. According to section 4(2) there shall be an abuse of dominant position under sub-section (1), if an enterprise or a group: (a) directly or indirectly, imposes unfair or discriminatory — (i) condition in purchase or sale of goods or service; or (ii) price in purchase or sale (including predatory price) of goods or service; (b) limits or restricts — (i) production of goods or provision of services or market therefore; or (ii) technical or scientific development relating to goods or services to the prejudice of consumers; or (c) indulges in practice or practices resulting in denial of market access in any manner; or (d) makes conclusion of contracts subject to acceptance by other parties of supplementary obligations which, by their nature or according to commercial usage, have no connection with the subject of such contracts; or (e) uses its dominant position in one relevant market to enter into, or protect, other relevant market.

Combinations that mar competition are forbidden by Section 6 and they are void. No person or enterprise shall enter into a combination which causes or is likely to cause an appreciable adverse effect on competition within the relevant market in India and such a combination shall be void.[246] The CCI has the responsibility of identifying such objectionable agreements or combinations.

Powers of the Commission

Power to Issue Interim Orders

Where during an inquiry, the Commission is satisfied that an act in contravention of sub-section (1) of section 3 or sub-section (1) of section 4 or section 6 has been committed and continues to be committed or that such act is about to be committed, the Commission may, by order, temporarily restrain any party from carrying on such act until the conclusion of such inquiry or until further orders, without giving notice to such party, where it deems it necessary.[247]

Power of Commission to Regulate its Own Procedure

In the discharge of its functions, the Commission shall be guided by the principles of natural justice and, subject to the other provisions of this Act and of any rules made by the Central Government, the Commission shall have the powers to regulate its own procedure.[248] The Commission shall have, for the purposes of discharging its functions under this Act, the same powers as are vested in a Civil Court under the Code of Civil Procedure, 1908, while trying a suit, in respect of the following matters, namely:

(a) summoning and enforcing the attendance of any person and examining him on oath;
(b) requiring the discovery and production of documents;
(c) receiving evidence on affidavit;

(d) issuing commissions for the examination of witnesses or documents; and
(e) requisitioning, subject to the provisions of sections 123 and 124 of the Indian Evidence Act, 1872, any public record or document or copy of such of record or document from any office.[249]

The Commission may call upon such experts, from the field of economics, commerce, accountancy, international trade or from any other discipline as it deems necessary to assist the Commission in the conduct of any inquiry by it.[250] The Commission may direct any person:

(a) to produce before the Director General or the Secretary or an officer authorized by it, such books, or other documents in the custody or under the control of such person so directed as may be specified or described in the direction, being documents relating to any trade, the examination of which may be required for the purposes of this Act; and
(b) to furnish to the Director General or the Secretary or any other officer authorized by it, as respects the trade or such other information as may be in his possession in relation to the trade carried on by such person, as may be required for the purposes of this Act.[251]

Competition Appellate Tribunal

Chapter VIII-A of the Act, inserted by the Competition (Amendment) Act, 2007, provides for the establishment, powers and functions of Competition Appellate Tribunal. The Central Government shall, by notification, establish an Appellate Tribunal to be known as Competition Appellate Tribunal —

(a) to hear and dispose of appeals against any direction issued or decision made or order passed by the Commission under sub-sections (2) and (6) of section 26, section 27, section 28, section 31, section 32, section 33, section 38, section 39, section 43, section 43A, section 44, section 45 or section 46 of the Act; and
(b) to adjudicate on claim for compensation that may arise from the findings of the Commission or the orders of the Appellate Tribunal in an appeal against any finding of the Commission or under section 42A or under sub-section (2) of section 53Q of

this Act, and pass orders for the recovery of compensation under section 53N of this Act.[252]

Composition of Appellate Tribunal

The Appellate Tribunal shall consist of a Chairperson and not more than two other members to be appointed by the Central Government.[253] The Chairperson of the Appellate Tribunal shall be a person, who is, or has been a Judge of the Supreme Court or the Chief Justice of a High Court. A member of the Appellate Tribunal shall be a person of ability, integrity and standing having special knowledge of, and professional experience of not less than twenty five years in, competition matters including competition law and policy, international trade, economics, business, commerce, law, finance, accountancy, management, industry, public affairs, administration or in any other matter which in the opinion of the Central Government, may be useful to the Appellate Tribunal.[254]

The Chairperson and members of the Appellate Tribunal shall be appointed by the Central Government from a panel of names recommended by a Selection Committee consisting of—

(a)	the Chief Justice of India or his nominee	*Chairperson*
(b)	the Secretary in the Ministry of Corporate Affairs	*Member*
(c)	the Secretary in the Ministry of Law and Justice	*Member*[255]

The Chairperson or a member of the Appellate Tribunal shall hold office as such for a term of five years from the date on which he enters upon his office, and shall be eligible for re-appointment. However, no Chairperson or other member of the Appellate Tribunal shall hold office as such after he has attained, in the case of the Chairperson, the age of sixty-eight years; and in the case of any other member of the Appellate Tribunal, the age of sixty-five years.[256]

Appeal to Appellate Tribunal

The Central Government or the State Government or a local authority or enterprise or any person, aggrieved by any direction, decision or order referred to in clause (a) of section 53A may prefer an appeal to the Appellate Tribunal. Every appeal shall be filed within a period of sixty days from the date on which a copy of the direction or decision or order made by the Commission is received by the Central Government or the State Government or a local authority or enterprise or any person referred to in that sub-section and it shall be in such form and be accompanied by such fee as may be prescribed. However, the Appellate Tribunal may entertain an appeal after the expiry of the said period of sixty days if it is satisfied that there was sufficient cause for not filing it within that period. On receipt of an appeal, the Appellate Tribunal may, after giving the parties to the appeal, an opportunity of being heard, pass such orders thereon as it thinks fit, confirming, modifying or setting aside the direction, decision or order appealed against. The Appellate Tribunal shall send a copy of every order made by it to the Commission and the parties to the appeal. The appeal filed before the Appellate Tribunal shall be dealt with by it as expeditiously as possible and endeavour shall be made by it to dispose of the appeal within six months from the date of receipt of the appeal.[257]

Appeal to Supreme Court

The Central Government or any State Government or the Commission or any statutory authority or any local authority or any enterprise or any person aggrieved by any decision or order of the Appellate Tribunal may file an appeal to the Supreme Court within sixty days from the date of communication of the decision or order of the Appellate Tribunal to them. The Supreme Court may, if it is satisfied that the applicant was prevented by sufficient cause from filing the appeal within the said period, allow it to be filed after the expiry of the said period of sixty days.[258]

Exclusion of Jurisdiction of Civil Courts

No civil court shall have jurisdiction to entertain any suit or proceeding in respect of any matter which the Commission or the Appellate Tribunal is empowered by or under this Act to determine and no injunction shall be granted by any court or other authority in respect of any action taken or to be taken in pursuance of any power conferred by or under this Act.[259]

Power of the Commission to impose penalties has been provided in Sections 42 to 48. Under section 63 of the Act the Central Government has the power to make rules to carry out the provisions of the Act. section 64 gives power to the Commission to make regulations consistent with this Act and rules made thereunder to carry out the purposes of this Act.

3.4.5. *Regulation of Ports*

In India, major ports are placed under the Union List of the Constitution, and ports other than the major ones are placed under the Concurrent List. The Indian Ports Act, 1908, extends automatically to all ports. This Act deals mainly with shipping safety and conservation of ports. The Major Port Trusts Act, 1963, (MPT Act) makes provisions for the constitution of port authorities at major ports to vest the administration, control, and management of such ports in such authorities and for matters connected therewith. Under this Act, a duly constituted Board of Trustees (BoT) comprising trustees drawn from the Government, trade, labour, and other interests is responsible for the management of the major port.

Before the April 1997 amendment of the MPT Act, the major port trusts were realizing charges for services rendered and for use of port property in accordance with rates proposed by the Trust, approved by the BoT, and sanctioned by the Union Government. In pursuance of its economic reforms policy, the Government of India stressed upon liberalizing the economy. In this context, it decided to open-up the port sector for privatization. The decision was taken not merely because of resource constraints for the development of additional port capacity but also because the Government wished to introduce healthy competition between the port trusts and private operators as also between the port trusts themselves.

However, in a situation of inadequate port capacity to deal with available/emerging traffic, unrestricted privatization can result in a transition from public to private monopoly. It will, therefore, be necessary to regulate both public ports and private terminal operators until competition develops. In a situation of "landlord ports", it may be possible for the port itself to be a regulator of terminal operators. But in operation ports where only some facilities are privatized, it may not be tenable for the port itself to be a regulator, since there will be a clash of interests arising from its position as a competitive operator. In such a situation, it became necessary to have a neutral third-party regulator. Accordingly, a neutral regulatory body was proposed for regulating tariffs.

In the event, the Government amended the MPT Act to provide for the constitution of such a regulatory mechanism. It provided that all tariffs (both vessel and cargo related) including rates for the lease of properties, should be so regulated. Accordingly, the Tariff Authority for

Major Ports (TAMP) was constituted in April 1997, as a corporate body under section 47A of the MPT Act, 1963, consisting of one full-time chairman and two part-time members. A person to be appointed as Chairperson should have been the Secretary to the Government of India or on any equivalent post in the Government of India. One of the member is required to be an economist having experience of not less than 15 years in the field of transport or foreign trade, and other having experience of not less than 15 years in the field of finance with special reference to investment or cost analysis. The term of appointment is for a period of 5 years or 65 years whichever is earlier. No bar is there on seeking other employment after the completion of tenure.

The jurisdiction of the Authority, as indicated by its very name, is restricted to major ports and BoT operators therein; it has nothing to do with minor ports, private or otherwise. Even in major ports, it has nothing to do with the 'safety' and 'conservancy' aspects of port management. Its attention is restricted to matters relating to tariffs. The TAMP is to fix the rates for services rendered by the ports as well as the charges for use of properties belonging to the Port Trusts. It is expected not only to notify the rates but also the conditionalities governing application of the rates. Besides, the TAMP is also mandated to regulate Terminal Handling Charges (THC) recovered from shoppers by shipping lines. The charges relating to Port Railways working are also to be regulated by the TAMP. The Authority is expected to streamline the tariff structure and systematize the tariff-setting process. There is an expectation that the Authority will use the tariff leverage to effect improvements in operational efficiency at the ports. The 'conditionalities' are expected to provide it with the manoeuverability required for this purpose. The general perception is that it will not be very meaningful to regulate tariffs if such regulation does not result in better quality of service and reduced costs. The rates are not (and cannot be) the same in all the major ports. The attempt is only to ensure that the principles adopted and practices followed in tariff matters are uniform everywhere. Although 'lease' is not 'tariff', even in the matter of lease of port properties, the Authority is expected to notify rates and conditionalities. The idea is apparently to ensure proper utilization of properties towards maximizing income-generation so that port trusts do not have to load the entire burden on to tariffs. The Tariff Authority is a statutorily autonomous quasi-judicial body. It is expected to introduce objectivity and transparency in its functioning.

Regulation of tariffs shall promote objectivity and transparency and emphasize predictability and universality. Objectivity and transparency will promote confidence in the system. Predictability will help the private terminal operators to plan for investments, and universality will ensure non-discrimination among users. Concessions, discounts etc. will be based on objective principles and criteria and be available to all equally.

The orders passed by the Authority are final and without provision for appeal within the system. Aggrieved parties will have to approach the High Court of law for redressal, but the Union Government has the power to issue "policy directives" on matters relating to port pricing.

3.4.6. *Regulation of Petroleum and Gas Sector*

The oil crisis of the 1970s was the major reason promoting the governments all over the world to intervene. As a result all the aspects of the petroleum industry in India like exploration and production, refining, marketing and distribution were closely regulated by the Government of India. Subsequent to 1991 reforms, oil consumption has been growing at an enormous rate. Meeting such a demand required massive investment, far beyond the scope of the public sector which required the involvement of the private sector, both domestic and foreign. To increase competition in the industry, attract private capital and remove constraints on the economic pricing of products and services deregulation of the sector was required. To kick start the deregulation process in the petroleum industry, the government appointed the R group with the experts drawn from the government and the private sector. The R group suggested major policy changes in its report submitted in 1996. The recommendations included the dismantling of the administered price mechanism and tariff reforms. The notification brought out by the government in November 1997 announced phased dismantling of the APM from April 1998. The other features in the notification included: fixed time frame for dismantling of APM; linking the price for domestic crude oil to the international price; abolishing the retention price for refineries; ex-refinery price of controlled products to be fixed by the OCC; adjusted import parity for existing refineries; tariff adjusted import parity for new refineries; decontrolled products-refineries free to set prices; rationalization of customs duty on crude oil and products to provide protection to refineries; marketing rights for new players subject to conditions; reduction in subsidies on Kerosene oil and LPG; and establishment of regulatory body. The regulatory body for the petroleum and natural gas has been set-up by the Petroleum and Natural Gas Regulatory Board Act enacted in 2006.

The Petroleum and Natural Gas Regulatory Board Act, 2006, provides for the establishment of Petroleum and Natural Gas Regulatory Board to regulate the refining, processing, storage, transportation, distribution, marketing and sale of petroleum, petroleum products and natural gas excluding production of crude oil and natural gas so as to protect the interests of consumers and entities engaged in specified activities relating to petroleum, petroleum products and natural gas and to ensure uninterrupted and adequate supply of petroleum, petroleum products and natural gas in all parts of the country and to promote competitive markets and for matters connected therewith or incidental thereto.

The Central Government shall establish, for the purposes of this Act, a Board to be called the Petroleum and Natural Gas Regulatory Board.[260] The Board shall be a body corporate by the name aforesaid, having perpetual succession and a common seal, with power, subject to the provisions of this Act, to acquire, hold and dispose of property, both movable and immovable, and to contract, and shall, by the said name, sue or be sued.[261] The Board shall consist of a Chairperson, a member (legal) and three other members to be appointed by the Central Government.[262] The head office of the Board shall be at New Delhi and regional offices at such places as the Board may deem necessary having regard to public interest and magnitude of the work.[263]

The Central Government shall appoint the Chairperson and other members of the Board from amongst persons of eminence in the fields of petroleum and natural gas industry, management, finance, law, administration or consumer affairs. However, no person shall be appointed as Member (Legal) unless he — (a) is qualified to be a Judge of a High Court; or (b) has been a member of the Indian Legal Service and has held a post in Grade I of that Service for at least three years.[264] Before appointing any person as the Chairperson or other member, the Central Government shall satisfy itself that such person does not have any financial or other interest which is likely to affect prejudicially his functions as Chairperson or such other member.[265] The Chairperson and other members shall hold office for a term of five years from the date on which they enter upon their offices or until they attain the age of sixty-five years, whichever is earlier. The Chairperson and other members shall not be eligible for re-appointment.[266]

According to Section 11 functions of the Board are to:

(a) protect the interest of consumers by fostering fair trade and competition amongst the entities;

(b) register entities to —

  (i) market notified petroleum and petroleum products and, subject to the contractual obligations of the Central Government, natural gas;
  (ii) establish and operate liquefied natural gas terminals;
  (iii) establish storage facilities for petroleum, petroleum products or natural gas exceeding such capacity as may be specified by regulations;

(c) authorize entities to —

  (i) lay, build, operate or expand a common carrier or contract carrier;
  (ii) lay, build, operate or expand city or local natural gas distribution network;

(d) declare pipelines as common carrier or contract carrier;
(e) regulate, by regulations, —

  (i) access to common carrier or contract carrier so as to ensure fair trade and competition amongst entities and for that purpose specify pipeline access code;
  (ii) transportation rates for common carrier or contract carrier;
  (iii) access to city or local natural gas distribution network so as to ensure fair trade and competition amongst entities as per pipeline access code;

(f) in respect of notified petroleum, petroleum products and natural gas —

  (i) ensure adequate availability;
  (ii) ensure display of information about the maximum retail prices fixed by the entity for consumers at retail outlets;
  (iii) monitor prices and take corrective measures to prevent restrictive trade practice by the entities;
  (iv) secure equitable distribution for petroleum and petroleum products;
  (v) provide, by regulations, and enforce, retail service obligations for retail outlets and marketing service obligations for entities;
  (vi) monitor transportation rates and take corrective action to prevent restrictive trade practice by the entities;

(g) levy fees and other charges as determined by regulations;

(h) maintain a data bank of information on activities relating to petroleum, petroleum products and natural gas;

(i) lay down, by regulations, the technical standards and specifications including safety standards in activities relating to petroleum, petroleum products and natural gas, including the construction and operation of pipeline and infrastructure projects related to downstream petroleum and natural gas sector; and

(j) perform such other functions as may be entrusted to it by the Central Government to carry out the provisions of this Act.

According to section 12(1) the Board shall have jurisdiction to: (a) adjudicate upon and decide any dispute or matter arising amongst entities or between an entity and any other person on issues relating to refining, processing, storage, transportation, distribution, marketing and sale of petroleum, petroleum products and natural gas according to the provisions of Chapter V, unless the parties have agreed for arbitration; and (b) receive any complaint from any person and conduct any inquiry and investigation connected with the activities relating to petroleum, petroleum products and natural gas on contravention of— (i) retail service obligations; (ii) marketing service obligations; (iii) display of retail price at retail outlets; (iv) terms and conditions subject to which a pipeline has been declared as common carrier or contract carrier or access for other entities was allowed to a city or local natural gas distribution network, or authorization has been granted to an entity for laying, building, expanding or operating a pipeline as common carrier or contract carrier or authorization has been granted to an entity for laying, building, expanding or operating a city or local natural gas distribution network; and (v) any other provision of this Act or the rules or the regulations or orders made thereunder.

While deciding a complaint under sub-section (1), the Board may pass such orders and issue such directions as it deems fit or refer the matter for investigation according to the provisions of Chapter V.[267] If any dispute arises, among entities or between an entity and any other person, such dispute shall be decided by a Bench consisting of the Member (Legal) and one or more members nominated by the Chairperson. If the members of the Bench differ on any point or points, they shall state the point or points on which they differ and refer the same to a member other than a member of the Bench for hearing on such point or points and such point or points shall be decided according to the opinion of that member.[268] The Bench shall exercise, on and from the appointed day, all such jurisdiction, powers and authority as were exercisable by a civil court on any matter relating to —

(a) refining, processing, storage, transportation and distribution of petroleum, petroleum products and natural gas by the entities;
(b) marketing and sale of petroleum, petroleum products and natural gas including the quality of service and security of supply to the consumers by the entities; and
(c) registration or authorization issued by the Board under section 15 or Section 19.[269]

The Board shall, while deciding a dispute under this Chapter, have due regard to the provisions of this Act and to the following factors, namely:

(a) the amount of disproportionate gain made or unfair advantage derived, wherever quantifiable, as a result of the default;
(b) the amount of loss caused to an entity as a result of the default; and
(c) the repetitive nature of the default.[270]

The Appellate Tribunal established under section 110 of the Electricity Act, 2003, shall be the Appellate Tribunal for the purposes of this Act and the said Appellate Tribunal shall exercise the jurisdiction, powers and authority conferred on it by or under this Act.[271] Any person aggrieved by an order or decision made by the Board under this Act may prefer an appeal to the Appellate Tribunal.[272] Every appeal under sub-section (1) shall be filed within a period of thirty days from the date on which a copy of the direction or order of decision made by the Board is received by the aggrieved person and it shall be in such form, verified in such manner and be accompanied by such fee as may be prescribed. However, the Appellate Tribunal may entertain an appeal after the expiry of the said period of thirty days if it is satisfied that there was sufficient cause for not filing it within that period.[273] The appeal filed under sub-section (1) shall be dealt with by the Appellate Tribunal as expeditiously as possible and endeavour shall be made by it to dispose of the appeal finally within ninety days from the date of receipt of appeal. Provided that where any such appeal could not be disposed of within the said period of ninety days, the Appellate Tribunal shall record its reasons in writing for not disposing of the appeal within the said period.[274]

An appeal shall lie against any order, not being an interlocutory order, of the Appellate Tribunal to the Supreme Court on one or more of the grounds specified in Section 100 of Code of Civil Procedure, 1908.[275] No appeal shall lie against any decision or order made by the Appellate Tribunal with the consent of the parties.[276] Every appeal under this section shall be preferred within a period of ninety days from the date of the decision or order appealed against. However, the Supreme Court may entertain the appeal after the expiry of the said period of ninety days, if it is satisfied that the appellant was prevented by sufficient cause from preferring the appeal in time.[277]

3.4.7. *Regulation of Aviation Sector*

Civil Aviation forms a crucial infrastructure segment in boosting trade and commerce, as well as, in enhancing overall international competitiveness and connectivity. India currently has 127 airports, including 16 international airports, 8 customs declared airports, 79 domestic airports, and 24 civil enclaves at the defence airfields, all of which are being managed by Airports Authority of India (AAI). Traditionally, airport development in the country has been in the public sector. However, the amendment to AAI Act and Aircraft Rules in 2004, has enabled private sector investments. Hundred per cent Foreign Direct Investment (FDI) is allowed in setting-up of greenfield airports. Growth of the Indian economy over the past few years has led to an interesting growth trend in the civil aviation industry also. Traffic at Indian airports has grown in all three segments, viz. passenger, aircraft movement, and freight. The airport sector has attracted considerable private interest. According to the Eleventh Plan projections, of the total investment requirement of ₹ 30,968 crore, as much as 70 per cent (₹ 21,630 crore) is envisaged by way of private investment. The PPP route has progressively gained importance and is being used either for modernization or construction of airports or only for city-side development at airports.[278]

Aviation as a sector is different from other economic sectors, in that its operations are an agglomeration of multiple distinct, yet intertwined, commercial functions in different segments, *viz.* airline companies, ground handling, air traffic control, competition, safety, security etc. Since, airports are natural monopoly, there is need for an effective regulatory mechanism that embodies the principles of fair competition and articulates explicit objectives. With the changing ownership structure, airport regulation now also includes economic regulation. On the recommendations of the Naresh Chandra Committee Report, the Airports

Economic Regulatory Authority (AERA) has been set-up as an independent regulator.

The Airports Economic Regulatory Authority of India Act, 2008, was notified on December 5, 2008. The Act authorized the establishment of an independent body to regulate tariffs and monitor the performance of airports areas that were previously under the purview of the Airports Authority of India. Pursuant to the Act, on May 12, 2009 the Airports Economic Regulatory Authority was established and its chairperson was appointed on June 17, 2009. The new regulatory authority will seek to remove anomalies that were prevalent during the Airports Authority of India's dual reign as service provider and regulator of domestic and international airports in India, where often the charges for aeronautical services did not match the quality of services provided. Without an independent regulator, India lacked the necessary professional environment for the development of an airport infrastructure that met global standards.

Section 3 of the Act provides that the Central Government shall, within three months from the date of commencement of this Act, by notification in the Official Gazette, establish an Authority, to be known as the Airports Economic Regulatory Authority, to exercise the powers conferred on, and the functions assigned to it, by or under this Act. The Authority shall consist of a Chairperson and two other Members to be appointed by the Central Government. Wherever the Authority is deciding a matter involving a civil enclave in a defence airfield, there shall be an additional Member, not below the rank of Additional Secretary to the Government of India, to be nominated by the Ministry of Defence. The Chairperson and Members of the Authority shall be appointed by the Central Government from amongst persons of ability and integrity having adequate knowledge of, and professional experience in, aviation, economics, law, commerce or consumers affairs. However, a person who is or has been in the service of Government shall not be appointed as a Member unless such person has held the post of Secretary or Additional Secretary to the Government of India or any equivalent post in the Central or State Government for a total period of not less than three years.[279] The Chairperson and other Members, shall hold office, as such, for a term of five years from the date on which he enters upon his office, but shall not be eligible for re-appointment. No Chairperson or other Member shall hold office, as such, after attains in the case of the Chairperson, the age of sixty-five years; and in the case of any other Member, the age of sixty-two years.[280]

The Authority shall perform the following functions in respect of major airports, namely: (a) to determine the tariff for the aeronautical services; (b) to determine the amount of the development fees in respect of major airports; (c) to determine the amount of the passengers service fee levied under rule 88 of the Aircraft Rules, 1937, made under the Aircraft Act, 1934; (d) to monitor the set performance standards relating to quality, continuity and reliability of service as may be specified by the Central Government or any authority authorized by it in this behalf; (e) to call for such information as may be necessary to determine the tariff under clause (a); and (f) to perform such other functions relating to tariff, as may be entrusted to it by the Central Government or as may be necessary to carry out the provisions of this Act.[281] The Authority shall determine the tariff once in five years and may if so considered appropriate and in public interest, amend, from time-to-time during the said period of five years, the tariff so determined.[282] While discharging its functions under sub-section (1) the Authority shall not act against the interest of the sovereignty and integrity of India, the security of the State, friendly relations with foreign States, public order, decency or morality.[283] The Authority shall ensure transparency while exercising its powers and discharging its functions.[284]

According to Section 17 of the Act, the Central Government shall, by notification in the Official Gazette, establish an Appellate Tribunal to be known as the Airports Economic Regulatory Authority Appellate Tribunal to: (a) adjudicate any dispute — (i) between two or more service providers; (ii) between a service provider and a group of consumers. The Appellate Tribunal may, if considers appropriate, obtain the opinion of the Authority on any matter relating to such dispute; (b) hear and dispose of appeal against any direction, decision or order of the Authority under this Act. The Appellate Tribunal shall consist of a Chairperson and not more than two Members to be appointed, by notification in the Official Gazette, by the Central Government.[285] A person shall not be qualified for appointment as the Chairperson or a Member of the Appellate Tribunal unless he — (a) in the case of Chairperson, is, or has been, a Judge of the Supreme Court or the Chief Justice of a High Court; (b) in the case of a Member, has held the post of Secretary to the Government of India or any equivalent post in the Central Government or the State Government for a total period of not less than two years in the Ministries or Departments dealing with aviation or economics or law or a person who is well-versed in the field of aviation or economics or law.[286] The Chairperson and every other

Member of the Appellate Tribunal shall hold office as such for a term not exceeding three years from the date on which he enters upon his office. However, no Chairperson or other Member shall hold office as such after he has attained, — (a) in the case of Chairperson, the age of seventy years; and (b) in the case of any other Member, the age of sixty-five years.[287]

The Central Government or a State Government or a local authority or any person may make an application to the Appellate Tribunal for adjudication of any dispute as referred to in clause (a) of Section 17.[288] The Central Government or a State Government or a local authority or any person aggrieved by any direction, decision or order made by the Authority may prefer an appeal to the Appellate Tribunal.[289] Every appeal under sub-section (2) shall be preferred within a period of thirty days from the date on which a copy of the direction or order or decision made by the Authority is received by the Central Government or the State Government or the local authority or the aggrieved person and it shall be in such form, verified in such manner and be accompanied by such fee as may be prescribed. However, the Appellate Tribunal may entertain any appeal after the expiry of the said period of thirty days if it is satisfied that there was sufficient cause for not filing it within that period.[290]

If the Chairperson and other Members differ in opinion on any matter, such matter shall be decided according to the opinion of the majority.[291] No civil court shall have jurisdiction to entertain any suit or proceeding in respect of any matter which the Appellate Tribunal is empowered by or under this Act to determine and no injunction shall be granted by any court or other authority in respect of any action taken or to be taken in pursuance of any power conferred by or under this Act.[292] The Appellate Tribunal shall not be bound by the procedure laid down by the Code of Civil Procedure, 1908, but shall be guided by the principles of natural justice and, subject to the other provisions of this Act, the Appellate Tribunal shall have powers to regulate its own procedure.[293] Notwithstanding anything contained in the Code of Civil Procedure, 1908 or in any other law, an appeal shall lie against any order, not being an interlocutory order, of the Appellate Tribunal to the Supreme Court on one or more of the grounds specified in Section 100 of that Code. No appeal shall lie against any decision or order made by the Appellate Tribunal with the consent of the parties. Every appeal under this section shall be preferred within a period of ninety days from the date of the decision or order appealed against. However, the Supreme

Court may entertain the appeal after the expiry of the said period of ninety days, if it is satisfied that the appellant was prevented by sufficient cause from preferring the appeal in time.[294]

3.4.8. *Regulation of Food Sector*

Earlier the food sector in India was governed by many laws under different ministries. This multiplicity in law in food sector resulted in many problems in the area of food standards maintenance. Need for a single regulatory body and an integrated food law was recognized as a remedy for this multiplicity of laws. The Food Safety and Standards Act, 2006, had been enacted by the Parliament on 23rd August, 2006 which became operational on August 5, 2011 with the notification of the Food Safety and Standard Rules, 2011. The Act is to consolidate the laws relating to food and to establish the Food Safety and Standards Authority of India for laying down science-based standards for articles of food and to regulate their manufacture, storage, distribution, sale and import, to ensure availability of safe and wholesome food for human consumption and for matters connected therewith or incidental thereto. The following laws have been repealed after coming into force of new Act — the Prevention of Food Adulteration Act, 1954, the Fruit Products Order, 1955, the Meat Food Products Order, 1973, the Vegetable Oil Products (Control) Order, 1947, the Edible Oils Packaging (Regulation) Order, 1998, the Soiled Meal and Edible Flour (Control) Order, 1967, the Milk and Milk Products Order, 1992 and any other order issued under the Essential Commodities Act, 1955 relating to food. The Act also aims to establish a single reference point for all matters relating to food safety and standards, by moving from multi-level, multi-departmental control to a single line of command. To this effect, the Act establishes an independent statutory Authority — the Food Safety and Standards Authority of India with head office at Delhi. Food Safety and Standards Authority of India (FSSAI) and the State Food Safety Authorities shall enforce various provisions of the Act.

All food items produced, distributed and sold now come under the scanner of this regulatory body. This includes restaurants, retail chains, food companies, and even roadside outlets. The Authority aided by several scientific panels and a central advisory committee will lay down standards for food safety. These standards will include specifications for ingredients, contaminants, pesticide residue, biological hazards and labels. The State Commissioners of Food Safety and other local level officials will enforce the law. Every entity in the food sector is required to get a licence or a registration under the Act. Till now the Authority has framed Regulations on:

- Licensing and Registration.
- Packaging and Labelling.
- Food Standards.
- Food Additives.
- Contaminants and Toxins.
- Prohibitions and Restrictions.
- Laboratory Sampling and Analysis.

According to the Section 4(1) of the Act, the Central Government shall, by notification, establish a body to be known as the Food Safety and Standards Authority of India to exercise the powers conferred on, and to perform the functions assigned to, it under this Act. The Food Authority shall be a body corporate by the name aforesaid, having perpetual succession and a common seal with power to acquire, hold and dispose of property, both movable and immovable, and to contract and shall, by the said name, sue or be sued.[295] The Food Authority shall consist of a Chairperson and twenty-two members out of which one-third shall be women, namely: (a) seven Members, not below the rank of a Joint Secretary to the Government of India, to be appointed by the Central Government, to respectively represent the Ministries or Departments of the Central Government dealing with — (i) Agriculture, (ii) Commerce, (iii) Consumer Affairs, (iv) Food Processing, (v) Health, (vi) Legislative Affairs, and (vii) Small Scale Industries, who shall be Members *ex-officio*; (b) two representatives from food industry of which one shall be from small scale industries; (c) two representatives from consumer organizations; (d) three eminent food technologists or scientists; (e) five members to be appointed by rotation every three years, one each in seriatim from the Zones as specified in the First Schedule to represent the States and the Union territories; (f) two persons to represent farmers' organizations; and (g) one person to represent retailers' organizations.[296] The Chairperson and other Members of the Food Authority shall be appointed in such a manner so as to secure the highest standards of competence, broad range of relevant expertise, and shall represent, the broadest possible geographic distribution within the country.[297] The Chairperson shall be appointed by the Central Government from amongst the persons of eminence in the field of food science or from amongst the persons from the administration who have been associated with the subject and is either holding or has held the position of not below the rank of Secretary to the Government of India.[298] The Chairperson and the Members other than *ex-officio* Members of the Food Authority shall be appointed by the Central Government on the recommendations of the Selection Committee.[299] The Chairperson or Members other than *ex-officio* Members of the Food Authority shall not hold any other office.[300] The Chairperson and the members other than *ex-officio* Members shall hold office for a term of three years from the date on which they enter upon their offices, and shall be eligible for re-appointment for a further period of three years. However, Chairperson or a member other than *ex-officio* Member shall not hold office as such after he has attained — (a) in the case of the Chairperson, the age of sixty-five years, and (b) in the case of a Member, the age of sixty-two years.[301]

Duties and Functions of Food Authority — It shall be the duty of the Food Authority to regulate and monitor the manufacture, processing, distribution, sale and import of food so as to ensure safe and wholesome food.[302] Without prejudice to the provisions of sub-section (1), the Food Authority may by regulations specify: (a) the standards and guidelines in relation to articles of food and specifying an appropriate system for enforcing various standards notified under this Act; (b) the limits for use of food additives, crop contaminants, pesticide residues, residues of veterinary drugs, heavy metals, processing aids, myco-toxins, antibiotics and pharmacological active substances and irradiation of food; (c) the mechanisms and guidelines for accreditation of certification bodies engaged in certification of food safety management systems for food businesses; (d) the procedure and the enforcement of quality control in relation to any article of food imported into India; (e) the procedure and guidelines for accreditation of laboratories and notification of the accredited laboratories; (f) the method of sampling, analysis and exchange of information among enforcement authorities; (g) conduct survey of enforcement and administration of this Act in the country; (h) food labelling standards including claims on health, nutrition, special dietary uses and food category systems for foods; and (i) the manner in which and the procedure subject to which risk analysis, risk assessment, risk communication and risk management shall be undertaken.[303]

The Food Authority shall also: (a) provide scientific advice and technical support to the Central Government and the State Governments in matters of framing the policy and rules in areas which have a direct or indirect bearing on food safety and nutrition; (b) search, collect, collate, analyze and summarize relevant scientific and technical data particularly relating to — (i) food consumption and the exposure of individuals to risks related to the consumption of food; (ii) incidence and prevalence of biological risk; (iii) contaminants in food; (iv) residues of various contaminants; (v) identification of emerging risks; and (vi) introduction of rapid alert system; (c) promote, coordinate and issue guidelines for the development of risk assessment methodologies and monitor and conduct and forward messages on the health and nutritional risks of food to the Central Government, State Governments and Commissioners of Food Safety; (d) provide scientific and technical advice and assistance to the Central Government and the State Governments in implementation of crisis management procedures with regard to food safety and to draw up a general plan for crisis management and work in close cooperation with the crisis unit set-up by the Central Government in this regard; (e) establish a system of network of organizations with the aim to facilitate a scientific cooperation framework by the coordination of activities, the exchange of information, the development and implementation of joint projects, the exchange of expertise and best practices in the fields within the Food Authority's responsibility; (f) provide scientific and technical assistance to the Central Government and the State Governments for improving cooperation with international organizations; (g) take all such steps to ensure that the public, consumers, interested parties and all levels of panchayats receive rapid, reliable, objective and comprehensive information through appropriate methods and means; (h) provide, whether within or outside their area, training programmes in food safety and standards for persons who are or intend to become involved in food businesses, whether as food business operators or employees or otherwise; (i) undertake any other task assigned to it by the Central Government to carry out the objects of this Act; (j) contribute to the development of international technical standards for food, sanitary and phyto-sanitary standards; (k) contribute, where relevant and appropriate, to the development of agreement on recognition of the equivalence of specific food related measures; (l) promote coordination of work on food standards undertaken by international governmental and non-governmental organizations; (m) promote consistency between international technical standards and domestic food standards while ensuring that the level of protection adopted in the country is not reduced; and (n) promote general awareness as to food safety and food standards.[304]

The Food Authority and the State Food Safety Authorities shall be responsible for the enforcement of this Act.[305] The Food Authority and the State Food Safety Authorities shall monitor and verify that the relevant requirements of law are fulfilled by food business operators at all stages of food business.[306] The authorities shall maintain a system of control and other activities as appropriate to the circumstances, including public communication on food safety and risk, food safety surveillance and other monitoring activities covering all stages of food business.[307] The Food Safety Officers shall enforce and execute within their area the provisions of this Act with respect to which the duty is not imposed expressly or by necessary implication on some other authority.[308] The regulations under this Act shall specify which of the Food Safety Officers are to enforce and execute them, either generally or in relation to cases of a particular description or a particular area, and any such regulations or orders may provide for the giving of assistance and information, by any authority concerned in the administration of the regulations or orders, or of any provisions of this Act, to any other authority so concerned, for the purposes of their respective duties under them.[309] The Commissioner of Food Safety and Designated Officer shall exercise the same powers as are conferred on the Food Safety Officer and follow the same procedure specified in this Act.[310]

The State Government shall appoint the Commissioner of Food Safety for the State for efficient implementation of food safety and standards and other requirements laid down under this Act and the rules and regulations made thereunder.[311] The Commissioner of Food Safety shall perform all or any of the following functions, namely: (a) prohibit in the interest of public health, the manufacture, storage, distribution or sale of any article of food, either in the whole of the State or any area or part thereof for such period, not exceeding one year, as may be specified in the order notified in this behalf in the Official Gazette; (b) carry out survey of the industrial units engaged in the manufacture or processing of food in the State to find out compliance by such units of the standards notified by the Food Authority for various articles of food; (c) conduct or organize training programmes for the personnel of the office of the Commissioner of Food Safety and, on a wider scale, for different segments of food chain for generating awareness on food safety; (d) ensure an efficient and uniform implementation of the standards and other requirements as specified and also ensure a high standard of objectivity, accountability, practicability, transparency and credibility;

(e) sanction prosecution for offences punishable with imprisonment under this Act; (f) such other functions as the State Government may, in consultation with the Food Authority, prescribe.[312] The Commissioner of Food Safety may, by order, delegate, subject to such conditions and restrictions as may be specified in the order, such of his powers and functions under this Act (except the power to appoint Designated Officer, Food Safety Officer and Food Analyst) as he may deem necessary or expedient to any officer subordinate to him.[313]

The Commissioner of Food Safety shall, by order, appoint the Designated Officer, who shall not be below the rank of a Sub-Divisional Officer, to be in-charge of food safety administration in such area as may be specified by regulations.[314] There shall be a Designated Officer for each district.[315] The functions to be performed by the Designated Officer shall be as follows, namely: (a) to issue or cancel licence of food business operators; (b) to prohibit the sale of any article of food which is in contravention of the provisions of this Act and rules and regulations made thereunder; (c) to receive report and samples of article of foods from Food Safety Officer under his jurisdiction and get them analyzed; (d) to make recommendations to the Commissioner of Food Safety for sanction to launch prosecutions in case of contraventions punishable with imprisonment; (e) to sanction or launch prosecutions in cases of contraventions punishable with fine; (f) to maintain record of all inspections made by Food Safety Officers and action taken by them in the performance of their duties; (g) to get investigated any complaint which may be made in writing in respect of any contravention of the provisions of this Act and the rules and regulations made thereunder; (h) to investigate any complaint which may be made in writing against the Food Safety Officer; and (i) to perform such other duties as may be entrusted by the Commissioner of Food Safety.[316] The Commissioner of Food Safety shall, by notification, appoint such persons as he thinks fit, having the qualifications prescribed by the Central Government, as Food Safety Officers for such local areas as he may assign to them for the purpose of performing functions under this Act and the rules and regulations made thereunder.[317] The State Government may authorize any officer of the State Government having the qualifications prescribed under sub-section (1) to perform the functions of a Food Safety Officer within a specified jurisdiction.[318]

For the purposes of adjudication under Chapter X, an officer not below the rank of Additional District Magistrate of the district where the alleged offence is committed, shall be notified by the State Government as the Adjudicating Officer for adjudication in the manner as may be prescribed by the Central Government.[319] The Adjudicating Officer shall, after giving the person a reasonable opportunity for making representation in the matter, and if, on such inquiry, he is satisfied that the person has committed the contravention of provisions of this Act or the rules or the regulations made thereunder, impose such penalty as he thinks fit in accordance with the provisions relating to that offence.[320]

The Central Government or as the case may be, the State Government may, by notification, establish one or more tribunals to be known as the Food Safety Appellate Tribunal to hear appeals from the decisions of the Adjudicating Officer under section 68.[321] The Central Government or the State Government, as the case may be, shall prescribe, the matters and areas in relation to which the Tribunal may exercise jurisdiction.[322] The Tribunal shall consist of one person only, referred to as the Presiding Officer of the Tribunal, to be appointed, by notification, by the Central Government or the State Government, as the case may be. No person shall be qualified for appointment as a Presiding Officer to the Tribunal unless he is or has been a District Judge.[323] The qualifications, appointment, term of office, salary and allowances, resignation and removal of the Presiding Officer shall be such as may be prescribed by the Central Government.[324] The procedure of appeal and powers of the Tribunal shall be such as may be prescribed by the Central Government.[325] The Tribunal shall not be bound by the procedure laid down by the Code of Civil Procedure, 1908, but shall be guided by the principles of natural justice and, subject to the other provisions of this Act and the rules made thereunder, the Tribunal shall have powers to regulate its own procedure including the place at which it shall have its sittings.[326] Any person aggrieved by any decision or order of the Tribunal may file an appeal to the High Court within sixty days from the date of communication of the decision or order of the Tribunal to him on any question of fact or law arising out of such order. The High Court may, if it is satisfied that the appellant was prevented by sufficient cause from filing the appeal within the said period, allow it to be filed within a further period not exceeding sixty days.[327] No civil court shall have jurisdiction to entertain any suit or proceeding in respect of any matter which an Adjudicating Officer or the Tribunal is empowered by or under this Act to determine and no injunction shall be granted by any court or other authority in respect of any action taken or to be taken in pursuance of any power conferred by or under this Act.[328]

The new regulator will also be responsible for imported and genetically modified food products, as well as food recalls in case unsafe or hazardous batches are discovered. The Quality Council of India (QCI) and Bureau of Indian Standards (BIS) will lend their expertise in laying standards for the regulator to administer.

3.4.9. *Regulation of the Service Sector through Ombudsmen*

(i) *Banking Ombudsman*

In exercise of the powers conferred by Section 35A of the Banking Regulation Act, 1949, the Reserve Bank of India introduced the Banking Ombudsman Scheme on June 14, 1995 thereby creating a redressal system of grievances against deficiency in banking services of all commercial banks, regional rural banks and scheduled primary cooperative banks. The scheme has since been revised twice in 2002 and 2005. The latest revised Scheme has come into force from January 1, 2006. In public interest and in the interest of banking policy, the extent and scope of the authority and functions of the Banking Ombudsman were enlarged on 14th June, 2002, empowering the Ombudsman to act as an arbitrator for specified disputes and putting regional Rural Banks also under the umbrella of the Banking Ombudsman Scheme. Thereafter, in 2006 Reserve Bank once again enlarged the extent, the scope of authority and functions of Banking Ombudsman by revising the Scheme with effect from 1st January, 2006. The Scheme envisages expeditious and satisfactory disposal of customer complaints in a time bound manner. It provides a free, fair and speedy forum free of procedural hurdles to consumers. For the purpose of promoting settlement of complaints, the Banking Ombudsman has been allowed to follow such procedures as he may consider appropriate and he is not bound by any legal rule of evidence.

The Reserve Bank may appoint one or more of its officers in the rank of Chief General Manager or General Manager to be known as Banking Ombudsmen to carry out the functions entrusted to them by or under the Scheme. The appointment of Banking Ombudsman may be made for a period not exceeding three years at a time.[329] There are 15 Ombudsman offices located at Ahmedabad, Bangalore, Bhopal, Bhubaneswar, Chandigarh, Chennai, Guwahati, Hyderabad, Jaipur, Kanpur, Kolkata, Mumbai, New Delhi, Patna and Thiruvananthapuram.

A complaint on anyone of the following grounds alleging deficiency in banking or other services may be filed with the Banking Ombudsman having jurisdiction:

1. non-payment or inordinate delay in the payment or collection of cheques, drafts, bills etc.;
2. non-acceptance, without sufficient cause, of small denomination notes tendered for any purpose, and for charging of commission in respect thereof;
3. non-acceptance, without sufficient cause, of coins tendered and for charging of commission in respect thereof;
4. non-payment or delay in payment of inward remittances;
5. failure to issue or delay in issue of drafts, pay orders or bankers' cheques;
6. non-adherence to prescribed working hours;
7. failure to honour guarantee or letter of credit commitments;
8. failure to provide or delay in providing a banking facility (other than loans and advances) promised in writing by a bank or its direct selling agents;
9. delays, non-credit of proceeds to parties' accounts, non-payment of deposits or non-observance of the Reserve Bank directives, if any, applicable to rate of interest on deposits in any savings, current or other account maintained with a bank;
10. delays in receipt of export proceeds, handling of export bills, collection of bills etc. for exporters provided the said complaints pertain to the bank's operations in India;
11. complaints from Non-Resident Indians having accounts in India in relation to their remittances from abroad, deposits and other bank-related matters;
12. refusal to open deposit accounts without any valid reason for refusal;
13. levying of charges without adequate prior notice to the consumers;
14. non-adherence by the bank or its subsidiaries to the instructions of Reserve Bank on ATM/Debit card operations or credit card operations;
15. non-disbursement or delay in disbursement of pension (to the extent the grievance can be attributed to the action on the part of the bank concerned, but not with regard to its employees);
16. refusal to accept or delay in accepting payment towards taxes, as required by Reserve Bank/Government;

17. refusal to issue or delay in issuing, or failure to service or delay in servicing or redemption of Government securities;
18. forced closure of deposit accounts without due notice or without sufficient reason;
19. refusal to close or delay in closing the accounts;
20. non-adherence to the fair practices code as adopted by the bank; and
21. any other matter relating to the violation of the directives issued by the Reserve Bank in relation to banking or other services.

A complaint on anyone of the following grounds alleging deficiency in banking service in respect of loans and advances may be filled with the Banking Ombudsman having jurisdiction:

1. non-observance of Reserve Bank Directives on interest rates;
2. delays in sanction, disbursement or non-observance of prescribed time schedule for disposal of loans applications;
3. non-acceptance of application for loans without furnishing valid reasons to the applicant; and
4. non-observance of any other direction or instruction of the Reserve Bank as may be specified by the Reserve Bank for this purpose from time-to-time.

The Banking Ombudsman may also deal with such other matter as may be specified by the Reserve Bank from time-to-time in this behalf.[330]

Any person who has a grievance against a bank on any one or more of the grounds mentioned in Clause 8 of the Scheme may, himself or through his authorized representative (other than an advocate), make a complaint to the Banking Ombudsman within whose jurisdiction the branch or office of the bank complained against is located. In case of credit cards the complaint shall be filed before the Banking Ombudsman within whose territorial jurisdiction the billing address of the card holder is located and not the place where the bank concerned or the credit card processing unit is located. The complaint in writing shall be duly signed by the complainant or his authorized representative and contain information about (i) the name and the address of the complainant; (ii) the name and address of the branch or office of the bank against which the complaint is made; (iii) the facts giving rise to the complaint; (iv) the nature and extent of the loss caused to the complainant; and (v) the relief sought for. A complaint can also be made through electronic means. The Banking Ombudsman shall also entertain complaints covered by this Scheme received by Central Government or Reserve Bank and forwarded to him for disposal. No complaint to the Banking Ombudsman shall lie unless the complainant had, before making a complaint to the Banking Ombudsman, made a written representation to the bank and the bank had rejected the complaint or the complainant had not received any reply within a period of one month after the bank received his representation or the complainant is not satisfied with the reply given to him by the bank. The complaint is to be made within one year after the complainant has received the reply of the bank to his representation or, where no reply is received, not later than one year and one month after the date of the representation to the bank.[331]

The Banking Ombudsman sends a copy of the complaint to the branch or office of the bank named in the complaint and tries to promote a settlement between the consumer and the bank named in the complaint through conciliation or mediation. If a complaint is not settled by agreement within a period of one month from the date of receipt of the complaint or such further period as the Banking Ombudsman may allow the parties, he may, after affording the parties a reasonable opportunity to present their case, pass an Award or reject the complaint. The Banking Ombudsman shall take into account the evidence placed before him by the parties, the principles of banking law and practice, directions, instructions and guidelines issued by the Reserve Bank from time-to-time and such other factors which in his opinion are relevant to the complaint. The award shall state the reasons for passing the award. The award passed shall contain direction(s), if any, to the bank for specific performance of its obligations and in addition to or otherwise, the amount, of any, to be paid by the bank to the complainant by way of compensation for any loss suffered by the complainant, arising directly out of the act or omission of the Bank. A copy of the Award shall be sent to the complainant and the bank. An award shall lapse and be of no effect unless the complainant furnishes to the bank concerned within a period of 30 days from the date of receipt of copy of the Award, a letter of acceptance of the Award in full and final settlement of his claim. No such acceptance may be furnished by the complainant if he has filed an appeal under sub-clause (1) of clause 14. The bank shall, unless it has preferred an appeal under sub-clause (1) of clause 14, within one month from the date of receipt by it of the acceptance in writing of the Award by the complainant comply with the Award and intimate compliance to the Banking Ombudsman.[332]

Any person aggrieved by an Award may within 30 days of the date of receipt of communication of Award, prefer an appeal before the Appellate Authority. The Deputy Governor in charge of the Department of the Reserve Bank implementing the Scheme is the Appellate Authority. In case of appeal by a bank, the period of thirty days for filing an appeal shall commence from the date on which the bank receives letter of acceptance of Award by complainant. The Appellate Authority may, if he is satisfied that the applicant had sufficient cause for not making the appeal within time, allow a further period not exceeding 30 days. The appeal may be filed by a bank only with the previous sanction of the Chairman or, in his absence, the Managing Director or the Executive Director or the Chief Executive Officer or any other officer of equal rank. The Appellate Authority shall, after giving the parties a reasonable opportunity of being heard (a) dismiss the appeal; or (b) allow the appeal and set aside the Award; or (c) remand the matter to the Banking Ombudsman for fresh disposal in accordance with such directions as the Appellate Authority may consider necessary or proper; or (d) modify the Award and pass such directions as may be necessary to give effect to the Award so modified; or (e) pass any other order as it may deem fit.[333]

(ii) *Insurance Ombudsman*

The Government of India, Ministry of Finance, Department of Economic Affairs, Insurance Division, under section 114(1) of Insurance Act, 1938, has framed the "Redressal of Public Grievance Rules, 1998", for appointment of Insurance Ombudsman, which came into force with effect from 11-11-1998. The Insurance Ombudsman has started functioning from 1999, to provide for efficient, cost effective and impartial settlement of claims and grievances of any person against a Life or General Insurer in public and private sector. Insurance Ombudsman has two types of functions to perform (1) conciliation, and (2) Award making. The insurance Ombudsman is empowered to receive and consider complaints in respect of personal lines of insurance from any person who has any grievance against an insurer. The complaint may relate to any grievance against the insurer, i.e. (a) any partial or total repudiation of claims by the insurance companies, (b) dispute with regard to premium paid or payable in terms of the policy, (c) dispute on the legal construction of the policy wordings in case such dispute relates to claims; (d) delay in settlement of claims and (e) non-issuance of any insurance document to customers after receipt of premium. Ombudsman's powers are restricted to insurance contracts of value not exceeding ₹ 20 lakh. (The insurance ombudsman has been discussed in detail in chapters 4 and 5.)

(iii) *SEBI Ombudsman*

The Securities and Exchange Board of India (SEBI) under Section 30 read with sub-section (1) of Section 11 of the SEBI Act, 1992, has framed the SEBI (Ombudsman) Regulations, 2003, which were notified on 21-08-2003. The Regulations provide for the establishment of the office of Ombudsman to redress the grievance of investors in securities and connected matters. The provisions of Ombudsman Regulations have been incorporated in the code of conduct of various market intermediaries for effective compliance of the Ombudsman award. The listed companies and registered stock market intermediaries have to disclose the name, address and other particulars of Ombudsman in their office for the benefit of investors.

The SEBI appoints one or more Ombudsmen and Stipendiary Ombudsman on the recommendation of a selection committee headed by a retired Judge of a High Court. "Stipendiary Ombudsman" Acts as Ombudsman in respect of a specific matter or matters in specific territorial jurisdiction. The office of the Ombudsman is to be located in Mumbai and other places to be decided by the SEBI. The SEBI is to provide the premises and other infrastructures including staff to the Ombudsman and Stipendiary Ombudsman. The Ombudsman and Stipendiary Ombudsman, meeting the prescribed qualifications, are to be appointed for a term of five years and are eligible for reappointment up to the age of 70 years.

An investor and recognized investors association can lodge complaint in writing on the following grounds:

(i) non-receipt of refund orders, allotment letters in respect of public issue of securities of companies or units of mutual funds or collective investment schemes;
(ii) non-receipt of share certificates, unit certificates, debenture certificates, bonus shares;
(iii) non-receipt of dividend by shareholders or unit-holders;
(iv) non-receipt of interest of debentures, redemption amount of debentures or interest on delayed payment of interest on debentures;

(v) non-receipt of interest on delayed refund of application monies;
(vi) non-receipt of annual reports or statements pertaining to the portfolios;
(vii) non-receipt of redemption amount from a mutual fund or returns from collective investment scheme;
(viii) non-transfer of securities by an issuer company, mutual fund, collective investment management company or depository within the stipulated time;
(ix) non-receipt of letter of offer or consideration in takeover or buy-back offer or delisting;
(x) non-receipt of statement of holding corporate benefits or any grievance in respect of corporate benefits etc.;
(xi) any grievance in respect of public rights or bonus issue of a listed company;
(xii) any of the matters covered under section 55A of the Companies Act, 1956; and
(xiii) any grievance in respect of issue or dealing in securities against an intermediary or a listed company.

An aggrieved party can file complaint on above matters himself or through his authorized representative or any investors association against listed company or an intermediary to the Ombudsman within whose jurisdiction registered or corporate office of such listed company or intermediary is located. The complaint has to be in writing and duly signed by the complainant or his authorized representative (not being a legal practitioner) in the specified form and supported by documents relied upon. A complainant, before making a complaint to the Ombudsman, has to make a written representation to the opposite party against whom complaint is to be lodged. In case the complainant's representation is rejected, reply is unsatisfactory or no reply is received within one month, the complainant can file complaint within six months from the date of rejection or within seven months after the receipt of complaint by the opposite party. A person whose complaint on the same subject matter is pending before a consumer forum, arbitrator or court or already decided by such authorities cannot approach the Ombudsman. The Ombudsman may dismiss a complaint *in limine* if the complaint is frivolous or vexatious.

The Ombudsman has the power to call for information from the company or intermediary or any person, institution or authority relating to the subject matter of complaint. The Ombudsman shall maintain the confidentiality of the information so received. The Ombudsman sends a copy of the complaint to the opposite party tries to amicably settle the dispute, and, pass consent order within one month, directing the parties to perform their obligations in terms of the consent award. The Ombudsman adjudicates the complaint, in case the matter cannot be resolved amicably, within one month from the date of receipt of complaint or extended period. The award is made within three months from the date of filing the complaint. The award of the Ombudsman is final and binding on the parties.

A party aggrieved by the Ombudsman's award can file a petition before the SEBI for review of the award on two grounds — (a) there is substantial miscarriage of justice, or (b) there is an error apparent on the face of the award. The petition has to be filed within one month from the receipt of the award. The Ombudsman and SEBI can award reasonable compensation along with interest, including future interest, till the date of satisfaction of the award at the rate of one per cent per annum. Further, cost of proceedings may also be awarded on merit. A party aggrieved by the order of the SEBI on review petition, can appeal before the SEBI Appellate Tribunal. The parties implement the award within one month of receipt of the award from the Ombudsman or SEBI.

(iv) *Electricity Ombudsman*

The Electricity Regulatory Commission, under section 181 read with sub-section (5) of section 42 of the Electricity Act, 2003, issues guidelines for establishment of Forums and Ombudsman for redressal of grievances of electricity consumers. The various State Electricity Regulatory Commissions have issued regulations for the establishment of Forum for redressal of grievances of the consumers and Ombudsman. Under these guidelines the institutions of Electricity Forums and Ombudsman have been created for the redressal of consumer grievances.

The nature and types of complaint include:

- unfair trade practice or a restrictive trade practice adopted by the licensee in providing electricity service;
- electricity services hired or availed of or agreed to be hired or availed of by him suffer from defect or deficiency in any respect;
- licensee has charged for electricity services mentioned in the complaint a price in excess of the price fixed by the Commission;

- electricity services which are hazardous to life and safety when availed, are being offered for use of the public in contravention of the provisions of any law for the time being in force or of any licence;
- violation of any law or license requiring the licensee to display the information in regard to the manner or effect of use of the electrical services; and
- breach of any obligation by the licensee which adversely affects any consumer or which may be considered as a complaintant.

An electricity consumer has to first approach the Electricity Forum for redressal of his grievance. In case he is not satisfied with the order of the Electricity Forum, he can approach Electricity Ombudsman by way of an appeal. He can himself or through his authorized representative file an appeal in writing stating the following: (a) name and address of the consumer, service connection number, category, name of the local licensee's office against whom the representation is made, the facts giving rise to the representation, the grounds thereof, the relief sought from the Ombudsman; and (b) name of the Forum, date of order or decision of the Forum. A consumer has to file appeal within one month from the date of receipt of the order concerned, but the delay can be condoned if there is sufficient reason for the delay. Second, he has to deposit with the licensee one-third of the amount assessed by the Forum and enclose documentary evidence of such deposit with the appeal.

The Ombudsman on registering the representation, calls records from the concerned Forum. He directs the parties to submit written statements. He passes speaking order after perusal of the documents and hearing the parties. Electricity Ombudsman in discharge of his functions is guided by the principles of natural justice. The Ombudsman normally gives award within three months from the date of receipt of appeal. The award of Ombudsman is final and binding on the parties and there is no provision of further appeal.

3.4.10. *Broader Regulatory Framework*

In addition to the above sector specific regulators there are a number of other regulatory bodies created under various statutes to regulate a range of industries and sectors. A few have been enlisted here briefly. Coastal Aquaculture Authority consisting of a Chairman and 10 members has been established under the Coastal Aquaculture Authority Act,

2005, to make regulations for the construction and operation of aquaculture farms within the coastal areas. The Khadi and Village Industries Commission has been constituted under the Khadi and Village Industries Commission Act, 1956, to plan, promote, facilitate, organize and assist in the establishment and development of Khadi and Village Industries in the rural areas in coordination with other agencies engaged in rural development wherever necessary. The Commission consists of Chairperson and ten members. The Veterinary Council of India constituted under the Indian Veterinary Council Act, 1984, consists of one President, one Vice-President and 25 members. The purpose is to make provision of veterinary practices and maintenance of registers of persons qualified to engage in veterinary practice for the whole of India and for matters connected therewith or ancillary thereto. The Agricultural and Processed Food Products Export Development Authority constituted under the Agricultural and Processed Food Products Export Development Authority Act, 1985, to undertake measures for the development and promotion of export of scheduled products. It consists of one chairperson and 38 members. The Atomic Energy Regulatory Board has been created under the Atomic Energy Act, 1962. The Central Pollution Control Boards act as regulatory authorities under the Water (Prevention and Control of Pollution) Act, 1974, for prevention and control of water pollution and maintaining and restoring of wholesomeness of water. The same Control Board also functions under the Air (Prevention and Control of Pollution) Act, 1981, for prevention and control of air pollution. The board consists of one Chairman, 15 members and one member secretary. The Protection of Plant Varieties and Farmers' Rights Authority under the Protection of Plant Varieties and Farmers' Rights Act, 2001, has been established to promote the development of new varieties of plants and to protect the rights of farmers and breeders. It consists of one Chairman and 15 members. The Information Technology Act, 2000, establishes Office of Controller of Certifying Authorities to exercise supervision over the activities of the Certifying Authorities and lay down the standards to be maintained by the Certifying Authorities.

The Parliament has enacted a number of statutes to regulate several professions and to provide for adjudicative machinery for enforcing discipline and regulating professional conduct among the practitioners of the concerned profession. In India there are many such statutes which provide for regulatory and disciplinary authorities for regulation of these professional service providers. Some of these statutes are the

Advocates Act, 1961; the Chartered Accountants Act, 1949; the Cost and Works Accountants Act, 1959; the Architects Act, 1972; the Pharmacy Act, 1948; the Medical Council Act, 1956; the Indian Medicine Central Council Act, 1970; the Dentists Act, 1948; and the Press Council Act, 1978. The Press Council Act creates Press Council to preserve the freedom of the press and to maintain and improve standard of newspapers. The Council consists of a Chairman and 28 members. All the members of the Council are selected in accordance with prescribed rules and the government has no power to select anyone of them. The body is thus genuinely independent of the government control. The Advocates Act, 1961, creates a State Bar Council at the State-level and a Bar Council of India at the Centre. Under the Chartered Accountants Act, 1949, the Institute of Chartered Accountants of India is constituted as an incorporated body. It has a Council and officers to manage its own affairs. Its functions, *inter alia*, include enforcing professional discipline and maintenance of the status and standard of professional qualifications. The Architects Act, 1972, creates a Council of Architecture. The Council may remove the name of an architect from the register of architects, or take any other disciplinary action against him, or account of professional misconduct after holding an inquiry as prescribed by the rules and after giving a hearing to the architect. The Indian Medical Council Act, 1956, creates Medical Council of India consisting of one President, one Vice-President and Members. The Council has power to regulate through regulations such as permission for establishment of new medical college, new course of study, non-recognition of medical qualification in certain cases, recognition of medical qualification granted by universities or medical institutions in India etc. The Council can even take disciplinary action and remove the name of a medical practitioner from the Indian Medical Register. The Indian Medicine Central Council Act, 1970, creates the Central Council of Indian Medicine which discharges similar functions with respect to practitioners of Indian Medicine as the Medical Council performs with respect to the other medical practitioners. The Dentists Act, 1948, creates the Dental Council of India and State Dental Councils. A State Dental Council may remove the name of a dentist from the register of dentists on the ground of misconduct etc. after giving him a reasonable opportunity of being heard and after such inquiry as it deems fit. Similarly, there is Pharmacy Council under the Pharmacy Act, 1948; Indian Nursing Council under the Indian Nursing Council Act, 1947; the Homoeopathy Central Council under the

Homoeopathy Central Council Act, 1973; to regulate the professionals in the area.

Commodity Boards, a kind of self-regulatory mechanism in the case of specific commodities has also been created by several statutes. Examples of such statutes are the Coffee Act, 1942; the Tea Act, 1953; the Rubber Act, 1947; the Coir Industry Act, 1953; the Cardamom Act, 1965; the Seeds Act, 1966; and the Tobacco Act, 1975.[334] Coir Board has been established under Coir Industry Act, 1953, to promote development of coir industry, facilitate export of coir fibre, coir mats and other articles made of coir. It consists of one chairperson and 40 members. Regulation of these commodities in their various facets involves adjudication by the respective statutory board which includes as its members representatives of the producers and the traders concerned. The several commodity boards regulate production, price, sale, import and export, storage etc. of the respective commodities. Some of these regulations involve licensing.

3.4.11. *Regulation — Emerging Dimensions*

India is the first country in Asia to establish independent regulator for pension sector to integrate the disparate components of the social security system into a fiscally, financially and economically sustainable multi-tier system. Established in 2004, Pension Fund Regulatory and Development Authority (PFDRA) will regulate the new civil service scheme, but over time is expected to turn into a regulator for entire pension sector.[335] The independent regulators are in contemplation for a number of other infrastructure sectors like railways, postal, housing, broadcasting etc. In the postal sector the *de jure* monopoly of the department has been eroded by a large number of private couriers who have taken away a good proportion of the high revenue yielding traffic from the state owned monopoly operator. Recognizing the *de facto* operation of a large number of couriers without rights and obligations imposed by law, a need is being felt within and outside government circles that postal operations in India must be brought under a licensed regime for proper regulation of activities.[336] To regulate the private entities and fly by night operators in the education sector, the University Grant Commission is set to regulate the admissions and fees in all professional courses in the private deemed universities. As per the draft regulations a retired Supreme Court Judge to be nominated by the Chief Justice of India will head the National Fee Committee to decide the fee for all deemed universities on the laid down criteria. To oversee the admissions, the UGC will constitute a national level Admission Monitoring Committee headed by a former Vice-Chancellor of a Central University.[337] To further regulate the investments by the foreign investors in the education sector the government also introduced Foreign Educational Institutions (Regulation of Entry and Operations, Maintenance of Quality and Prevention of Commercialization) Bill in March 2007. It would clarify regulations for setting-up campuses in India, a process which many U.S. University have found to be an obstacle. One proposed provision of the Bill is that foreign educational institutions would invest 51 per cent of the capital for a project and all profit would be reinvested in the Indian partner institution in most cases, encouraging only serious educators. They have to ensure that the quality of the programme in India is comparable to those on the home campus. The government is also working towards setting-up an independent regulatory mechanism to rein in vulgarity and obscenity on television. The Ministry has hoped to put in place an independent and credible regulatory mechanism in the form of Broadcasting Authority of India through the Broadcasting Bill, with some teeth to take care of violations by content providers and advertisers.[338]

Till now the real estate sector was largely unregulated in India. If a consumer had a complaint against a developer he would had to make rounds of consumer or civil courts. Also absence of standardization and lack of adequate consumer protection has constrained the healthy and orderly growth of the industry.[339] To protect the interest of the allottees/purchasers by promoting transparency, accountability and efficiency in the construction and execution of real estate projects by promoters, the Parliament has enacted the Real Estate (Regulation and Development) Act, 2016. The Act provides for the establishment of the "Real Estate Regulatory Authority" which one year from the date of coming into force of the Act, a specialized regulator for monitoring of the sector. The promoter has to register their project, both residential and commercial where the land is over 500 sq.m. or eight apartments, with the Regulatory Authority before booking, selling or offering apartments for sale in such projects. This law makes it mandatory for developers to post all information on issues such as project plan, layout, Government approvals, land title status, sub-contractors to the project, schedule for completion with the State Real Estate Regulatory Authority (SRERA) and then in effect pass this information on to the consumers. The present practice of selling on the basis of ambiguous super built-up area for a real estate project will come to a stop as this law makes it illegal. Carpet area has been clearly defined in the law. Currently, if a project is delayed, then the developer does not suffer in any way. Now, the law ensures that any delay in project completion will make the developer liable to pay the same interest as the EMI being paid by the consumer to the bank back to the consumer. The maximum jail term for a developer who violates the order of the appellate tribunal of the SRERA is three years with or without a fine. The buyer can contact the developer in writing within one year of taking possession to demand after sales service if any deficiency in the project is noticed. The developer cannot make any changes to the plan that has been sold without the written consent of the buyer. This puts paid to a common and unpopular practice by developers to increase the cost of projects.[340]

Many of vital infrastructure projects are delayed due to repeated and prolonged litigation, which slows down development. To deal with it the government has proposed the draft Public Contracts (Resolution of Disputes) Bill, 2015. The draft suggests setting-up a tribunal for public contracts with a chairperson, vice-chairpersons and members. The tribunal will have four key functions to discharge: adjudicate upon disputes and differences; refer disputes and differences to arbitration and adjudicate upon awards arising from such proceedings; adjudicate upon disputes involving a public authority, service provider or contractor; and exercise supervisory control over the arbitral proceedings. The jurisdiction of the dispute-resolution tribunal will include disputes arising from a public contract that has been executed or entered into by the Centre, State, any local or other statutory authority, any corporation, society or trust owned or controlled by the Centre/State, or by any entity in which such a government is a joint signatory. It will extend to any dispute arising from a public contract, including execution, specific performance of terms of the contract, termination, cancellation, repudiation, and claims for damages for breach of contract. It will also extend to disputes that involve an amount of ₹ 5 crore or more, or any lower amount in respect of any class or category of cases, as prescribed. The draft prescribes a timeline of 120 days for completion of the arbitration process and announcement of award. There is also a time limit of 180 days (which can be extended by a maximum of 15 days) for the tribunal to complete the proceeding and issue an order. An appeal against this order can be made only in the Supreme Court.[341]

NOTES

1. Majone, G. (ed.) (1989), *Deregulation or Re-regulation*, London, Pinter, pp. 1-2.
2. See Noll, R. (1987), *The Political Foundations of Regulatory Policy* in K. McCubbins and T. Sullivan (ed.), *Congress*, Cambridge, Cambridge University Press, p. 464.
3. See Ayres and Braithwaite (1992), *Responsive Regulation*, Oxford University Press, New York, pp. 7-12.
4. Majone, G. (ed.) (1989), *Deregulation or Re-regulation*, London, Pinter, q. in C. Hood (1994), *Explaining Economic Policy Reversals*, Open University Press, Buckingham, p. 20.
5. Böllhoff, D., "The New Regulatory Regime — The Institutional Design of Telecommunications Regulation at the National Level", in Héritier, A. (ed.) (2002), *Common Goods: Reinventing European and International Governance*, Lanham, Rowman & Littlefield Publishers, pp. 227-57.
6. Prosser, T. (1997), *Law and the Regulators*, Oxford: Clarendon Press, p. 46.
7. John F. McEldowney (1998), *Public Law*, Sweet and Maxwell, London, 2nd Edn., pp. 387-88.
8. *Ibid.*, p. 388.
9. David Parker (1999), "Regulating Public Utilities: Lessons from the UK Experience", *International Review of Administrative Sciences*, 65(1), pp. 117-18.
10. *Ibid.*, p. 118.
11. *Ibid.*, p. 120.
12. Thatcher, M. (1998), "Institutions, Regulation, and Change: New Regulatory Agencies in the British Privatized Utilities", *West European Politics*, 21(1), pp. 120-47, 123.
13. David Coen, Adrienne Héritier and Dominik Böllhoff (2002), *Regulating the Utilities: UK and Germany Compared*, Anglo-German Foundation for the Study of Industrial Society, October, pp. 5-6.
14. The Communications Act, 2003, Section 3(1).
15. David Coen, Adrienne Héritier and Dominik Böllhoff (2002), *Regulating the Utilities: UK and Germany Compared*, Anglo-German Foundation for the Study of Industrial Society, October, p. 9.
16. Hogwood, B.W. (1990), "Developments in Regulatory Agencies in Britain", *International Review of Administrative Sciences*, 56, p. 600.
17. Gilland, T., "The Regulatory Regime of the Electricity Industry in England and Wales", in Sturm, R. and Wilks, S. (eds.) (1996), *Wettbewerbspolitik und die Ordnung der Elektrizitätswirtschaft in Deutschland und Großbritannien*, Baden-Baden, Nomos, p. 244.
18. Prosser, T. (1997), *Law and the Regulators*, Oxford, Clarendon Press, pp. 185ff.
19. The Railway Act, 1993, Section 1.
20. *Ibid.*, section 4(1)(a).
21. Thatcher, M. (1998), "Institutions, Regulation, and Change: New Regulatory Agencies in the British Privatized Utilities", *West European Politics*, 21(1), pp. 120-47.
22. Knill, C., "Reforming Transport Policy in Britain: Concurrence with Europe but Separate Development", in Héritier, A.; Kerwer, D.; Knill, C.; Lehmkuhl, D.; Teutsch, M. and Douillet, A.C. (eds.) (2001), *Differential Europe: New Opportunities and Restrictions for Policy-Making in Member States*, Rowman & Littlefield Publishers, Lanham, pp. 113-87.

23. David Coen, Adrienne Héritier and Dominik Böllhoff (2002), *Regulating the Utilities: UK and Germany Compared*, Anglo-German Foundation for the Study of Industrial Society, October, p. 15.
24. Héritier, A. (1998), *After Liberalization: Public-Interest Services in the Utilities*. Bonn, Preprint, Max Planck Project Group Common Goods: Law, Politics, Economics, pp. 15f; Héritier, A. and Schmidt, S.K., "After Liberalization: Public Interest Services and Employment", in Scharpf, F.W. and Schmidt, V.A. (2000), *Welfare and Work in the Open Economy: Diverse Responses to Common Challenges*, Oxford: Oxford University Press, p. 562.
25. ORR (1997), *Inquiry into the Proposed Strategic Rail Authority and Railway Regulation*, Office of the Rail Regulator, London.
26. SRA (2000), *Annual Report 1999/2000*, Strategic Rail Authority, London, p. 15.
27. Wade and Forsyth (2005), *Administrative Law*, 9th edn., Oxford University Press, pp. 148-50.
28. Articles 81 and 82 EC Treaty.
29. Replacing the regime established in the Fair Trading Act, 1973.
30. Act of 1998, Section 2 and Section 3 providing that this prohibition does not apply to the bodies and agreements listed in four schedules (two of which can be amended by the Secretary of State). Individual exemption may be granted by the Director-General of Fair Trading (Section 4).
31. *Ibid.*, Section 2(4).
32. *Ibid.*, Section 2(2)
33. *Ibid.*, Section 18. Once more provision is made for exclusion from the reach of Section 18 by Schedule (generally liable to be altered by the Secretary of State): Section 19.
34. *Ibid.*, Section 18(2).
35. *Ibid.*, Section 25. The Director may require the production of documents or information from 'any person' [Sec. 26(1) and may enter premises under a warrant without notice (Sec. 28) or without a warrant but with notice (Sec. 27)].
36. *Ibid.*, Sections 32 and 33.
37. *Ibid.*, Sections 36-38.
38. *Ibid.*, Section 34.
39. *Ibid.*, Section 12 Where the Director has given guidance that a particular agreement does not infringe Chapter One, then no further action will be taken and no penalty imposed unless there has been a material change of circumstances (or like development) (Section 16).
40. *Ibid.*, Section 35.
41. See Enterprise Act, 2002, Sections 12, 21 and Schedule 5 read with Section 46 of the 1998 Act.
42. The Competition Act,1998 Section 47, read with Schedule 5 of the 2002 Act.
43. *Ibid.*, Section 49.
44. Act of 2002, Section 131(1).
45. Act of 2002, Section 22. In addition there must be a "relevant merger situation" which requires in broad terms that "two or more enterprises have ceased to be distinct enterprises" and the "turnover in the United Kingdom of the enterprise being taken over exceeds & 70 million" (Sec. 23). Similar rules apply where the merger is simply anticipated (Sec. 33).
46. Act of 2002, Schedule 8. The normal method in the case of mergers is to seek an undertaking that an enterprise divest itself of certain assets, etc. but if undertakings

are not given orders may be made. The OFT has the duty of enforcing the orders made (Sec. 162).

47. For the structure of the Tribunal see Act of 2002, Part Two and Schedule 4.
48. Act of 2002, Section 120(4).
49. Act of 2002, Section 120(6).
50. These include the Self-Regulating Organizations (SROs) [such as the Personal Investment Authority (PIA), the Investment Management Regulatory Organization (IMRO) and the Securities and Futures Authority (SFA)], the Supervision and Surveillance Branch of the Bank of England, the Building Societies Commission. The Authority takes the place of the former Securities and Investments Board.
51. Wade and Forsyth (2005), *Administrative Law*, 9th edn., Oxford University Press, pp. 151-53.
52. Financial Services and Markets Act, 2000, Sec. 1, 1st Schedule Sets out the requirements of the FSA's constitution. Its executive members and chairman are appointed by the Treasury.
53. FSM Act of 2000, Section 2(1).
54. FSM Act of 2000, Section 2(2). The objectives are defined in detail in Sections 3-6.
55. FSM Act of 2000, Section 8. To this end there must be maintained a standing 'Practitioner Panel' and a 'Consumer Panel' for consultation purposes: Sections 9 and 10.
56. FSM Act, 2000, Section 14(2).
57. FSM Act, 2000, Section 14(3).
58. The Treasury may exempt specified persons or classes of person (Section 38).
59. FSM Act, 2000 Section 20. A breach of this section is a crime (up to two years' imprisonment on indictment) but it is a defence for a defendant to show that he took "all reasonable precautions and exercised all due diligence" (Sec. 23). Elsewhere in the Act there are many criminal sanctions, e.g. Sec. 346.
60. Regulated activities are defined in Section 22 and 2nd schedule and include the provision of most forms of financial service.
61. A person is 'authorized' if he has been given permission to carry on a regulated activity by the Authority (Sec. 31). The procedure for obtaining permission is set out in Part IV of the Act. The 3rd schedule and 4th schedule contain special provision for the authorization of firms situated in European Economic Area states and authorized by their home states to carry on the activity in question.
62. Part V.
63. FSM Act, 2000 Sections 91, 100, 206. A penalty is recoverable as a debt (Section 180).
64. *Ibid.*, Section 45 and Section 33.
65. *Ibid.*, Section 132. The members are appointed by the Lord Chancellor and the President (and chairmen of panels) must be legally qualified (11th Schedule).
66. *Ibid.*, Section 395.
67. *Ibid.*, Section 56.
68. *Ibid.*, Section 57(5).
69. *Ibid.*, Section 137.
70. *Ibid.*, Section 138. Rules can also be made about non-regulated activities to authorized person to ensure that there is no adverse effect on regulated activity [Sec. 138(1)(b)].

71. *Ibid.*, Section 143.
72. *Ibid.*, Sections 144-46.
73. *Ibid.*, Section 151(2); and a breach of a rule is not an offence [Section 151(1)].
74. *Ibid.*, Section 149.
75. *Ibid.*, Section 150(2).
76. *Ibid.*, Section 150(1).
77. *Ibid.*, Section 155(4).
78. *Ibid.*, Section 157.
79. *Ibid.*, Section 213.
80. See the Bill's explanatory notes, paragraph 5.
81. Phillip Hampton (2005), *Reducing Administrative Burdens: Effective Inspection and Enforcement*, March.
82. *Introduction to the Regulatory Programme of the United State Government*, April 1, 1987-March 1988, US Office of Management and Budget (1988).
83. *Background Report on Government Capacity to Assure High Quality Regulation*, OECD, 1999, p. 13.
84. Data from the Washington University Centre for the Study of American Business (1999), q. in *Background Report on Government Capacity to Assure High Quality Regulation*, OECD, p. 13.
85. President Ronald Reagan (1998), "The Regulatory Message of the President", *Regulatory Programme*, April 1-March 31, p. vii.
86. Phillip J. Cooper (2000), *Public Law and Public Administration*, 3rd Edn., F.E. Peacock Publishers, p. 110.
87. *Ibid.*
88. Breyer Stephen (1982), *Regulation and Its Reform*, Cambridge M.A.: Harvard University Press, p. 205.
89. Ralph Bradburd and David R. Ross (1991), *Regulation and Deregulation in Industrial Countries — Some Lessons from LDCs*, WPS 699, World Bank, June p. 75.
90. Levine Richard (1989), "Unfinished Business: Reagan's Regulatory Relief", *Management Review*, March, p. 18.
91. *Report to Congress on the Costs and Benefits of Federal Regulations*, US Office of Information and Regulatory Affairs, Office of Management and Budget, September 30, 1997.
92. Statement by the Vice-President, *The Regulatory Plan*, 29 October, 1997, ER 57003.
93. President Ronald Reagan, Executive Order No. 12498, *Regulatory Planning Process*, January 4, 1985.
94. White House, Memorandum for Heads of Executive Departments and Agencies, *Development of Administration's Regulatory Programme*, January 4, 1985.
95. President Executive Order 12866, *Regulatory Planning and Review*, September 30, 1993.
96. The SEBI Act, 1992, Section 3.
97. *Ibid.*, Section 4(1).
98. *Ibid.*, Section 4(4).
99. *Ibid.*, Section 4(5).
100. *Ibid.*, Section 5(1).
101. *Ibid.*, Section 5(2).
102. *Ibid.*, Section 11.

103. *Ibid.*, Section 20A.
104. *Ibid.*, Section 15K.
105. *Ibid.*, Section 15L.
106. *Ibid.*, Section 15M.
107. *Ibid.*, Section 15N.
108. *Ibid.*, Section 15U(1).
109. *Ibid.*, Section 15Y.
110. *Ibid.*, Section 15Z.
111. *Ibid.*, Section 29(1).
112. *Ibid.*, Section 30(1).
113. TRAI Act, 1997, Section 3(1).
114. *Ibid.*, Section 3(2).
115. *Ibid.*, Section 3(3).
116. *Ibid.*, Section 3(4).
117. *Ibid.*, Section 4 as amended by the TRAI (Amendment) Act, 2000.
118. *Ibid.*, Section 4 proviso.
119. *Ibid.*, Section 5(1).
120. *Ibid.*, Section 5(2).
121. *Ibid.*, Section 6(1).
122. *Ibid.*, Section 11(1).
123. *Ibid.*, Section 14.
124. *Ibid.*, Section 18.
125. *Ibid.*, Section 14.
126. *Ibid.*, Section 14-A(1).
127. *Ibid.*, Section 14-A(2).
128. *Ibid.*, Section 14-A(3).
129. *Ibid.*, Section 14-A(3) Proviso.
130. *Ibid.*, Section 14-A(4).
131. *Ibid.*, Section 14-A(5).
132. *Ibid.*, Section 14-A(6).
133. *Ibid.*, Section 14-A(6) Proviso.
134. *Ibid.*, Section 14-A(7).
135. *Ibid.*, Section 14-B.
136. *Ibid.*, Section 14-B(2).
137. *Ibid.*, Section 14-D.
138. *Ibid.*, Section 14-C Proviso.
139. *Ibid.*, Section 14-C.
140. *Ibid.*, Section 14-B(3)(a).
141. *Ibid.*, Section 14-B(3)(b).
142. *Ibid.*, Section 14-B(3)(c).
143. *Ibid.*, Section 14-B(4).
144. *Ibid.*, Section 14-I.
145. *Ibid.*, Section 14-J.
146. *Ibid.*, Section 14-M.
147. *Ibid.*, Section 14-M First Proviso.
148. *Ibid.*, Section 14-M Second Proviso.
149. *Ibid.*, Section 15.
150. *Ibid.*, Section 16(1).
151. *Ibid.*, Section 18(1).

152. *Ibid.*, Section 18(2).
153. *Ibid.*, Section 18(3).
154. The Electricity Act, 2003, Preamble.
155. *Ibid.*, Section 76(1).
156. *Ibid.*, Section 82(1).
157. *Ibid.*, Section 83(1).
158. *Ibid.*, Section 76(2).
159. *Ibid.*, Section 76(2) Proviso.
160. *Ibid.*, Section 76(3).
161. *Ibid.*, Section 76(4).
162. *Ibid.*, Section 76(5).
163. *Ibid.*, Section 76(6).
164. *Ibid.*, Section 77(1).
165. *Ibid.*, Section 77(2).
166. *Ibid.*, Section 77(3).
167. *Ibid.*, Section 77(4).
168. *Ibid.*, Section 78(1) read with Clauses (2), (3) and (4).
169. *Ibid.*, Section 78(9) Proviso.
170. *Ibid.*, Section 79(1).
171. *Ibid.*, Section 79(2).
172. *Ibid.*, Section 79(3).
173. *Ibid.*, Section 79(4).
174. *Ibid.*, Section 178(1).
175. *Ibid.*, Section 80(1).
176. *Ibid.*, Section 80(2).
177. *Ibid.*, Section 80(3).
178. *Ibid.*, Section 81.
179. *Ibid.*, Section 82(1), appointed date defined in Section 2(2).
180. *Ibid.*, Section 82 First Proviso.
181. *Ibid.*, Section 82 Second Proviso.
182. *Ibid.*, Section 82(2).
183. *Ibid.*, Section 82(3).
184. *Ibid.*, Section 82(4).
185. *Ibid.*, Section 85(1).
186. *Ibid.*, Section 85(2), (3) and (4).
187. *Ibid.*, Section 86(1).
188. *Ibid.*, Section 86(2).
189. *Ibid.*, Section 86(3).
190. *Ibid.*, Section 86(4).
191. *Ibid.*, Section 87.
192. *Ibid.*, Section 83(1).
193. *Ibid.*, Section 83(1) Proviso.
194. *Ibid.*, Section 83(2).
195. *Ibid.*, Section 83(4).
196. *Ibid.*, Section 89(1).
197. *Ibid.*, Section 110.
198. *Ibid.*, Section 111(1).
199. *Ibid.*, Section 111(2).
200. *Ibid.*, Section 111(2) Proviso.

201. *Ibid.*, Section 111(3).
202. *Ibid.*, Section 111(4).
203. *Ibid.*, Section 111(5).
204. *Ibid.*, Section 111(5) Proviso.
205. *Ibid.*, Section 112(1).
206. *Ibid.*, Section 112(2)(a).
207. *Ibid.*, Section 112(2)(b).
208. *Ibid.*, Section 112(2)(b) Proviso.
209. *Ibid.*, Section 112(2)(c).
210. *Ibid.*, Section 112(3).
211. *Ibid.*, Section 113(1)(a).
212. *Ibid.*, Section 113(1)(b).
213. *Ibid.*, Section 113(2).
214. *Ibid.*, Section 113(3).
215. *Ibid.*, Section 114(1).
216. *Ibid.*, Section 114(1) First Proviso.
217. *Ibid.*, Section 114(1) Second Proviso.
218. *Ibid.*, Section 120(1).
219. *Ibid.*, Section 120(3).
220. *Ibid.*, Section 120(4).
221. *Ibid.*, Section 121.
222. *Ibid.*, Section 123.
223. *Ibid.*, Section 124(1).
224. *Ibid.*, Section 124(2).
225. *Ibid.*, Section 125.
226. *Ibid.*, Section 125 Proviso.
227. Statement of Objects and Reasons of the Competition Act, 2002.
228. Competition Act, 2002, Section 7(1).
229. *Ibid.*, Section 7(2).
230. *Ibid.*, Section 7(3).
231. *Ibid.*, Section 7(4).
232. *Ibid.*, Section 9(1).
233. *Ibid.*, Section 10(1).
234. *Ibid.*, Section 12.
235. *Ibid.*, Section 10(5).
236. *Ibid.*, Section 11(1).
237. *Ibid.*, Section 11(2).
238. *Ibid.*, Section 11(3).
239. *Ibid.*, Section 13.
240. *Ibid.*, Section 22(1).
241. *Ibid.*, Section 22(2).
242. *Ibid.*, Section 22(3).
243. *Ibid.*, Section 35.
244. *Ibid.*, Preamble and Section 18.
245. S.P. Sathe (2004), *Administrative Law*, 7th Edn, Lexis Nexis Butherworths, p. 352.
246. The Competition Act, 2002, Section 6(1).
247. *Ibid.*, Section 33.
248. *Ibid.*, Section 36(1).

249. *Ibid.*, Section 36(2).
250. *Ibid.*, Section 36(3).
251. *Ibid.*, Section 36(4).
252. *Ibid.*, Section 53A(1).
253. *Ibid.*, Section 53C.
254. *Ibid.*, Section 53D.
255. *Ibid.*, Section 53E.
256. *Ibid.*, Section 53F.
257. *Ibid.*, Section 53B.
258. *Ibid.*, Section 53T.
259. *Ibid.*, Section 61.
260. PNGRB Act, 2006, Section 3(1).
261. *Ibid.*, Section 3(2).
262. *Ibid.*, Section 3(3).
263. *Ibid.*, Section 3(4).
264. *Ibid.*, Section 4(1).
265. *Ibid.*, Section 5(1).
266. *Ibid.*, Section 5(2).
267. *Ibid.*, Section 12(2).
268. *Ibid.*, Section 24(1).
269. *Ibid.*, Section 24(2).
270. *Ibid.*, Section 27.
271. *Ibid.*, Section 30(1).
272. *Ibid.*, Section 33(1).
273. *Ibid.*, Section 33(2).
274. *Ibid.*, Section 33(5).
275. *Ibid.*, Section 37(1).
276. *Ibid.*, Section 37(2).
277. *Ibid.*, Section 37(3).
278. *IIFCL Infra Newsletter*, Vol. II, No. 2 April-June, 2009, Indian Infrastructure Finance Company Ltd., pp. 2-4.
279. The AERA Act, 2008, Section 4.
280. *Ibid.*, Section 6(1).
281. *Ibid.*, Section 13(1).
282. *Ibid.*, Section 13(2).
283. *Ibid.*, Section 13(3).
284. *Ibid.*, Section 13(4).
285. *Ibid.*, Section 19.
286. *Ibid.*, Section 20.
287. *Ibid.*, Section 21.
288. *Ibid.*, Section 18(1).
289. *Ibid.*, Section 18(2).
290. *Ibid.*, Section 18(3).
291. *Ibid.*, Section 26.
292. *Ibid.*, Section 28.
293. *Ibid.*, Section 29(1).
294. *Ibid.*, Section 31.
295. FSSAI Act, 2006, Section 4(2).
296. *Ibid.*, Section 5(1).

297. *Ibid.*, Section 5(2).
298. *Ibid.*, Section 5(3).
299. *Ibid.*, Section 5(4).
300. *Ibid.*, Section 5(5).
301. *Ibid.*, Section 7(1).
302. *Ibid.*, Section 16(1).
303. *Ibid.*, Section 16(2).
304. *Ibid.*, Section 16(3).
305. *Ibid.*, Section 29(1).
306. *Ibid.*, Section 29(2).
307. *Ibid.*, Section 29(3).
308. *Ibid.*, Section 29(4).
309. *Ibid.*, Section 29(5).
310. *Ibid.*, Section 29(6).
311. *Ibid.*, Section 30(1).
312. *Ibid.*, Section 30(2).
313. *Ibid.*, Section 30(3).
314. *Ibid.*, Section 36(1).
315. *Ibid.*, Section 36(2).
316. *Ibid.*, Section 36(3).
317. *Ibid.*, Section 37(1).
318. *Ibid.*, Section 37(2).
319. *Ibid.*, Section 68(1).
320. *Ibid.*, Section 68(2).
321. *Ibid.*, Section 70(1).
322. *Ibid.*, Section 70(2).
323. *Ibid.*, Section 70(3).
324. *Ibid.*, Section 70(4).
325. *Ibid.*, Section 70(5).
326. *Ibid.*, Section 71(1).
327. *Ibid.*, Section 71(6).
328. *Ibid.*, Section 72(1).
329. Banking Ombudsman Scheme, 2006, Clause 4.
330. *Ibid.*, Clause 8.
331. *Ibid.*, Clause 9.
332. *Ibid.*, Clauses 11 & 12.
333. *Ibid.*, Clause 14.
334. Also the Coconut Development Board Act, 1979, provides for the creation of a board to promote and develop the coconut industry.
335. Mukul Asher and Deepa Vasudevan, "The Role of Pension Regulators", *Margin*, Vol. 38, No. 1, pp. 1-11.
336. B.B. Dave (2008), "Policy Framework for Regulation of Courier Services", *Economic and Political Weekly*, January 19, Vol. XLIII, No. 3, pp. 24-27.
337. Chetan Chauhan (2009), "Government to Regulate Fee Structure of Private Varsities", *The Hindustan Times*, February 9, pp. 1 & 14.
338. "Regulatory Body for TV: Minister", *The Hindustan Times*, July 28, 2009.
339. Moushumi Das Gupta, "Here's How the Real Estate Bill will Benefit Buyers", *The Hindustan Times*, New Delhi, March 10, 2016, http://www.hindustantimes.com/india/all-you-need-to-know-about-real-estate-bill-listed-for-re-passage-today/story-bvr7LwbdLpH7bLc02B97zN.html, accessed on August 1, 2016.

340. Sudip Mullick and Amit Wadhwani, *Salient Features of the Real Estate (Regulation and Development) Bill, 2016*, 21 March 2016. http://www.mondaq.com/india/x/475724/real+estate/Salient+Features+Of+The+Real+Estate+Regulation+And+Development+Bill+2016 accessed on Aug 1, 2016; "Real Estate Regulator Bill: 10 Things You Should Know About It", *The Economic Times*, March 10, 2016. http://economictimes.indiatimes.com/wealth/real-estate/real-estate-regulator-bill-10-things-you-should-know-about-it/articleshow/51344872.cms accessed on August 1, 2016.

341. Shishir Sinha (2015), *Public Contracts: Speedy Dispute Resolution Mechanism on Anvil*, June 25. http://www.thehindubusinessline.com/economy/public-contracts-speedy-dispute-resolution-mechanism-on-anvil/article7354687.ece accessed on August 1, 2016.

4

REGULATION OF INSURANCE SECTOR
An Analysis of Indian Legal Framework

4.1. Introduction

The law governing insurance has gradually developed as a result of the interaction of the conflicting interests of the insurers and insuring public over the years. On the one hand, the insurers are inclined to condition and limit the risks they are prepared to assume and on the other hand, the insuring public requires to be protected in view of the wide disparity in economic power between the insurance corporations and the individual insured. Governments have also intervened at various stages. All these have contributed to the development of law governing the business of insurance. The task undertaken in this chapter is to provide broadly the different kinds of insurance and the development of legal framework in a gradual process.

Insurance, in law and economics, is a form of risk management primarily used to hedge against the risk of a contingent loss. Insurance is defined as the equitable transfer of the risk of a loss, from one entity to another, in exchange for a premium, and can be thought of as a guaranteed small loss to prevent a large, possibly devastating loss. An insurer is a company selling the insurance; an insured is the person or entity buying the insurance. The insurance rate is a factor used to determine the amount to be charged for a certain amount of insurance coverage, called the premium. Risk management, the practice of appraising and controlling risk, has evolved as a discrete field of study and practice. It may also be said that insurance is a cooperative device to spread the loss, caused by an uncertain event which is covered by insurance, over a large number of persons who are also exposed to the same risk and insure themselves against the risk. Thus, it is "a contract by which one party in consideration of a price (called the premium) paid to him adequate to the risk becomes security to the other that he shall not suffer loss, damage or prejudice by the happening of the perils specified to certain things which may be exposed to them".[1] Every contract of insurance, except life assurances, is a contract of indemnity; every contract of insurance is a contract of absolute good faith and requires some insurable interest to support it, without which it will be mere wager.

Insurance business and the need for insurance cover are growing with the growing complexity of life and commerce. As a consequence there is now a bewildering variety of insurance cover. Keeping in view the development of civilization, economic growth and nature of interest, the contract of insurance can be broadly classified as follows:[2]

1. *Life Insurance* — The contract of life insurance is a mutual agreement by which the insurer undertakes to pay a given sum to the insured or his nominee upon the happening of a particular event. It is also called endowment insurance.
2. *Employer's Liability Insurance* — It is one against loss arising from injury suffered by the employee in the course of his employment. Such a liability would be covered under ESI Act, Workmen's Compensation Act.
3. *Property Insurance* — Property insurance relates to fire, burglary, house-breaking, and crop insurance.
4. *Marine Insurance* — Marine insurance is one against loss by injury to ship, cargo, or freight by perils of the sea.
5. *Fidelity Insurance* — It is one against loss arising from default or dishonesty of employees.
6. *Motor Accident Insurance* — In insurance under Motor Vehicle Act, 1988, as amended in 1994, compensation is payable on account of injury sustained, permanent or partial disablement and death caused in the accident, or damage to property during the course of accident. Under this Act, third party is also covered for compensation.
7. *Railway Accidents* — Compensation is payable in case the victim suffers an injury, permanent or partial disablement, loss of limb, death arising out of the railway accident or damage to goods etc. For this Railways Accidents and Untowards Incidents (Compensation) Rules, 1990, have been framed.
8. *Miscellaneous Insurance* — This includes variety of new insurances under 'social insurance' or 'liability Insurance', Industrial Insurance, Aviation Insurance etc.

4.2. Indian Insurance Industry: A Perspective

4.2.1. *Life Insurance*

Life insurance in its existing form came to India from the United Kingdom (UK) with the establishment of a British firm, Oriental Life Insurance Company in Kolkata in 1818 followed by Bombay Life Assurance Company in 1823, the Madras Equitable Life Insurance Society in 1829 and Oriental Government Security Life Assurance Company in 1874. All of these operated in India but did not insure the lives of Indians. They were insuring the lives of the Europeans living in India. Prior to 1871 Indian lives were treated as sub-standard and charged an extra premium of 15 per cent to 20 per cent. Bombay Mutual Life Assurance Society, an Indian insurer which came into existence in 1871, was the first to cover Indian lives at normal rates.[3]

After the start of the Swadeshi Movement in 1905, indigenous enterprises sprang-up in many industries. The Movement also touched the insurance industry leading to formation of dozens of life insurance companies along with provident fund companies (provident fund companies are pension funds). The United India in Chennai, National Indian and National Insurance in Kolkata and the Cooperative Assurance at Lahore were established in 1906. In 1907, Hindustan Cooperative Insurance Company came into being in one of the rooms of the Jorasanko, house of the great poet Rabindranath Tagore, in Kolkata. The Indian Mercantile, General Assurance and Swadeshi Life (later Bombay Life) were some of the companies established during the same period. The Indian Life Assurance Companies Act, 1912 was the first statutory measure to regulate life insurance business. Later, in 1928, the Indian Insurance Companies Act was enacted, *inter alia*, to enable the Government to collect statistical information about both life and non-life insurance business transacted in India by Indian and foreign insurers, including the provident insurance societies. In 1938, with a view to protect the interest of insuring public, earlier legislation was consolidated and amended by the Insurance Act, 1938, with comprehensive provisions for detailed and effective control over the activities of insurers. In order to administer the aforesaid legislation, an insurance wing was established and attached first with the Ministry of Commerce and later with the Ministry of Finance. This insurance wing was administratively responsible for deciding policy matters pertaining to insurance. The actuarial and operational matters relating to insurance industry were looked after by an attached office at Shimla headed first by the Actuary to the Government of India, then by the Superintendent of Insurance and finally by the Controller of Insurance.

The Insurance Act, 1938, was amended in 1950, making far-reaching changes, such as requirement of equity capital for companies carrying on life insurance business, ceilings on share holdings in such companies, stricter controls on investments of life insurance companies, submission of periodical returns relating to investments and such other information to Controller as he may call for, appointment of administrators for mismanaged companies, ceilings on expenses of management and agency commission, incorporation of the Insurance Association of India and formation of councils and committees thereof.

By 1956, 154 Indian insurers, 16 non-Indian insurers and 75 provident societies were carrying on life insurance business in India. Life insurance business was confined mainly to cities and better off segments of the society. On 19th January, 1956 the management of life insurance business of 245 Indian and foreign insurers and provident societies was taken over by the Central Government and then nationalized on 1st September, 1956. LIC was formed in September 1956 by an Act of Parliament and with capital contribution of ₹ 5 crore from the Government of India.

The then Finance Minister, Shri C.D. Deshmukh, while piloting the Bill for nationalization, outlined the objectives of LIC thus: to conduct the business with the utmost economy, in a spirit of trusteeship; to charge premium not higher than warranted by strict actuarial considerations; to invest the funds for obtaining maximum yield for the policy-holders consistent with safety of the capital; to render prompt and efficient service to policy-holders, thereby making insurance widely popular. In 1974, LIC formulated its objectives in pursuance of recommendations of the Administrative Reforms Commission as under:

(i) To spread life insurance much more widely and in particular to the rural areas, and to the socially and economically backward classes with a view to reaching all insurable persons in the country. and providing them, at a reasonable cost, adequate financial cover against death.

(ii) To maximize mobilization of people's savings by making insurance linked savings adequately attractive.

(iii) To bear in mind, in the investment of funds, the primary obligation to its policy-holders, whose money it holds in trust, without losing sight of the interest of the community as a whole; the funds to be deployed to the best advantage of the investors as well as the community as a whole, keeping in view national priorities and obligations of attractive return.

(iv) To contract business with utmost economy and with the full realization that the moneys belong to the policy-holders.

(v) To act as trustees of the insured public in their individual and collective capacities.

(vi) To meet the various life insurance needs of the community that would arise in the changing social and economic environment.

(vii) To involve all people working in the Corporation to the best of their capability in furthering the interest of the insured public by providing efficient service with courtesy.

(viii) To promote amongst all agents and employees of the Corporation a sense of participation, pride and job satisfaction through discharge of their duties with dedication towards achievement of corporate objectives.

4.2.2. *General Insurance*

General insurance has developed with the industrial revolution in the West and consequent growth of seafaring trade and commerce in the seventeenth century.[4] It came to India from UK. To begin with this business was transacted by British and other foreign insurance companies through their agencies in India. The first general insurance company, *viz.* Triton Insurance Company Ltd. was established in Kolkata in 1850 whose shares were held mainly by the British. The first insurance company to be set-up by Indians for transacting all classes of general insurance business was Indian Mercantile Insurance Company Ltd., Mumbai, 1907. The British and other foreign insurers had a share of about 40 per cent in insurance business at the time of Independence which declined progressively thereafter.

In 1957, the General Insurance Council, a wing of the Insurance Association of India, framed a code of conduct for ensuring fair conduct and sound business practices in the general insurance industry. An administrative set-up headed by the Controller of Insurance was set-up in 1957 at Delhi with branch offices at Mumbai, Kolkata and Chennai for administering the code of conduct. Further, in order to increase retention of general insurance business in India, the insurers started a reinsurance company, *viz.* India Reinsurance Corporation Ltd. in 1956 to which they all voluntarily ceded 10 per cent of their gross direct business. In 1961, by an amendment to the Insurance Act, this voluntary arrangement was formalized by notifying the Indian Guarantee and General Insurance Company Ltd., a Government company, along with the India Reinsurance Corporation as "Indian Reinsurers". The cession to each of them was about 10 per cent. Besides, the insurers also had a pooling arrangement in terms of which a percentage of their fire and marine hull insurance business was ceded to the Fire Insurance Pool and the Marine Hull Insurance Pool, respectively. Such business was retroceded among the same insurers thereby spreading a portion of the risk under every policy among the members of the pool. In 1968, the Insurance Act was amended again to provide for extension of social control over insurers transacting general insurance business. The amendments provided, *inter alia*, for regulation of investment of assets, setting-up of the Tariff Advisory Committee (TAC) under the chairmanship of the Controller of Insurance, minimum solvency margin, licensing of surveyors and payment of premium before commencement of risk. The Insurance Act also gave powers to the Controller of Insurance, to carry out inspection, investigation, and search and seizure of books. These amendments to the Act came into force w.e.f. June 1, 1969. Before, however, they could be effectively implemented, management of non-life insurers was taken over by the Central Government in 1971 as a prelude to nationalization. General insurance business was nationalized with effect from January 1, 1973 by the General Insurance Business (Nationalization) Act, 1972.

Prior to 1973, general insurance was, by and large, city-oriented, catering mainly to the needs of organized trade and industry. One hundred and seven insurers including branches of foreign companies operating within the country were amalgamated and grouped into four companies, *viz.* the National Insurance Company Ltd., the New India Assurance Company Ltd., the Oriental Insurance Company Ltd., and the United India Insurance Company Ltd. with head offices at Kolkata, Mumbai, New Delhi and Chennai, respectively. GIC was incorporated as a company in November 1972 and it commenced business w.e.f. January 1, 1973. The capital of GIC was subscribed by the Government of India, and that of the four companies, by GIC. All the five entities are Government companies registered under the Companies Act.

The purpose of establishment of GIC as a holding company of the four operation (subsidiary) companies, as stated in the General Insurance Business (Nationalization) Act, is superintending, controlling and carrying on the business of general insurance. The functions of GIC as enunciated in the said Act are as follows:

(a) the carrying on of any part of general insurance business as deemed desirable;
(b) aiding, assisting and advising the companies in the matter of setting-up of standards of conduct and sound practice in general insurance business and in rendering efficient customer service;
(c) advising the acquiring companies in the matter of controlling their expenses including the payment of commission and other expenses;
(d) advising the acquiring companies in the matter of the investment of funds; and
(e) issuing directions to acquiring companies in relation to the conduct of general insurance business.

4.2.3. *Regulation of Insurance Business*

Insurance business was conducted in India without any specific regulation.[5] They were subject to Indian Companies Act, 1866. Regulation of insurance in India was introduced with the promulgation of the Indian Life Assurance Companies Act in 1912. In 1912, two sets of legislation were passed: the Indian Life Assurance Companies Act and the Provident Insurance Societies Act. There are several striking features of these legislations. First, they were the first legislations in India that particularly targeted the insurance sector. Second, they left general insurance business out of it. The Government did not feel the necessity to regulate general insurance. Third, they restricted activities of the Indian insurers but not the foreign insurers even though the model used was the British Act of 1909.

Comprehensive arrangements were, however, brought into effect only with the enactment of the Insurance Act, 1938. Efforts in this direction continued progressively till 1956 for life insurance business and till 1968 for general insurance. During this period, an office of the Controller of Insurance evolved, through its various phases, as an attached office firstly of the Ministry of Commerce and then of the Ministry of Finance of the Government of India. The Controller was a statutory functionary whose duties, powers, and responsibilities as regards supervision and regulation of insurance business are defined in the Insurance Act. On the nationalization of life insurance business and creation of LIC in 1956, followed by the nationalization of general insurance business and formation of GIC and its subsidiaries in 1973, application of the Insurance Act, 1938 was greatly modified by the nationalizing enactments and government notifications issued thereunder from time-to-time. Most of the regulatory functions were taken away from the Controller and vested in LIC and GIC themselves.

The Controller of Insurance was the supervisory and regulatory authority for the insurance industry till 1999. The 1968 amendment to the Insurance Act sought to enlarge his role to curb the ills of the general insurance industry such as malpractice in claims settlement, unhealthy rate cutting and misuse of insurance funds for speculative and other purposes. The nationalization of the general insurance industry in 1972, however, changed the position. The Controller's office moved from Shimla to Delhi and started shrinking in all respects. The Controller and Assistant Controller now became a part of the Insurance Division of the Ministry of Finance and performed a few residual functions under law which, in practice, were not of much importance. These developments also created some functional anomalies. The Joint Secretary in the Insurance Division of the Ministry and *ex-officio* Controller of Insurance was on the Board of two of the four general insurance companies. From his earlier position of the Chairman, he was relegated to the position of a member of TAC which was then headed by the Chairman of GIC.

The Insurance Act did seek to create a strong and powerful supervisory and regulatory authority as the Controller of Insurance. His role and responsibilities were set out in several sections of the Act. It empowered him to direct, advise, caution, prohibit, investigate, inspect, prosecute, search, seize, fine, amalgamate, authorize, register, and liquidate insurance companies. The powers and position of the Controller of Insurance had undergone drastic curtailment after nationalization of the industry. This presumably happened in the belief that the nationalized industry did not require any supervision and that its accountability to government through the Insurance Division of the Finance Ministry would be adequate. There were, however, operations which required professional regulation even in the nationalized insurance sector, particularly in areas relating to expenses, customer service, claim settlements, resolution of disputes, reasonableness of tariffs, and prevention of restrictive trade practices. The need was even greater if the insurance sector was to be liberalized and the private sector was to be allowed entry into the business. Special dispensations given to LIC and GIC and its subsidiary companies by Government notifications were required to be withdrawn to create a level playing field for all insurers. Further, the Acts of Parliament which nationalized life and general insurance industries, also required substantial amendments.

4.2.4. *Recommendations of Malhotra Committee*

Although Indian markets were privatized and opened up to foreign companies in a number of sectors in 1991, insurance remained out of bounds on both counts. With pressure from the opposition, the Government decided to set-up a committee in 1993 headed by Mr. R.N. Malhotra, former Finance Secretary and RBI Governor. The Committee was formed to evaluate the Indian insurance industry and recommend its future direction with the objective of complementing the reforms initiated in the financial sector.

I. Recommendation of the Committee as regards Regulation of Business

As regards the regulation of insurance business, the Committee recommended as follows:

(i) There is an urgent need to activate the insurance regulatory apparatus even in the present set-up of nationalized insurance sector. For this purpose and as an interim measure, the office of Controller of Insurance should be restored its full functions under the Insurance Act and it should be set-up as a separate office as a matter of high priority.

(ii) Legislation and Government notifications, through which LIC and general insurance companies were exempted from several provisions of the Insurance Act in derogation of the functions of the Controller, should be withdrawn.

(iii) Meanwhile, step should be initiated for the establishment of a strong and effective insurance regulatory authority in the form of a statutory autonomous board on the lines of SEBI.

(iv) The insurance regulatory authority should be highly professional and compact organization with adequate information technology support.

(v) The insurance regulatory authority should have an independent source for financing its establishment and activities. For this purpose it should be permitted to levy a charge of say 0.05 per cent of the yearly Indian premium income of the insurance industry.

II. Recommendations with regard to Liberalization of the Industry

As regards the liberalization of the industry, the Committee recommended as follows:

(i) The private sector should be allowed to enter insurance business. No single company should be allowed to transact both life and general insurance business. The number of new entrants should be controlled.

(ii) The minimum paid-up capital for new entrant should be ₹ 100 crore. However, a lower capital requirement can be prescribed for state level cooperative institutions taking up life insurance business.

(iii) The promoters' holding in a private insurance company should not exceed 40 per cent of the total. However, if the promoters wish to start with a higher holding, they should be permitted to do so provided their holding is brought down to 40 per cent within a specified period of time through public offering. No person other than the promoters should be allowed to hold more than 1 per cent of the equity. Promoters should at no time hold less than 26 per cent of the paid-up capital.

(iv) If and when entry of foreign insurance companies is permitted, it should be done on selective basis. They should be required to float an Indian company for purpose, preferably in joint venture with Indian partner.

(v) Before the private sector is allowed to enter the insurance field, the Controller of Insurance should start functioning effectively.

(vi) Regulatory and prudential norms as well as conditions for ensuring level playing fields among insurers should be finalized early so that intending entrants into the insurance business would be aware of the stipulations they would have to comply with. These conditions should aim to ensure that life insurers do not neglect the small man or the rural business and that the general insurers have balanced portfolios.

(vii) Though nationalized insurance companies are in a position to face competition, it is essential that they quickly upgrade their technology, reorganize themselves on more efficient lines and are enabled to operate as board-run enterprises.

4.2.5. *Mukherjee Committee, 1997*

Immediately after the publication of the Malhotra Committee Report, a new committee (called the Mukherjee Committee) was set-up to make concrete plans for the requirements of the newly formed insurance companies. Recommendations of the Mukherjee Committee were never made public. But, from the information that filtered out it became clear that the committee recommended the inclusion of certain ratios in insurance company balance sheets to ensure transparency in accounting. But the Finance Minister objected. He argued (probably on the advice of some of the potential entrants) that it could affect the prospects of a developing insurance company.

4.2.6. *190th Report of Law Commission of India, 2004*

In the changing economic scenario, it was felt that the IRDA would have to play a vital role for the regulation and development of insurance business and accordingly, the Insurance Act, 1938, would require review and revision. This prompted the reference to the Law Commission of India. In 2002 Insurance Regulatory and Development Authority requested the Law Commission to examine the Insurance Act, 1938. At the instance of the Insurance Regulatory Development Authority, the Law Commission of India undertook the exercise of examining the Insurance Act, 1938, and to make recommendations for revision of the Act and for consequential amendments thereto.

The Law Commission in the Report dealt with the following issues:

(i) Changes in definitions including replacement of references in the Insurance Act, 1938, to older enactments by corresponding new legislations and reclassification of insurance businesses including changed definitions of the terms 'insurance' and 'insurer';

(ii) Deletion of provisions of the Insurance Act, 1938, that are redundant and deletion of transitional provisions of the Act;

(iii) Merger of relevant provisions of IRDA Act with the Insurance Act, 1938;

(iv) Setting-up of an independent grievance redressal mechanism with an appeal to an Insurance Appellate Tribunal and further appeal to the Supreme Court of India;

(v) Repudiation of policies by insurers on account of misstatement of facts or failure to make disclosure of the material information would render the contract void or voidable;

(vi) Assignment and transfer and nomination of beneficiaries under insurance policies; and

(vii) Provisions relating to penalties and other changes.

4.2.7. *KPN Committee, 2005*

The Insurance Act, 1938, notwithstanding many an amendment since its enactment, has retained a basic structure, despite its vintage in the context of contemporary insurance legislation across the globe. The amendments in 1950, 1956, and 1972 have varied from minor changes to substantial overhaul, dictated by the necessities of various times. The last exercise was undertaken in the year 1999 and some modifications in the year 2002 did leave an imminent need to make a thorough review of the Act for removal of perceived incongruities and inconsistencies and come up with a possible integrated set of provisions to take in what had been separately legislated for in the IRDA Act, 1999. The Law Commission was requested to undertake this exercise of reviewing the Act, in the context particularly of the IRDA Act, 1999, and the Commission in its report in 2004 has made specific recommendations in regard to many an area requiring legislative intervention. However, it has been of the considered view that as regards the following specialized domain areas, a detailed examination by experts would be necessary for suggesting amendments to the statutory framework of the Act: Provisions relating to Investments, Shareholders' Funds and Policy-holders' Funds, Sufficiency of Assets, Insurance Surveyors, Tariff Advisory Committee. Accordingly, the Insurance Regulatory and Development Authority in 2005 constituted this Committee, *inter alia*, to examine in detail all the aforesaid five areas and recommend changes that are warranted in the statutory framework. Further, the Committee was also called upon to indicate any other sections of the Act, which need to be amended, in the light of the developments that have taken place in the insurance scene, other than those covered by the Law Commission's recommendations. The Chairman of IRDA had also desired and empowered the Committee to also give its views, suggestions and recommendations on such of the areas examined by the Law Commission, as are considered necessary by the Committee, in the light particularly of submissions made in regard thereto.[6]

4.3. Insurance Industry: Present Scenario

It was felt in 1990s that the scale of economic activity attained in the mid-eighties and the momentum generated through the reforms process in other sectors of the economy cannot be sustained by state controlled insurance industry and that insurance penetration and enlargement of the market can be accomplished only when a large number of companies compete with each other. Thus, the insurance sector was opened up for private participation on the ground that inspite of enormous contributions made by the public sector to expand the coverage and spread awareness about insurance, the interests of the consumers would be better served if there is competition among the insurers. It was also recognized that the country has a vast potential waiting to be tapped and this can be done only when we have a large number of companies spreading their wings across the country and offering a variety of products catering to the demands of different sections of the population. It was also felt that competition would generate a healthy attitude towards redressal of consumer grievances and improve the quality of service.

The champions of change finally prevailed and the Insurance Regulatory and Development Authority Act was notified in April 2000. While the long debates in the 90s; and the twists and turns that surrounded the opening up of the sector for private participation had, at times, thrown up serious concerns about the implementation of insurance reforms in this country, once the legislation was put through, the actual process of inducting private players into the market had gone off smoothly. After that the transition from state monopoly to free market of the insurance sector has been as hassle free.

Supervision and regulation of insurance is a relatively new experience in India. It is the job of the regulator to ensure that the insurers have, at any point of time, sufficient resources to meet the liabilities and that all customers are treated in an equitable manner. When the state enterprises controlled the entire industry, the safety of the policy-holders' fund was ensured through state guarantee while the fair dealings with the customers were achieved through parliamentary oversight of the state enterprises. The opening of the sector for private participation naturally raised issues about ensuring solvency of the companies and fair treatment to the insured. The Regulations framed by the Authority deal with both the issues in a comprehensive way. The former is addressed by stipulating a high level of capital requirement for entry into the field and rigorous enforcement of the solvency requirements, while the latter is covered by the regulations put in place for protection of policy-holder's interests.

The opening up of the market for private players has encouraged international insurance giants to enter the Indian market through the medium of joint ventures with Indian promoters. However, the foreign promoters' equity in an Indian insurance company is limited by law to 26 per cent. The market has attracted participants from across the globe. A rich tapestry of foreign promoters from U.K., U.S.A., Canada, France, Germany, Netherlands, South Africa, Australia have descended on the Indian scene. All these promoters have probably sought to re-establish themselves in the Indian market where they had a presence prior to the nationalization of the industry.

The foreign perceive that the India market is expected to grow rapidly and thus provide business opportunities in the long run. The foreign partners have rich experience in the insurance market, which will enable the ventures promoted within the country to offer new products and provide better services for the policy-holders. These companies have varied and rich experience in insurance underwriting and administration and by joining hands with the Indian promoters have brought to Indian insurance market new management techniques and practices, underwriting standards, risk analysis and risk management techniques — all of which will indeed strengthen the Indian insurance market and afford the Indian customers risk covers at competitive costs. The India partners have vast experience as industrial groups. Thus, the joint ventures have been promoted by financially sound groups which are fully aware of the need for commitment of resources — technical, monitory and human in the long-run.

4.3.1. *Growth of Premium*

A remarkable feature of the post-liberalization landscape is the unprecedented growth in the premium. The growth is primarily significant in life insurance. Life insurance industry recorded a premium income of ₹ 2,01,351.41 crore during 2007-08 as against ₹ 1,56,075.85 crore in the previous year, recording a growth of 29.01 per cent. The significant increase in the insurance market in last 7-8 years has reinforced the arguments of pro-reform groups that there is vast market waiting to be exploited and that a single, state driven entity will not, by itself, be able to cater to the requirements of that market. It also established that so far as life insurance market is concerned, the growth of the private sector need not be at the expense of the public sector. The public and the private sector can together experience high growth rates for a long time to come.

In the case of general insurance industry, the premium growths have been significant though not as impressive as in the case of life insurance. The general insurance has underwritten a total premium of ₹ 27,823.74 crore in 2007-08 as against ₹ 24,905.47 in 2006-07 exhibiting a growth rate of 11.72 per cent. The premium had grown from ₹ 9,450 crore in 1999-2000 to ₹ 25,000 crore in 2006-07. The growth in the premium has, therefore, come through increased volumes, especially under motor and health sectors. In 2007-08 the private insurers had a market share of 39.51 per cent. The portfolio mix also indicates that the private sector had succeeded in acquiring a share in the more profitable segments. Private insurers have also attempted to bring in product innovation especially in the areas of liability covers and crop insurance. Further, significant changes in non-life insurance can be ushered in when the tariffs are removed and the companies are permitted to tailor the products to meet specific requirements of the customers.

4.3.2. *Removal of Tariffs*

There has been a persistent demand for freeing the general insurance market from the rigidities inherent in a regime where tariffs are prescribed by an outside agency. It has been argued that the insurers should be able to determine what risks they are prepared to underwrite and the rate at which they would underwrite the risk. It was also pointed out that the present system of having tariffs in some risks and free rates in others is leading to distortions in pricing as the insurers are willing to underwrite risks not covered by tariff at throwaway prices in order to gain access to lucrative fire and engineering covers which were covered by tariff. The Authority recognized that the consumer would normally stand to gain when there is a free market and de-tariffing is an essential pre-requisite for the healthy growth of the market. With this the de-tariffing of the general insurance industry was made effective from January 1, 2007, which is one of the most important events post-opening up of the insurance sector. Now, the insurers can determine their rates for all risks that they undertake.

4.3.3. *Insurance Penetration*

With large population and untapped market, insurance is a big opportunity in India. The life insurance business (measured in the context of first year premium) registered an impressive growth of 23.88 per cent as against 94.96 per cent in 2006-07. The general insurance business has registered growth of 11.72 per cent in 2007-08 as against 3.52 per cent achieved in 2006-07. This has resulted in increasing insurance penetration in the country. Insurance penetration or premium volume as a ratio of GDP, for the year 2007 stood at 4.00 per cent for life insurance and 0.60 for non-life insurance and for the year 2006 stood at 4.10 per cent for life insurance and 0.60 per cent for non-life insurance. The level of penetration, particularly in life insurance, tends to rise as income levels increase. India, with its huge middle class households, has exhibited growth potential for the insurance industry. Saturation of markets in many developed economies has made the Indian market even more attractive for global insurance majors. The insurance market in India has witnessed dynamic changes including presence of a number of insurers in both life and non-life segment. While insurance penetration was 1.93 per cent in 1999 it rose to 4.8 per cent in the year 2007. It has thus more than doubled in 7 years. While the increase is impressive in the case of life, where it increased from 1.39 to 4.0 per cent, it remained stagnant at nearly 0.6 per cent in the case of non-life.

4.3.4. *Insurance Density*

In the area of insurance density, significant contribution has been made by the private sector. We had the problem of not only absence of risk protection through insurance, but also a considerable amount of under insurance. During the pre-liberalization era, the nationalized companies were unable to target niche markets and were content to sell a large number of low ticket items spread over the whole country. The private sector has, on the contrary, started looking at the requirements of various segments of the population, and introduced need-based selling through excellent counselling. Most of the private insurance companies are joint ventures with recognized foreign players across the globe. Consumer awareness has improved.

4.3.5. *Innovation in Products*

Competition has brought more products and improved the customer service. It has a positive impact on the economy in terms of income generation and employment opportunities in the sector. Growth in insurance industry has been spurred by product innovation, active sales and distribution channels coupled with targeted advertising and marketing campaigns by the insurers. Innovations have come not only in the form of benefits attached to the products, but also in delivery mechanisms which have emanated from various marketing tie-ups both within the realm of financial services and outside. All these have taken life insurance closer to the customer as well as making it more relevant. The insurance companies are increasingly tapping the semi-urban and rural areas to take across the message of protection of life through insurance cover. The insurers have also introduced special products aimed at the rural markets. Particularly, unit linked products have attracted the attention of the insured. While this is a product for the discerning public, there seems to be appetite for this product from all sections. Availability of riders, particularly health riders, has been a positive development. In the non-life segment crop insurance-based on rainfall and temperature, experiments in health insurance, Directors and Officers liability covers have made their entry and have come to stay. The removal of tariffs will give a further boost to development of tailor made products in the years to come.

4.3.6. *Agents' Training*

The expanding market demands a large agency force. The insurers have, therefore, been recruiting agency force on a continuous basis. Presently, there are more than 20 lakh individual agents and nearly 5,000 Corporate Agents. In order to introduce an element of professionalism in the insurance intermediaries elaborate training and testing arrangements were introduced by the Authority. The Authority had, during 2004, streamlined the system of training and impressed upon the insurers the need for greater attention being paid to the training of their agency force. The revised guidelines were issued after extensive consultations with the stakeholders and it is hoped that this effort would result in improving the quality of the agency force. The Authority is keen that the agency force should be properly equipped as the insurance products are no longer simple and the agent should be able to assess the requirements and advise on the appropriate policy.

The opening of the sector is accompanied by entry of new set of intermediaries in the insurance market. The institution of corporate agents was a new experiment started by the Authority to facilitate sale of insurance policies through existing institutions which are in contact with a large section of the population in the discharge of their normal activities.

The introduction of brokers in the Indian insurance industry in the liberalized scenario is another significant development. Brokers act as representatives of the policy-holders although they are paid by the insurers. As a result, they are expected to bring better service to the clients in several areas like: (i) Monitoring the insurance market, the credibility of the players and the quality of services they render; (ii) Analyzing the various products available in the market and assist the clients in choosing the products that suit their requirement; (iii) Helping the client in the completion of the proposals, conclusion of the contract and render subsequent service, if any; and (iv) Assisting the client in the settlement of claims. Although the agent is also expected to render most of these services, for several reasons this has not been achieved in the Indian context. Being better equipped with higher level of training and with no obligations to the insurers, the brokers are expected to deliver these services to the client in a more objective fashion.

4.3.7. *Rural and Social Focus*

One of the concerns expressed with opening of the insurance sector was that the competition generated with the entry of private insurers would result in all the insurers including the public sector insurers to chase the niche markets in the relatively well-off regions and their activities would, therefore, be mostly urban centric and they would ignore the rural markets and the weaker sections of the society. It was then argued by many academicians that all business relating to rural areas and weaker sections need not be loss making and all insurers should have the obligation to serve the rural areas and weaker sections. The Insurance Act was, therefore, amended authorizing the Regulator to lay down certain obligations on the insurers towards rural areas and weaker sections.

The Authority notified the regulations on obligations of insurers towards the rural and social sectors in the year 2000. The definition of rural area is in accordance with the one provided by the Census of India. It is mandatory for all insurers to comply with the rural and social sector obligations which are linked to the year of commencement of operations of the respective company.

In respect of the public sector insurers (four non-life insurers and LIC), the Regulations provide that the quantum of insurance business to be done in the rural and social sectors shall not be less than what was recorded by them for the accounting year ended 31st March, 2002. The Authority monitors the performance of the insurers in fulfilling their obligations to these sectors. The insurance companies have over the last seven years set-up systems to explore and exploit the potential of the rural markets. The obligation has not been viewed merely as a statutory requirement. The insurers recognized the potential of the rural markets; particularly in the context of these markets having exhibited the ability to procure goods and services with the growing income levels. There is also awareness about the need for insurance particularly life and health. The new players are making an effort to tap these markets in a commercial way. This fact is duly reflected in the premium underwritten in the rural sectors/lives covered in the social sectors by some of the insurers which is in excess of the stipulated obligations.

4.3.8. *Micro Insurance Regulations*

Proper implementations by the insurers of the social and rural obligations would depend on the development of products suited to the requirements of the target population and the commitment on the part of the intermediary to bring the product and the consumer together. In the absence of an appropriate product and a willing and dedicated intermediary the observance of obligations could degenerate into adherence to the letter of the law and not its spirit. To avoid such a situation the Authority came out with micro-insurance regulations defining the micro-insurance product and giving the insurer access to various channels for fulfilling the obligations in the spirit in which they were mandated.

The regulations are aimed at facilitating the insurers' efforts to bring down the costs of transactions, thereby achieving the objective of offering reduced premium rates to the targeted policy-holders. Micro-insurance aims at meeting the insurance needs of the rural and targeted section of the population to cover the risks of loss of life, their main income earning assets their habitats and to cover them for their health needs. Availability of composite insurance products is, therefore, one of the requirements/prerequisites of the rural and targeted market segments. The regulations provide the framework by allowing one class of insurer (say life) to tie-up with another class of insurer (say non-life) for offering their respective products. The micro-insurance regulations also aim at developing self-sustainable standalone institutional micro-insurance delivery channels.

4.4. Regulatory Framework for the Insurance Sector

The Constitution of India is of federal type, wherein there is division of powers between the Centre and the States so that each of them is independent of other within its own sphere. Articles 245 and 246 of the Constitution lay down the principle of distribution of powers. The Seventh Schedule of the Constitution contains three lists of subjects which are within the exclusive legislative competence of the Union and the States and the Concurrent List. Subjects of all India relevance have been kept in the Union List. The winding-up of trading corporations including banking, insurance (Item 43) and Insurance (Item 47) are items of the Union List. Hence, only the Union Legislature can enact laws relating to insurance. Thus, the business and various other aspects relating to insurance are regulated by Central Laws, namely the Insurance

Act, 1938, the Life Insurance Corporation Act, 1956, the General Insurance Business (Nationalization) Act, 1972, the Marine Insurance Act, 1963, and the Motor Vehicles Act, 1988. The Indian Contract Act, 1872, governs most of the aspects of the insurance contract. Additionally, the Transfer of Property Act, 1882, the Foreign Exchange Management Act, 2000, Income Tax Act, 1961, Indian Stamp Act and the Hindu and Indian Succession Act and few other laws also govern some aspects involved in insurance.

4.4.1. *Insurance Act, 1938*

The law relating to insurance in British India was contained in Indian Life Assurance Companies Act in 1912 and the Indian Provident Insurance Societies Act, 1912. Due to increase in the volumes of life insurance business and the development of other forms of business in British India it became necessary to enact more comprehensive legislation. In 1925, a Bill was prepared to extend to other classes of insurance business the supervision already exercised over life insurance. Almost simultaneously, in England a departmental committee was appointed presided over by Mr. A.C. Clauson, K.C. to report on the amendment of the Insurance Companies Act, 1909, on which the Indian Provident Insurance Societies Act, 1912, had been largely based. On account of this development in England the Government of India decided to postpone that Bill, and await the legislation resulting from the Clauson enquiry. The enquiry, though completed in 1927, was not immediately followed by and did not result in legislation in England, although the report of the committee contained a draft bill embodying the recommendations of the committee for the re-enactment of 1909 Act with extensive modifications. In the meanwhile, Act of 1928 was passed by Indian legislature and it was hoped that the information collected through it would be of value when the time came to consider the problems affecting Indian insurance.

In 1935 the Government decided to proceed with reform of insurance law without waiting for the enactment of legislation in England. Mr. S.C. Sen was placed on special duty to examine the material which had been collected concerning the amendment of company law in general, and insurance law in particular. In 1936, the Indian Companies (Amendment) Act was passed. The project of revising the insurance law was at once taken up. A small advisory committee of experts representing various interests was assembled in the autumn of 1936 to consider in detail various recommendations contained in Mr. Sen's report. This Bill embodying the proposal which the Government has decided to submit to the Legislature after consideration of Mr. Sen's recommendations and opinions of the advisory committee was prepared. The Insurance Bill was passed by the Legislature and received its assent on 26th February, 1938 and came into force on 1st July, 1939. Since, then the Act has been amended from time to time. Lastly, it has been amended in 2002. The Insurance (Amendment) Act, 2002, which came in force on August 9, 2002 permitted, by way of insertion of Section 2(8A) in the Insurance Act, 1938, insurance cooperative societies, registered under the Cooperative Societies Act, 1912 or Multi-State Cooperative Societies Act, 1984 or under any state law relating to cooperative society, to carry on any class of insurance business. However, the IRDA has been empowered to exempt an insurance cooperative society from the application of any of the provisions of the Insurance Act or application of its provisions with exceptions, modifications or adaptations [see proviso to S.94A(2)]. The Insurance (Amendment) Act, 2002, provided for insurance intermediaries, including insurance brokers and consultants, and provisions for the payment of commission, brokerage or fee to them, thereby introducing in this country the business practice adopted the world over in this area. Further, Section 49 of the Act has been modified to provide shareholders an entitlement of actuarial surplus. By virtue of amendment to Section 64VB of the Act, the IRDA has been authorized to prescribe the mode of payment of premium, i.e. through credit cards or through the internet which in turn might result in an increase in the insurance business.

The Act applies to all types of insurance business — life, fire, marine etc. done by companies incorporated in India or elsewhere. It also governs the provident companies, mutual offices and cooperative societies.

Requirement as to Capital

According to Section 6 of the Act no insurer carrying on the business of life insurance, general insurance or re-insurance in India on or after the commencement of the Insurance Regulatory and Development Authority Act, 1999, shall be registered unless he has —

(i) a paid-up equity capital of rupees one hundred crore, in case of a person carrying on the business of life insurance or general insurance; or

(ii) a paid-up equity capital of rupees two hundred crore, in case of a person carrying on exclusively the business as a reinsurer.

In determining the aforesaid capital requirement, the deposit to be made under section 7 and any preliminary expenses incurred in the formation and registration of the company shall be excluded.[7] Further, an insurer carrying on business of life insurance, general insurance or re-insurance in India before the commencement of the Insurance Regulatory and Development Authority Act, 1999 and who is required to be registered under this Act, shall have a paid-up equity capital in accordance with aforesaid capital requirement within six months of the commencement of that Act.[8]

Deposits

To prevent the growth of insurers of small financial resources or speculative concerns, the Act provided for registration of all insurers and a substantial deposit with the Reserve Bank. Every insurer shall, in respect of the insurance business carried on by him in India, deposit and keep deposited with the Reserve Bank of India in one of the offices in India of the bank for and on behalf of the Central Government, the amount hereafter specified, either in cash or in approved securities, estimated at the market value of the securities on the day of deposit or partly in cash and partly in approved securities so estimated —

- in the case of life insurance business, a sum equivalent to one per cent of his total gross premium written in India in any financial year commencing after the 31st day of March, 2000, not exceeding rupees ten crore;
- in the case of general insurance business, a sum equivalent to three per cent of his total gross premium written in India, in any financial year commencing after the 31st day of March, 2000, not exceeding rupees ten crore;
- in the case of re-insurance business, a sum of rupees twenty crore; and
- where the business done or to be done is marine insurance only and relates exclusively to country craft or its cargo or both, the amount to be deposited under this sub-section shall be one hundred thousand rupees only.[9]

These deposits will be held by the RBI though for the credit of the insurer and are returnable to the insurer in the event the provisions of the Insurance Act mandate such return. Interest accruing, due and collected on deposited securities will be paid to the insurer, subject to any deductions of the normal commission chargeable for the realization of interest. In addition, it is important to note that the deposits will:

- not be susceptible to any assignment or charge, or
- not be available for the discharge of any liability of the insurer other than liabilities arising out of policies of insurance issued by the insurer so long as any such liabilities remain undischarged, or
- not be liable to attachment in execution of any decree except a decree obtained by a policy-holder of the insurer in respect of a debt due upon a policy which debt the policy-holder has failed to realize in any other way.

Where the insurer has ceased to carry on all classes of insurance business in India, the deposit made with the RBI shall, on an application being made to the Court, be returned to the insurer after satisfaction of all his liabilities in India in respect of all classes of insurance business.[10]

Registration

Section 3 provides that, no person shall, after the commencement of this Act, begin to carry on any class of insurance business in India and no insurer carrying on any class of insurance business in India shall after the expiry of three months from the commencement of this Act, continue to carry on any such business, unless he has obtained from the Authority a certificate of registration for the particular class of insurance business. In the case of an insurer who was carrying on any class of insurance business in India at the commencement of this Act, failure to obtain a certificate of registration in accordance with the requirements of this sub-clause shall not operate to invalidate any contract of insurance entered into by him if before such date as may be fixed in this behalf by the Central Government by notification in the Official Gazette, he has obtained that certificate.

Every application for registration shall be accompanied by:

(a) a certified copy of the memorandum and articles of association;
(b) name, address and occupation of directors;
(c) a statement of the class or classes of insurance business done or to be done and a statement that the amount required to be deposited with RBI has been deposited;
(d) a declaration that the provisions of those sections as to paid-up equity capital or working capital have been complied with;

(e) in the case of an insurer having principal place of business or domicile outside India a statement by the principal officer setting forth the requirements (if any) not applicable to nationals of the country in which such insurer is constituted, incorporated or domiciled which are imposed by the laws or practice of that country upon Indian nationals as a condition of carrying on insurance business in that country;

(f) a certified copy of the published prospectus and of standard policy forms and statement of assured rates, advantages, terms and conditions to be offered in connection with insurance policies;

(g) the receipt showing payment of fee as may be determined by the regulations which shall not exceed fifty thousand rupees for each class of business as may be specified by the regulations made by the Authority; and

(h) such other documents as may be specified by the regulations made by the Authority.

The Authority may register the applicant as an insurer and grant him a certificate of registration if, on receipt of an application for registration and after making such inquiry as the Authority may deem fit, it is satisfied that —

(a) the financial condition and the general character of management of the applicant are sound;

(b) the volume of business likely to be available to, and the capital structure and earning prospects of, the applicant will be adequate;

(c) the interests of the general public will be served; and

(d) the applicant has complied with the provisions of sections 2C, 5, 31-A and 32 and has fulfilled all the requirements of this section applicable to him.[11]

The Authority shall cancel the registration of an insurer either wholly or in so far as it relates to a particular class of insurance business as the case may be:

(a) if the insurer fails to comply with the provisions of Section 7 or 98 as to deposits; or

(b) if the insurer fails, at any time, to comply the provisions of Section 64-VA as to the excess of the value of his assets over the amount of his liabilities; or

(c) if the insurer is in liquidation or is adjudged as insolvent; or

(d) if the business or class of business has been transferred to any other person or has been transferred to or amalgamated with the business of any other insurer; or

(e) if the whole of the deposit made in respect of insurance business has been returned to the insurer under section 9; or

(f) if, in the case of an insurer specified in sub-clause (c) of clause (9) of section 2, the standing contract referred to in that sub-clause is cancelled or is suspended and continues to be suspended for a period of six months; or

(g) if the Central Government so directs under sub-section (4) of section 33,

and the Authority may cancel the registration of an insurer —

(h) if the insurer makes default in complying with, or acts in contravention of any requirement of this Act or of any rule or any regulation or order made or, any direction issued thereunder; or

(i) if the Authority has reason to believe that any claim upon the insurer arising in India under any policy of insurance remains unpaid for three months after final judgement in regular course of law; or

(j) if the insurer carries on any business other than insurance business or any prescribed business; or

(k) if the insurer makes a default in complying with any direction issued or order made, as the case may be, by the Authority under the Insurance Regulatory and Development Authority Act, 1999; or

(l) if the insurer makes a default in complying with, or acts in contravention of, any requirement of the Companies Act, 1956, or the Life Insurance Corporation Act, 1956, or the General Insurance Business (Nationalization) Act, 1972, or the Foreign Exchange Regulation Act, 1973.[12]

Submission of Returns

According to section 15 the audited accounts and balancesheet referred to in section 11 or sub-section (5) of section 13 and abstract of actuarial report and statement in case of insurer carrying on life insurance business referred to in section 13 shall be printed and four copies thereof shall be furnished as returns to the Authority within six months from the end of the period to which they refer. The period of submission may be extended by three months in the case of insurers having their principal place of business or domicile outside India and in the case of insurers constituted, incorporated or domiciled in India, but also carrying on business outside India. Further, the Central Government may in any case extend the time allowed by this sub-section for the furnishing of such returns by a further period not exceeding three months.

Of the four copies so furnished one shall be signed in the case of a company by the Chairman and two directors and by the principal officer of the Company and, if the company has a managing director or managing agent, by that director or managing agent, in the case of a firm, by two partners of the firm, and, in the case of an insurer being an individual, by the insurer himself and one shall be signed by the auditor who made the audit or the actuary who made the valuation, as the case may be.

Restriction of Commission and Prohibition of Rebating

No person shall, after the expiry of six months from the commencement of this Act, pay or contract to pay any remuneration or reward whether by way of commission or otherwise for soliciting or procuring insurance business in India to any person except an insurance agent or an intermediary or insurance intermediary.[13]

No Insurance agent shall be paid or contract to be paid by way of commission or as remuneration in any form an amount exceeding in the case of life Insurance business, 40 per cent of the first year's premium payable on any policy or policies effected through him and 5 per cent of a renewal premium, payable on such a policy, or, in the case of business of any other class, 15 per cent of the premium. However, insurers, in respect of life insurance business only, may pay, during the first ten years of their business, to their insurance agents 55 per cent of the first year's premium payable on any policy or policies effected through them and 6 per cent of the renewal premium payable on such policies. However, nothing in this sub-section shall apply in respect of any policy of life insurance issued after the 31st day of December, 1950, or in respect of any policy of general insurance issued after the commencement of the Insurance (Amendment) Act, 1950.[14] Further, no insurance agent or intermediary or insurance intermediary shall be paid or contract to be paid by way of commission or as remuneration in any form any amount in respect of any policy not effected through him.[15]

Limitations of Expenditure on Commission

No person shall pay or contract to pay to an insurance agent, and no insurance agent shall receive or contract to receive by way of commission or remuneration in any form in respect of any policy of life insurance issued in India by an insurer after the 31st day of December, 1950, and effected through an insurance agent, an amount exceeding:

(a) where the policy grants an immediate annuity or a deferred annuity in consideration of a single premium, or where only one premium is payable on the policy, 2 per cent of that premium;
(b) where the policy grants a deferred annuity in consideration of more than one premium, 7½ per cent of the first year's premium, and 2 per cent of the each renewal premium, payable on the policy; and
(c) in any other case, 35 per cent of the first year's premium, 7½ per cent of the second and third year's renewal premium, and thereafter 5 per cent of each renewal premium payable on the policy.

However, in a case referred to in clause (c), an insurer, during the first 10 years of his business, may pay to an insurance agent, and an insurance agent may receive from such an insurer, 40 per cent of the first year's premium payable on the policy. Further, in case referred to in clause (c) where the rate of commission payable on the first year's premium is equal to or less than twenty-one per cent thereof, and the rate on the fourth and fifth year's premiums does not exceed six per cent thereof, the Life Insurance Corporation of India may pay to an insurance agent, and the insurance agent may receive from it, commission on the sixth and subsequent year's renewal premiums payable on the policy at a rate not exceeding six per cent of each renewal premium.[16]

No person shall pay or contract to pay to a special agent, and no special agent shall receive or contract to receive, by way of commission or as remuneration in any form, in respect of any policy of life insurance issued in India by an insurer after the 31st day of December, 1950 and elected through a special agent, on amount encoding —

(a) in a case referred to in clause (a) of sub-section (1), one-half per cent of the premium;
(b) in a case referred to in clause (b) of sub-section (1), two per cent of the first year's premium payable on the policy; and
(c) in a case referred to in clause (c) of sub-section (1), fifteen per cent of the first year's premium payable on the policy.

However, in a case referred to in clause (c), an insurer, during the first ten years of his business, may pay to a special agent, and a special agent may receive from such an insurer, seventeen and a half per cent of the first year's premium payable on the policy.[17]

No person shall pay or contract to pay to a special agent, and no special agent, shall receive or contract to receive, by way of commission or remuneration in any form in respect of any policy of general insurance issued in India by an insurer after the commencement of Insurance (Amendment) Act, 1968, and effected through an insurance agent, an amount not exceeding fifteen per cent of the premium payable on the policy, where the policy relates to fire or marine insurance or miscellaneous insurance.[18]

No person shall pay or contract to pay to a principal agent, and no principal agent shall receive or contract to receive, by way of commission or remuneration in any form, in respect of any policy of general insurance issued in India by an insurer after the commencement of the Insurance (Amendment) Act, 1950, and effected through a principal agent, an amount exceeding —

(a) in the case referred to in clause (a) of sub-section (3), twenty per cent of the premium payable on the policy; and
(b) in the case referred to in clause (b) of that sub-section, fifteen per cent of the policy, less any commission payable to any insurance agent in respect of the said policy.

However, the Authority may, in such circumstances and to such extent and for such period as may be specified, authorize the payment of commission or remuneration exceeding the limits specified in this sub-section to a principal agent of an insurer incorporated or domiciled elsewhere than in India, if such agent carries out and has continuously carried out in his own office duties on behalf of the insurer which would otherwise have been performed by the insurer.[19]

A contravention of any of the provisions of the preceding sub-sections by an insurer, any insurance agent who contravenes the provisions of sub-section (1) or sub-section (3) shall be punishable with fine which may extend to one hundred rupees.[20]

Prohibition of Rebates

No person shall allow or offer to allow either directly or indirectly, as an inducement to any person to take out or renew or continue an insurance in respect of any kind of risk, relating to lives or property in India, any rebate of the whole or part of the commission payable or any rebate of the premium shown on the policy, nor shall any person taking out or renewing or continuing a policy accept any rebate, except such rebate, as may be allowed in accordance with the published prospectuses or tables of the insurer. Provided that acceptance by an insurance agent of commission in connection with a policy of life insurance taken out by himself on his own life shall not be deemed to be acceptance of a rebate of premium within the meaning of this sub-section if at the time of such acceptance the insurance agent satisfies the prescribed conditions establishing that he is *bona fide* insurance agent employed by the insurer. Any person making default in complying with the provisions of this section shall be punishable with fine which may extend to five hundred rupees.[21]

Licensing of Insurance Agents

The Authority or an officer authorized by him in this behalf shall, in the manner determined by regulations made by it and on payment of the fee determined by the regulations, which shall not be more than two hundred and fifty rupees, issue to any person making an application in the manner determined by the regulations, a licence to act as an insurance agent for the purpose of soliciting or procuring insurance business, provided that:

- (i) in the case of an individual, he does not suffer from any of the disqualification; and
- (ii) in the case of a company or firm, any of its directors or partners does not suffer from any of the said disqualifications.

However, any licence issued immediately before the commencement of the Insurance Regulatory and Development Authority Act, 1999 shall be deemed to have been issued in accordance with the regulations which provide for such licence.[22]

The disqualifications mentioned in Section 42(4) are:

- (a) that the person is a minor;
- (b) that he is found to be of unsound mind by a court of competent jurisdiction;
- (c) that he has been found guilty of criminal misappropriation or criminal breach of trust or cheating or forgery or an abatement of or attempt to commit any such offence by a court of competent jurisdiction;

However, where at least five years have elapsed since the completion of sentence imposed on any person in respect of such offence, the Authority shall ordinarily declare in respect of such person that his conviction shall cease to operate as a disqualification.

- (d) that in the course of any judicial proceedings relating to any policy of insurance or the winding-up of an insurance company or in the course of an investigation of the affairs of an insurer it has been found that he has been guilty of or has knowingly participated in or connived at any fraud, dishonesty or misrepresentation against an insurer or an insured;
- (e) that he does not possess the requisite qualifications and practical training for a period not exceeding twelve months, as may be specified by the regulations made by the Authority in this behalf;
- (f) that in the case of a company or firm making an application, a director or a partner or one or more of its officers or other employees so designated by it and in the case of any other person, the chief executive, by whatever name called, or one or more of his employees designated by him, do not possess the requisite qualifications and practical training and have not passed such an examination as required under clauses (e) and (f) of sub-section (4);
- (g) that he had not passed such examination as may be specified by the regulations made by the Authority in this behalf; and
- (h) that he violates the code of conduct as may be specified by the regulations made by the Authority.

A licence issued under this section shall entitle the holder to act as an insurance agent for any insurer. A licence issued under this section, after the commencement of the Insurance Regulatory and Development Authority Act, 1999, shall remain in force for a period of three years only from the date of issue, but shall, if the applicant, being an individual does not, or being a company or firm any of its directors or partners does not suffer from any of the disqualification mentioned in clauses (b), (c), (d), (e), (ea) and (f) of sub-section (4) and the application for renewal of the licence reaches the issuing authority at least thirty days before the date on which the licence ceases to remain in force, be renewed for a period of three years at any one time on payment of the fee determined by regulations made by the Authority, which shall not be more than two hundred and fifty rupees, and an additional fee of an amount determined by regulations made by the Authority, not exceeding one hundred rupees by way of penalty if the application for renewal of the licence does not reach the issuing authority at least thirty days before the date on which the licence ceases to remain in force. No application for the renewal of a licence under this section shall be entertained if the application does not reach the issuing authority before the licence ceases to remain in force. However, the Authority may, if satisfied that undue hardship would be caused otherwise, accept any application in contravention of this provision on payment by the applicant of a penalty of seven hundred and fifty rupees.[23]

Investments

Every insurer shall invest and at all times keep invested assets equivalent to not less than the sum of:

(a) the amount of his liabilities to holders of life insurance policies in India on account of matured claims; and
(b) the amount required to meet the liability on policies of life insurance maturing for payment in India,
less:
    (i) the amount of premiums which have fallen due to the insurer on such policies, but have not been paid and the days of grace for payment of which have not expired; and
    (ii) any amount due to the insurer for loans granted on and within the surrender values of policies of life insurance maturing for payment in India issued by him or by an insurer whose business he has acquired and in respect of which he has assumed liability,

in the manner following, namely, twenty-five per cent of the said sum in Government securities, a further sum equal to not less than twenty-five per cent of the said sum in Government securities or other approved securities and the balance in any of the approved investments specified in sub-section (1) of section 27A, or subject to the limitations, conditions and restrictions specified in sub-section (2) of that section, in any other investment.[24]

The insurer shall invest or keep invested any part of his controlled fund in any of the following approved investment, namely:

(a) approved securities;

(b) securities of, or guaranteed as to the principal and interest by Government of the UK;

(c) debentures or other securities for money issued with the permission of the State Government by any Municipality in a State;

(d) debentures or other securities for money issued by any authority constituted under any housing or building scheme approved by the Central or a State Government, or by any authority or body constituted by any Central Act or Act of a State Legislature;

(e) first mortgage on immovable property situated in India under any housing or building scheme of the insurer approved by the Authority or a State Government;

(f) debentures secured by a first charge on any immovable property plant or equipment of any company which has paid interest in full for the five years immediately preceding or for at least five out of the six or seven years immediately preceding on such or similar debentures issued by it;

(g) debentures secured by a first charge on any immovable property, plant or equipment of any company where either the book value or the market value, whichever is less, of such property, plant or equipment is more than three times the value of such debentures;

(h) first debentures secured by a floating charge on all its assets of any company which has paid dividends on its ordinary shares for the five years immediately preceding or for at least five out of the six or seven years immediately preceding;

(i) preference shares of any company which has paid dividends on its ordinary shares for the five years immediately preceding or for at least five out of the six or seven years immediately preceding;

(j) preference shares of any company on which dividends have been paid for the five years immediately preceding or for at least five out of the six or seven years immediately preceding and which have priority in payment over all the ordinary shares of the company in winding-up;

(k) shares of any company which have been guaranteed by another company, such other company having paid dividends on its ordinary shares for the five years immediately preceding or for at least five out of the six or seven years immediately preceding.

(l) shares of any company on which dividends of not less than four per cent including bonus have been paid for the seven years immediately preceding or for at least seven out of the eight or nine years immediately preceding;

(m) first mortgages on immovable property situated in India or in any other country where the insurer is carrying on insurance business;

(n) immovable property situated in India or in any other country where the insurer is carrying on insurance business;

(o) loans on life interests, or on policies of life insurance within their surrender values issued by him or by an insurer whose business he has acquired and in respect of which business he has assumed liability;

(p) life interests;

(q) fixed deposits with banks included for the time being in the Second Schedule to the Reserve Bank of India Act, 1934 or with cooperative societies registered under the Indian Cooperative Societies Act, 1912, or under any other law for the time being in force, the primary object of which is to finance other cooperative societies similarly registered;

(r) debentures of, or shares in cooperative societies registered under the Indian Cooperative Societies Act, 1912, or under any other law for the time being in force;

(s) such other investments as the Authority may, by notification in the Official Gazette, declare to be approved investments for the purposes of this section.[25]

Prohibition of Loan

No insurer shall grant loans or temporary advances either on hypothecation of property or on personal security or otherwise, except loans on life policies issued by him within their surrender value, to any director, manager, managing agent, actuary, auditor, or officer of the insurer if the company or where the insurer is a firm, to any partner therein, or to any other company or firm in which any such director, manager, managing agent, actuary, officer or partner holds such position.[26]

Investigation

The Authority may, at any time, by order in writing, direct any person (Investigating Authority) specified in the order to investigate the affairs of any insurer and to report to the Authority on any investigation made by him provided that the Investigating Authority may, whenever necessary employ any auditor or actuary or both for the purpose of assisting him in any investigating under this section.[27]

Insurance Association of India, Councils of the Association and Committees thereof

Incorporation of the Insurance Association of India

All insurers and provident societies incorporated or domiciled in India are members of the Insurance Association of India, and all insurers and provident societies incorporated or domiciled elsewhere than in India are associate members of that Association.[28]

Councils of the Insurance Association of India

There shall be two Councils of the Insurance Association of India, namely:

(a) the Life Insurance Council consisting of all the members and associate members of the Association, who carry on life insurance business in India; and
(b) the General Insurance Council consisting of all the members and associate members of the Association who carry on general insurance business in India.[29]

The Life Insurance Council may, with the approval of the Authority authorize its Executive Committee to hold examinations for individuals wishing to qualify themselves as insurance agents for the purpose of procuring life insurance business.[30]

The functions of the Executive Committee of the Life Insurance Council shall be:

(a) to aid, advise and assist insurers carrying on life insurance business in the matter of setting-up standards of conduct and sound practice and in the matter of rendering efficient service to holders of life insurance policies;
(b) to render advice to the Authority in the matter of controlling the expenses of insurers in respect of their life insurance business in India;
(c) to bring to the notice of the Authority the case of any insurer acting in a manner prejudicial to the interests of holders of life insurance policies; and

(d) to act in any matter incidental or ancillary to any of the matters specified in clauses (a) to (c) as, with the approval of the Authority, may be notified by the Life Insurance Council in the Gazette of India.[31]

The functions of the Executive Committee of the General Insurance Council shall be:

(a) to aid and advise insurers, carrying on general insurance business, in the matter of setting-up standards of conduct and sound practice and in the matter of rendering efficient service to holders of policies of general insurance;
(b) to render advice to the Authority in the matter of controlling the expenses of such insurers carrying on business in India in the matter of commission and other expenses;
(c) to bring to the notice of the Authority the case of any such insurer acting in a manner prejudicial the interests of holders of general insurance policies; and
(d) to act in any matter incidental or ancillary to any of the matters specified in clauses (a) to (c) as with the approval of the Authority may be notified by the General Insurance Council in the Gazette of India.[32]

Tariff Advisory Committee

The Advisory Committee is a body corporate having perpetual succession and a common seal, with power to acquire, hold and dispose of property, both movable and immovable, and to contract, and may, by the said name, sue and be sued. The Committee is to control and regulate the rates, advantages, terms and conditions that may be offered by insurers in respect of general insurance business.[33]

The Advisory Committee may, from time-to-time and to the extent it deems expedient, control and regulate the rates, advantages, terms and conditions that may be offered by insurers in respect of any risk or any class or category of risks, the rates, advantages, terms and conditions of which, in its opinion, it is proper to control and regulate, and any such rate, advantages, terms and conditions shall be binding on all insurers.[34] Every decision of the Advisory Committee shall be valid only after and to the extent it is ratified by the Authority, and every such decision shall take effect from the date on which it is so ratified by the Authority, or if the Authority so orders in any case, from such earlier date as he may specify in the order.[35] The decisions of the Advisory Committee in pursuance of the provisions of this section shall be final.[36] Where an insurer is guilty of breach of any rate, advantage, term or condition fixed by the Advisory Committee, he shall be deemed to have contravened the provisions of this Act.[37]

4.4.2. *The Life Insurance (Emergency Provisions) Act, 1956*

The insurance industry was facing problems in its role as an affective instrument in mobilizing people's saving and putting them to use in a constructive manner. The Government made a study of the problems being faced by the insurance industry, which found the management of the industry wanting in several respects. In 1950 by amending the Insurance Act, 1938, the Government took powers to appoint administrators to manage companies where the interests of the policy-holders were in grave jeopardy. Investigations into the affairs of the companies put under administrator revealed gross mismanagement even embezzlement very often resulting in insolvency. It was observed that the Indian Life Insurers were virtually being controlled by individuals who were prone to utilize the funds of these companies to subsidize or prop-up their investments in other ventures to the detriment of the industry and the policy-holder. Tightening the provisions of the Insurance Act, 1938, was not found a proper remedy. Therefore, the Government decided to nationalize the Life Insurance Business. Before the Bill to nationalize the insurance business was introduced in the Parliament, it was found essential to issue an ordinance to save the interests of the policy-holders from damage. Therefore, the Life Insurance (Emergency Provisions) Ordinance, 1956, was promulgated vesting the management of all Life Insurance Business in India, including the business managed by foreign insurers, in the Government and for appointment of custodians to manage the business on behalf of the Government. To replace the Ordinance, the Life Insurance (Emergency Provisions) Bill was introduced in the Parliament, having been passed by both the Houses of Parliament, received the assent of the President on 21st March, 1956. The Act was enacted with the objective to provide for taking over, in the public interest, of the management of life insurance business pending nationalization thereof. The Act provided that on and from appointed day, the management of the controlled business of all insurers shall vest in the Central Government.[38] The Central Government may appoint any person as custodian for the purpose of taking over the management of the controlled business of an insurer.[39]

4.4.3. *The Life Insurance Corporation Act, 1956*

An Ordinance was promulgated on 1st January, 1956 pending passing of a Bill, to nationalize insurance business. The management of the life insurance in India was vested in the Central Government. A separate Bill was introduced to replace that Ordinance and for setting-up a Life Insurance Corporation of India as a step for the permanent arrangement for the nationalization of insurance business. The Life Insurance Corporation Bill, having been passed by both the Houses of Parliament, was assented by the President on 18th June, 1956 and came into effect on 1st July, 1956 as the Life Insurance Corporation Act, 1956.

Under this Act a Life Insurance Corporation was set-up, with a share capital provided entirely by the Central Government to undertake life insurance business in India as a monopoly and to integrate all the insurance companies engaged in life business and also the organizations functioning under the control of State Government and conducting such business for the benefit of the public. By virtue of section 3 of the Act, the Central Government established a Corporation called the Life Insurance Corporation of India with effect from September 1, 1956 as a body corporate having perpetual succession and a common seal with power to acquire, hold and dispose of property and to sue by its name and be sued. The original capital of the Corporation was Rupees Five crore which was provided by the Central Government on terms and conditions determined by it.[40] The Corporation is to be guided by the Central Government in matters of policy involving public interest.[41] The sums insured by all policies issued by or taken over by the Corporation were guaranteed as to payment in cash by the Central Government.[42] The Corporation shall not be placed in liquidation save by the order of the Central Government and in such manner as the Government may direct.[43] Thus, the creation, control and extinction of the Corporation is completely in the hands of the Central Government giving LIC a status of statutory corporation owned by the Central Government.

Chapter IV consisting of sections 7 to 17 and sections 35, 36 of Chapter VII were of historic interest only as they provided for various problems that arose in nationalization of life insurance business, namely taking over the assets and liabilities of the existing insurers, fixing and paying compensation for the acquisition and constituting Tribunals for settling disputes arising therefrom, transfer of service of existing employees of the insurers and of their chief agents and refixing their terms and conditions of service, right to modify contracts and seek relief in respect of imprudent transactions entered into on the eve of the nationalization and so on.

Powers and Functions of the Corporation

The general duty of the Corporation shall be to carry on life Insurance business, whether in or outside India, and the Corporation shall so exercise its powers under this Act as to secure that life insurance business is developed to the best advantage of the community.[44] The Corporation shall have the following powers:[45]

(a) to carry on capital redemption business, annuity certain business or reinsurance business in so far as such reinsurance business appertains to life insurance business;

(b) subject to the rules, if any, made by the Central Government in this behalf, to invest the funds of the Corporation in such manner as the Corporation may think fit and to take all such steps as may be necessary and expedient for the protection or realization of any investment; including the taking over of and administering any property offered as security for the investment until a suitable opportunity arises for its disposal;

(c) to acquire, hold and dispose of any property for the purpose of its business;

(d) to transfer the whole or any part of the life insurance business carried on outside India to any other person or persons, if in the interests of the Corporation it is expedient so to do;

(e) to advance or lend money upon the security of any movable or immovable property or otherwise;

(f) to borrow or raise any money in such manner and upon such security as the Corporation may think fit;

(g) to carry on either by itself or through any subsidiary any other business in any case where such other business was being carried on by a subsidiary of an insurer whose controlled business has been transferred to and vested in the Corporation under this Act;

(h) to carry on any other business which may seem to the Corporation to be capable of being conveniently carried on in connection with its business and calculated directly or indirectly to render profitable the business of the Corporation; and

(i) to do all such things as may be incidental or conducive to the proper exercise of any powers of the Corporation.

Management of the Corporation

On the appointed day, i.e. September 1, 1956, all the assets and liabilities appertaining to the controlled business of all life insurances shall be transferred to and vested in the Corporation.[46] The Corporation shall consist of such number of persons not exceeding sixteen as the Central Government may think fit to appoint and one of them shall be appointed by the Central Government to be Chairman thereof.[47] The Central office of the Corporation shall be at such place as the Central Government may, by notification in the Official Gazette, specify. The Central office of the Corporation is at Mumbai. The Corporation shall establish a Zonal Office at Mumbai, Kolkata, Delhi, Kanpur and Chennai and may establish such other Zonal Offices as it thinks fit, subject to the previous approval of the Central Government. The territorial limits of each zone shall be specified by the Corporation. There may be established as many divisional offices and branches in each zone as the Zonal Manager thinks fit.[48] At present the LIC has one corporate office, seven zonal offices, 100 divisional offices and 2048 fully computerized branch offices.

The Corporation may entrust the general superintendence and direction of its affairs and business to an Executive Committee consisting of not more than five of its members and the Executive Committee may exercise all powers and do all such acts and things as may be delegated to it by the Corporation. The Corporation may also constitute an Investment Committee for advising it in matters relating to investment of its funds. The Investment Committee shall consist of not more than eight members of whom not less than four shall be members of the Corporation and the remaining members shall be persons, whether members of the Corporation or not, who have special knowledge and experience in financial matters, particularly matters relating to investment of funds. The Corporation may constitute such other Committees as it may think fit for the purposes of discharging such other functions as may be delegated to them such as the Service and Budget Committee, Public Relations Committee, etc.[49] The Corporation may appoint one or more persons to be the Managing Director or Directors of the Corporation, and every Managing Director shall be whole time officer of the Corporation and shall exercise such powers and perform such duties as may be entrusted or delegated to him by the Executive Committee of the Corporation.[50] Section 22 provides for the appointment of a Zonal Manager for each zone to superintend and direct the affairs and business of the zonal office. The Zonal Manager may or may not be a member of the Corporation. The Zonal Manager shall perform all such functions of the Corporation as may be delegated to him with respect of the area within the jurisdiction of the Zonal Office. The Corporation may also constitute for each zone a Zonal Advisory Board for advising the Zonal Manager in respect of such matters as may be referred to it under the regulations made by the Corporation. The Corporation shall constitute in prescribed manner for each zonal office an Employees and Agents Relations Committee consisting of representatives of the Corporations and of its employees and agents and the duty of the Committee shall be to advise the Zonal Manager on matters which relate to the welfare of the employees and agents of the Corporation or which are likely to promote and secure amity and good relation between them and the Corporation.

In discharge of its functions under the Act, the Corporation shall be guided by such directions in matters of policy involving public interest as the Central Government may give in writing; and if any question arises whether a direction relates to matter of policy involving public interest, the decision of the Central Government thereon shall be final.[51]

Exclusive Privilege of the Corporation

Section 30 of the Act laid down that from the appointed day that is, September 1, 1956, the Corporation shall have the exclusive privilege to carry on life insurance business in India. However, section 30A added by consequential amendment in 1999 provides that this exclusive privilege of carrying on life insurance business in India by the Corporation ceased on and from the commencement of the Insurance Regulatory and Development Authority Act, 1999 and thereafter, the Corporation has to carry on life insurance business in India in accordance with the provisions of the Insurance Act, 1938.

Power to make Rules and Regulations

The Central Government has power to make rules to carry out the purpose of this Act. The rules may provide for all or any of the following matter:

(a) the terms of office and the conditions of service of members;
(b) the manner in which the moneys and other assets belonging to any such fund as referred in Section 8 shall be apportioned between the trustees of the fund and the Corporation;

(c) the services which the chief agent should have rendered for the purposes of the proviso to section 12;
(d) the terms and conditions of service of the employees and agents of the Corporation, including those who become employees and agents of the Corporation on the appointed day under the Act;
(e) the jurisdiction of the Tribunals constituted under section 17;
(f) the manner in which, and the persons to whom, any compensation under this Act may be paid;
(g) the time within which any matter which may be referred to a Tribunal for decision under this Act may be so referred;
(h) the manner in which and conditions subject to which investments may be made by the Corporation;
(i) the manner in which an Employees and Agents Relations Committee may be constituted for each zonal office;
(j) the form in which the report giving an account of the activities of the Corporation shall be prepared;
(k) the conditions subject to which the Corporation may appoint employees;
(l) the fees payable under this Act and the manner in which they are to be collected; and
(m) any other matter which has to be or may be prescribed.[52]

The Corporation, may with the previous approval of the Central Government, make regulations not inconsistent with the Act and the rules made thereunder to provide for all matters for which provision is expedient for the purpose of giving effect to the provisions of this Act. Such regulations may provides for —

(a) the powers and functions of Corporation which may be delegated to the Zonal Managers;
(b) method of recruitment of employees and agents of the Corporation;
(c) the numbers, term of office and conditions of service of members of Boards constituted under section 22;
(d) the territorial limits of each zone established under this Act and the business to be transacted in each zone;
(e) the manner in which the fund of the Corporation shall be maintained;
(f) the maintenance of separate funds and accounts at each of the zonal offices;

(g) the jurisdiction of each divisional office and the establishment of councils representative of policy-holders in each area served by a divisional office for the purpose of advising the divisional office in respect of any matter which may be referred to it;

(h) the conduct of business at meetings of the Corporation;

(i) the formation of Committees of the Corporation and the delegation of powers and functions of the Corporation to such Committees, and the conduct of business at meetings of such Committees;

(j) the form and manner in which policies may be issued and contracts binding on the Corporation may be executed;

(k) the classification of policies, whether issued by the Corporation or by any insurer whose controlled business has been transferred to and vested in the Corporation for the purposes of declaring differential bonuses, wherever necessary;

(l) the manner in which and the intervals within which the accounts of the various zonal offices, divisional offices and branch offices may be inspected and their accounts audited; and

(m) the conditions subject to which any payment may be made by the Corporation.[53]

4.4.4. *The General Insurance Business (Nationalization) Act, 1972*

An Ordinance was promulgated by the President of India on 13 May, 1971 whereby the management of the undertaking of all insurers carrying out general insurance business was vested in the Central Government, pending nationalization of, the general insurance business. The ordinance was replaced by the General Insurance (Emergency Provisions) Act, 1971 empowering the Central Government to appoint custodians of take-over and carry on the management of the undertaking of insurers for and on behalf of the Central Government. To complete the process of nationalization the General Insurance Business (Nationalization) Bill was introduced in the Parliament. The Bill was passed by both the Houses of Parliament and received the assent of the President on 20th September, 1972. As per the Preamble of the Act, the Act is to provide for the acquisition and transfer of shares of Indian insurance companies and undertakings of other existing insurers in order to serve better the needs of the economy by securing the development of general insurance business in the best interests of the community and to ensure that the operation of the economic system does not result in the concentration of wealth to the common detriment, for the regulation and control of such business and for matters connected therewith or incidental thereto.

As per the section 4 of the Act, on the appointed day, i.e. January 1, 1973, all the shares in the capital of every Indian Insurance Company shall stand transferred to and vested in the Central Government free of all trusts, liabilities and encumbrances affecting them. A few shares, however, would thereafter be formally transferred to the nominees of the Central Government in order to enable each of the Indian insurance companies to function as a government company.[54] Further, the undertaking of every existing insurer who is not an Indian insurance company shall also stand transferred to and vested in the Central Government and the Central Government shall provide for the transfer of and vesting in such Indian insurance company as it may specify in notification.[55] Section 9 of the Act directs that the Central Government shall form a government company in accordance with the provisions of the Companies Act, 1956, known as the General Insurance Corporation for the purpose of superintending, controlling and carrying on the business of general insurance. The authorized capital of the corporation shall be rupees two hundred and fifty crore, divided into two hundred and fifty lakhs fully paid-up shares of one hundred rupees each, out of which rupees five crore shall be the initial subscribed capital of the Corporation. The Corporation has been exempted from adding the word limited as the last word of its name. The GIC in thus a Company registered under the Companies Act where as LIC is a statutory corporation. On the formation of the Corporation, the shares of the Indian insurance companies, vested in the Central Government except a few shares dealt with under section 4(2) would stand automatically transferred to and vested in the Corporation and all the Indian Insurance Companies would become the subsidiaries of the Corporation.[56] Thus, the GIC became the holder of these shares of Indian Insurance Companies which in consequence had to rectify their register of members. Section 16 of the Act was an enabling provision which empowered the Central Government to frame one or more schemes whereby the Indian insurance companies would get so merged in one another that ultimately there will be only four Indian companies, so situated as to promote competition between them so that effective services in the field of general insurance may be rendered by them in all parts of India. All the Insurance Companies were thereafter merged into four "Acquiring Companies" namely (1) the New India Assurance Co. Ltd., Mumbai; (2) the United India Fire and General Insurance Co. Ltd., Chennai; (3) the Oriental Fire and General Insurance Co. Ltd., New Delhi; and (4) the National Insurance Co. Ltd., Kolkata from 1st January, 1974 for the more efficient and effective carrying on of general insurance business in all parts of India by virtue of four schemes framed by the Central Government on 31 December, 1973.

The functions of the Corporation shall, *inter alia*, include:

(a) the carrying on of any part of the general insurance business, if it thinks it desirable to do so;
(b) aiding, assisting and advising the acquiring companies in the matter of setting-up standards of conduct and sound practice in general insurance business and in the matter of rendering efficient service to holders of policies of general insurance;
(c) advising the acquiring companies in the matter of controlling their expense including the payment of commission and other expenses;
(d) advising the acquiring companies in the matter of the investment of their funds; and
(e) issuing directions to acquiring companies in relation to the conduct of general insurance business.[57]

Section 24 of the Act provides that the Corporation and the acquiring companies shall have the exclusive privilege of carrying on general insurance business in India. However, section 24A inserted by 1999 amendment provided that this exclusive privilege shall cease on and from commencement of the Insurance Regulatory and Development Authority Act, 1999 and the Corporation and the acquiring companies shall, thereafter, carry on general insurance business in India in accordance with the provisions of the Insurance Act, 1938.

The power to make rules under the Act has been given to the Central Government. The Central Government may make rules to carry out the provisions of this Act. In particular the rules may provide for:

(a) the manner in which the profits, if any, and other moneys received by the Corporation may be dealt with;
(b) the conditions if any, subject to which the Corporation and the acquiring companies shall carry on general insurance business;
(c) the terms and conditions subject to which any reinsurance contracts or treaties may be entered into;
(d) the form and manner in which any notice or application may be given or made to the Central Government;
(e) the reports which may be called for by the Central Government from the corporation and the acquiring companies; and
(f) any other matter which is required to be, or may be, prescribed.[58]

4.4.5. *Marine Insurance Act, 1963*

Since, the eighteenth century, London happened to be the world centre of marine insurance where various customs and usages of trade took place. There the law regulating the marine insurance was known as English Marine Insurance Act, 1906. Since, Independence, the Indian Navy and Indian Shipping had undergone considerable expansion but as there had been no Indian legislation governing marine insurance the Indian marine insurance continued to be governed by the British Marine Insurance Act, 1906. At the same time the insurance contracts in India also became subject to the provisions of Indian Contract Act, 1872. The insurance policy form used in India was the English form based on mercantile customs and business conventions. They at times were in conflict with the provisions of Indian Contract Act, 1872. The result was that the courts had to put their own interpretations. Due to this unsatisfactory position it was considered essential to have a, comprehensive legislation consistent to Indian conditions. To achieve this objective the Marine Insurance Bill was introduced in the Parliament. It was passed by both Houses of Parliament and received the assent of the President on 18th April, 1963. It came into force on 1st August, 1963. The objective of the Act was to codify law relating to marine insurance. The Indian Marine Insurance Act, 1963 was enacted by bodily adopting most of the provisions of the English Act of 1906 except for very minor and inconsequential differences.

Maritime perils has been defined under the Act as the perils consequent on, or incidental to, the navigation of the sea, that is to say, perils of the seas, fire, war perils, pirates, rovers, thieves, captures, seizures, restraints and detainments of princes and peoples, jettisons, barratry and any other perils which are either of the like kind or may be designated by the policy.[59] Marine insurance has been defined under section 3 of the Act as an agreement whereby the insurer undertakes to indemnify the assured, in the manner and to the extent thereby agreed, against marine losses, that is to say, the losses incidental to marine adventure. A contract of marine insurance may, by its express terms, or by usage of trade, be extended so as to protect the assured against losses on inland waters or on any land risk which may be incidental to any sea voyage.[60] Section 4(2) makes it clear that nothing in this Act shall alter or affect any rule of law applicable to any contract of insurance other than a contract of marine insurance as by this Act defined. Subject to the provisions of this Act, every lawful marine adventure may be the subject of a contract of marine insurance.[61]

Every contract of marine insurance by way of wagering is void. A contract of marine insurance is deemed to be a wagering contract—(a) where the assured has not an insurable interest as defined by this Act, and the contract is entered into with no expectation of acquiring such an interest; or (b) where the policy is made "interest or no interest", or "without further proof of interest than the policy itself", or "without benefit of salvage to the insurer", or subject to any other like term. Provided that, where there is no possibility of salvage, a policy may be effected without benefit of salvage to the insurer.[62]

Every person has an insurable interest who is interested in a marine adventure. In particular, a person is interested in a marine adventure where he stands in any legal or equitable relation to the adventure or to any insurable property at risk therein, in consequence of which he may benefit by the safety or due arrival of insurable property, or may be prejudiced by its loss, or by damage thereto, or by the detention thereof, or may incur liability in respect thereof.[63]

The assured must be interested in the subject-matter insured at the time of the loss, though he need not be interested when the insurance is effected. However, where the subject-matter is insured "lost or not lost", the assured may recover although he may not have acquired his interest until after the loss, unless at the time of effecting the contract of insurance the assured was aware of the loss, and the insurer was not. Where the assured has no interest at the time of the loss, he cannot acquire interest by any act or election after he is aware of the loss.[64]

Sections 9 to 16 of the Marine Insurance Act, 1963, give some instances of an insurable interest by way of illustrations. A defeasible interest is insurable, as also is a contingent interest. In particular, where the buyer of goods has insured them, he has an insurable interest, notwithstanding that he might, at his election, have rejected the goods, or have treated them as at the seller's risk, by reason of the latter's delay in making delivery or otherwise.[65] A partial interest of any nature is insurable.[66] The insurer under a contract of marine insurance has an insurable interest in his risk, and may re-insure in respect of it. Unless the policy otherwise provides, the original assured has no right or interest in respect of such re-insurance.[67] The lender of money on bottomry or respondentia has an insurable interest in respect of the loan.[68] The master or any member of the crew of a ship has an insurable interest in respect of his wages.[69] In the case of advance freight, the person advancing the freight has an insurable interest, in so far as such freight is not repayable in case of loss.[70] The assured has an insurable interest in the charges of any insurance which he may effect.[71]

Where the subject-matter insured is mortgaged, the mortgagor has an insurable interest in the full value thereof, and the mortgagee has an insurable interest in respect of any sum due or to become due under the mortgage. A mortgagee, consignee, or other person having an interest in the subject-matter insured may insure on behalf and for the benefit of other persons interested as well as for his own benefit. The owner of insurable property has an insurable interest in respect of the full value thereof, notwithstanding that some third person may have agreed, or be liable to indemnify him in case of loss.[72]

Where the assured assigns or otherwise parts with his interest in the subject-matter insured, he does not thereby transfer to the assignee his rights under the contract of insurance, unless there be an express or implied agreement with the assignee to that effect. But the provisions of this section do not affect transmission of interest by operation of law.[73]

A contract of marine insurance is a contract based upon the utmost good faith, and if the utmost good faith be not observed by either party, the contract may be avoided by the other party.[74] The assured must disclose to the insurer, before the contract is concluded, every material circumstance which is known to the assured, and the assured is deemed to know every circumstance which, in the ordinary course of business, ought to be known to him. If the assured fails to make such disclosure, the insurer may avoid the contract. Every circumstance is material which would influence the judgement of a prudent insurer in fixing the premium, or determining whether he will take the risk. In the absence of inquiry the following circumstances need not be disclosed, namely: (a) any circumstance which diminishes the risk; (b) any circumstance which is known or presumed to be known to the insurer. The insurer is presumed to know matters of common notoriety or knowledge, and matters which an insurer in the ordinary course of his business as such, ought to know; (c) any circumstance as to which information is waived by the insurer; and (d) any circumstance which it is superfluous to disclose by reason of any express or implied warranty. Whether any particular circumstance, which is not disclosed, be material or not is, in each case, a question of fact.[75]

A contract of marine insurance is deemed to be concluded when the proposal of the assured is accepted by the insurer, whether the policy be then issued or not; and for the purpose of showing when the proposal was accepted, reference may be made to the slip, covering note or other customary memorandum of the contract, although it be unstamped.[76] A contract of marine insurance shall not be admitted in evidence unless it is embodied in a marine policy in accordance with this Act. The policy may be executed and issued either at the time when the contract is concluded, or afterwards.[77] A marine policy must specify — (1) the name of the assured, or of some person who effects the insurance on his behalf; (2) the subject-matter insured and the risk insured against; (3) the voyage, or period of time, or both, as the case may be, covered by the insurance; (4) the sum or sums insured; and (5) the name or names of the insurer or insurers.[78]

Where the contract is to insure the subject-matter at and from, or from one place to another or others, the policy is called a "voyage policy", and where the contract is to insure the subject-matter for a definite period of time, the policy is called a "time policy". A contract for both voyage and time may be included in the same policy. A time policy which is made for any time exceeding twelve months is invalid.[79] The subject-matter insured must be designated in a marine policy with reasonable certainty. The nature and extent of the interest of the assured in the subject-matter insured need not be specified in the policy. Where the policy designates the subject-matter insured in general terms, it shall be construed to apply to the interest intended by the assured to be covered. In the application of this section regard shall be had to any usage regulating the designation of the subject-matter insured.[80]

A policy may be either valued or unvalued. A valued policy is a policy which specifies the agreed value of the subject-matter insured. Subject to the provisions of this Act, and in the absence of fraud, the value fixed by the policy is, as between the insurer and assured, conclusive of the insurable value of the subject intended to be insured, whether the loss be total or partial. Unless the policy otherwise provides, the value fixed by the policy is not conclusive for the purpose of determining whether there has been a constructive total loss.[81] An unvalued policy is a policy which does not specify the value of the subject-matter insured, but subject to the limit of the sum insured, leaves the insurable value to be subsequently ascertained.[82] A floating policy is a policy which describes the insurance in general terms, and leaves the name or names of the ship or ships and other particulars to be defined by subsequent declaration. The subsequent declaration or declarations may be made by endorsement on the policy, or in other customary manner. Unless the policy otherwise provides, the declarations must be made in the order of dispatch or shipment. They must, in the case of goods, comprise all consignments within the terms of the policy, and the value of the goods or other property must be honestly stated, but an omission or erroneous declaration may be rectified even after loss or arrival, provided the omission or declaration was made in good faith. Unless the policy otherwise provides, where a declaration of value is not made until after notice of loss or arrival, the policy must be treated as an unvalued policy as regards the subject-matter of that declaration.[83]

Where two or more policies are effected by or on behalf of the assured on the same adventure and interest or any part thereof, and the sums insured exceed the indemnity allowed by this Act, the assured is said to be over-insured by double insurance. Where the assured is over-insured by double insurance — (a) the assured, unless the policy otherwise provides, may claim payment from the insurers in such order as he may think fit, provided that he is not entitled to receive any sum in excess of the indemnity allowed by this Act; (b) where the policy under which the assured claims is a valued policy, the assured must give credit as against the valuation, for any sum received by him under any other policy, without regard to the actual value of the subject-matter insured; (c) where the policy under which the assured claims is an unvalued policy he must give credit, as against the full insurable value, for any sum received by him under any other policy; and (d) where the assured receives any sum in excess of the indemnity allowed by this Act, he is deemed to hold such sum in trust for the insurers, according to their right of contribution among themselves.[84]

4.4.6. *Indian Contract Act, 1872*

The Indian Contract Act, 1872 governs the relationship between the parties to an Insurance contract generally except in regard to some of its special features. The intimation of proposer's intention to buy insurance is the 'offer' and insurer's readiness to undertake risk is 'acceptance'. The offer in case of insurance is called proposal. If other party accepts this proposal, it is transformed into an agreement. Section 2(h) of the Act defines contract as an agreement enforceable by law and Section 10 prescribes the requirements for a valid contract.

According to Section 10 of the Act, conditions which must be fulfilled for the formation of contracts are: (1) The parties must be competent to contract; (2) The agreement must be with their free consent; (3) It must be for a lawful consideration and with a lawful object; (4) It should not have been expressly declared to be void by any law for the time being in force. A person is competent to contract who is of the age of majority according to the law to which he is subject, and is of sound mind and is not disqualified from contracting by any law to which he is subject.[85] When two persons agree upon the same thing in the same sense they are said to consent.[86] As per Section 14 of the Act, consent is said to be free when it is not caused by coercion, undue influence, fraud, misrepresentation or mistake as provided under sections 15-20 of the Indian Contract Act, 1872. Thus, when a proposal is made by the insured and accepted by the insurer in the same sense in which it is made without any coercion, misrepresentation etc. a valid insurance contract can arise. To convert the proposal into a contract, the acceptance must be absolute and unqualified and must be expressed in some usual and reasonable manner, unless proposal prescribes the manner in which it is to be accepted.[87] Another ingredient of a valid contract is that it should be for lawful consideration and with a lawful object. The consideration or object of an agreement is lawful unless it is forbidden by law or is of such nature that, if permitted it would defeat the provisions of any law or is fraudulent or involves or implies, injury to the person or property of another or the court regards it as immoral, or opposed to public policy. In each of these cases, the consideration or object of an agreement is said to be unlawful. Every agreement of which the object or consideration is unlawful is void.[88]

In the contract of insurance, the insured's promise to pay premium is the consideration for the insurer's promise to pay a sum assured or indemnify the insured and these are lawful considerations. The object of the agreement, that is the ultimate purpose, which the contract subserves must also be lawful. It must not tend to be immoral or involve injury to the person of property of another etc.

Another ingredient of a valid contract is that it should not be expressly declared to be void by the Act. Section 30 states that "agreement by way of wager is void". Anson defines 'wager' as a promise to give money or money's worth upon the determination or ascertainment of an uncertain event. An insurance interest not supported by insurable interest amounts to a wagering agreement and is, therefore, void. If one or more requirements prescribed by section 10 are not satisfied the agreement may be either void or voidable. According to section 2(g) a void agreement is one which is not enforceable by law, e.g. where the parties have no personal competence to contract like the proposer of insurance is a minor, where the parties are incompetent, the object or consideration to not lawful, where both the parties to an agreement are under mistake as to the matter of fact essential to the agreement.[89] According to section 2(i) a voidable contract is one which is enforceable by law at the option of one or more of the parties thereto, but not at the option of the other or others. The contract is voidable if the consent is not free but is caused by coercion, undue influence, fraud or misrepresentation.[90] The contract is voidable at the option of the party whose consent was so caused. The party entitled to avoid the contract on account of fraud or misrepresentation, may affirm it if he thinks fit, in which case he may insist that the contract shall be performed and that he shall be put in the position in which he would have been if the representation made had been true.[91]

Performance of Contracts

Chapter IV of the Contract Act consisting of sections 37 to 67 deals with the different aspects of performance, such as, by whom, when, how and what contracts have to be performed and what contracts need not be performed. These provisions govern insurance contracts also. Primarily, it is the parties to a contract that must perform or offer to perform their respective promises. It is insured or his representative that must pay the premium and not any stranger. It is, however, open to the insurer to accept performance from a stranger. Promises bind the representative of the promisor in case of death of such promisor before performance, unless a contrary intention appears from the contact.[92] Where the periodic premium on a life policy is payable on the due date or within the period of 30 days thereafter and would lapse if remains unpaid. The insured dies after due date without paying the premium, his representatives may pay it within the grace period to prevent the policy from lapsing.[93]

Where a promisor has made an offer of performance to the promisee, and the offer has not been accepted, the promisor is not responsible for non-performance, nor does thereby lose his right under the contract.[94] Thus, if insurer refuses to accept the premium duly offered by the insured, the insured does not thereby lose his right under the policy and if a loss occurs thereafter the insurer is still liable to indemnify the insured. According to section 62 of the Act, if parties to a contract agree to substitute a new contract for it or to rescind or alter it, the original contract need not be performed. The novation, alteration or rescission of the original contract requires the assent of both the parties, namely, the insurer and the insured and that completely puts an end to the original contract which need not be performed. Thus, conversion of whole life into an endowment policy, the surrender of a policy or making it paid-up or extending its term can be done only by agreement of both parties.

According to section 64 of the Act when a person at whose option a contract is voidable rescinds it, the other party thereto need not perform any promise therein contained in which he is a promisor. The party rescinding the voidable contract shall, if he has received any benefit thereunder from another party to such contract, restore such benefit, so far as may be, to the person from whom it was received. Thus, when the insurer comes to know about the misrepresentation regarding material facts, the insurer may refuse to receive the premium and rescind the contract and return the premium already received. But insurer can forfeit the premiums received if the policy contains a condition to that effect.[95] Such a condition is included in LIC policies. The, rescission of a voidable contract may be communicated or revoked in the same manner, and subject to same rules, as apply to the communication or revocation of the proposal.[96] Section 65 of the Act lays down that when an agreement is discovered to be void or when a contract becomes void any person who has received any advantage under such agreement or contract is bound to restore it or to make compensation for it, to the person from whom he received it.

Discharge of Contracts

Discharge of contract is the bringing to an end of the relationship brought into existence by the formation of the contract. Discharge[97] of insurance contract usually takes place in following ways:

(i) *By Agreement* — When the insured surrenders his policy for cash payment to which the insurer must consent, the policy is discharged by agreement. A fire or motor policy is terminated before its normal term by either party if that is a condition of the policy, is also discharged by agreement. By agreement a policy may also be substituted by a new policy with different terms.

(ii) *By Breach of Contract* — Where one party is willing to abide by the contract but the other breaks it, the contract comes to an end, e.g. insured not paying the premium or insurer not accepting premium, by breach of warranty by insured.

(iii) *By Performance* — In life insurance policy, the payment of claim on maturity or death of the insured brings the policy to an end. The payment of sum is discharged by performance. In a non-life policy when the insured is indemnified on the loss, the policy is fully discharged if the indemnity covers full sum insured or discharged to the extent of the sum insured paid as indemnity and policy continues to be in force on normal terms for the balance of sum insured.

(iv) *By Impossibility* — A contract ends when its performance becomes impossible or unlawful.[98]

4.4.7. *Insurance Ombudsman under the Redressal of Public Grievance Rules, 1998*

Rule 6 of the Redressal of Public Grievance Rules, 1998 provides that the governing body of the Insurance Council shall appoint one or more persons as Ombudsman. The Ombudsman selected may be drawn from a wider circle including those who have experience or have been exposed to the industry, civil service, administrative service, etc. in addition to those drawn from judicial service.[99] An Ombudsman shall be appointed for a term of three years and shall be eligible for reappointment. However, no person shall hold office as Ombudsman after he has attained the age of 65 years.[100] An Ombudsman may be removed from service for gross misconduct committed by him during his term of office.[101] The office of the Ombudsman shall be located at such place as may be specified by the Insurance Council from time-to-time. The governing body shall specify the territorial jurisdiction of each Ombudsman. The Ombudsman may hold sitting at various places within his area of jurisdiction in order to expedite disposal of complaints jurisdiction in order to expedite disposal of complaints.[102] The governing body has appointed twelve Ombudsmen across the country allotting them different geographical areas as their areas of jurisdiction. The Ombudsman may hold sitting at various places within their area of jurisdiction in order to expedite disposal of complaints. The offices of the twelve insurance Ombudsmen are located at: (1) Bhopal, (2) Bhubaneswar, (3) Cochin, (4) Guwahati, (5) Chandigarh, (6) New Delhi, (7) Chennai, (8) Kolkata, (9) Ahmedabad, (10) Lucknow, (11) Mumbai, and (12) Hyderabad.

Insurance Ombudsman has two types of functions to perform: (1) Conciliation, and (2) Award-making. The Ombudsman has power to receive and consider — complaints under rule 13; any partial or total repudiation of claims by an insurer; any dispute in regard to premium paid or payable in terms of the policy; any dispute on the legal construction of the policies in so far as such disputes relate to claims; delay in settlement of claims; non-issue of any insurance document to customers after receipt of premium. The Ombudsman shall act as counsellor and mediator. The Ombudsman decision whether the complaint is fit and proper for being considered by it or not, shall be final.[103] Any person who has a grievance against an insurer, may himself or through his legal heirs make a complaint in writing to the

Ombudsman within whose jurisdiction the branch or office of the insurer complained against is located. The complaint shall state clearly the name and address for the complainant, the name of the branch or office of the insurer against which the complaint is made, the fact giving rise to the complaint supported by documents, if any, relied on by the complainant, the nature and extent of the loss caused to the complainant and the relief sought from the Ombudsman.

Ombudsman's powers are restricted to insurance contracts of value not exceeding ₹ 20 lakh. The insurance companies are required to honour the awards passed by an Insurance Ombudsman within three months.

No complaint to the Ombudsman shall lie unless —

(a) The complainants had before making a complaint to the Ombudsman made a written representation to the insurer named in the complaint and either insurer has rejected the complaint or the complainant had not received any reply within a period of one month after the insurer concerned received his representation or the complainant in not satisfied with the reply given to him by the insurer;
(b) The complaint is made not later than one year after the insurer had rejected the representation or sent his final reply on the representation of the complainant; and
(c) The complaint is not on the same subject-matter, for which any proceedings before any court, or Consumer Forum or arbitrator is pending or were so earlier.[104]

When a complaint is settled through mediation of the Ombudsman, the Ombudsman shall make a recommendation which he thinks fair in the circumstances of the case. The copies of the recommendation shall be sent to the complainant and the insurance company concerned. Such recommendation shall be made not later than one month from the date of the receipt of the complaint. If the complainant accepts the recommendation of the Ombudsman, he will send a communication in writing within 15 days of the date of receipt of the recommendation. He will confirm his acceptance to Ombudsman and state clearly that the settlement reached is acceptable to him, in totality, in terms of recommendations made by the Ombudsman in full and final settlement of complaint. The Ombudsman shall send to the insurance company a copy of the recommendation along with the acceptance letter received from the complainant. The insurer shall thereupon comply with the terms of the recommendations immediately not latter than 15 days of the receipt of such recommendation and the insurer shall inform the Ombudsman of its compliance.[105]

Where the complaint is not settled by agreement under rule 15, the Ombudsman shall pass an award which he thinks fair in the facts and circumstances of a claim. The award shall be passed within a period of three months from the receipt of the complaint in writing stating the amount awarded to the complainant. Copy of the award shall be sent to the complainant and the insurer. The complainant shall furnish to the insurer within a period of one month from the date of receipt of the award, a letter of acceptance that the award is in full and final settlement of his claim. The insurer shall comply with the award within 15 days of the receipt of the acceptance letter and it shall intimate the compliance to the Ombudsman.[106] If the complainant does not intimate the acceptance, the award may not be implemented by the insurance company.[107]

The Ombudsman shall furnish a report every year containing a general review of the activities of the office of the ombudsman during preceding financial year of the Central Government and such other information as may be considered necessary by it. In the annual report, the Ombudsman will make an annual review of the quality of services rendered by the insurer and make recommendations to improve there services.[108]

4.4.8. *Consumer Protection Act, 1986*

The Consumer Protection Act, 1986 is a benevolent, unique and highly progressive piece of social welfare legislation providing for simple, speedy and less expensive remedy for the redressal of consumer grievances in relation to defective goods and deficient services. Consumer Protection Act is a weapon in the hands of consumers to fight against exploitation by traders, manufacturers and sellers on one hand and providers of services on the other. The Act provides effective, people oriented, broad-based and efficient remedy to consumers against unfair dealings and exploitation. It was enacted with an objective to provide better protection of the interests of the consumers and to make provision for the establishment of Consumer Councils and other authorities for the settlement of consumer disputes. Unlike other laws, which are basically punitive or preventive in nature the provisions of the Act are compensatory. It is a matter of great satisfaction that we can legitimately boast that we now have in our country a statute, which provides more effective protection to the consumers than any corresponding legislation in force in countries, which are considered to be much more advanced and industrialized. CPA has been to operation for about 22 years. A number of deficiencies and shortcoming in respect of its operation have come to light thereby requiring amendments in 1991, 1993 and 2002. Despite all this it is a handy weapon for consumers to ensure accountability of producers of goods and providers of services.

The Act was enacted on 24th December, 1986 with an objective to provide for better protection of the interests of consumers and for that purpose to make provision for the establishment of consumer councils and other authorities for the settlement of consumers' disputes and for matters connected therewith. The Act contemplates establishment of adjudicatory and advisory structures in the form of consumer fora and council structure respectively for the protection of consumers' rights. Since, then the Act has been thrice amended in 1991, 1993 and 2002. It extends to the whole of India except the State of Jammu & Kashmir which has its own Consumer Protection Act. The Act applies to all goods and services unless any good or service is expressly excluded by the Central Government by notification. The Act extends to all sectors — public, private or cooperative. The Consumer Protection Act is an alternative and additional remedy to the remedies already available to the aggrieved persons/consumers by way of civil suit.

The Act postulates establishment of councils at three levels — Central Consumer Protection Council, the State Consumer Protection Councils and District Consumer Protection Council for the purpose of spreading consumer awareness. The object of this three-tier Council structure is to promote and protect the rights of the consumers. The Central Council is headed by Minister in-charge of the Consumer Affairs in the Central Government and in the State it is the Minister in-charge of the Consumer Affairs in the State Government who heads State Council. The District Consumer Protection Council is headed by the Collector of the District. The provision of District Consumer Protection Council has been added by the 2002 amendments to CPA.

To provide cheap, speedy and simple redressal to consumer disputes, three-tier quasi-judicial machinery is set-up at each District, State and National levels called District Forums, State Consumer Disputes Redressal Commission and National Consumer Disputes Redressal Commission respectively. At present, there are 617 District Forums, 35 State Commissions with apex body as a National Consumer Disputes Redressal Commission (NCDRC). These quasi-judicial bodies are required to follow summary procedure and Principles of Natural Justice to provide quick and speedy justice to the consumers.

The District Forums are headed by the person who is or has been or is eligible to be appointed as a District Judge. Besides the President, there are two other members, one of whom shall be a woman. The qualifications and disqualifications for the members have been specified by the third amendment. Every appointment to the District Forum shall be made by the State Government on the recommendation of a Selection Committee consisting of the President of the State Commission as Chairman, Secretary, Law Department of the State as Member and Secretary in-charge of the Department dealing with Consumer Affairs in the State as Member. Every member of the District Forum shall hold office for a term of five years or up to the age of sixty-five years, whichever is earlier. A member shall be eligible for re-appointment for another term of five years or up to the age of sixty-five years, whichever is earlier, subject to the condition that he fulfils the qualifications and other conditions for appointment and such re-appointment is also made on the basis of the recommendation of the Selection Committee.

The State Commissions are headed by a person who is or has been a Judge of High Court. In addition, there are not less than two, and not more than such number of members, as may be prescribed, and one of whom shall be a woman. The qualifications and disqualifications for the members of the State Commission are same as that of the District Forum. Every member of the State Commission shall hold office for a term of five years or up to the age of sixty-seven years, whichever is earlier. A member shall be eligible for re-appointment for another term of five years or up to the age of sixty-seven years, whichever is earlier subject to the condition that he fulfils the qualifications and other conditions for appointment and such re-appointment is made on the basis of the recommendation of the Selection Committee. The President of the State Commission shall also be eligible for re-appointment.

The National Commission is headed by a sitting or retired Judge of the Supreme Court of India. The National Commission shall have not less than four and not more than such number of members, as may be prescribed, and one of whom shall be a woman. The National Commission was constituted in the year 1988. Every member of the National Commission shall hold office for a term of five years or up to the age of seventy years, whichever is earlier. The President and Members of the National Commission shall be eligible for re-appointment for another term of five years or up to the age of seventy years, whichever is earlier.

The provisions of this Act cover 'Products' as well as 'Services'. A complaint under the Act can be filed for 'defects in goods' or 'deficiency in service'. The consumer has been defined under section 2(1)(d) of the Act. As regards the goods it includes within its ambit any person who buys any goods for a consideration and includes any user of such goods when such use is made with the approval of buyer. In relation to services consumer means any person who hires or avails of any services for a consideration and includes any beneficiary of such services when such services are availed of with the approval of the first mentioned person. But does not include a person who avails of such goods or services for any commercial purpose. The products are those which are manufactured or produced and sold to consumers through wholesalers and retailers. The service means service of any nature which are of the nature of transport, telephones, electricity, constructions, banking, insurance, medical treatment etc. The services are, by and large, include those provided by professionals such as doctors, engineers, architects, lawyers etc.

Jurisdiction of Quasi-Judicial Bodies

A written complaint in relation to a product or in respect of a service, as amended by Consumer Protection (Amendment) Act, 2002, can be filed before the District Consumer Forum if the value of the goods or services and the compensation claimed does not exceed rupees twenty lakh, before the State Commission if the value of claim is more than twenty lakh up to one crore and before the National Commission if it is above rupees one crore. As regards the territorial jurisdiction is concerned, a complaint shall be instituted in a District Forum/State Commission within the local limits of whose jurisdiction, (a) the opposite party or each of the opposite parties, where there are more than one, at the time of the institution of the complaint, actually and voluntarily resides or carries on business or has a branch office or personally works for gain; or (b) any of the opposite parties, where there are more than one, at the time of the institution of the complaint, actually and voluntarily resides, or carries on business or has a branch office, or personally works for gain, provided that in such case either the permission of the District Forum/State Commission is given, or the opposite parties who do not reside, or carry on business or have a branch office, or personally work for gain, as the case may be, acquiesce in such institution; or (c) the cause of action, wholly or in part, arises. The District Forum, the State Commission or the National Commission shall not admit a complaint unless it is filed within two years from the date on which the cause of action has arisen. However, a complaint may be entertained after the period specified, if the complainant satisfies that he had sufficient cause for not filing the complaint within such period.

The National Commission, State Commissions and District Forums are required to decide complaint, as far as possible, within a period of three months from the date of notice received by the opposite party where complaint does not require analysis or testing of commodities and within five months if it requires analysis or testing of commodities. The Appeals are allowed within 90 days against the order of the District Forum to the State Commission and against the order of the State Commission, to the National Commission. Appeal can also be preferred to the Supreme Court against the order of the National Commission within a period of 30 days. No appeal by a person who is required to pay any amount in terms of an order of the National Commission shall be entertained by the Supreme Court unless that person has deposited in the prescribed manner fifty per cent of that amount or rupees fifty thousand, whichever is less. Similarly, there is a requirement for depositing ₹ 35,000 and ₹ 25,000 in case of appeals to National Commission and State Commission respectively.

Majority of complaints relating to service sector before the Forums and Commission under Consumer Protection Act, 1986 (CPA) are from the insurance sector. A number of complaints against the insurance companies are reaching before consumer courts and relief is being given to the complainants. The Consumer Courts have begun to take a closer look at the insurance sector to judge whether decisions taken by an insurer, in cases of claims, are reasonable in the context of the facts and circumstances of the cases. Therefore, it has become incumbent on the insurance companies to ensure that the decision taken by them stand the test of legal scrutiny by the quasi-judicial machinery under CPA. In medi-claim cases, one of the most common ground given by the insurance companies, for repudiating a claim, is the alleged suppression of information regarding pre-existing diseases.[109] In one of the case,[110] the insurance company repudiated the claim on the ground that he suppressed the fact regarding his pre-existing diseases such as diabetes, hypertension etc. and the fact that he was suffering from giddiness and had taken medical leavc. The repudiation was rejected by the National Commission on the ground that the insured used medical leave for other genuine reasons and not for actual medical treatment. Since, there was no proof of the insured of having taken treatment for various diseases which he was allegedly suffering from, the revision petition of the Life

Insurance Corporation was dismissed and the claim was allowed as per the policy.

There are also a number of complaints before the consumer courts relating to motor vehicle theft or accident. For example in case[111] where the vehicle got stolen on day when it was registered, the insurance company assessed the market price at ₹ 3,05,000 after deducting ₹ 60,000, the NC held that there was no reason for the insurance company to deduct the amount. The NC allowed the complaint where the car met with an accident while waiting for a permanent Registration Number and the insured was not informed about the strict condition of the insurance contract that the registration number has to be made permanent otherwise the policy would be cancelled.[112]

The cases also relate to agriculture and animal insurances. These include rejection of claim by the insurance company in case of failure of crop,[113] repudiation of claim of death of goats due to eating some poisonous grass, on the ground that there were no tags in the ears of the goats,[114] repudiation of claim without any reason in case of death of buffaloes due to flood,[115] where the insurance company did not dispute the cause of death of the fish in the ponds but repudiated the claim relying on an exclusion clause wherein it was stated that the insurance company shall not be liable in respect of loss arising out of Asphyxia[116] etc. The complaints before the Forums and Commissions also include difficulties in getting claims against accident,[117] burglary,[118] and fire[119] insurances.

4.4.9. *Regulations Dealing with Compulsory/Accidental Insurance*

I. The Personal Injuries (Compensation Insurance) Act, 1963

The liability of an employer to pay compensation for personal injury (i.e. war injuries) under section 4 of the Personal Injuries (Emergency Provisions) Act, 1962, the Workmen's Compensation Act, 1923, and the Employees' State Insurance Act, 1948 having been removed, it became imperative to provide for payment of compensation on a uniform basis irrespective of the fact whether a workmen is covered by the Workmen's Compensation Act, 1923 or the Employees' State Insurance Act, 1948. In order to achieve this objective the Personal Injuries (Compensation Insurance) Bill was introduced in the Parliament with objectives to:

(i) impose on the employers of workmen in factories, mines, major ports, plantations, essential services etc. the liability to pay compensation in respect of personal injuries to the extent the amount of compensation payable under the Workmen's Compensation Act, 1923, exceeds the amount of compensation payable under the Personal Injuries (Emergency Provisions) Act, 1962; and

(ii) provide for a scheme of insurance of the liability by the employers with the Government based on premium rates which can bc varied with reference to the actual nature or extent of the liability as it may exist from time-to-time.

The Personal Injuries (Compensation Insurance) Bill having being passed by both the Houses of Parliament received the assent of the President on 8th October, 1963. It came into force on 1st day of January, 1965 as the Personal Injuries (Compensation Insurance) Act, 1963. The Act provides for payment of compensation on a uniform basis irrespective of the fact whether the workman is covered by the Workmen's Compensation Act, 1923, or the Employees' State Insurance Act, 1948. This has been considered necessary from the point of view of the practicability, equity and the fact that the quantum of benefits under the latter Act is not fixed automatically as in case of the former Act. The premium payable by the employers for compulsory insurance is collected at quarterly intervals as is being done under the Emergency Risks (Factories) Insurance Act, 1962. Exemption from compulsory insurance is granted to small establishments whose total wages bill for any quarter is less than ₹ 1,500 because the cost of collecting premium and the administration charges in their case is likely to be out of proportion to the realization made.

According to Section 3, the Act applies to the workmen who are:

(a) employed in any employment or class of employment which is, or has been declared to be, an essential service under rule 126AA of the Defence of India Rules, 1962 or under rule 119 of the Defence of India Rules, 1971;

(b) employed in any factory as defined in clause (m) of section 2 of the Factories Act, 1948;

(c) employed in any mine within the meaning of the Mines Act, 1952;

(d) employed in any major port;

(e) employed in any plantation as defined in clause (f) of section 2 of the Plantations Labour Act, 1951; and

(f) employed in any employment specified in this behalf by the Central Government by notification.

Under the Act compensation of the amount in addition to any relief provided under the Personal Injuries (Emergency Provisions) Act, 1962 shall be payable by an employer in respect of personal injury sustained by a gainfully occupied person who is a workman to whom this Act applies.[120] Where any person has a right apart from the provisions of this Act and of the Personal Injuries (Emergency Provisions) Act, 1962 to receive compensation or damages from an employer in respect of a personal injury in respect of which compensation is payable under this Act, the right shall extend only to so much of such compensation or damages as exceed the amount of compensation payable under this Act.[121]

Compensation Insurance Scheme

The Central Government shall, by notification, put into operation a scheme to be called the Personal Injuries (Compensation Insurance) Scheme whereby provision is made for all matters necessary to give effect to the purposes of this Act and whereby the Central Government undertakes, in relation to employers of workmen to whom the Act applies, the liabilities of insuring such employers against liabilities incurred by them to workmen under this Act. Provided different schemes shall be put into operation in relation to different periods of emergency. The scheme shall secure that any liability of the Central Government as insurer under the scheme is determined by a policy of insurance issued in the prescribed form by person acting on behalf of the Central Government. The scheme may provide the date on which it shall come into operation or shall be deemed to have come into operation on such date as may be specified therein. The scheme may be amended at any time by the Central Government. The scheme may:

(a) make provisions regulating the payment of the compensation payable under this Act and the scheme including provisions for the punishment by fine not exceeding two thousand rupees for the contravention of any requirement of the scheme;
(b) make provisions specifying the persons to whom and the proportions and manner in which payments under this Act shall be made;
(c) make provisions for determining the value in lump-sum of the amount payable under the Personal Injuries (Emergency Provisions) Act, 1962;
(d) specify conditions or circumstances which will disentitle a workman to the compensation payable under this Act, and

make it an express or implied condition of any policy of insurance issued under this scheme that the payment of compensation in defiance of such specification is not covered by the policy;

(e) specify the conditions or circumstances under which the compensation payable to a workman may be withheld, cancelled, reduced or reviewed if the award made under the Personal Injuries (Emergency Provisions) Act, 1962, is withheld, cancelled, reduced or reviewed;

(f) provide for cases in which an employer has of his own accord undertaken a part or the whole of the liability imposed by this Act;

(g) provide for the final assessment of the total premium due on a policy of insurance under the scheme either as the equivalent of all advance payments of premium already made by the employer, or as a percentage of total wages bills of an employer for the periods with reference to which the amount of any advance payments made by him was fixed or as a percentage of the total wages bill of an employer for a period of not less than twelve or more than fifteen months immediately, preceding the expiry of the emergency, and for the assessment of the total premium due on policy which has ceased to be in force before the expiry of the period of the emergency owing to the employer having gone out of business; and

(h) provide for the recovery from an employer of the total premium due on a policy of insurance including provision for its recovery by periodic advance payments of an amount based on a percentage of his total wages bill for any prescribed period, the separate funding of the payments so made by each employer, and the eventual adjustment of the total premium as finally assessed against the total of such periodic payments.[122]

Every employer of workmen to whom this Act applies except an employer whose total wages bill for any quarter has never exceeded fifteen hundred rupees, shall take out a policy of insurance in accordance with the scheme. He is insured until the expiry of the period of the emergency or until the date, if any, prior to the expiry of the period of the emergency at which he ceases to be an employer, against all liabilities imposed on him by this Act. Whosoever fails to take out a policy or having taken out the policy of insurance as required, fails to make any payment by way of premium in accordance with the provisions of the scheme, shall be punishable with fine which may extend to two thousand rupees and shall also be punishable with a further fine which may extend to one thousand rupees for everyday after having being so convicted on which the contravention or failure continues. However, this section shall not bind the government.[123]

The Central Government may, after due appropriation made by the Parliament by law in this behalf, transfer in each financial year to a fund to be called the Personal Injuries (Compensation Insurance) Fund such sums, as may be considered necessary, not exceeding the sums received by the Central Government by way of insurance premiums under the scheme, or by way of payments made on composition of offences under section 18 or by way expenses or compensation awarded by a court under section 545 of the Code of Criminal Procedure, 1898, out of any fine imposed in any prosecution under this Act or by way of penalties imposed under the Scheme. From the fund all sums shall be paid for the discharge by the Central Government of any of its liabilities under this Act or the scheme or for the payment by the Central Government of the remuneration and expenses of agents employed for the purposes of the scheme or for the payment by the Central Government of the cost of administrating the scheme. However, no payment from the fund shall be made in discharge of any liability of the Government to pay compensation to workmen employed by it.[124]

Where an employer has failed to take out a policy of insurance as required by sub-section (1) of Section 9, or having taken out a policy of insurance as required by that sub-section, has failed to make the payments by way of premium thereon which are subsequently due from him in accordance with the provisions of the scheme, payment of any compensation for the payment of which he is liable under this Act may be made out of the fund, and the sum so paid together with a penalty of such amount not exceeding the sum so paid may be determined by an officer authorized in this behalf by the Central Government shall be recoverable from the employer as an arrear of land revenue for payment into the fund.[125]

Under section 22, the Central Government has power to make rules. The Central Government may by notification make rules to carry into effect the provisions of this Act. Such rules may prescribe for —

(a) the principles to be followed in ascertaining the total wages bill of an employer, including provision for the exclusion therefrom of certain categories of the wages or of certain elements included in the definition of wages;

(b) the form of the policies of insurance referred in sub-section (2) of section 8;
(c) the period referred to in clause (g) of sub-section (5) of section 8;
(d) the date and the period referred in sub-section (1) of section 9;
(e) the form and the manner of preparing and publishing the account referred to in sub-section (3) of section 13;
(f) the periods referred to in sub-section (3) of section 15; and
(g) any other matter which has to be or may be prescribed.

II. The Public Liability Insurance Act, 1991

The growth of hazardous industries, processes and operations in India has been accompanied by the growing risks from accidents, not only to workmen employed in the undertaking, but also to the public who may be in the vicinity. Such accidents lead to death and injury to human beings and other living beings and damage to private and public properties. Very often, the majority of people affected is from economically weaker sections and suffer great hardships because of delayed relief and compensation. While the workers and employees of hazardous installations are protected under separate laws, members of the public are not assured of any relief except through long legal processes as industrial units are seldom willing to compensate the victims of the accidents. Some units may not have the financial resources to provide even the minimum relief.

It was only when accidents of the impact like the Bhopal catastrophe, the worst industrial disaster in human history and Oleum Gas Leak Case had taken place that the environmentalists, social workers, general public and government institutions woke-up to a new awareness. This led to legislative and administrative activism. Compensation to the victims of Bhopal disaster raised an enigma in Indian tort law which was still based on the English Common Law Principles. It was only in *M.C. Mehta* vs. *Union of India (oleum gas leakage case)*,[126] the Principle of Absolute Liability for the harm caused by the industry engaged in hazardous and inherently dangerous activities was formulated which was a new doctrine free from the exceptions of Strict Liability Rule of England. Industries engaged in hazardous and inherently dangerous activities are "absolutely liable" to compensate those who are affected by the harm arising from such activity and such liability is not subject to any exception. Further, the court held that the measure of compensation must be correlated to the magnitude and the capacity of the enterprise. This principle of absolute liability was later included in enactments like Public Liability Insurance Act, 1991, and the National Environment Tribunal Act, 1995.

To ameliorate the sufferings of members of public due to accidents which take place in hazardous installations it was found essential to provide for mandatory Public Liability Insurance for installations handling hazardous substances to provide minimum relief to victim. Such insurance, apart from safeguarding the interests of the victim of accidents would also provide cover and enable the industry to discharge its liability to settle large claims arising out of major accidents. To achieve this objective the Public Liability Insurance Bill was introduced in the Parliament, having been passed by both the Houses of Parliament, received the assent of the President on 22nd January, 1991. Under the Act, the mandatory public liability is based on the principle of "no fault" liability as it is limited to only relief on a limited scale.

Where death or injury to any person other than workmen or damage to any property has resulted from an accident, the owner shall be liable to give specified relief for such death, injury or damage. In the claim for relief, the claimant shall not be required to plead or establish that the death, injury or damage in respect of which claim has been made was due to any wrongful act, neglect or default of any person.[127] The following relief has been specified under the schedule of the Act:

1. Reimbursement of medical expenses incurred up to a maximum of ₹ 12,500 in each case.
2. For fatal accidents the relief will be ₹ 25,000 per person in addition to reimbursement of medical expenses, if any, incurred on the victim up to a maximum of ₹ 12,500.
3. For permanent total or permanent partial disability or other injury or sickness, the relief will be:
   (i) reimbursement of medical expenses incurred, if any, up to a maximum of ₹ 12,500 in each case; and
   (ii) cash relief on the basis of percentage of disablement as certified by an authorized physician. The relief for total permanent disability will be ₹ 25,000.
4. For loss of wages due to temporary partial disability which reduces the earning capacity of victim, there will be a fixed monthly relief not exceeding ₹ 1,000 per month up to a maximum of 3 months, provided the victim has been hospitalized for a period exceeding 3 days and is above 16 years of age.

5. Up to ₹ 6,000 depending on the actual damage, for any damage to private property.

Under section 4 every owner is under an obligation to take out, before he starts handling any hazardous substance, one or more policies providing for contracts of insurance whereby he is insured against liability to give relief under sub-section (1) of section 3. Every owner shall get the insurance policy renewed from time-to-time, throughout the period during which such handling is continued. No insurance policy taken out or renewed by an owner shall be for an amount less than the amount of the paid-up capital of the undertaking handling any hazardous substance and owned or controlled by that owner, and more than the amount, not exceeding fifty crore rupees, as may be prescribed.[128] The liability of the insurer under one insurance policy shall not exceed the amount specified in the terms of the contract of insurance in that insurance policy.[129] Every owner shall also, together with the amount of premium pay to the insurer, for being credited to the Relief Fund established under section 7A, such further amount, not exceeding the sum equivalent to the amount of premium, as may be prescribed. The Central Government may, by notification, exempt the following from taking out insurance policies:

(a) the Central Government;
(b) any State Government;
(c) any corporation owned or controlled by the Central Government or a State Government; or
(d) any local authority.

However, the exemption will be applicable only if a fund has been established and is maintained by that owner in accordance with the rules made in this behalf for meeting any liability under sub-section (1) of Section 3.[130]

Claim for Relief: Where an accident has occurred at any place within jurisdiction of the Collector, it shall be his duty to verify the occurrence of accident and to invite applications under section 6(1) by causing publicity.[131] An application for claim for relief may be made: (a) by the person who has sustained the injury; (b) by the owner of the property to which the damage has been caused; (c) where death has resulted from the accident by all or any of the legal representatives of the deceased; or (d) by any agent duly authorized by such person or owner of such property or all or any of the legal representatives of the deceased; as the case may be. Such application shall be made to the Collector and shall be in Form-1 prescribed under Rule 4, containing such particulars and accompanied by such documents as may be prescribed. The application for relief shall be made within 5 years of the occurrence of the accident.[132] On receipt of the application for claim, Collector is required to hold the enquiry and make an award determining the amount of relief which is reasonable. The claim for relief shall be disposed of as expeditiously as possible and every endeavour shall be made to dispose of such claim within three months of the receipt of the application. When an award is made under this section:

(a) the insurer, who is required to pay any amount in terms of such award and to the extent specified under section 4 (2B), shall, within a period of thirty days of the date of announcement of the award, deposit the amount in such manner as the Collector may direct;

(b) the Collector shall arrange to pay from the Relief Fund, in terms of such award and in accordance with the scheme under section 7A, to the person or persons referred to in sub-section (1) such amount as may be specified in that scheme; and

(c) the owner shall, within such period, deposit such amount in such manner as the Collector may direct.[133]

Environment Relief Fund: The Central Government may by notification, establish a fund to be known as the Environment Relief Fund. The Relief Fund shall be utilized for paying, in accordance with the provisions of this Act and the scheme, relief under the award made by the Collector under section 7. The Central Government may, by notification, make a scheme specifying the authority in which the Relief Fund shall vest, the manner in which money shall be drawn from the Relief Fund and for all other matters connected with or incidental to the administration of the Relief Fund and the payment of relief therefrom.[134]

The relief under the Act, shall be in addition to any other right to claim compensation under any other law for the time being in force. However, the amount of compensation paid under any other law shall be reduced by an amount of relief paid under this Act.[135]

Penalty under the Act: If the employer or the owner does not take out insurance policies or does not keep them alive during the continuation of hazardous process or fails to pay amount to Relief Fund or fails to comply with any direction issued by Central Government under section 12, he shall be punishable with imprisonment for a term which shall not less than one year and six months but which may extend upto six years, or with fine which shall not be less than one lakh rupees, or with both. Whosoever, having already been convicted of offence is convicted for the second offence or any offence subsequent to the second offence, he shall be punishable with imprisonment for a term which shall not be less than two years but which may extend to seven years and with fine which shall not be less than one lakh rupees.[136]

Where any offence under this Act has been committed by a company then every person, who at the time when the offence was committed was directly in-charge of or was responsible to, the company for the conduct of its business, the company itself and every such person shall be deemed to be guilty of the offence. If the offence has been committed by any department of the government, the head of the department shall be deemed to be guilty of the offence and he shall be punished accordingly. However, no suit, prosecution or other legal proceeding shall lie against the government or the person, officer, authority or agency in respect of anything done or intended to be done in good faith under this Act.[137]

Advisory Committee: The Central Government may, from time-to-time, constitute an Advisory Committee on the matters relating to the insurance policy under this Act. The Advisory Committee shall consist of — (a) three officers representing the Central Government; (b) Two persons representing the insurers; (c) Two persons representing the owners; and (d) Two persons from amongst the experts of insurance or hazardous substances, to be appointed by the Central Government. The Chairman of the Advisory Committee shall be one of the members representing the Central Government, nominated in this behalf by that Government.[138]

Power to Make Rules: The Central Government may, by notification, make rules for carrying out the purposes of this Act. In particular, such rules may provide for all or any of the following matters:

(a) the maximum amount for which an insurance policy may be taken out by an owner under sub-section (2A) of section 4;

(b) the maximum amount required to be paid by an owner for being credited, to the Relief Fund under sub-section (2C) of section 4;

(c) the manner in which and the period within which the amount received from the owner is required to be remitted by the insurer under sub-section (2D) of section 4;

(d) establishment and maintenance of fund under sub-section (3) of section 4;

(e) the form of application and the particulars to be given therein and the documents to accompany such application under sub-section (2) of section 6;

(f) the procedure for holding an inquiry under sub-section (4) of section 7;

(g) the purposes for which the Collector shall have powers of a civil court under sub-section (5) of section 7;

(h) the manner in which notice of the offence and of the intention to make a complaint to the Central Government shall be given under clause (b) of section 18; and

(i) any other matter which is required to be, or may be, prescribed.[139]

In exercise of the power conferred by section 23 of the Act, the Central Government has made the Public Liability Insurance Rules, 1991.

III. Motor Vehicle Act, 1988

Compulsory Insurance of Motor Vehicles

According to Section 146 of the Motor Vehicle Act, 1988 no vehicle can be used in a public place without a policy of insurance complying with requirements of Chapter XI of the Act. No person shall use, except as a passenger, or cause or allow any other person to use, a motor vehicle in a public, unless there is in force in relation to the use of the vehicle by that person or that other person, as the case may be, a policy of insurance complying with the requirements of this Chapter. Unlike other properties which may be insured or not at the option of the owner, a motor vehicle is required by law to be insured in respect of the user's liability for death of or bodily injury to third parties in accordance with the Chapter XI of the 1988 Act. With effect from March 2, 1970, it has been compulsory to insure also in respect of damage to any property of the third party. Act liability, therefore, means liability in respect of the death of or bodily injury to the person or damage to property of a third party caused by or arising out of the use of a vehicle in a public place.[140] This is also referred to as "compulsorily insurable risk". Using an uninsured motor vehicle in a public place has been made an offence by Section 196 of the Act punishable with imprisonment which may extend to three months, or with fine which may extend to one thousand rupees, or with both.

Sub-sections (2) and (3) of section 146 provide certain exceptions to the rule of compulsory insurance. Accordingly, vehicles belonging to the Central and State Governments and used by them for the purposes unconnected with their commercial enterprises need not be insured. The appropriate Government may also exempt from insurance government vehicles used for commercial enterprises or belonging to any State Transport Undertaking or to any local authority, provided such authority has made provision to meet their 'Act liabilities'.

According to section 147 of the Act the policy of insurance must be one issued by an 'authorized insurer'. Such an insurer on and from January 1, 1973 is the General Insurance Corporation of India together with its four subsidiary companies and any Government Insurance fund authorized to do general insurance business under the General Insurance Business (Nationalization) Act, 1972. As per section 147(1)(b)(ii) a policy of insurance must be a policy which is issued by a person or classes of persons specified in the policy: (i) against any liability which may be incurred by him in respect of the death of or bodily injury to any person, including owner of the goods or his authorized representative carried in the vehicle or damage to any property of a third party caused by or arising out of the use of the vehicle in a public place; (ii) against the death of or bodily injury to any passenger of a public service vehicle caused by or arising out of the use of the vehicle in a public place. However, a policy shall not be required — (i) to cover liability in respect of the death, arising out of and in the course of his employment, of the employee of a person insured by the policy or in respect of bodily injury sustained by such an employee arising out of and in the course of his employment other than a liability arising under the Workmen's Compensation Act, 1923 (8 of 1923) in respect of the death of, or bodily injury to, any such employee — (a) engaged in driving the vehicle; or (b) if it is a public service vehicle engaged as conductor of the vehicle or in examining tickets on the vehicle; or (c) if it is a goods carriage, being carried in the vehicle; or (ii) to cover any contractual liability. According to section 147(2) a policy of insurance shall cover any liability incurred in respect of any accident, up to the following limits, namely: (a) save as provided in clause (b), the amount of liability incurred; (b) in respect of damage to any property of a third party, a limit of rupees six thousand.

Section 149 lays down the duty of insurers to satisfy judgements and awards against persons insured in respect of third party risks as are required to be covered by a policy under section 147(1)(b) "as if he were the judgement debtor, in respect of the liability", notwithstanding that the insurer may be entitled to avoid or cancel or may have avoided or cancelled the policy. Section 149(2) states that no sum shall be payable by an insurer under sub-section (1) in respect of any judgement or award unless, before the commencement of the proceedings in which the judgement of award is given the insurer had notice through the Court or, as the case may be, the Claims Tribunal of the bringing of the proceedings, or in respect of such judgement or award so long as execution is stayed thereon pending an appeal; and an insurer to whom notice of the bringing of any such proceedings is so given shall be entitled to be made a party thereto and to defend the action on any of the following grounds, namely:

(a) that there has been a breach of a specified condition of the policy, being one of the following conditions; namely:

  (i) a condition excluding the use of the vehicle —

    (a) for hire or reward, where the vehicle is on the date of the contract of insurance a vehicle not covered by a permit to ply for hire or reward; or
    (b) for organized racing and speed testing; or
    (c) for a purpose not allowed by the permit under which the vehicle is used, where the vehicle is a transport vehicle; or
    (d) without side-car being attached where the vehicle is a motor cycle; or

  (ii) a condition excluding driving by a named person or persons or by any person who is not duly licensed, or by any person who has been disqualified for holding or obtaining a driving licence during the period of disqualification; or

  (iii) a condition excluding liability for injury caused or contributed to by conditions of war, civil war, riot or civil commotion; or

(b) that the policy is void on the ground that it was obtained by the non-disclosure of a material fact or by a representation of fact which was false in some material particular.

No Fault Liability under Chapter X of the Motor Vehicle Act, 1988

According to section 140 where death or permanent disablement of any person has resulted from an accident arising out of the use of a motor vehicle or motor vehicles, the owner of the vehicle shall, or, as the case may be, the owners of the vehicles shall, jointly and severally, be liable to pay compensation in respect of such death or disablement in accordance with the provisions of this section. The amount of compensation which shall be payable in respect of the death of any person shall be a fixed sum of fifty thousand rupees and the amount of compensation payable in respect of the permanent disablement of any person shall be a fixed sum of twenty five thousand rupees. In any claim for compensation, the claimant shall not be required to plead and establish that the death or permanent disablement in respect of which the claim has been made was due to any wrongful act, neglect or default of the owner or owners of the vehicle or vehicles concerned or of any other person. Further, a claim for compensation shall not be defeated by reason of any wrongful act, neglect or default of the person in respect of whose death or permanent disablement the claim has been made nor shall the quantum of compensation recoverable in respect of such death or permanent disablement be reduced on the basis of the share of such person in the responsibility for such death or permanent disablement. This section is a beneficial provision in order to meet to some extent the responsibility of the society to death or injuries caused by road accidents. Section 140 has been enacted with a view to confer benefit of expeditious payment of a limited amount by way of compensation to the victims of an accident arising out of the use of motor vehicle on the basis of "no fault liability".

The right to claim compensation under section 140 in respect of death or permanent disablement of any person shall be in addition to any other right, except the right to claim under the scheme referred to in Section 163A (such other right hereafter in this section referred to as the right on the principle of fault) to claim compensation in respect thereof under any other provision of this Act or of any other law for the time being in force.[141]

The Act provides for the Motor Accidents Claims Tribunal with the object of the providing a cheap and speedy mode of enforcing the liability of the person who caused the accident. Section 165 empowers the State Government to constitute by notification in the Official Gazette, one or more Motor Accidents Claims Tribunals for such area as may be specified in the notification for the purpose of adjudicating upon claims for compensation in respect of accidents involving the death of, or bodily injury to, persons arising out of the use of motor vehicles, or damages to any property of a third party so arising, or both. A Claims Tribunal shall consist of such number of members as the State Government may think fit to appoint and where it consists of two or more members, one of them shall be appointed as the Chairman thereof. A person is qualified to be appointed as member of the Claims Tribunal only if he is, or has been, a Judge of a High Court, or is, or has been a District Judge, or is qualified for appointment as a High Court Judge or as a District Judge. As per section 175 of the Act, where any Claims Tribunal has been constituted for any area, no Civil Court shall have jurisdiction to entertain any question relating to any claim for compensation which may be adjudicated upon by the Claims Tribunal for that area, and no injunction in respect of any action taken or to be taken by or before the Claims Tribunal in respect of the claim for compensation shall be granted by the Civil Court.

IV. The Workmen's Compensation Act, 1923

The Workmen's Compensation Act is the first piece of legislation towards social security. It deals with compensation for workers who are injured in the course of duty. The scheme of the Workmen's Compensation Act is not to compensate the worker in lieu of wages. The general principle is that a worker who suffers an injury in the course of his employment, which results in a disablement, should be entitled to compensation and in the case of a fatal injury his dependants should be compensated. Under the Workmen's Compensation Act, it is the employer who is responsible to pay compensation as opposed to the Employees State Insurance. The meaning of compensation in this Act is limited to compensation granted under the Act for employment injuries sustained during the course of work. It is also limited to specifically monetary compensation other than a salary, travel allowance, and any other form of remuneration that could be paid under normal circumstances of employment. The compensation is in proportion to the wages drawn by the employee. Under the Act the employer's liability is absolute and irrespective of negligence on his part.

All establishments hiring 20 workers and above must compulsorily register themselves under the Employees' State Insurance Act (ESI Act). It is only those establishments, which employ a lesser number of workers, and therefore, do not come within the purview of the ESI Act that the Workmen's Compensation Act applies to. Also if employers fail to register themselves under the ESI Act, then they will be responsible to pay compensation under the Workmen's Compensation Act. However, the Workmen's Compensation Act will only apply to those persons considered "workers" and those Employers considered 'Employers', as defined under the Act.

For the purpose of the Act the "workman" means any person (other than a person whose employment is of a casual nature and who is employed otherwise than for the purposes of the employer's trade or business), who is: (i) a railway servant as defined in clause (34) of

Section 2 of the Railways Act, 1989, not permanently employed in any administrative, district or sub-divisional office of a railway and not employed in any such capacity as is specified in Schedule II, or (ia) (a) a master, seaman or other member of the crew of a ship, (b) a captain or other member of the crew of an aircraft, (c) a person recruited as driver, helper, mechanic, cleaner or in any other capacity in connection with a motor vehicle, (d) a person recruited for work abroad by a company, and who is employed outside India in any such capacity as is specified in Schedule II and the ship, aircraft or motor vehicle, or company, as the case may be, is registered in India; or (ii) employed in any such capacity as is specified in Schedule II, whether the contract of employment was made before or after the passing of this Act and whether such contract is expressed or implied, oral or in writing; but does not include any person working in the capacity of a member of the Armed Forces of the Union; and any reference to a workman who has been injured shall, where the workman is dead, include a reference to his dependants or any of them.[142]

If personal injury is caused to a workman by accident arising out of and in the course of his employment, his employer shall be liable to pay compensation.[143] However, the employer shall not be so liable: (a) in respect of any injury which does not result in the total or partial disablement of the workman for a period exceeding three days; (b) in respect of any injury, not resulting in death or permanent total disablement, caused by an accident which is directly attributable to: (i) the workman having been at the time thereof under the influence of drink or drugs; or (ii) the wilful disobedience of the workman to an order expressly given, or to a rule expressly framed, for the purpose of securing the safety of workmen; or (iii) the wilful removal or disregard by the workman of any safety guard or other device which he knew to have been provided for the purpose of securing the safety of workmen.

Subject to the provisions of this Act, the amount of compensation shall be as follows, namely: (a) where death results from the injury an amount equal to fifty per cent of the monthly wages of the deceased workman multiplied by the relevant factor; or an amount of eighty thousand rupees, whichever is more; (b) where permanent total disablement results from the injury an amount equal to sixty per cent of the monthly wages of the injured workman multiplied by the relevant factor, or an amount of ninety thousand rupees, whichever is more; (c) where permanent partial disablement results from the injury — (i) in the case of an injury specified in Part II of Schedule I, such percentage of the compensation which would have been payable in the case of permanent total disablement as is specified therein as being the percentage of the loss of earning capacity caused by that injury; and (ii) in the case of an injury not specified in Schedule I, such percentage of the compensation payable in the case of permanent total disablement as is proportionate to the loss of earning capacity (as assessed by the qualified medical practitioner) permanently caused by the injury; and (d) where temporary disablement whether total or partial, results from the injury, a half monthly payment of the sum, equivalent to twenty five per cent of monthly wages of the workman, to be paid.[144]

Compensation under section 4 shall be paid as soon as it falls due.[145] In cases where the employer does not accept the liability for compensation to the extent claimed, he shall be bound to make provisional payment-based on the extent of liability which he accepts, and, such payment shall be deposited with the Commissioner or made to the workman, as the case may be, without prejudice to the right of the workman to make any further claim.[146] Where any employer is in default in paying the compensation due under this Act within one month from the date it fell due, the Commissioner shall — (a) direct that the employer shall, in addition to the amount of the arrears, pay simple interest thereon at the rate of twelve per cent per annum or at such higher rate not exceeding the maximum of the lending rates of any scheduled bank as may be specified by the Central Government, by notification in the Official Gazette, on the amount due; and (b) if, in his opinion, there is no justification for the delay, direct that the employer shall, in addition to the amount of the arrears and interest thereon, pay a further sum not exceeding fifty per cent of such amount by way of penalty.[147]

Under section 17 any contract or agreement whereby a workman relinquishes right of compensation from the employer for personal injury in so far as it purports to relinquish or reducing the liability of any person to pay compensation under the Act is null or void.

V. Employee's State Insurance Act, 1948

The Employee's State Insurance Scheme comes under the class of Compulsory Insurance, made compulsory by statute and administered by Employee's State Insurance Corporation which is a Central Government Undertaking. The scheme was brought into force by the enactment of the Employee's State Insurance Act, 1948 enacted in April 1948. It is a compulsory scheme of health insurance to provide for certain benefits in the event of sickness, maternity and employment injury to the workmen employed in or in connection with the work in factories including those belonging to the government, other than seasonal factories. The insurance fund for this purpose is made-up from the contributions from the employers and workmen, each workman's contribution being fixed on the basis of his average wage during the previous 12 months. The monthly wage limit for coverage under the ESI Act is ₹ 6,500 per month.[148] An employee covered at the beginning of a contribution period shall continue to remain covered till the end of that contribution period notwithstanding the fact that his wages may exceed the prescribed ceiling at any time after the commencement of that contribution period.

The ESI Corporation comprises members representing vital interest groups that include, employees, employers, the Central and State Government, besides, representatives of Parliament and medical profession. The Corporation is headed by the Union Minister of Labour, as its Chairman, whereas the Director-General, appointed by the Central Government functions as its chief executive officer. A standing committee constituted from amongst the members of the corporation, acts as an executive body. The medical benefit council, constituted by the Central Government, is yet another statutory body that advises the corporation on matters related to effective delivery to the beneficiary population.

The insured workmen will have the following benefits:

(a) a cash benefit for sickness, for a period not exceeding 8 weeks in any continuous 12 months' period;
(b) maternity benefits for women workers for a period of 12 weeks and also medical aid at the medical institutions provided for the purposes of the Act; and
(c) disablement and dependent's benefit where the workman is disabled by employment injury totally or partially. In the case of death resulting from employment injury a pension will be payable to the widow and minor children.

Under the Act the insured or their dependants are barred from receiving or recovering whether from the employer of the insured person or from any other person, any compensation or damages under the Workmen's Compensation Act, 1923 or Provident Fund Act or any other law for the time being in force or otherwise in respect of an employment injury sustained by the insured person or an employee under the Act.[149]

VI. Railways Act, 1989

The Act and Rules framed under the Act are beneficial provisions for providing monitory help in the event of a passenger suffering injuries in an accident or granting compensation to the dependents of a decreased in the event of an accident taking place. Under the scheme of the Act compensation is payable in case the victim suffers an injury, permanent or partial disablement, loss of limb, death arising out of railway accident or damage to goods, non-delivery of goods. Rules framed under the provisions of the Act prescribe the maximum benefit that a person would be entitled to under the relevant statutory provisions.

The provisions of section 124 and rules 3 and 4 of the Railway Accidents and Untoward Incidents (Compensation) Rules, 1990 are like contract of insurance, whereby one person, i.e. the railways called insurer undertakes to return for the agreed consideration on the premium to pay to the assured the sum of money on the happening of a specified event. In such cases the person insured cannot claim more than what has been insured. Similarly, a passenger carrying a valid ticket or a pass cannot claim more than what specifically provided.

Section 93 of the Act there provides the general responsibility of a railway administration as carrier of goods. Under section the nature of responsibility of the railways has been changed from that of a bailee into that of insurer. So long as, there is failure on the part of the railways, it cannot escape its liability. For a person to claim damages in respect of goods consigned at owner's risk, he must prove that the negligence or misconduct on the part of the railway administration or any of its servants was the cause for the loss, damage, destruction, deterioration or non-delivery. A railway administration shall be responsible for the loss, destruction, damage or deterioration in transit, or non-delivery of any consignment, arising from any cause except the following, namely (a) act of God; (b) act of war; (c) act of public enemies; (d) arrest, restraint or seizure under legal process; (e) orders or restrictions imposed by the Central Government or a State Government or by an officer or authority subordinate to the Central Government or a State Government authorized by it in this behalf; (f) act or omission or negligence of the consignor or the consignee or the endorsee or the agent or servant of the consignor or the consignee or the endorsee; (g) natural deterioration or wastage in bulk or weight due to inherent defect, quality or vice of the goods; (h) latent defects; and (i) fire, explosion or any unforeseen risk. However, even where such loss, destruction, damage, deterioration or non-delivery is proved to have arisen from anyone or more of the aforesaid causes, the railway administration shall not be relieved of its responsibility for the loss, destruction, damage, deterioration or non-delivery unless the railway administration further proves that it has used reasonable foresight and care in the carriage of the goods.

The liability of the railway administration in respect of the accidents to trains carrying passengers is provided in section 124. The Act casts a "no fault liability" on the railway administration and entitles a person who has suffered a loss to maintain an action to claim compensation by approaching the Railway Claim Tribunal. When in the course of working a railway, an accident occurs the railway administration shall be liable to pay compensation to such extent as may be prescribed and to that extent only for loss occasioned by the death of a passenger dying as a result of such accident, and for personal injury and loss, destruction, damage or deterioration of goods owned by the passenger and accompanying him in his compartment or on the train, sustained as a result of such accident, whether or not there has been any wrongful act, neglect or default on the part of the railway administration.

When in the course of working a railway an untoward incident occurs, then whether or not there has been any wrongful act, neglect or default on the part of the railway administration such as would entitle a passenger who has been injured or the department of a passenger who has been killed to maintain an action and recover damages in respect thereof, the railway administration shall, notwithstanding anything contained in any other law, be liable to pay compensation to such extent as may be prescribed and to that extent only of loss occasioned by the death of, or injury to, a passenger as a result of such untoward incident. Provided that no compensation shall be payable under this section by the railway administration if the passenger dies or suffers injury due to: (a) suicide or attempted suicide by him; (b) self-inflicted injury; (c) his own criminal act; (d) any act committed by him in a state of intoxication or insanity; and (e) any natural cause or disease or medical or surgical treatment unless such treatment becomes necessary due to injury caused by the said untoward incident.[150] For the purpose of this section, "passenger" includes: (i) a railway servant on duty; and (ii) a person who has purchased a valid ticket for travelling, by a train carrying passengers, on any date or a valid platform ticket and becomes a victim of an untoward incident.[151]

Rule 3 of the Railway Accidents (Compensation) Rules, 1990 provides the amount of compensation payable in case of railway accident in respect of death or injury. The amount of compensation payable in respect of death or injuries, shall be as specified in the Schedule. The amount of compensation payable for an injury not specified in Part II or Part III of the Schedule but which, in the opinion of the Claims Tribunal is such as to deprive a person of all capacity to do any work, shall be rupees two lakh. The amount of compensation payable in respect of any injury other than an injury specified in the Schedule or referred to in sub-rule (2) resulting in pain and suffering shall lie as the Claims Tribunal may after taking into consideration medical evidence, besides other circumstances of the case, determine to be reasonable. Provided that if more than one injury is caused by the same accident, compensation shall be payable in respect of each such injury. Provided further that the total compensation in respect of all such injuries shall not exceed rupees forty thousand. Where compensation has been paid for any injury which is less than the amount which would have been payable as compensation if the injured person had died and the person subsequently dies as a result of the injury, a further compensation equal to the difference between the amount payable for death and that already paid shall become payable. Compensation for loss, destruction or deterioration of goods or animals shall be paid to such extent as the Claims Tribunal may, in all the circumstances of the case, determine to be reasonable. Rule 4 provides the limit of compensation. The total compensation payable under rule 3 shall in no case exceed rupees two lakh in respect of anyone person.

An application for compensation under section 124 or section 124A may be made to the Claims Tribunal — (a) by the person who has sustained the injury or suffered any loss; or (b) by any agent duly authorized by such person in this behalf; or (c) where such person is a minor, by his guardian; or (d) where death has resulted from the accident, or the untoward incident by any dependant of the deceased or where such a dependant is a minor, by his guardian. Every application by a dependant for compensation under this section shall be for the benefit of every other dependant.[152] An application before the Claims Tribunal for compensation for the loss of life or personal injury to a passenger, may be instituted against, — (a) the railway administration from which the passenger obtained his pass or purchased his ticket; or (b) the railway administration on whose railway the destination station lies or the loss or personal injury occurred.[153]

Where a person who has made an application for compensation under section 125 desires to be paid interim relief, he may apply to the railway administration for payment of interim relief along with a copy of the application made under that section. Where, on the receipt of an application made under sub-section (1) and after making such inquiry as it may deem fit, the railway administration is satisfied that circumstances exist which require relief to be afforded to the applicant immediately, it may, pending determination by the Claims Tribunal of the actual amount of compensation payable under section 124 or section 124A pay to any person who has sustained the injury or suffered any loss, or where death has resulted from the accident, to any dependant of the deceased, such sum as it considers reasonable for affording such relief, so however, that the sum paid shall not exceed the amount of compensation payable at such rates as may be prescribed. The railway administration shall, as soon as may be, after making an order regarding payment of interim relief under sub-section (2), send a copy thereof to the Claims Tribunal. Any sum paid by the railway administration under sub-section (2) shall be taken into account by the Claims Tribunal while determining the amount of compensation payable.[154] Subject to such rules as may be made, the rates of compensation payable in respect of any injury shall be determined by the Claims Tribunal. The compensation payable in respect of any loss of goods shall be such as the Claims Tribunal may, having regard to the circumstances of the case, determine to be reasonable.[155]

The right of any person to claim compensation under section 124 or section 124A shall not affect the right of any such person to recover compensation payable under the Workmen's Compensation Act, 1923, or any other law for the time being in force; but no person shall be entitled to claim compensation more than once in respect of the same accident. Nothing in sub-section (1) shall affect the right of any person to claim compensation payable under any contract or scheme providing for payment of compensation for death or personal injury or for damage to property or any sum payable under any policy of insurance.[156]

The Central Government may, by notification, make rules to carry out the purposes of this Chapter. In particular, and without prejudice to the generality of the foregoing power, such rules may provide for all or any of the following matters, namely: (a) the compensation payable for death; and (b) the nature of the injuries for which compensation shall be paid and the amount of such compensation.[157]

4.4.10. *Some Other Legislations on Insurance*

I. The Deposit Insurance and Credit Guarantee Corporation Act, 1961

In 1954 Shroff Committee on Finance for the Private Sector made some recommendations on the question of establishing statutory corporation for insuring deposits in the commercial banks. These recommendations were examined by the Government in consultation with the Reserve Bank and representatives of commercial banks and it was considered that the scheme should be implemented at a very early date. Thus, the Deposit Insurance and Credit Guarantee Corporation Act was passed on 7th December, 1961 to provide for the establishment of a corporation for the purpose of insurance of deposits and guaranteeing of credit facilities and for other matters connected therewith or incidental thereto. The Act provides for establishment of Deposit Insurance Corporation by the Central Government as a wholly owned subsidiary of the Reserve Bank with the paid-up capital of a crore of rupees. It will insure all deposits in commercial banks including the deposits belonging to the Central Government or to a State or Foreign Government or to the insured banks. Every insured bank is to pay a premium to the Corporation on its deposits at the notified rates. But the premium payable by any insured bank for any period is not to exceed fifteen naya paise per annum for every hundred rupees of the total amount of the deposits in the bank at the end of that period. The premium is to be paid for prescribed periods at prescribed times and in the prescribed manner.

In case of default in payment the insured bank is to pay interest on such amount at the rate of eight per cent over and above the bank rate.[158] On the order for winding-up or liquidation of the insured bank the corporation is to pay to every depositor of that bank an amount equal to the amount due to him in respect of him deposit in that bank. But the total amount payable by the corporation to anyone depositor in respect of his deposit in that bank is not to exceed one thousand and five hundred rupees. The corporation can raise the aforesaid limit of ₹ 1,500 having regard to its financial position and to the interest of the banking system of the country as a whole.[159] The Deposit Insurance and Credit Guarantee Corporation is to act as agent for the Central Government in guaranteeing the due performance by any small scale industrial concern or other institution or undertaking of its obligations to any credit institution in respect of loans and advances made or other credit facilities provided to it and in making of payments in connection with such guarantee.[160]

II. The Industrial Disputes (Banking and Insurance Companies) Act, 1949

Prior to promulgation of Industrial Disputes (Banking and Insurance Companies) Ordinance on the 30th April, 1949, the disputes in banks and insurance companies were the responsibility of Provincial Governments. The Provincial Governments were the "appropriate authority" under the Industrial Disputes Act, 1947. Besides Central enactment, three Provinces, *viz.* Bombay, the United Provinces and the Central Provinces and Berar, had provincial labour relations enactments of their own under which also control over disputes in bank and insurance companies rested with Provincial Governments. Thus, bank or insurance company with several branches in several Provinces had, therefore, to deal with a number of provincial Governments and a number of agencies including tribunals set-up by them for settlement of disputes arising in its establishments. It was difficult for an organization with country-wide establishments to maintain any principle of uniformity in matters of wages, allowances, and other terms and conditions of employment of its staff. For removing this drawback the Industrial Disputes (Banking and Insurance Companies) Ordinance, 1949 was promulgated on 30th April, 1949 which was replaced by a second ordinance on expiry. That Ordinance was replaced by an Act, Industrial Disputes (Banking and Insurance Companies) Act passed on 14th December, 1949. Under section 4 of the Act it shall not be competent for a State Government or any officer or authority subordinate to such government to refer an industrial dispute concerning any banking or insurance company or any matter relating to such dispute, to any tribunal or other authority for adjudication, inquiry or settlement.

NOTES

1. Lawrence J. (1806) in *Lucena* vs. *Graufurd*, 2 Bos & PNR 269 at p. 301.
2. M.N. Srinivasan (2002), *Principles of Insurance Law*, 7th edn., Wadhwa and Co., Nagpur, pp. 38-39.
3. *Report of the Committee on Reforms in the Insurance Sector (Malhotra Committee Report)*, Ministry of Finance, GoI, January 1994, pp. 6-11.
4. *Ibid.*, pp. 12-16.
5. *Ibid.*, pp. 75-76.
6. *KPN Committee on Provisions of the Insurance Act, 1938*; IRDA, 2005.
7. The Insurance Act, 1938, Proviso 1 to Section 6.
8. *Ibid.*, Proviso 2 to Section 6.
9. *Ibid.*, Section 7.
10. *Ibid.*, Sections 8 and 9.
11. *Ibid.*, Section 3(2A).
12. *Ibid.*, Sub-section 4 of Section 3.
13. *Ibid.*, Section 40(1).
14. *Ibid.*, Section 40(2).
15. *Ibid.*, Section 40(2A).
16. *Ibid.*, Section 40A(1).
17. *Ibid.*, Section 40A(2).
18. *Ibid.*, Section 40A(3).
19. *Ibid.*, Section 40A(4).

20. *Ibid.*, Section 40A(5).
21. *Ibid.*, Section 41.
22. *Ibid.*, Section 42(1).
23. *Ibid.*, Sub-sections (2), (3) and (3A) of Section 42.
24. *Ibid.*, Section 27.
25. *Ibid.*, Section 27A.
26. *Ibid.*, Section 29(1).
27. *Ibid.*, Section 33.
28. *Ibid.*, Section 64A(2).
29. *Ibid.*, Section 64C.
30. *Ibid.*, Section 64I.
31. *Ibid.*, Section 64J.
32. *Ibid.*, Section 64L.
33. *Ibid.*, Section 64U.
34. *Ibid.*, Section 64UC(1).
35. *Ibid.*, Section 64UC(3).
36. *Ibid.*, Section 64UC(4).
37. *Ibid.*, Section 64UC(5).
38. The Life Insurance (Emergency Provisions) Act, 1956, Section 3.
39. *Ibid.*, Section 4.
40. The Life Insurance Corporation Act, 1956, Section 5.
41. *Ibid.*, Section 21.
42. *Ibid.*, Section 37.
43. *Ibid.*, Section 38.
44. *Ibid.*, Section 6(1).
45. *Ibid.*, Section 6(2).
46. *Ibid.*, Section 7(1).
47. *Ibid.*, Section 4(1).
48. *Ibid.*, Section 18.
49. *Ibid.*, Section 19.
50. *Ibid.*, Section 20.
51. *Ibid.*, Section 21.
52. *Ibid.*, Section 48.
53. *Ibid.*, Section 49.
54. The General Insurance Business (Nationalization) Act, 1972, Section 4.
55. *Ibid.*, Section 5.
56. *Ibid.*, Section 10.
57. *Ibid.*, Section 18.
58. *Ibid.*, Section 39.
59. The Marine Insurance Act, 1963, Section 2(e).
60. *Ibid.*, Section 4(1).
61. *Ibid.*, Section 5.
62. *Ibid.*, Section 6.
63. *Ibid.*, Section 7.
64. *Ibid.*, Section 8.
65. *Ibid.*, Section 9.
66. *Ibid.*, Section 10.
67. *Ibid.*, Section 11.
68. *Ibid.*, Section 12.
69. *Ibid.*, Section 13.
70. *Ibid.*, Section 14.

71. *Ibid.*, Section 15.
72. *Ibid.*, Section 16.
73. *Ibid.*, Section 17.
74. *Ibid.*, Section 19.
75. *Ibid.*, Section 20.
76. *Ibid.*, Section 23.
77. *Ibid.*, Section 24.
78. *Ibid.*, Section 25.
79. *Ibid.*, Section 27.
80. *Ibid.*, Section 28.
81. *Ibid.*, Section 29.
82. *Ibid.*, Section 30.
83. *Ibid.*, Section 31.
84. *Ibid.*, Section 34.
85. The Indian Contract Act, 1872, Section 11.
86. *Ibid.*, Section 13.
87. *Ibid.*, Section 7.
88. *Ibid.*, Section 23.
89. *Ibid.*, Sections 23, 30, 20.
90. *Ibid.*, Sections 19 and 19A.
91. *Ibid.*, Second para of Section 19.
92. *Ibid.*, Section 37.
93. *Stewart* vs. *Freeman*, (1903) 1 KB 47.
94. The Indian Contract Act, 1872, Section 38.
95. *Mithoolal Nayak* vs. *LIC*, AIR 1962 SC 814.
96. The Indian Contract Act, 1872, Section 66.
97. M.N. Srinivasan, *Principles of Insurance Law*, 7th Edn., Wadhwa & Co., p. 46, see also Avatar Singh (2002), *Law of Contract*, 8th Edn, p. 324.
98. The Indian Contract Act, 1872, Section 56.
99. The Redressal of Public Grievance Rules, 1998, Rule 6(1) and (2).
100. *Ibid.*, Rule 7.
101. *Ibid.*, Rule 8(1).
102. *Ibid.*, Rule 10.
103. *Ibid.*, Rule 12.
104. *Ibid.*, Rule 13.
105. *Ibid.*, Rule 15.
106. *Ibid.*, Rule 16.
107. *Ibid.*, Rule 17.
108. *Ibid.*, Rule 20.
109. *Praveen Damani* vs. *Oriental Insurance Co. Ltd.*, IV (2006) CPJ 189 (NC); *United India Insurance* vs. *Ramesh Chand Gupta*, RP No. 711 of 2008, decided on 19-2-2008, *Life Insurance Corporation of India* vs. *Smt. Tejalben Kananbhai Patel*, I (2007) CPJ 275 (NC).
110. *Life Insurance Corporation of India* vs. *Sajida Begum*, III (2007) CPJ 319 (NC).
111. *Oriental Insurance Company* vs. *Indu Devi*, R.P. No. 631 of 2008, decided on 19-2-2008.
112. *HDFC Chubb General Insurance Co. Ltd.* vs. *Ila Gupta*, I (2007) CPJ 274 (NC).
113. *Agricultural Insurance Co. of India Ltd.* vs. *Kemlegowda*, IV (2006) CPJ 313 (NC).

114. *New India Assurance Co.* vs. *Surtu*, IV (2004) CPJ 158.
115. *Leela Devi* vs. *State Bank of India*, I (2006) CPJ 435.
116. *National Insurance Co. Ltd.* vs. *Shri Nachhattar Singh*, II (2006) CPJ 120 (NC).
117. *Mayadevi* vs. *Life Insurance Corporation of India Ltd.*, Revision Petition No. 2824 of 2007, decided on 21-5-2008.
118. *National Insurance Co. Ltd.* vs. *Padmavathi Jewellers*, III (2007) CPJ 368 (NC).
119. *Kochar Woollen Mills P. Ltd.* vs. *United India Insurance Co. Ltd.*, III (2007) CPJ 60 (NC).
120. The Personal Injuries (Compensation Insurance) Act, 1963, Section 4(1).
121. *Ibid.*, Section 5.
122. *Ibid.*, Section 8.
123. *Ibid.*, Section 9.
124. *Ibid.*, Section 13.
125. *Ibid.*, Section 16.
126. AIR 1987 SC 1086.
127. The Public liability Insurance Act, 1991, Section 3.
128. *Ibid.*, Section 4(2A).
129. *Ibid.*, Section 4(2B).
130. *Ibid.*, Section 4.
131. *Ibid.*, Section 5.
132. *Ibid.*, Section 6.
133. *Ibid.*, Section 7.
134. *Ibid.*, Section 7A.
135. *Ibid.*, Section 8.
136. *Ibid.*, Section 14.
137. *Ibid.*, Sections 16, 17, and 20.
138. *Ibid.*, Section 21.
139. *Ibid.*, Section 23.
140. The Motor Vehicle Act, 1988, Section 147.
141. *Ibid.*, Section 141(1).
142. The Workmen Compensation Act, Section 2(1)(n).
143. *Ibid.*, Section 3(1).
144. *Ibid.*, Section 4(1).
145. *Ibid.*, Section 4A(1).
146. *Ibid.*, Section 4A(2).
147. *Ibid.*, Section 4A(3).
148. ESI Central Rules, 1950, Rule 50.
149. ESI Act, Sections 53 and 61.
150. Railways Act, 1989, Section 124A.
151. *Ibid.*, Explanation to Section 124A.
152. *Ibid.*, Section 125.
153. *Ibid.*, Section 109.
154. *Ibid.*, Section 126.
155. *Ibid.*, Section 127.
156. *Ibid.*, Section 128.
157. *Ibid.*, Section 129.
158. The Deposit Insurance and Credit Guarantee Corporation Act, 1961, Section 15.
159. *Ibid.*, Section 16(1).
160. *Ibid.*, Section 21B.

5

WORKING OF THE INSURANCE REGULATORY AND DEVELOPMENT AUTHORITY

5.1. Introduction

The nationalized insurance companies did contribute to the spread of the insurance business beyond the metropolitan areas. They to a great extent succeeded in popularizing the concept in rural and semi-urban areas. However, the public sector companies had numerous problems and in the absence of competition the consumers were not benefited to desired extent. In early 1990s the Government reviewed its policy and initiated a process of liberalization. This encouraged private participation in various sectors. It was felt necessary that insurance penetration and enlargement of the market can be accomplished only when a large number of companies compete with each other. Thus, the insurance sector was opened-up for private participation on the ground that the interests of the consumers would be better served, if there is competition among the insurers. It was also recognized that the country has a vast potential waiting to be tapped and this can be done only when we have a large number of companies spreading their wings across the country and offering a variety of products catering to the demands and needs of different sections of the population. It was also felt that competition would generate a healthy attitude towards redressal of consumer grievances and improve the quality of service.

The Committee on Reforms in the Insurance Sector, commonly known as the Malhotra Committee made a major recommendation[1] that there was an urgent need to activate the insurance regulatory apparatus even in the then prevailing nationalized insurance sector. A strong, effective, autonomous, compact and highly professional statutory body with independent source of funding should be established. The

Government ultimately decided to do so. Finally, the Insurance Regulatory and Development Authority Act was notified in April 2000. Once, the legislation was put through, the actual process of inducting private players into the market was started and the transition from state monopoly to free market of the insurance sector began. Supervision and regulation of insurance is a relatively new experience in India. It is the job of the regulator to ensure that the insurers have, at any point of time, sufficient resources to meet the liabilities and that all customers are treated in an equitable manner. The regulations framed by the Authority deal with both the issues in a comprehensive way. The former is addressed by stipulating a high level of capital requirement for entry into the field and rigorous enforcement of the solvency requirements, while the latter is covered by the regulations put in place for protection of policy-holder interests. From time-to-time, the Authority is coming out with a number of regulations to ensure smooth functioning of the insurance business.

5.2. The Insurance Regulatory and Development Authority Act, 1999

The insurance industry requires a high degree of regulation. The Insurance Act, 1938, provided for the institution of Controller of Insurance to act as a strong and powerful supervisory and regulatory authority with powers to direct, advise, caution, prohibit, investigate, inspect, prosecute, search, seize, fine, amalgamate, authorize, register and liquidate insurance companies. However, after the nationalization of the life insurance industry in 1956 and the general insurance industry in 1972, the role of Controller of Insurance diminished in significance over a period of time.

The recommendations of the Malhotra Committee were discussed at different forums including the Consultative Committee of the Parliament attached to the Ministry of Finance. The recommendation to set-up an autonomous Insurance Regulatory Authority found wide support. In view of the general support received, the then Government decided to bring in a legislation to establish an independent regulatory authority for the Insurance Industry. Since, enacting legislation for creating the Insurance Regulatory Authority would take time, the then Government constituted through a resolution an Interim Insurance Regulatory Authority pending the enactment of a comprehensive legislation.

In pursuance of the Budget Speech in July 1996, the then Government introduced on December 20, 1996, the Insurance Regulatory Authority Bill, 1996, for establishment of an Authority to protect the interests of holders of Insurance policies and to regulate, promote and ensure orderly growth of the insurance industry and for matters connected therewith or incidental thereto. The Bill was referred to the Department related Standing Committee on the Ministry of Finance. The Committee submitted its report on May 9, 1997. However, the said Bill incorporating therein the recommendations of the said Standing Committee was taken for consideration, but could not be passed and the Bill was withdrawn by the then Government.

In order to provide better insurance coverage to citizens and also to augment the flow of long-term resources for financing infrastructure, in the Budget Speech, 1998, the policy of the Government was announced to open-up the insurance sector and also to establish a statutory regulatory authority. Accordingly, the Insurance Regulatory Authority Bill, 1998, was introduced in the Lok Sabha on the 15th December, 1998 providing for setting a statutory Insurance Regulatory Authority and contained three schedules incorporating amendment to the Insurance Act, 1938; the Life Insurance Corporation Act, 1956; and the General Insurance Business (Nationalization) Act, 1972, to permit the entry of private Indian companies into the insurance sector and to make certain consequential amendments to the Insurance Act, 1938. The Bill was referred to the Standing Committee on Finance on 4th January, 1999 for examination and report. The Standing Committee while recommending the Bill suggested some amendments. These were accepted by the Government and amendments to the Bills were circulated on the 18th March, 1999. However, the Bill could not be taken-up for consideration consequent on dissolution of the Lok Sabha.

It was then proposed to reintroduce a fresh Bill by incorporating the provisions of the Insurance Regulatory Authority Bill, 1998, and the amendments suggested by the Standing Committee on Finance. The Bill was titled Insurance Regulatory and Development Authority Bill on the basis of the recommendation of the Standing Committee. In the main text of the Bill, provisions were incorporated to give a statutory character to the Interim Insurance Regulatory Authority and the three Schedules contained amendments to the Insurance Act, 1938; the Life Insurance Corporation Act, 1956; and the General Insurance Business (Nationalization) Act, 1972.

The Insurance Regulatory and Development Authority Bill having passed by both the Houses of Parliament received the assent of the President on 29th December, 1999. As per Preamble of the Act, the objective of the Act is to provide for the establishment of an authority to protect the interests of the holders of insurance policies, to regulate, promote and insure orderly growth of the insurance industry and for matters connected therewith or incidental thereto and further to amend the Insurance Act, 1938; the Life Insurance Corporation Act, 1956; and the General Insurance Business (Nationalization) Act, 1972.

5.2.1. *Constitution and Composition of the Authority*

Under the Act the Central Government has been mandated to establish an authority to be called "the Insurance Regulatory and Development Authority".[2] The Authority shall be a body corporate having perpetual succession and common seal with power to acquire, hold and dispose of property both movable and immovable and to contract, and by the said name sue or be sued.[3] The head office of the Authority shall be at the place to be decided by the Central Government from time-to-time. It is empowered to establish offices at other places in India.[4]

The Insurance Regulatory and Development Authority shall consist of a Chairman and other members not exceeding nine of whom not more than five shall be full-time and not more than four shall be part-time to be appointed by the Central Government from amongst persons of ability, integrity and standing and who have knowledge or experience in life insurance, general insurance, actuarial science, finance, economics, law, accountancy, administration or any other discipline which would be useful to the Authority.[5] The Chairman and every whole-time member shall hold office for a term of five years or until the age of 65 years in the case of Chairman and 62 in the case of other whole-time members, whichever is earlier and they shall be eligible for reappointment subject to age consideration. A part time member shall hold office for a term not exceeding five years.[6] Any member can relinquish his office by giving in writing notice of not less than three months.[7] Any member of IRDA can be removed from office by the Central Government who is or has been adjudged as an insolvent, or who has become physically or mentally incapable, or who has been convicted of any offence which involves moral turpitude or who has acquired any financial or other interest which is likely to affect prejudicially his functions as members or who has abused his position as to render his continuation in office detrimental to office.[8]

5.2.2. *Duties, Powers and Functions of Authority*

The Authority shall have the duty to regulate, promote and ensure orderly growth of the insurance business and re-insurance business.[9] The powers and functions of the Authority shall include:

(a) issuc to the applicant a certificate of registration, renew, modify, withdraw, suspend or cancel such registration;
(b) protection of the interests of the policy-holders in matters concerning assigning of policy, nomination by policy-holders, insurable interest, settlement of insurance claim, surrender values of the policy and other terms and conditions of contracts of insurance;
(c) specify requisite qualifications, code of conduct and practical training for intermediary or insurance intermediaries and agents;
(d) specify the code of conduct for surveyors and loss assessors;
(e) promoting efficiency in the conduct of insurance business;
(f) promoting and regulating professional organizations connected with insurance and re-insurance business;
(g) levying fees and other charges for carrying out the purposes of this Act;
(h) calling for information from, undertaking inspection of, conducting enquiries and investigations including audit of the insurers, intermediaries, insurance intermediaries and other organizations connected with the insurance business;
(i) control and regulation of rates, advantages, terms and conditions that may be offered by insurers in respect of general insurance business not so controlled and regulated by the Tariff Advisory Committee under section 64U of the Insurance Act, 1938;
(j) specify the form and manner in which books of account shall be maintained and statement of account shall be rendered by insurers and other insurances intermediaries;
(k) regulating investment of funds by insurance companies;
(l) regulating maintenance of margin of solvency;
(m) adjudication of disputes between insurers and intermediaries or insurance intermediaries;
(n) supervising the functioning of the Tariff Advisory Committee;
(o) specifying the percentage of premium income of the insurer to finance schemes for promoting and regulating professional organizations referred to in Clause (f);
(p) specifying the percentage of life insurance business and general insurance business to be undertaken by the insurer in the rural or social sector; and
(q) exercising such other powers as may be prescribed.[10]

The powers and functions mentioned under the Act enable the Authority to perform the role of effective watchdog and regulation for the insurance sector in India. Pursuant to its powers under the IRDA Act, the IRDA has framed atleast 27 sets of Regulations on various topics like preparation and submission of actuarial reports, obligations of insurers to rural and social sectors, registration of Indian insurance companies, preparation of financial statements and auditors report of insurance companies, form of annual statements of account and record, insurance brokers etc. These regulations are important constituents of the regulatory regime.

5.2.3. *Power to Issue Directions and Power of Suppression*

The Authority in exercise of its powers and the performance of its functions is bound by such directions on questions of policy, other than those relating to technical and administrative matter, as the Central Government may give in writing to it from time-to-time. However, the Authority shall be given an opportunity to express its view before direction is given. The decision of Central Government shall be final.[11]

If at any time the Central Government is of the opinion that on account of circumstances beyond the control of the Authority, it is unable to discharge the functions or perform the duties imposed on it by or under the provisions of the Act or the Authority has persistently defaulted in complying with any direction given by the Central Government or in discharge of the functions or performance of duties imposed on it by or under the provisions of the Act and as a result of such default the financial position of the Authority or the administration of the Authority has suffered or some circumstances exist which render it necessary in public interest so to do, the Central Government can by notification and for reasons to be specified therein, supersede the Authority for a period not exceeding six months and appoint a person to be Controller of Insurance under section 2B of the Insurance Act, 1938.[12]

5.2.4. *Delegation of Powers by the Authority*

The Authority may, by general or special order in writing, delegate such of its powers and functions under this Act to the Chairman or any other member or officer of the Authority subject to such conditions as may be specified in the order.[13] The Authority may by an order in writing form committees of the members and delegate to them the powers and functions of the Authority as may be specified by the regulations.[14]

5.2.5. *Rule-making Powers of the Central Government*

The Central Government may, by notification, make rules for carrying out the provisions of the Act.[15] Such rules may provide for the following matters:

(a) the salary and allowances and other terms and conditions of service of the members other than part-time members;
(b) the allowances to be paid to the part-time members;
(c) such other powers that may be exercised by the Authority under clause (q) of sub-section (2) of Section 14;
(d) the form of annual statement of accounts to be maintained by the Authority under sub-section (1) of Section 17;
(e) the form and the manner in which and the time within which returns and statements and particulars are to be furnished to the Central Government under sub-section (1) of Section 20;
(f) the matters under sub-section (5) of Section 25 on which the Insurance Advisory Committee shall advise the Authority; and
(g) any other matter which is required to be, or may be prescribed, or in respect of which provision is to be or may be made by rules.[16]

5.2.6. *Insurance Advisory Committee*

The Authority may establish a Committee to be known as the Insurance Advisory Committee. The Insurance Advisory Committee shall consist of not more than twenty-five members excluding *ex-officio* members to represent the interests of commerce, industry, transport, agriculture, consumer fora, surveyors, agents, intermediaries, organizations engaged in safety and loss prevention, research bodies and employees' association in the insurance sector. The Chairperson and the members of the Authority shall be *ex-officio* chairperson and *ex-officio* members of the Insurance Advisory Committee. The objects of the Insurance Advisory Committee shall be to advise the Authority on matters relating to making of the regulations under section 26. The Insurance Advisory Committee may also advise the Authority on such other matters as may be prescribed.[17]

5.2.7. *Power to Make Regulations*

The Authority may, in consultation with the Insurance Advisory Committee, by notification make regulations consistent with this Act and Rules made thereunder to carry out the purposes of this Act. Such regulations may provide for all or any of the following matters:

(a) the time and places of meeting of the Authority and the procedure to be followed at such meetings including the quorum necessary for transaction of business under sub-section (1) of Section 10;
(b) the transaction of business at its meetings under sub-section (4) of Section 10;
(c) the terms and other conditions of service of officers and other employees of the Authority under sub-section (2) of section 12;
(d) the powers and functions which may be delegated to committees of the members under sub-section (2) of section 23; and
(e) any other matter which is required to be or may be, specified by regulations or in respect of which provision is to be or may be made by regulations.[18]

5.2.8. *Schedules to the IRDA Act*

The First Schedule appended to the IRDA Act listed out several amendments to the Insurance Act, 1938. The Second Schedule to the IRDA Act inserted section 30A in the Life Insurance Corporation Act, 1956, whereby the exclusive privilege of LIC to carry on life insurance business in India was to cease. The Third Schedule to the IRDA Act inserted a similar provision, section 24A, in the General Insurance Business (Nationalization) Act, 1972, whereby the exclusive privilege of the GIC and its subsidiaries in relation to general insurance business ceased.

The amendments made by the IRDA Act, 1999, to the Insurance Act, 1938, prohibited insurers other than companies registered under the Companies Act, 1956, to carry on insurance business in India and investment of funds of the policy-holders outside India. Foreign participation has been restricted to 26 per cent of the paid-up equity capital of an insurance company. The amendments provided for —

(a) requirements as to paid-up equity capital for both insurers and reinsurers;
(b) manner of divesting of excess shareholding by promoters;
(c) manner and conditions of investment;
(d) maintenance of required solvency margin at all times by the insurers;
(e) issue of licence to insurance agents, intermediary or insurance intermediary and surveyors by the Authority as also suspension and cancellation thereof;

(f) obligations of insurers to compulsorily undertake specified percentage of insurance business in rural and social sector;
(g) enhanced penalties for contravention of and failure to comply with the provisions of the Act and offences by companies; and
(h) powers of the Authority to make regulations as required by the Act.

5.2.9. *Grievance Redressal under Insurance Regulatory and Development Authority*

A. Grievance Redressal Cell

The Grievance Redressal Cell of the Insurance Regulatory and Development Authority looks into complaints from policy-holders. Complaints against life and non-life insurers are handled separately. This Cell plays a facilitative role by taking-up complaints with the respective insurers.

Policy-holders who have complaints against insurers are required to first approach the Grievance/Customer Complaint Cell of the concerned insurer. If they do not receive a response from insurer(s) within a reasonable period of time or are dissatisfied with the response of the company, they may approach the Grievance Cell of the IRDA. Only cases of delay/non-response regarding matters relating to policies and claims are taken-up by the Cell with the insurers for speedy disposal. As claims/policy contracts in dispute require adjudication and the IRDA does not carry out any adjudication, insured are advised to approach the available quasi-judicial or judicial channels, i.e. the Insurance Ombudsmen, Consumer fora or the Civil courts for such complaints. Only complaints from the insured themselves or the claimants are entertained by the cell. The Cell does not entertain complaints written on behalf of policy-holders by advocates or agents or any third parties. The complaints can also be sent through e-mail, complete in all details of the complaint as required in the complaint's registration form. Without this the Cell will not be in a position to register the complaint.

B. Insurance Ombudsman

The institution of Insurance Ombudsman was created by Government of India notification dated 11th November, 1998 with the purpose of quick disposal of the grievances of the insured customers and to mitigate their problems involved in redressal of those grievances. This institution is of great importance and relevance for the protection of interests of policy-holders and also in building their confidence in the system. The institution has helped to generate and sustain the faith and confidence amongst the consumers and insurers.

The governing body of Insurance Council issues order of appointment of the Insurance Ombudsman on the recommendations of the committee comprising of Chairman, IRDA; Chairman, LIC; Chairman, GIC; and a representative of the Central Government. Insurance Council comprises members of the Life Insurance Council and General Insurance Council formed under section 40C of the Insurance Act, 1938. The governing body of insurance council consists of representatives of insurance companies.

Ombudsmen are drawn from insurance industry, civil services and judicial services. Insurance Ombudsman is appointed for a term of three years or till the incumbent attains the age of sixty five years, whichever is earlier. Reappointment is not permitted. The governing body has appointed twelve Ombudsmen across the country allotting them different geographical areas as their areas of jurisdiction. The Ombudsman may hold sitting at various places within their area of jurisdiction in order to expedite disposal of complaints. The offices of the twelve insurance Ombudsmen are located at: (1) Bhopal, (2) Bhubaneswar, (3) Cochin, (4) Guwahati, (5) Chandigarh, (6) New Delhi, (7) Chennai, (8) Kolkata, (9) Ahmedabad, (10) Lucknow, (11) Mumbai, and (12) Hyderabad.

The Ombudsman has a secretarial staff provided to him by the insurance council to assist him in discharging his duties. The total expenses on Ombudsman and his staff are incurred by the insurance companies who are members of the insurance council in such proportion as may be decided by the governing body. An Ombudsman may be removed from service for gross misconduct committed by him during his term of office. The governing body may appoint such person as it thinks fit to conduct enquiry in relation to misconduct of the Ombudsman. All enquiries on misconduct will be sent to Insurance Regulatory and Development Authority which may take a decision as to the proposed action to be taken against the Ombudsman. On recommendations of the IRDA, the governing body may terminate his services, in case he is found guilty.

Insurance Ombudsman has two types of functions to perform first, conciliation, and second award-making. The insurance Ombudsman is empowered to receive and consider complaints in respect of personal lines of insurance from any person who has any grievance against an insurer. The complaint may relate to any grievance against the insurer, i.e. (a) any partial or total repudiation of claims by the insurance companies; (b) dispute with regard to premium paid or payable in terms of the policy; (c) dispute on the legal construction of the policy wordings in case such dispute relates to claims; (d) delay in settlement of claims; and (e) non-issuance of any insurance document to customers after receipt of premium. Ombudsman's powers are restricted to insurance contracts of value not exceeding ₹ 20 lakh. The insurance companies are required to honour the awards passed by an Insurance Ombudsman within three months.

Manner of Lodging Complaint

The complaint by an aggrieved person has to be in writing, and addressed to the insurance Ombudsman of the jurisdiction under which the office of the insurer falls. The complaint can also be lodged through the legal heirs of the insured. Before lodging a complaint the complainant should have made a representation to the insurer named in the complaint and the insurer either should have rejected the complaint or the complainant has not received any reply within a period of one month after the concerned insurer has received his complaint or he is not satisfied with the reply of the insurer. The complaint cannot be made later than one year after the insurer has replied. The same complaint on the subject should not be pending before any court, consumer forum or arbitrator.

When a complaint is settled through the mediation of the Ombudsman, he shall make the recommendations which he thinks fair in the circumstances of the case. Such a recommendation shall be made not later than one month and copies of the same shall be sent to complainant and the insurance company concerned. If the complainant accepts recommendations, he will send a communication in writing within 15 days of the date of receipt accepting the settlement.

The Ombudsman shall pass an award within a period of three months from the receipt of the complaint. The awards are binding upon the insurance companies. If the policy-holder is not satisfied with the award of the Ombudsman he can approach other avenues like Consumer Forums and Courts of Law for redressal of his grievances. As per the policy-holder's protection regulations, every insurer shall inform the policy-holder along with the policy document in respect of the Insurance Ombudsman in whose jurisdiction his office falls for the purpose of grievances redressal arising if any subsequently.

Steady increase in number of complaints received by various Ombudsman shows that the policyholders are reposing their confidence in the institution of Insurance Ombudsman. During 2007-08, 10,865 complaints were lodged with the Ombudsmen against the insurers both life and non-life. As on April 1, 2007, there were 1,947 complaints pending with the Ombudsmen for disposal. Of the total 12,812 complaints, the Ombudsmen have disposed of 11,393 complaints during 2007-08. Of the disposed complaints, 5,778 were against the life insurers and 5,615 were against the non-life insurers. Of the total complaints the Ombudsmen have given awards in 2,664 cases, dismissed 1,156 cases and 352 cases have been recommended to the companies for settlement at their end.[19] Similarly, during 2006-07 — 10,187 complaints were lodged with the Ombudsmen out of which 5,433 were against life insurers and rest against non-life insurers. Of the total 12,116 complaints pending before the Ombudsmen at the end of March 2007, 10,169 complaints have been disposed of. In 1,867 complaints the Ombudsmen have passed awards and 1,112 cases have been dismissed. In 338 cases the Ombudsmen recommended to the companies for settlement at their end.[20]

C. Appellate Authority for IRDA

The Union Government has set-up an Appellate Authority for the insurance industry.[21] The Authority will be the mechanism for addressing any ruling of the Insurance Regulatory and Development Authority (IRDA). The function of the Authority will be similar to that of a system which was earlier in operation in the Ministry of Finance (MoF) for capital market players to challenge the orders of the Security and Exchange Board of India (SEBI) before setting-up the Securities Appellate Tribunal headed by a judge. The Central Government, through a notification, has set-up both a single and division bench of the Appellate Authority for the insurance industry. Joint Secretary, MoF, will constitute the single bench, while on the division bench, he will be joined by Joint Secretary, the Ministry of Law. Though the Government has planned to set-up a full-fledged appellate tribunal for domestic insurance, the move to announce an Appellate Authority with its own official will boost the process of transparency of IRDA, which has to regulate a fast expanding complex industry.

5.3. Analysis of the Views on the Working of the IRDA Obtained through the Questionnaire

To better understand the working of the Insurance Regulatory and Development Authority a questionnaire was developed having twenty four questions on different aspects of the functioning of the Authority. The same was sent to the Research and Development Unit of IRDA and was promptly replied by them. However, few questions on the powers of the Authority to function as the watchdog and regulation, powers needed to make it more effective and efficient, procedural steps being followed by the Authority in formulating regulations and suggestions by the Authority to improve the functioning of the insurers and insurer intermediaries were not answered by the Authority on the ground that these questions are policy issues and are under debate. The replies to rest of the questions are placed below:

5.3.1. *Exercise of Power of Renewal, Modification, Withdrawal, Suspension or Cancellation of Certificate of Registration by IRDA*

After liberalization of the market in 1990s the insurance market has attracted financial institutions, big industrial establishments etc. to enter the insurance sector. Participation of banks and other financial institutions in the floatation of insurance companies is also subject to clearance from the industry regulator, *viz.* Reserve Bank of India or National Housing Bank.

The Authority has divided the examination process into two distinct phases — a preliminary satisfaction on the credibility and stability of the promoters followed by an in-depth assessment of the business plans submitted. Upon satisfaction that the management is fit and proper and after exhaustive discussions between the promoters' representative and the officers of the Authority, the application is accepted. All applications that are filed with IRDA have to undergo through a first, a second or even third revision to accommodate market realities, solvency requirements, market products, pricing, aspects relating to technology, geographical spread etc. The Authority seeks to satisfy itself that an insurer would not only be committed to long-term stay in the market, but would bring to the market new techniques in insurance underwriting and administration to make the Indian market also reflect the international trends and flavour.

The performance of insurance companies is regularly monitored to ensure compliance of various requirements as provided in the regulations. Failure on the part of the insurance company to comply with these regulations leads to suspension, cancellation, modification, withdrawal of certificate of registration and imposition of penalty. The regulations further require each insurer to seek renewal of certificates of registration before 31st December each year.

Cases relating to Insurers in each Category:

Sl. No.	*Category*	*Year*				
		2007-08	*2006-07*	*2005-06*	*2004-05*	*2003-04*
1.	Certificate of Commencement	10	1	2	–	2
2.	Modification	–	–	–	–	–
3.	Withdrawal	–	–	–	–	–
4.	Suspension	–	–	–	–	–
5.	Cancellation	–	–	–	–	–
6.	Renewal	All existing	All existing	All existing	All existing	All existing

5.3.2. *Steps Taken by the Authority to Protect the Interests of the Policy-holders (Consumers) and the Areas where Positive Intervention of Authority is Needed*

IRDA's main mission is to protect the interests of the policy-holders. The following are some of the steps taken by the Authority for the protection of the interests of the policy-holders:

- The Authority through regulations has mandated the insurers to put in place effective mechanisms for redressal of grievances. With a view to strengthen the regulations for protection of the interests of the policy-holders, the Authority notified the IRDA (Protection of Policy-holders' Interests) Regulations, 2002. While laying down guidelines for both, new as well as existing insurance contracts the regulations provide for the manner of presentation of prospectus of any insurance product, mode of furnishing details therein and claims procedure in respect of life and general insurance policies. The regulations also require each insurer to set-up in-house grievance redressal machinery, review of speed of settlement of claims and prompt service to the policy-holders. The regulations also provide for penal provisions in case of delay in settlement of claim amount by the insurer. The Authority carried out modifications in the Protection of Policy-holders Regulations in October 2002 to make them more robust.
- In another initiative, the office of the Appellate Authority has been constituted under section 110H of the Insurance Act, 1938. The Appellate Authority has been set-up to review, on appeal, the directives given by the Authority.

- In November 2002, the Authority has set-up a grievance cell to facilitate resolution of policy-holders' complaints. The Cell is headed by a Deputy Director to receive complaints/grievances from the policy-holders. The Cell receives complaints from the policy-holders/insurance customers, insurance intermediaries and from other sources against different insurance companies, irrespective of the nature of the complaints and forwards them to the insurance companies to ensure early resolution of the public grievances. On receipt of the complaints the cell functions in two ways: (a) facilitates an early resolution of the complaint by the insurer through direct interaction with the policy-holder; and (b) analyses the complaints based on: (i) duration of disposal; (ii) functional area. The insurer-wise analysis for duration of complaints evaluates the effectiveness and simplicity of the process adopted by the insurer in handling the complaints. It also evaluates how insurer is complying with the provisions of Regulation 5 of IRDA (Protection of Policy-holders' Interests) Regulations, 2002. The Regulation requires speedy and efficient handling of the complaints by the insurer. The analysis of the complaints-based on functional area indicates: (a) the weakness in market practices, and (b) the inadequacies of the insurance companies, which may require regulatory intervention for necessary corrective action.

  The Grievance Cell plays a facilitative role by registering the complaint and tracking down the same with the insurer for its early resolution. In case of dispute on any issue between the insurer and the complainant, the cell informs the complainant to take-up the matter with quasi-judicial (insurance Ombudsman/consumer forums) or judicial bodies, since IRDA does not have the power of adjudication. The Cell looks into genuine cases of delay in the settlement of grievances. The Authority receives and takes-up the complaints with the insurance companies. The nature of complaints reflects on the happenings in the market. Most of the complaints in respect of life insurance relate to repudiation of death claims, especially early death. In the case of general insurance, most grievances relate to personal insurances, health (Mediclaim) being the most prominent, followed by Motor. However, the Cell does not function as an underwriter nor does it decide on issues like adoption of underwriting practices, the claims procedure etc. by the insurers. The Authority has set-up grievance cells separately for life and non-life insurance. There is a separate channel set-up in the IRDA to deal with complaints of senior citizens in respect of health insurance policies.

- Making it compulsory for every life insurer to make available the premium rates with a facility of a premium calculator on its website for the information of public.
- Insurers to have a consumer representative on their Board.
- Making it obligatory for insurance companies to disclose clearly the benefits, terms and conditions of the policy document.
- Advertisements issued by the insurers are required to make proper disclosures. The Authority is conscious of the fact that the fine print should not take away what the bold print promises. In this regard it has come out with the Insurance Advertisement and Disclosure Regulations [IRDA (Insurance Advertisements and Disclosure) Regulations, 2000]. The regulations ensure that the insurance companies adhere to fair trade practices and transparent disclosure norms while addressing the policy-holders on the prospects. Companies have been mandated to comply with the Advertisement Code as prescribed by the ASCI (Advertisement Standard Council of India). Insurers have also been made responsible to vet any advertisement issued by their agents or where cross-promotions are involved, to ensure that misleading advertisements are not issued.
- For redressal of the complaints of the individual policy-holders, the Ombudsman Scheme has been put in place by the Central Government. The implementation of the scheme is being supervised by the Authority.
- Insurers are required to set-up proper grievance redressal machinery at their head office and at their other offices and set benchmarks for efficient and effective service.
- Introducing Third Party Administrators in the health sector, to provide improved health insurance services, *viz.* cashless cover, and other add on facilities.
- Licensing brokers as intermediaries to serve better the interests of the insured public in general and insurance industry in particular. The broker renders advice on appropriate insurance cover and terms thereof, keeps up to date on the variety of available insurance products and submits quotations received from insurers for consideration of the client.
- The Authority also protects the interests of the policy-holders by ensuring that the insurers maintain the prescribed solvency margin.

Maintenance of the solvency margins by the insurers is an indication that they are in a position to meet their obligations towards policy-holders with regard to payment of claims.

- To protect the interests of holders of insurance policies and to regulate, promote and ensure orderly growth of the insurance industry, the Authority has inducted a leading consumer activist into the Insurance Advisory Committee. In addition to this member, this committee has drawn representation from the industry, insurance agents, women's organizations and other interest groups.
- All insurance intermediaries, before obtaining a licence, or at the time of renewal of license, are required to undergo compulsory training to ensure that they can serve the policyholders better by being well trained and informed. They are also required to adhere to a code of conduct which also involves aspects related to policy-holder servicing.
- In exercise of the power under sections 64UM and 102 of the Insurance Act, 1938, the Authority has in specific instances issued instructions to the insurers to discharge their liabilities under the policies issued by them.
- The Authority also directed the life insurers to display the latest Net Asset Value (NAV) of unit linked policies along with the date of valuation. Other initiatives taken by the Authority include directives to ensure that life insurers do not offer premium rates other than those filed with the Authority; and inform the policy-holders about the sources from which NAV can be accessed through insertions in the premium Notices/Receipts issued to them. These initiatives are made public by the Authority through its website.
- Non-life insurers and the TPAs have been advised against entering into any agreement at the instance of their clients for the sake of business consideration and charging separate fees in addition to insurance premium. Such Agreements are considered to be outside the scope of IRDA (TPA Health Insurance) Regulations, 2001.
- From time-to-time, insurers were directed to strictly adhere to the File and Use procedure and not to introduce any product or amend the existing products without prior approval of the Authority. Guidelines have been issued to insurers to file their existing and new products with the Authority. In case of new products insurers are required to submit details of premium rating, policy conditions, proposal form, claim form, underwriting manual

and the system in vogue to review the rates, terms and conditions in future. In addition to this, they are required to furnish certificates from advocates and actuaries that the statements made are true and accurate and are not in violation of any law and that the policy wordings are simple and easily understandable to a policy-holder.

5.3.3. *Steps Taken by the Authority to Ensure Observance of Code of Conduct, Requisite Qualifications and Training for the Intermediary or Insurance Intermediaries and Agents*

For the observance of code of conduct, requisite qualifications and training for the intermediary or insurance intermediaries and agents the IRDA has formulated following regulations:

- Insurance Regulatory and Development Authority (Licensing of Insurance Agents) Regulations, 2000.
- Insurance Regulatory and Development Authority (Licensing of Corporate Agents) Regulations, 2002.
- Insurance Regulatory and Development Authority (Insurance Brokers) Regulations, 2002.

5.3.4. *Experience of the Authority in the Implementation of the Code of Conduct by the Intermediary or Insurance Intermediaries and Agents*

Intermediaries associated with insurance business are brokers, third party administrators (TPAs) and surveyors. The insurance agents, including the corporate agents, are in the nature of intermediaries but are not so defined in the IRDA Act. However, since the agents represent their principals, i.e. the insurers, and their functions are akin to intermediaries they are treated as intermediaries. A critical element of insurance sector reforms is the development of a pool of human resources having right skill and expertise in each segment of the industry to provide quality intermediation to market participants. Quality intermediation requires personnel working in the industry need to (i) follow a certain code of conduct; and (ii) have an understanding of business and skills to serve different constituents in the market. It was recognized that agents are a critical link between the insurer and the insured and they should be fully equipped to sell insurance.

The Authority has prescribed qualifications and training for agents as per Regulations 4 and 5 of the IRDA (Licensing of Insurance Agents)

Regulations, 2002. Similarly, in case of Corporate Agents, Regulation 4 of IRDA (Licensing of Corporate Agents) Regulations, 2002, prescribes minimum qualifications for the corporate insurance executive/specified person. The agent, corporate executive and the specified persons shall also not suffer from any of the disqualifications specified under section 42D of the Insurance Act, 1938. The Authority has issued guidelines for offline agents' training institutes in the October 2004 and for online agents' training institutes in May 2005.

The guidelines provide for a minimum training period, coverage of training, maintenance of attendance record of the trainees, appointment of one qualified faculty for each stream to solve the online queries of the trainees, maintenance of database by the web administrator, barring of marketing fee/consultancy fee payment for getting the trainees etc. The accreditation for offline institutes will be for three years and the accreditation for online training institutes will be for one year.

The Authority also prescribed technical checks to be complied with by the online training institutes. In addition to that IRDA issued a Circular on 23rd June, 2006 stating that (i) Opening of more than one Login (multiple Login) on same computer as well as Login by same user ID/Password on different machines at the same time is not permissible; and (ii) that the training institutes must have only one domain to launch the IRDA accredited online training for Life and General Insurance. Use of more than one domain is not permissible.

5.3.5. *Observance of the Code of Conduct as Specified by the Authority by the Surveyors and Loss Assessors*

The Authority issues licences to surveyors and loss assessors in terms of Section 64UM of the Insurance Act, 1938. An individual, a company or a firm wanting to Act as surveyor and loss assessor has to make an application to the Authority in the prescribed format for the purpose. The Insurance Surveyors and Loss Assessors (Licensing, Professional Requirements and Code of Conduct) Regulations, 2000, lay down the process of application for procurement of licence. During financial year 2007-08, the Authority has enrolled 773 applicants as trainee surveyors and issued 286 fresh licences to trainee surveyors on completion of practical training and passing of the requisite examinations. The Authority also received 1907 requests for renewal of licences during the financial year 2007-08 and 1651 licences have been renewed and issued on fulfilment of all the regulatory requirements. Further, for the first half of

2008-09, 1178 requests for renewals have been received and 1201 requests have been processed and issued renewed licences.

The code of conduct regarding the professional and ethical requirements for conduct of their professional work is specified in Chapter VI of the IRDA Surveyors and Loss Assessors (Licensing, Professional Requirements and Code of Conduct) Regulations, 2000. They should strive for objectivity in professional and business judgement while behaving ethically and with integrity in their professional pursuit acting impartially and complying with due diligence, care and skill with regard to technical and professional standards expected of them.

The Authority at the behest of the Ministry of Finance (which accepted the recommendations of the Bhandari Committee) had set-up the Indian Institute of Insurance Surveyors and Loss Assessors (IIISLA) on 4th October, 2005 in order to promote self-regulation and professionalism amongst the surveyors as a part of further reforms in the insurance sector. The elections for putting in place the first elected council of the Institute (IIISLA), were held during 2007-08 and the affairs of the Institute were formally handed over by IRDA to the first elected council on 15 December, 2007. The Council is expected to meet the mandate to establish the necessary infrastructure, to inculcate professionalism, discipline, and disseminate information relating to the profession of surveyors and loss assessors amongst its members. Both, the IRDA and IIISLA Institute are making efforts to ensure that the Institute develops the profession further and take on responsibilities envisaged in its charter.

5.3.6. *Steps Taken by the Authority to Promote Efficiency in the Conduct of Insurance Business*

- While setting in motion detariffing of the general insurance business the Authority simultaneously addressed the problem in regard to denial of motor insurance cover by some insurers. As data becomes important while moving towards detariffed regime, the Authority stressed the need for supply of quality data from the insurers. The tariffs for fire, engineering and motor were withdrawn with effect from 1st January, 2007. This resulted in the end of cross-subsidization era wherein profitable fire and engineering portfolios supported loss-making motor, health and marine cargo insurances. This was followed by complete relaxation of premium rates with effect from 1st January, 2008. There was apprehension that the statutory motor third party cover would be denied to the policy-holders. The Authority has been taking cognizance of complaints received regarding denial of third party cover and has resolved the complaints by taking-up with the concerned insurers. The Authority issued the direction that except for Motor Third Party risks for all other new insurances and renewals effective on or after January 1, 2008, insurers shall be free to quote rates of premium in accordance with the rate schedules and rating guidelines that have been filed with the Authority. Further, the premium rates for motor third party risks will continue to be regulated by the Authority. The initiatives taken by the Authority in regulating the third party motor premium have been upheld by several High Courts.

- The Authority's directives to the general insurers to participate in motor third party pooling arrangement for commercial vehicles segment has resulted in availability of third party cover for the policy-holders as well as an increase in such covers. The Pool has been set-up with state of the art hardware and software. The Authority has stressed the need for collection and collation of qualitative data by the insurers especially in the area of motor insurance.
- The Authority has also been taking initiatives in leading the life insurance council and the general insurance council towards becoming self-regulatory organizations. They are advised to discuss issues relating to bringing in efficiency into the insurance markets and convey the views of the industry to the Authority.
- The Authority has also put in place regulations on micro-insurance and expect that micro-insurance if spread in a proper way would provide relief to the vulnerable sections of the population. The Micro-insurance regulations put in place by the Authority in 10th November, 2005 [IRDA (Micro-Insurance) Regulations, 2005] has provided framework for insurers to design suitable micro-insurance products for the poor. This is a logical extension of the idea of social and rural sector obligations imposed by the Authority on insurers. These regulations enable the mechanisms and modalities to spread this protection among targeted sections of the population. The regulations have resulted in the mainstream general insurance companies submitting micro-insurance products to the Authority for approval. This augurs well for the low-income population as they can get the existing insurance products at affordable premium. The Authority has constituted a Committee

to look into issues relating to Health Insurance of Senior Citizens in procuring health insurance.

- A circular was issued on 28th December, 2006 to all life insurers advising them that the decision for closure/relocation of their places of business should be taken after due consideration of all the factors including the possible inconveniences to its clientele. It is essential that such a decision is appropriately appraised to the Board for information with the reasons, therefore, since the proposal for opening the branches/offices is initially approved by the Board. Adequate notice of a minimum of two months on the proposed relocation/closure should be given to policy-holders serviced by that branch along with the alternate arrangements being made to service them.
- In the specific context of hardships in complying with the Know Your Customer (KYC) requirement by small value policy-holders as per Anti-Money Laundering Guidelines and with possible implication for the spread of insurance into rural and low-income domains, especially the micro-insurance sector, the Authority, has *vide* circular dated 2nd March, 2007 decided to provide exemption upto a total Annual Premium of ₹ 10,000 on all the life insurance policies held by a single individual from the requirement of recent photograph and proof of residence.
- Consequent to circulation of misleading sales literature among the public by some of the life insurers representatives projecting high returns on unit linked products, the Authority has come out with a press release on 2nd March, 2007 cautioning members of the public not to be carried away by such projections and to take an informed decision-based on proper disclosure of projected returns as per guidelines of the Life Insurance Council.
- Advertisement guidelines were issued on 14th May, 2007 reinforcing the existing regulations on advertisements with a view to protect the interests of the insuring public, enhance their level of confidence on the nature of sales material that is made available to them and ultimately to encourage fair business practices.
- Rural/social sector obligations have been benchmarked-based on micro-insurance parameters for minimum/maximum cover and also micro-insurance agents have been permitted to issue joint sale advertisements. A circular dated 11th May, 2007 was issued clarifying certain key issues concerning policy-holders to ensure protection of their interests and to remove inconsistencies in implementation of ULIP guidelines across the industry.

- Consequent upon devastation caused due to flash floods in Surat, Gujarat, heavy rains in Mumbai and Tsunami in 2004-05 a number of claims were reported against losses sustained by them. All the insurers have announced steps to ensure speedy settlement of claims by setting-up special cells besides waiving some of the procedural requirements in case of genuine claims. On its part, the IRDA has (*vide* order dated 3rd August, 2005) permitted the in-house Surveyors to assess damage upto ₹ 50,000 against the normal limit of ₹ 20,000 to facilitate expeditious clearance of claims. The Authority has also directed all insurance companies to submit returns on a weekly basis giving the number of claims reported, number of claim settled, claims outstanding both in number and in quantum with a view to monitoring settlement of claims on a weekly basis.
- Another initiative the Authority has taken is tc nurture the concept of self-regulation among various classes of stakeholders. The Authority is actively pursuing this concept, enabled by the Insurance Act, 1938, The Life Insurance Council has been tackling issues of significance like mis-selling (uniform benefit illustrations during selling process) and disclosure (bringing clarity into the potentially confusing area of complex products). The General Insurance Council will be setting-up their own infrastructure shortly. The Authority has already set in motion the system of dealing with one organization in each segment that will comprehensively represent the interests of that sector and insurance brokers and third party administrators (TPAs) are at various stages of building their self-regulatory organizations. In the case of intermediaries like brokers, the Authority has insisted on their formulating suitable code of conduct for market discipline and conducting their business in a healthy and responsible way. Code of conduct for individual and corporate agents has been incorporated in the regulations. In the case of insurers, the Authority has worked to catalyze the councils into becoming self-regulatory organizations (SROs) that consider, determine and maintain market discipline, codes of conduct, and best practices. The incorporation of Indian Institute of Insurance Surveyors and Loss Assessors (IIISLA) is another milestone in this area.
- Payment of insurance was a tedious work for the insured. To make it easier the Authority has allowed payment of insurance premium through cheques, demand drafts, pay orders, banker's

cheques, postal money orders, credit/debit cards, and through internet and e-transfer. The insured can also issue standing instructions to the banks for direct transfers towards installments. These efforts are likely to bring down the costs of procuring insurance cover, thereby reducing the premium costs. These efforts indirectly increase to some extent insurance penetration.

- All insurers are required to file their products with the Authority under the "File & Use" procedure. Deficiencies in interpretation of the requirements provided for in the regulations, and inadequacies on account of complete details not being furnished to the Authority resulted in avoidable delays in clearing the products. In order to reduce such delays, guidelines were issued to the life insurers to comply with specific requirements while filing products under the File & Use procedures. Rating guidelines were issued to the life insurance companies for standardizing market practices on profit sharing/experience. These guidelines are required to be complied with while filing products under the Group Insurance schemes.

5.3.7. *Steps Taken by the Authority to Promote and Regulate Professional Organizations connected with Insurance and Reinsurance Business*

I. Institute of Insurance and Risk Management

The establishment of IIRM was in response to the needs of enhancing expertise in the subjects of insurance, actuarial science, risk management and related disciplines in the context of the contemporary challenges facing the Indian insurance industry. The knowledge and competencies in critical areas of underwriting, claims, investment, asset-liability management, marketing and customer service etc. are likely to play a significant role in the process of value creation in insurance and financial services sector. IIRM, to achieve this vision, has actively sought the collaboration and cooperation of relevant institutions and individuals. It has received local and international support in its initiative, as is reflected in the activities and programmes conducted jointly with international bodies, namely UNCTAD, World Bank, IAIS, OECD, INPRS, FSI and other insurance regulatory authorities. IIRM is in the process of strengthening its linkages with universities and insurance institutes to develop its educational, training and research projects. The Institute, through its collaborative network, is involved in providing services in the fields of Research and Consultancy; Advanced Technical and Management Programmes; Post-Graduate Education; Conference and Events; Insurance Regulators' and Supervisors' Training; and Publications.

Institute of Insurance and Risk Management was established as a joint venture of IRDA and Government of Andhra Pradesh for providing opportunities to students wishing to pursue Diploma in Insurance. During the year 2006-07 it has been granted affiliation by the Chartered Institute of Insurance (CII), London. This is in addition to the earlier accreditation accorded by the CII to the International Post-Graduate Diploma in Insurance conducted by IIRM. Efforts are on to obtain accreditation from some Universities in the United States to the IIRM Courses. A Distance Learning Wing has been opened in IIRM to provide opportunities to students wishing to pursue the diploma in the distance mode. Diploma obtained from this mode also has received accreditation from the CII, London. Recognizing the need for more actuaries in the insurance industry, International School of Actuarial Sciences was inaugurated at IIRM in August 2007. IIRM in collaboration with IRDA conducted a seminar on grievances redressal of insurance sector to educate the public on grievances redressal mechanism followed by IRDA. The Authority also conducted a Seminar on the accounting issues of insurance companies in coordination with the Institute of Chartered Accountants. IIRM also provides the facility for online registration of applications by prospective candidates.

II. The Life Insurance Council and the General Insurance Council

The Life Insurance Council and the General Insurance Council are the platforms available for the industry participants to interact and to set-up practices for the healthy growth of the industry. Development of these self-regulatory bodies augurs well for the industry to put across its view point on critical areas for the growth of the industry. Life Insurance Council is a statutory body under section 64J of the Insurance Act, 1938. It is a forum of licensed life insurers with functions of setting-up Codes of Conduct, Standards of Service, advising IRDA on management expenses of life Insurers, brings to the attention of IRDA matters relating to errant insurers etc. All registered life insurers are members and are represented by CEOs. There are two nominees from IRDA, one of whom is Chairman of the Council. The Secretary General functions as the chief executive of the Council. The Council has formed several standing sub-committees and working groups to discuss emerging issues from time-to-time. The committee-based approach ensures wider participation in providing valuable contribution. The Executive Committee of the General Insurance Council comprises apart from the nominees of IRDA [*viz.* Member (non-life) as Chairman and Executive Director (non-life) as Secretary General of the Council], the CEOs of the all the non-life insurance companies licensed by IRDA.

III. Insurance Broker Association of India

The brokers licensed by the Authority are necessarily required to be a member of the Insurance Broker Association of India (IBA). IBA conducted an Annual Conference during 2007-08. The Association is functioning as a Self-Regulatory Organization (SRO) with a Disciplinary Committee in place. A representative of the Authority is also a member of the Committee.

IV. Indian Institute of Insurance Surveyors and Loss Assessors (IIISLA)

The IRDA has promoted the establishment of the Indian Institute of Insurance Surveyors and Loss Assessors (IIISLA) in order to promote professionalism amongst surveyors. The "Indian Institute of Insurance Surveyors and Loss Assessors" was incorporated on 4th October, 2005 under section 25 of the Companies Act, 1956. The Institute has its registered office at Hyderabad. The main objectives of the Institute are: (1) to promote quality in the profession of Surveyors and Loss Assessors through education and training, facilitate introduction of best practices amongst its members and to disseminate technical information among its members to upgrade their skills and knowledge; (2) to conduct professional examination relating to the profession of Surveyors and Loss Assessors; (3) to promote research and studies in loss control and minimization techniques and measures and share the same with the insurance industry and general public and to update its members on application of new technologies for improving service to the users and consumers; (4) to bring out guidance notes, instructions manuals, periodicals for the use and benefit of members and others connected with the profession of surveyors and loss assessors; and (5) to develop and administer the code of conduct and ethics from time to time with the concurrence of the IRDA and ensure compliance of the same by its members and also ensure that the members maintain/adhere to high standards of integrity, transparency, discipline and professional conduct. The Promotee Council of IIISLA has handed over the functioning of the

Institute to the Council that consists of elected as well as nominated members. During the Financial Year 2007-08, the Elected Council met four times.

However, the Authority has not prescribed any percentage of the premium income of the insurer to finance schemes for promoting and regulating professional organizations connected with the insurance and re-insurance business.

5.3.8. *Exercise of Power of Calling of Information from, Undertaking Inspection, Enquiries and Investigations Including Audit of Insurers, Insurance Intermediaries and Other Organizations connected with Insurance Business by the Authority*

Section 14(2)(h) of the IRDA Act, 1999, and section 110C of the Insurance Act, 1938, empowers the Authority to conduct inspections and investigations to ensure that there are no breaches/non-compliance with the applicable Act/Regulations. Accordingly, the Authority has been conducting targeted inspections of insurers and intermediaries based on complaints/information received. With the initiation of the process of grant of registration to the new insurers, a need was also felt to put in place the supervisory systems for regulatory oversight to ensure that the regulated entities maintain robust financial health and serve the interests of the policy-holders. Broadly the process of oversight can be segregated into on-site and off-site supervision. These processes are laid down to ensure that the regulated entities are compliant with the regulatory framework to ensure protection of the interest of the policyholders on an on-going basis.

Inspections of insurance companies would, in general cover assessment of the financial position of an insurer, compliance with solvency requirements, besides the company's adherence to accepted principles of market conduct, corporate governance and internal control etc. These inspections could be either annually or at such periodicity as may become necessary. The Authority would endeavour to gradually move towards meeting the objective of comprehensive inspections. The detailed coverage of insurance companies operating in India periodically requires strengthening of the human resources with the Authority. While steps have been initiated in this regard, the Authority has in the mean time carried out focused inspections of certain portfolios of insurance companies. The inspections were also conducted consistent with the contemporary regulatory initiatives such as detariffing, AML guidelines etc. to ensure that there are no breaches and the transition is smooth.

While the Authority has been contemplating commencement of comprehensive on-site inspection, it was considered that the registered entities should be allowed time to stabilize operations prior to taking on full scale inspection. In the meantime, as an interim measure, based on concerns which arose at different points in time, the Authority has taken up targeted on-site inspections. The Authority has been conducting on-site inspections wherever: (i) the findings of off-site inspections necessitated a more detailed on-site inspection; (ii) where the Authority has received specific complaints; and (iii) investment audit as part of the annual exercise. Other than targeted inspections (including those related to market conduct issues), the Authority has been carrying on Investment Audit of the regulated insurance entities effective from the financial year 2001-02.

For conducting Investment Audit of insurers the Authority took into account the following aspects: constitution of Investment Committee; decision support systems; investment policy, its review in the light of investment performance; delegation of authority for day-to-day functioning; methodology adopted for Asset Liability Management; review of Investment Systems; adequacy of Internal Audit/Concurrent Audit; outsourcing of investment functions; adherence to Act, Regulations, Guidelines and Circulars; transfer between funds from the end of adherence; and filing of returns and its completeness.

The designing of various formats of reporting have been derived from the different aspects of operations of an insurance company. Broadly, the scope of off-site supervision has been focused on four segments, *viz.* (i) financial reporting, (ii) investment functions, (iii) actuarial and solvency aspects, and (iv) re-insurance. Derived from the regulations notified in this regard, insurance companies are required to file reports and statements as prescribed on a periodic basis (monthly, quarterly and annually). Additional formats of reporting have also been prescribed to obtain information which has not been specifically spelt out in the regulations, but is necessary to monitor the operations of the insurance companies. These statements form the basis for off-site supervision.

As part of its efforts to strengthen the regulatory framework through access to specific information, the Authority has been issuing instructions to the insurers (both life and non-life) to submit additional reports as per the prescribed formats. These include:

1. particulars of all persons paid remuneration whether by way of commission or otherwise where such remuneration exceeded

such sum as required under section 217(2A)(a) of Companies Act, 1956, read with Companies (Particulars of Employees) Rules, 1975, as part of the annual accounts of the insurers;

2. details of equity holding pattern of insurers to reflect the foreign equity holding in insurance companies, on a quarterly basis. As part of the quarterly returns, the insurers are also required to furnish the particulars of the equity holding pattern of the Indian promoters of insurance companies; and
3. all non-life insurers are required to furnish details of any deviations from the annual reinsurance programme filed with the Authority.

In addition to the submission of periodic statements, the Authority reserves the right to call for any other information as it may deem necessary in carrying out its functions. Thus, broadly, the inspections have been in the nature of: (i) overall inspection of the insurance companies; and (ii) targeted inspections, carried out to verify or otherwise the specific instances of breach of the provisions of the Insurance Act, 1938 and the regulations framed thereunder or specific instructions issued by the Authority.

On-site inspection of life insurance companies was carried out to address issues of regulatory concern, which include manner of reporting in financial statements, deficiencies noticed in the actuarial and investment returns filed with the Authority, non-compliance with the specific provisions of the Insurance Act, 1938, and the manner in which the business of the insurers was being carried out, including issues of market conduct. The on-site inspections are followed-up by interaction with the insurers at regular intervals to ensure that the anomalies pointed out by the inspection teams are rectified/clarified.

Specific cases of inspection included, enquiry in the context of the compliance with the requirements of the rural sector obligations under sections 32B and 32C of the Insurance Act, 1938, and imposition of penalty on insurer under section 105B of the Insurance Act for non-compliance of obligations towards rural and social sectors. The penalty was later withdrawn after being satisfied through on-site inspection that the said insurer had actually complied with the obligation.

The IRDA (Assets, Liabilities, and Solvency Margin of Insurers) Regulations, 2000, lay down the manner in which non-life insurers are required to create reserves for outstanding claims and reserve for Incurred But Not Reported (IBNR) claims. In such determination, the appointed actuary is required to follow the Guidance Notes issued by the Actuarial

Society of India in concurrence with the Authority, and within the framework of the directions issued by the Authority on the same. To assess the adequacy of the reserves created, inspection of non-life insurers is carried out. The Authority has on many occasions drawn the attention of the non-life insurers to the need to make adequate provision for claims. Following numerous complaints against Third Party Administrators (TPAs), activities of the TPAs, adequacy of infrastructure and the network to provide value added services to the insured were inspected. The claims handling procedures and the grievances of the insured were also looked into during the on-site inspections.

Similar on-site inspections of the licensed insurance brokers were also carried out covering areas such as, availability of infrastructure, human resources-presence of professionals as provided for in the regulations and their ability to perform the assigned duties in line with the details furnished at the time of registration, and whether the brokers are abiding by the code of conduct laid down in the regulations.

Inspections of the agents' training institutes were also carried out by the Authority to check compliance with the requirements laid down for training of agents in both the life and non-life insurance business. On coming across gross violations, which included absence of mandatory infrastructure and facilities; non-availability of mandatory records; deficiencies in the training imparted; and functioning of training institutes on basis of franchisee agreement, the Authority took steps to ensure that the quality of training of the agency force was improved. In this background, fresh guidelines have been issued regarding accreditation of the agents' training institutes.

5.3.9. *Regulation of the Investment Funds of the Insurer Companies by the Authority*

The insurance sector, by its business nature attracts long-term funds, which are required to be invested in a manner to ensure asset liability match and equip the insurers to meet their obligations to their policy-holders, in case of claims. The requirements laid down by the Authority address the dual objective of safety and returns to the insurers combined with their meeting the socio-economic objectives. The regulations framed under the Insurance Act, 1938, the Regulations of Investment of Funds by the insurance companies issued by the Authority in 2000, provide for investments in government securities, approved securities, approved investments and in infrastructure and social sectors. The regulations have laid down the pattern of investment of life fund; funds relating to pension and general annuity business; and unit linked life insurance business. In the case of unit linked life insurance business, every insurer is required to invest as per the pattern of investment offered to and approved by the policy-holders, with a proviso that total investment in "other than approved category" shall at no time exceed 25 per cent of the fund. Prescriptions have also been laid down on the pattern of investments in the case of non-life insurers and the re-insurer.

The regulations also require that the insurers carry out all functions related to insurance business in-house. As the insurers were in the process of building-up in-house capacities, they had earlier outsourced investment functions. Noticing this, the Authority instructed all insurers to take steps to ensure that outsourcing of such functions be discontinued by 31st December, 2004. The Authority has also laid down the requirement for demarcation of the "front" and "back" office investment functions of an insurer to ensure that adequate internal checks and controls are in place. The Investment Committee of an insurer frames the Investment Policy on an annual basis and reviews it periodically. The requirements have been prescribed to facilitate prudent investment decisions with adequate checks and balances thereby ensuring Asset Liability Management.

The Authority has initiated steps towards investment audit on a periodic basis with a view to monitor the investment decisions of the insurers, compliance with the regulations, prudent investment of the funds and adequate provisioning on a regular basis. The audits are carried out by chartered accountants drawn from a panel maintained by the Authority. An officer of the Authority is also a part of the inspection team. The inspection audits enable the Authority to make on-site assessment of the compliance with the regulations and to initiate corrective action.

The Authority has also been issuing clarifications/guidance notes to the insurers from time to time covering maintenance of section 7 deposits, investments in mutual funds and reconciliation of insurer's books with those of the custodian. In addition, the Investment regulations were amended in January, 2004 to provide for investments in Collateralized Borrowing and Lending Operations. Additional disclosure requirements were laid down and formats were prescribed, including details of non-performing assets and provisions made against them. The Authority also expanded the list of approved investments for life and non-life insurers.

The Regulations of investment of funds by the insurance companies were issued by the Authority in 2000. Subsequently, the innovations in the financial markets led to new instruments. As such the insurance companies approached the Authority to allow them to invest their funds in the new instruments also. In the light of this, the Authority had set-up a Working Group to review the existing statutory prescriptions on investments for insurance companies, constraints faced by them and to suggest changes, if necessary. The Working Group suggested amendments to the Regulations by providing flexibility to the Authority in prescribing the manner in which funds can be invested by the insurance companies. The Working Group while making suggestions has also examined the present returns prescribed for monitoring the information on investments and suggested certain changes in the format which will facilitate the Authority in supervision purposes. The Authority examined the recommendations. Some of the recommendations required changes in the Regulations. A suitable framework for implementation was also proposed. Accordingly, the Authority has issued new regulations on investment of funds by insurance companies *vide* "IRDA (Investment) (Fourth Amendment) Regulations, 2008".

The Authority closely monitors timely submission of returns by the insurers including e-submission. The Authority has been accepting 'e-mail' with attachments as a means of timely submission of returns. This is to ensure that there is no delay in sending the returns through conventional channels like post or courier. Compliance checking is done only after receipt of signed hardcopies. All Insurers have adhered to the pattern of investment laid down in Form 3A/Form 3B. The companies are required to submit Certificate under sections 28(2A)/(2B) and 28B(3) of Insurance Act, 1938 (FORM 6).

The returns provide useful data on the quantum of investments of the sector by way of various instruments and the direction of investments. The scrutiny of the yearly returns by the IRDA is focused on compliance of the companies with the prescribed pattern of investments and other prudential norms as laid down by the Authority. Other than certain minor non-compliance with procedural requirements relating to investments, the scrutinies have not revealed any significant deficiencies or non-compliances by insurers. The insurers have also taken action to comply with IRDA instructions before submission of the returns for the next quarter.

5.3.10. *Regulation of Margin of Solvency by the Authority*

Every insurer is required to maintain a required Solvency Margin as per the section 64VA of the Insurance Act, 1938. Every insurer shall maintain an excess of the value of assets over the liabilities. The excess prescribed by the IRDA, is referred to as Required Solvency Margin. The IRDA (Assets, Liabilities and Solvency Margin of Insurers) Regulations, 2000, describe in detail the method of computation of the Required Solvency Margin. The IRDA (Assets, Liabilities and Solvency Margin of Insurers) Regulations, 2000, require all life insurers to maintain a solvency margin to the extent of not less than ₹ 50 crore, or a sum equivalent-based on the prescribed formula given in the IRDA (Actuarial Report and Abstracts) Regulations, 2000. Similarly, in respect of non-life insurers, a minimum solvency margin of ₹ 50 crore is required to be maintained (₹ 100 crore in case of a re-insurer) or a sum equivalent-based on the formula given in the IRDA (Assets, Liabilities and Solvency Margin of Insurers) Regulations, 2000. Thus, in case of Life Insurers the Required Solvency Margin is the higher of an amount of ₹ 50 crore and a sum which is based on a formula given in the said Regulations. In case of General Insurers the Required Solvency Margin, shall be highest of the following amounts:

1. fifty crore of rupees (one hundred crore of rupees in case of re-insurer); or
2. a sum equivalent to twenty per cent of net premium income; or
3. a sum equivalent to thirty per cent of net incurred claims,

subject to credit for re-insurance in computing net premiums and net incurred claims being actual, but a percentage, determined by the regulations, not exceeding fifty per cent.

IRDA has set a working Solvency Margin Ratio (Ratio of Actual Solvency Margin to the Required Solvency Margin) of 1.5 for all insurers.

At the time of registration it was felt that the new insurance companies would take five to seven years to stabilize their operations, and may have to fund their initial losses through additional inflow of funds. Despite the initial strain in setting-up of operations, the insurers are required to meet the solvency margin requirements at all times, and the Authority places considerable importance on this parameter as an indicator of the health of an insurer and also as an adequate buffer to ensure protection of the interests of policyholders. Thus, monitoring solvency margin certified by the appointed actuary of the insurer is an important function of the Authority.

All insurers file with the Authority an annual statement as per the IRDA (Assets, Liabilities and Solvency Margin of Insurers) Regulations,

2000, giving their solvency position as on 31st March of each financial year. The ratio is monitored on annual basis. Considering the importance of monitoring this ratio on a continuous basis, the Authority has now asked the insurers to submit quarterly returns on solvency margins. The lower level of solvency for pure term products would provide significant relief to the life insurers both under individual products and under group products. This will also help the insurers in launching more pure term products for sufficiently longer periods and at affordable rates. Till now all insurers have complied with the solvency requirements as provided for in the Insurance Act, 1938. However, in a few instances there was a shortfall in meeting the required solvency margin of 1.5 as stipulated by the Authority.

Life insurance industry, by its very nature is capital intensive, and insurers have been injecting fresh equity at frequent intervals to ensure compliance with the solvency requirements and to finance their operating expenses. Ability of the insurers to bring in further capital has facilitated their ability to expand their operations. In the case of non-life insurers, on the other hand, given the size of their operations, the initial capital base has broadly enabled them to meet the requirements of solvency.

5.3.11. *System for Adjudication of Disputes between the Insurer and the Intermediaries or Insurance Intermediaries*

The IRDA does not carryout any adjudication in case of disputes between insurers and intermediaries or insurance intermediaries. Insurers are advised to approach the available quasi-judicial or judicial channels like Insurance Ombudsmen. In case of any disputes between insurers and intermediaries the Authority seeks clarifications from the concerned. Whenever a reference comes to the Authority relating to disputes between insurers and intermediaries or insurance intermediaries, the Authority examines the nature of the disputes. If only clarification is sought, the same is sent immediately through the Grievance Cell of the Authority. However, in cases involving any violation of Regulations, the Authority takes the reference seriously and action is initiated as per the laid out process and explanations are sought. Serious cases of disputes have been few.

5.3.12. *Experience of the Authority in Exercising its Powers of Supervision over the Tariff Advisory Committee*

In December 2006, it was decided that the rates, terms, conditions and regulations applicable to Fire, Engineering, Motor, Workmen's

Compensation and other tariff classes of business shall be withdrawn effective from 1st January, 2007. With the abolition of tariffs, the role of Tariff Advisory Committee has undergone a change. It is expected that TAC may perform the following functions in the changed scenario:

- collection of data on premiums and claims, analysis of such data and dissemination of the results to the insurers;
- report to IRDA on the underwriting health of the market and any aberrations in market behaviour;
- constitution of Expert Groups at the request of the General Insurance Council, to look into underwriting issues and recommend necessary action;
- organize training to underwriters at the market level; and
- attend to public grievances on non-availability of insurance and try to resolve the issues by discussion with insurers.

With the removal of tariffs the Tariff Advisory Committee has been designated by the Authority as the data repository for maintenance of database for various classes of general insurance. The TAC maintains a web enabled declined lives database for exclusive use of the life insurers. This database has incorporated the suggestions of Life Council and enlarged its scope of use. Consequent to a demand from insurers, the General Insurance Council and with the approval of Chairman, IRDA, TAC has developed a web search system for stolen insured vehicles. Tariff Advisory Committee has compiled the stolen vehicles database from the data submitted by the insurance companies for the year 2005-06 and stolen vehicles records submitted by insurers through General Insurance Council for the period up to 31st March, 2007. The users can access the search page by entering user name and password provided by TAC. The login designated access officers of insurance companies as per names received from General Insurance Council are provided with the user name and password to access the site.

5.3.13. *Penalties Imposed on the Insurance Companies for the Violation of Regulations of the Authority*

Following companies have been penalized in the last four years for the violation of provisions of Insurance Act, 1938, and various regulations framed by the Authority:

2007-08

Sl. No.	Name of the Insurance Company	Amount of Penalty	Brief Particulars of the Violation Committed
1.	Bajaj Allianz Life Insurance Co. Ltd.	₹ 5,00,000	Penalty for violation of Section 64VC of the Insurance Act, 1938 (which imposes restriction on opening of a new place of business without obtaining the prior permission of the Authority)
2.	New India Assurance Co. Ltd.	₹ 5,00,000	Penalty charged under section 105B for violation of section 32B of the Insurance Act, 1938, which imposes obligation on insurer to undertake life insurance and general insurance in the rural and social sector as may be specified by the Authority
3.	Shriram Life Insurance Co. Ltd.	₹ 5,00,000	Penalty charged under section 105B for violation of section 32B of the Insurance Act, 1938
4.	ICICI Lombard General Insurance Co. Ltd.	₹ 5,00,000	In response to Authority's order ref. no. 15/INSP/ICICI/On SITE INSPECTION/2007-08 dated 22.1.2008
5.	ICICI Lombard General Insurance Co. Ltd.	₹ 5,00,000	Penalty charged under section 105B for violation of IRDA's regulations and guidelines relating to reinsurance of risks pertaining to Indian Oil Corporation Ltd.
6.	ICICI Lombard General Insurance Co. Ltd.	₹ 5,00,000	Penalty charged under section 105B for violation of IRDA's File & Use guidelines in case of Pravsai Bhartiya Bima Yojana
7.	Max New York Life Insurance Co. Ltd.	₹ 5,00,000	Penalty charged under section 102(b) for violating directions issued by the Authority in respect of ULIP
8.	Shriram Life Insurance Co. Ltd.	₹ 1,85,150	For late submission of the renewal of registration application

2006-07

Though the Certificate of Registration issued to all the existing life and non-life insurance companies was renewed in term of section 3A of the Insurance Act, 1938, but penalties were imposed on the following insurers for the reasons mentioned as under:

Sl. No.	*Name of the Insurance Company*	*Amount of Penalty*	*Brief Particulars of the Violation Committed*
1.	Star Health & Allied Insurance Co. Ltd.	₹ 5,000	For late submission of the renewal of registration application
2.	Agriculture Insurance Corporation of India Ltd.	₹ 5,55,833	For late submission of the renewal of registration application
3.	Reliance General Insurance Co. Ltd.	₹ 1,62,331	For late submission of the renewal of registration application

Non-Life Department has acted as nodal department for levy of penalty for the following insurers for the reasons mentioned against their names:

Sl. No.	*Name of the Insurance Company*	*Amount of Penalty*	*Brief Particulars of the Violation Committed*
1.	Bajaj Allianz Life Insurance Co. Ltd.	₹ 5,00,000	Penalty under section 102(b) of the Insurance Act, 1938, for opening of offices without prior permission of the Authority
2.	United India Insurance Co. Ltd.	₹ 5,00,000	Lower charging of premium for Pravasiya Bhartiya Bima Yojana
3.	Bajaj Allianz General Insurance Co. Ltd.	₹ 5,00,000	Violation of IRDA Advertisement Regulations
4.	Reliance General Insurance Co. Ltd.	₹ 5,00,000	Violating provisions of Section 102 of the Insurance Act, 1938
5.	IFFCO Tokio General Insurance Co. Ltd.	₹ 5,00,000	Penalty for engaging a non-licensed entity as intermediary

2005-06

The Authority has not imposed any penalty on any insurer due to late submission of application for renewal of registration. The Authority did not modify, withdraw, suspend or cancel the certificate of registration of any insurer.

2004-05

The Authority imposed penalty equivalent to the ten per cent of the renewal fee on one life insurer due to late submission of the application for renewal of registration.

To sum up the above discussion it may be emphasized that the powers and functions assigned to the Authority are with a view to enable it to perform the role of effective watchdog and regulation of the insurance sector in India in the best interest of the consumers in particular and the economy in general. It may, however, be mentioned that there is need for effective redressal mechanism to give more teeth to the Authority. The adjudicatory and punitive powers of the Authority need to be further strengthened to make it more effective and efficient regulator. Further, the power of the Central Government in the matter of giving directions and supersession of the Authority need to be exercised very carefully in the interest of the independence and autonomy of the Authority. Again, this is a matter of utmost importance that the requirement of fairness and the importance of the maxim *nemo judex in re sua* in the matters of appeal against the decisions of the Authority should be respected.

NOTES

1. See *Report of the Committee on Reforms in the Insurance Sector (Malhotra Committee Report)*, Ministry of Finance, GoI, January 1994.
2. IRDA Act,1999, section 3(1).
3. *Ibid.*, Section 3(2).
4. *Ibid.*, Sections 3(3) and (4).
5. *Ibid.*, Section 4.
6. *Ibid.*, Section 5.
7. *Ibid.*, Section 5(3).
8. *Ibid.*, Section 6.
9. *Ibid.*, Section 14(1).
10. *Ibid.*, Section 14(2).
11. *Ibid.*, Section 18.
12. *Ibid.*, Section 19(1).
13. *Ibid.*, Section 23(1).
14. *Ibid.*, Section 23(2).
15. *Ibid.*, Section 24(1).
16. *Ibid.*, Section 24(2).
17. *Ibid.*, Section 25.
18. *Ibid.*, Section 26.
19. *Annual Report 2007-08*, IRDA, December 10, 2008, pp. 66-67.
20. *Annual Report 2006-07*, IRDA, December, 2007, pp. 58-59.
21. *IRDA Journal*, January 2004, p. 42.

6

CONCLUSIONS AND SUGGESTIONS

6.1. Conclusions

The main purpose of this chapter is to summarize previous discussions in regard to regulations in its different forms and phases conceptually, structurally, with policy and operational thrusts with a view to enhance readability and understanding. Regulation has been an area of policy boom in recent years. With international institutions, such as the Organization for Economic Cooperation and Development (OECD) and the World Bank, have promoted arm's-length rule-based governance claiming to be a more effective replacement to both public ownership and broad governmental discretion.[1] So, intense has been the growth in regulation that it has spawned also programmes in regulatory reform or better regulation, again through the OECD and other inter-governmental groups such as Asia-Pacific Economic Cooperation (APEC), within the European Union and at national levels. Both regulation and rights discourses have moved somewhat from traditional conceptions of centralized state power as the power of non-state actors is increasingly recognized in regimes where such actors have regulatory capacity and have expectations on them that they will honour rights of others. Regulation can, of course, also be understood as part of the legal system. But "regulatory law" substantially rejects the universalistic ambitions of the classical legal understanding and displaces it with a more targeted and instrumental idea of law. Regulation scholars are more concerned with questions of economic efficiency, the evaluation of results, rational design of institutions and bureaucratic or discretionary modes of pursuing generalized public interests. However, it should be remembered that the programme of deregulation of any sector or activity starts first with the regulation. Even the process of deregulation needs to be started only with the help of regulations.

Regulation is very wide term, having no accepted or straightforward definition. The term has multiple interpretations influenced by the country of origin and level of aggregation. It has been defined differently among policy researchers for different purposes. Regulation is a subject which calls for multi-disciplinary approach. It has stimulated interest in a number of disciplines like law, economics, political science, sociology, history, psychology, geography, management and public administration. Among the three branches of government, the legislature is responsible for laying down the law in general and executive to implement the law to achieve the purpose. However, in the present scenario extensive law-making power is being delegated by the legislature to the executive. Thus, the law-making power is now vested in local authorities, utility regulators, professional bodies and various other authorities so empowered by the national, regional and local legislative bodies.

The term "regulation" thus, refers to various instruments by which government imposes requirements on enterprises, institutions in public and private domains and citizens. It thus, includes within its ambit laws, formal and informal orders, administrative guidance and subordinate rules issued by all levels of government. It also refers to rules issued by non-governmental or professional self-regulatory bodies to which the government has delegated the powers. In Indian context, all doubts as regard to the ambit of "regulation" has been clarified by Article 13 of the Constitution. Article 13(3)(a) of the Constitution says "Law" includes any ordinance, order, bye-law, rule, regulation, notification, custom or usage having in the territory of India the force of law. The government may regulate for different motives, such as influence by the economically powerful, developed as a means for political elections or combinations of both. A number of issues and concerns are addressed by the government through these regulations. These include to regulate the monopolies, to eliminate the waste and to protect society suffering from externalities, to protect the consumers against information inadequacies, to produce socially desirable levels of continuity and availability of service, to sustain competition and protect consumers from the ill-effects of market domination, for public good and prevent moral hazards, to provide equal bargaining power, for fair allocation of resources and rationing, to prevent discrimination and distributional justice, to rationalize production processes and coordinate the market, and to protect the interest of future generations. The quality of regulatory regimes and actions can be assessed on five criterions, i.e. (i) support of legitimate authority; (ii) accountability; (iii) fairness, accessibility and openness of action; (iv) expertise of the regulator; and (v) efficiency of the regime.

Regulations can generally be categorized in three categories based on the different types of objectives they pursue. These are economic regulation, social regulation and administrative regulation. The economic regulation focuses on the direct government intervention in corporations and market decisions such as pricing, competition, market entry or exit etc. Social regulations are related to government protection of citizen and social values such as health, safety, housing, labour etc. Social regulations aim at protecting new values and addressing concerns and problems resulting from modern industrial society. The emergence of regulatory state in 1930s has been related to development of economic regulations whereas 1960s and 1970s saw expansion in social regulations. The third type of regulation, administrative regulation, relates to government formalities and paperwork. These regulations have increased complexity of public programme operation and requirements of financial and legal accountability.

The 1990s has seen the emergence of "new-style" regulation through regulatory commissions/authorities in place of the system of implementation as a part of the government department. Under old-style regulation the traditional administrator enjoyed only legislative and administrative powers. However, the regulation through independent regulatory commissions wields regulatory powers with legislative, executive and judicial powers. These authorities thus are termed as quasi-judicial authorities. Thus, contrary to the principle of separation of powers, a commission assumes the task of an administrator, a judge and a legislator. Expertise, economy, speed in decision-making, quick adoption to changing conditions, freedom from technicalities and procedural complexities, independence are some of the characteristics of independent commissions which make them more effective than the traditional administrators. Thus, there has been a significant loss of faith in state-centred and legal approaches to regulation and an interest in harnessing the capacities of a wider range of actors not only to secure the objectives of the regulatory regime but also to define those objectives.

The growth of regulations before the period of liberalization, privatization and globalization, can be traced in two phases, phase I which gives an account of its growth from early age up to Second World War and phase II captures the development after Second World War to 1980. Development of regulations in the latter part of the nineteenth century in USA was a reaction to industrialization, urbanization and economic changes. The national railroad system helped to create regional and national markets where the migrated rural populations provided cheap source of labour. During the period of 1870s and 1880s the dissatisfied groups of workers, farmers and small businessman started unionization and agitations began for regulation of different aspects of economic affairs. The prolonged protests resulted in the enactment of the Interstate Commerce Act, 1887, establishing Interstate Commerce Commission, the first National Commission for regulation of economic affairs. Thus, regulation was largely a product of the clash of organized private economic interests seeking to utilize governmental powers for enhancement of private interests. Though during the post-civil war period, there was close association of the government and economic life, still economic affairs were nurtured on the myths of *laissez faire*. The myth that persisted during the era was that the government and business lived in two separate spheres and would co-exist in place so long as government made no attempt to usurp the functions of the private business. However, during the nineteenth century the character of economic regulation shifted gradually from legislative and judicial to administrative control.

President Roosevelt's New Deal, undertaken in 1930s in context of the Great Depression, represented a fundamental restructuring of the American legal system. In the 1930s the power of the national government were expanded in an extraordinary way, to the point where the nation exercised something close to general authority to accomplish whatever tasks it thought important. The system of checks and balances also came under sharp criticism. Congress delegated enormous policy-making power to the President and also created a large number of powerful executive and independent agencies. Congress attempted to design these agencies so as to limit the consequences of the system of checks and balances by allowing a high degree of administrative autonomy. Thus, the new agencies had a large degree of discretionary authority under open ended statutory standards. They also combined traditionally separated powers of adjudication, execution and legislation. These institutional shifts resulted from a crucial national judgement made during the depression that individual rights, properly conceived, included not merely the common law catalogue of private interests, but also governmental protection against many of the harms and risks of market economy. These harms and risks included unemployment, poverty, lack of adequate nutrition, homelessness, lack of education, lack of access to medical care and many more.

An astonishing feature of the New Deal was its relative rapidity. Many of the changes came in brief period from 1932 to 1936. Rapid change was possible partly because it is a relatively simple step for a legislature to create a range of new bureaucratic institutions, atleast if the legislature does not specify their duties in advance. The New Deal entities in fact operated pursuant to little statutory guidance, Congress usually contended itself with open-ended delegation of authority. The U.S. despite its reputation as quintessential free market economy was in fact ahead of other developed countries in many areas of regulation. In contrast to other developed countries which adhered to *laissez faire* policies during the inter-war period, the reformist forces in the US had already succeeded by the late 1930s in establishing an extensive regime of natural monopoly regulation in various utilities (telecommunications, water electricity, gas, oil), transport (trucking, airlines, railways), wholesale and retail distribution, and finance. In addition, the enforcement of anti-trust regulation was significantly strengthened during the period.

The quarter century after the end of Second World War, i.e. up to 1970s can be termed as the "age of regulation", as it witnessed a general rise in the level of government across the world. During this period the governments of many countries began to practice more activist macro-economic policies, nationalized many enterprises or established new public enterprises, increased spending and most importantly increased the range and depth of regulatory activities. In developed countries, there was marked swing of political opinion against *laissez faire* economic policies, which were associated with the spectacular failures of capitalism during the interwar period. During this period the countries in Western Europe nationalized a large number of enterprises in 'strategic' industries, in order to provide the government with a "commanding height". Many countries also used various regulatory measures in order to control the 'excesses' of capitalist institutions, and more importantly for countries other than the US and the UK, to modernize their economics.

In India and other developing countries, developmental objectives played a much more important role in shaping the regulatory framework than in the developed countries during this period, given their desire to gain economic as well political independence from their former colonial masters. Deliberate attempts were made to promote industrial development through a wide range of regulatory and other policy measures. A large proportion of investment decisions were either taken or regulated through its controls over public enterprises, public sector investment programmes, and sometimes the financial sector. Regulations on imports and foreign direct investments were imposed in order to shelter 'infant' industries from foreign competition, control the pace and form of technology imports, and promote the development of indigenous technological capabilities. Domestically industrial licensing and other forms of entry regulations were issued in order to induce manufacturing investments by guaranteeing profit to investors who would otherwise invest in less risky non-manufacturing activities, to coordinate complementary investment decision, and to influence the amounts and types of investments in accordance with the overall industrial strategy.

The regulatory regime that was established across countries during this period and for some ex-colonial countries by 1960s, after their independence, worked reasonably well. Many developed countries of Europe achieved spectacular success with economic modernization. It is considered that the regulatory regime in USA largely accomplished its own objectives of providing high quality, widely available services, secure contractual arrangements and stable pricing during this period. The picture in the developing world was more mixed, but in most countries, the post-war regulatory regimes worked reasonably well during the period, and were indeed very successful in quite a few countries. At the end of the period there was a general consensus that an activist regulatory regime was necessary in order to improve efficiency, promote growth, and spread the fruits of economic progress more evenly to maintain individual equality and also regional balances.

The period of 1970s was a period of transition. The world economy withered the end of its 'Golden Age'. Politically, in many countries, there was noticeable shift to the Right, which advocated a substantial reduction in state intervention and wider application of market principles. Intellectually, also, this period witnessed an upsurge in pro-market theories which challenged the post-war orthodoxy of "regulated capitalism". In support of the market it was strongly pleaded that the public is bad and private is good.

In the collapse of Golden Age excessive government regulations played only secondary role. Partly because of the failings in the existing regulatory regimes, which became more apparent during the period of crisis, but mainly because of the changing political regime, a growing opinion was that the existing regulatory regimes were not working well and were even impairing the effective functioning of the economy. In many developed countries, with rise in affluence, there was a serious reassessment of the human and environmental costs of rapid industrialization, and a resulting rise in political movements which demanded a reduction in such costs. As a result, an increasingly wide range of 'social' issues like consumer protection, environment protection, health and safety, labour standards; have been brought into the realm of regulation which was previously occupied by 'economic' issues. Thus, during this period there was broadening of regulatory mandate of the government in social areas, while there was shrinkage in such a mandate in economic areas. The developing countries also started witnessing disillusionment with the existing models of state-led industrialization. However, in the case of developing countries, major deregulation drives came later than in the developed countries, that is, in the 1980s.

The political and intellectual tidal wave against regulation and government intervention in general that started to surge during the 1970s began to sweep the whole world from the early 1980s. The 1980s was an age of deregulation. Since, the 1980s, most countries, developed and developing alike, deregulated their economy, atleast to a degree. Deteriorating economic performances during the 1970s were often attributed to excessive government involvement in the economy, and consequently attempts were made to cut government spending, privatize public enterprise and deregulate economy. During this period, following various external and internal pressures, many countries embarked on the path of extensive restructuring of the relation between state and economy including regulatory reforms, budget cuts and privatization. By the early 1980s, the US and the UK were in the middle of a significant drive for deregulation, corporatization and privatization. Other developed countries also moved, in varying degrees and speeds, towards deregulation and in general reduction in government involvement in the economy, through spending cuts, sales of state assets (if not wholesale privatization), introduction of more 'commercial' criteria into the operations of public enterprises and welfare provision, and the introduction of more 'market-oriented' methods of regulation. Simultaneously, there was a significant reduction in the 'developmental' activities of the government in many developed countries.

Although regulatory reform in 1980s went under the slogan of 'deregulation' regulation was massively extended in some areas, notably safety and pollution.[2] Far from living in an age of deregulation, we live in golden age of regulation.[3] From environmental protection to consumer protection, safety and health, labour standards and social justice rules, no governmental activity has grown faster since 1980 than governmental regulatory functions. During the administrations of Reagan and Thatcher, the quintessential "deregulation", the quantity of regulations measured in number of rules and their length increased both in USA and UK.

Regulatory standards have never been higher in the developed countries than they are today. International standards are increasing rapidly.[4] The number and scope of government (domestic and international) regulations have increased so rapidly in almost all OECD countries that the term "regulatory inflation" was coined by the OECD in the early 1990s.[5] And even in areas of regulatory reform, what happened was not so much a complete withdrawal of government interest in areas such as telecommunications or aviation, but rather a change in the way the public authority was used to shape these markets. Many have pointed out that 're-regulation' would be a more accurate term.[6]

With the move towards network liberalization and privatization in most public utilities, the major policy focus is on the role of the old monopolies. In this process, the role of state owned enterprises is changing. Most have been commercialized, some are partly or fully privatized, and new entrants emerge, changing the face of competition. New regulatory institutions and traditional antitrust institutions aim to control monopoly power and facilitate entry as competition is emerging. In addition to this behavioural, often asymmetric regulation, that attempts to foster the emergence of a more competitive industry structure, governments are helping the emergence of competition also *via* structural policies. Examples are the restructuring of the industry prior to privatization and/or the divesting of important facilities, so that they may be available to new entrants. (Like the divestiture of telephone networks or related industries, for example from railroads, electricity and highway systems.) But some countries have pursued structural policies that point in the opposite direction, for example concentrated the industry itself before liberalization and privatization and supported the incumbent in the restructuring process.

Privatization policies have continued to evolve since the 1980s. New regulatory agencies and legal framework to regulate the utilities have been put in place. A wide range of statutory powers, contracts, licences and conditions provide the main legal mechanisms which govern the relationship between regulator, the company and the consumers. Regulating the privatized utilities has proved to be a complex and detailed process. The result is a complex hotch potch of legislation, regulation, rules, guidance, codes and licences, far removed from the consolidation and simplification that was hoped might result after privatization. It may be noted that 1980s was the period known for privatization and the 1990s was the period emphasizing for ethics in corporate governance. In recent years there has been a shift in regulation with an emphasis in protecting the consumer and environmental concerns. In the last two decades the independent regulation through independent regulatory authorities has emerged as the fourth branch of government. countries have constituted or contemplated independent regulatory authorities to catalyze the movement through competition or privatization.

Liberalization of Indian economy in 1990s lead to reforms in the service sectors like power, telecom which were gradually thrown open to private investment and competition. As a result the independent regulatory agencies have been set-up in a number of sectors. These agencies were set-up for electricity and telecommunications in 1990s. A semi-autonomous tariff regulator was established for the port sector in 1997. Recently, the regulators have been established in petroleum, natural gas, and aviation industries. India has also established the Competition Commission under the Competition Act, 2002, for the regulation of competition in general. Such, regulators for the railways, housing, postal, broadcasting industries and other service sectors are also under active consideration.

6.2. Suggestions

The reform experience of the last three decades has provided evidence to show the difficulty of government regulation and the challenges of regulatory reform. There is no one best way to resolve the many problems of government regulation because of the different nature of the economic and social problems involved. To address these problems, policy-makers need to consider not just the implementation of deregulation strategies, but also the development of an integrated and balanced regulatory system.

Deregulation alone is insufficient in resolving the problems of regulation. In principle, deregulation is considered as a reactive approach because it addresses problems developed in the past and focuses on instruments and technique issues. Deregulation policy offers no suggestion about the overall regulatory system and about new issues or challenges in the society. In practice, the implementation of deregulation in many sectors and industries has produced problems, which require additional governmental action. While not abandoning deregulation, policy-makers in other states have delayed the implementation of deregulation and have considered other supporting mechanisms (e.g. multi-state trading zones) to avoid the same problem in the future.

To overcome the problems of deregulation and to include other reform ideas, it is important for policy-makers to develop a balanced and integrated regulatory system. The balanced approach requires regulators to balance various interests between public and business groups as well as different concerns between economic and social factors. The balanced approach also includes the considerations of new reform policies that encourage compliance-oriented regulation, in addition to the traditional control requirements. The new approach emphasizes voluntary compliance by businesses and attempts to achieve the regulation purposes through enforced self-regulation and incentives.

The integrated approach refers to the development of a better regulatory management system by introducing changes in regulatory institutions and process. The integrated system will improve management capacities in the process of regulation design, implementation, monitoring and enforcement. The integrated system will also require the integration and involvement of different institutions, talents and groups to produce good performance and better results. Unlike the deregulation strategy, the integrated regulatory management system is more sophisticated in scope and emphasizes a proactive approach in its long-term development. Major features of this system include: managing aggregate regulatory effects (e.g. total costs on a sector); upgrading effectiveness of regulatory regimes; setting frameworks to guide relevant actors; improving flexibility in regulatory regimes; implementing longer-term structural reform; developing a wider range of alternatives; improving transparency and accountability; and creating longer-term cultural change. To assure the success of regulatory management system, reformers need to seek strong support from political leaders, develop a holistic and comprehensive approach, and provide good communication about the need, purpose, and sequence of reforms.

6.2.1. *Legislative Reforms*

This section exclusively highlights the need of legislative reforms in the area of insurance laws:

(i) **An integrated approach to revise the insurance laws is the need of the hour.** In changing economic scenario where vital role is played by the Insurance Regulatory and Development Authority in regulation and development of insurance sector, the Insurance Act, 1938, requires revision and review. The revision of the Act has to be carried out in such a manner that it not only promotes insurance business but also protects policy-holders and strengthens the Authority to ensure financial stability. While revising the Act, the other related laws also need to be reviewed and the relevant provisions of the IRDA Act, 1999, are also required to be merged into the principal Act after necessary modifications.

(ii) The Insurance Act, 1938, being a legislation of colonial era, contains certain *provisions that are redundant and accordingly require deletion*.

(iii) Some of the provisions of the Insurance Act, 1938 are *transitional* in nature and should, therefore, be *deleted*. Further, certain matters covered in the Regulations framed by the IRDA should be deleted from the Act, in order to avoid duplication. Further, the IRDA Act, 1999, has inserted some provisions in the Insurance Act, 1938, the effect of which was to nullify some existing provisions. They have not been deleted, thus giving rise to anomalies; such provisions require to be deleted.

(iv) References in the Insurance Act, 1938, to older enactments have to be replaced by references to the corresponding new legislations that have replaced such enactments.

(v) The IRDA exercises its powers by and large under the provisions of the principal Act. Therefore, it is appropriate as well as necessary that the *relevant provisions of IRDA Act be merged in the Insurance Act, 1938*. With the IRDA exercising many of the key functions assigned to it under the Insurance Act, 1938, there is no justification for continuing to have a separate legislation concerning the constitution and functions of the IRDA. Thus, there is a need to merge the provisions of the IRDA Act, 1999, with the Insurance Act, 1938, in order to bring about an integrated approach to the task of formulating a legislative regime that can encompass the key facets of the functioning of the Regulatory Authority even while strengthening the regulatory regime.

(vi) The IRDA while regulating the business activities of the insurers exercises quasi-judicial powers, in addition to the administrative powers, e.g. issue, renewal and cancellation of registration certificate to insurers, order in regard to investigation of the affairs of the insurers, making application to the court for the winding up of the insurance companies, grant of licences to the insurance agents etc. It is felt necessary that there must be a *provision of appeal against the decisions of the IRDA to an independent body constituted under the Act itself*. The appellate body at present set-up by the Central Government by notification headed by the Joint Secretary, MoF cannot be called as an independent body. The correctness of the system may be questioned on the ground of *nemo judex in re sua* (rule against bias).

(vii) **Grievance Redressal Mechanism.** The insurance business has increased several folds even while policy-holders have not been entirely satisfied with the manner of functioning of insurance companies, particularly in the area of settlement of claims. At present the IRDA is not performing any adjudicatory functions. It is not taking up any dispute either between the insurer and insurance intermediary or insurer and policy-holder. Only role played by the IRDA is that of facilitator through the grievance redressal cell. As a result the stake-holders are forced to approach other judicial and quasi-judicial bodies for redressal of their grievances. Notwithstanding the appointment of Ombudsmen under the Redressal of Public Grievances Rules, 1998, in exercise of powers under section 114(1) of the Insurance Act, 1938, the existing machinery for addressing the grievances of policy-holders has not been found to be satisfactory. The remedy under the Consumer Protection Act, 1986, also does not prove to be effective given the large number of cases pending decision. It is, therefore, suggested that there should be a composite, effective and independent grievance redressal mechanism like that set-up under the Securities and Exchange Board of India Act, 1992. There is need to strengthen the adjudicatory powers of the IRDA to make it more effective and efficient institution with teeth. The Appellate Authority, to review the rulings of the IRDA, set-up by the Central Government is far from satisfactory in terms of having an independent and impartial adjudicatory appellate body. In such a scenario, there is a need to set-up effective grievance redressal machinery to deal with the numerous complaints and appeals of policy-holders, which had hitherto not been satisfactorily dealt with.

(viii) **In-house grievance redressal mechanism.** It should be statutorily mandatory for every insurance company to put in place an in-house grievance redressal mechanism under the overall supervision of the IRDA. It will be incumbent for every person seeking to file a claim before available Grievance Redressal Authority (GRA) to first approach the in-house mechanism. Only after exhausting the remedy of approaching the in-house mechanism, it will be open to the claimant to approach the GRA.

6.2.2. *Administrative Measures — Policy Level Reforms*

In the era of deregulation and privatization accompanied with "downsizing of government" philosophy, there is a popular belief that fewer the regulations better it is. However, it should be remembered that well functioning markets need effective regulations regarding certain basic aspects of their operation, and therefore, less regulation is not necessarily better. Complex modern economics need an array of 'rules' in order to function at all. Many of these rules can be, and often are, provided by the private sector itself, e.g. the regulations in the stock market are often provided by the stock exchange itself. Many professions in many countries impose "self-regulation" on their members' qualifications and practices. Thus, many markets which are apparently regulation-free are, in fact, heavily regulated although not necessarily by the government. Choosing between government regulation and self-regulation is at one level a matter of relative efficiency. However, government regulation and self-regulation are not, in the final analysis, full substitutes, because self-regulation has ultimately to be backed by the government through legislation and other directives that draw boundaries around 'permissible' behaviour. In this sense, deregulation should not be equated with abolition of all government regulations, although which are strictly 'necessary' regulation is another, very difficult, question. It should also be pointed out that the deregulation in certain areas may require increased government regulation in other areas, e.g. deregulation of industry and finance may require increased regulation regarding protection of consumers and depositors respectively. It has also been argued on the basis of the experiences of UK and other countries, that privatization often needs to be accompanied by fortified rather weakened regulatory regimes, since it leads to a 'significant' increase in the number, scope and complexity of contractual relations, as relations which were previously internal to publicly owned industries are now the subject to market contracts between private firms, or of "contracts" between regulator and provider.

Asia is lagging behind in liberalizing the utility sectors, largely because countries in the region have neglected the underlying policy and governance reforms as carried out in Europe and Latin America. Markets in utility sector are confused mix of public and private enterprises, concessions and competition, and protectionism and openness. Most Asian countries suffer from partial privatization as well as severe conflict of interests in the operation, ownership, and regulation of utilities. Governments still assume many risks that should be borne by private firms. These problems undermine the credibility of a competitive market, regardless of the regulator's capacities. To enable utility regulators to do their jobs, structural reforms should be completed to create a potentially competitive environment in which markets and regulations can function. Independent regulators cannot succeed in the absence of broader policy and governance reforms that address half-furnished structural reforms, conflict of interests, and uncertain political commitment. Some of policy and governance reforms are listed below.

- **Multi-sector Regulator.** Regulation in India has come so far in the shape of SSRs (single-sector regulators). There are separate regulators for electricity, telecom, ports, insurance, and financial securities. The case for an MSR has been made on several grounds. Regulatory skills are said to be in short supply. Therefore, it makes sense to have an MSR to make best use of these skills. Common problems relating to economics, law, and finance can be tackled by a central pool, which can lend its services to the various sectors or industry-specific problems. Further, the narrow technical skills required for regulation can be outsourced, and, in fact, many regulators in India have made extensive use of outside expertise. In the same vein, keeping in mind the fact that the regulator has to play a role in the development of the sector, more than regulatory skills, what is required is knowledge of the sector, its problems, and the capacity to ensure its development to meet the objectives of government. These factors would prompt the need for an SSR. Regulatory capture, by the government or by the industry is said to be easier when there are SSRs, since these are smaller and more closely identified with one industry or department of the government.

Financial costs can also be much lower with an MSR since common resources can be economized. On the other hand, it can also be argued that these costs are so small in relation to the turnover of the sectors, thus the saving from these cannot be a material input affecting the choice of an SSR or MSR. Convergence of technologies or markets can be a very powerful argument for an MSR. Therefore, in areas like telecommunications, information technology and broadcasting, it would be difficult to have SSRs because the same resource can be put to multiple use.

Uniformity in rules can also be useful when there are several industries that compete with each other. Such uniformity makes for fair competition as different rules can give one or the other sector an unfair advantage. Thus, in India, coal and oil can be said to be competing in certain segments. Vertical integration can give a powerful impetus to the creation of an MSR if all the segments require a similar degree of regulation. Thus, in the energy sector in India, there are strong vertical linkages between the electricity and the coal industries. Both require regulation due to the absence of competitive markets. Without a common regulatory structure, many issues regarding coal supply, which impact the electricity consumers, are not being addressed.

- **Operational Autonomy and Management.** The regulatory functions of the authorities include problem identification, fact-finding, rule-making and enforcement. The regulator requires detailed knowledge and continuous monitoring of the activities concerned. Operational autonomy is required to be maintained in these sectoral specialized agencies. At the same time there is need to set up a mechanism for monitoring the agency as well.

- **Funding and Resources.** The funding of the regulatory commissions should be independent of the budget. The funding of the regulatory agency could be from the fees provided by the sponsor/operator on an annual basis, licence fees, recurring charges, and royalty payable by the operator as a percentage of annual turnovers. The fees and costs must be retained in corpus and not required to be paid into the Consolidated Fund of India. While levying fees, it must be kept in view that fees are not in the nature of taxes and must be in proportion to the service rendered. Government funding should be avoided to the extent possible.

- **Task Force.** The Government of India should constitute a Task Force not only to look into the sectors where regulation is already in place but also where there are chances of introducing regulations. It should (i) review the existing regulatory laws and formulate government's view on each aspect of regulation; (ii) identify the sectors where regulatory reforms are required and spell out the process of restructuring the sector; (iii) examine the need for integration of regulators in view of convergence; and (iv) suggest mechanisms for providing platform to deal with overlapping issues. The task force should review the experience of selected countries both developed and developing, in order to recommend the appropriate structuring and staffing of the regulatory authorities in each sector, both at Central and State levels.

- **Development of Regulatory Skills.** A Training Fund should be established possibly in cooperation with the multilateral and bilateral funding agencies, to finance in-depth training of staff of each of the regulatory authorities. The training of the regulators and various stakeholders such as regulated agencies, consumer groups, government officials etc. on various regulatory issues is must. Further, the government should encourage institutions to conduct research on various regulatory aspects.

- **Dispute Resolution.** Mechanism to settle disputes quickly must be set-up. The regulatory authorities must be provided with judicial powers. If the regulatory body does not have judicial powers, this mechanism should be incorporated within the legal system. A tribunal could also be created for each sector on the same lines as the Appellate Tribunal for the securities market.

- **Enforcement Powers.** The regulatory authority in each sector must also be vested with punitive powers to be effective. To make these regulatory commissions more effective the penal powers should be substantially increased.

- **Legislative Framework.** To have a simple legislative framework, existing sector specific enactments be unified into a single statute. Government of India should consider of enacting an umbrella regulatory legislation covering all the infrastructure sectors. The sector-specific differences can be covered by subordinate legislations.

The positioning of an independent regulator should precede the sectoral restructuring process as was done in the case of insurance sector.

- **Regulatory Autonomy and Capture.** Given government's continued dominance in infrastructure, are independent regulators really workable? For example, the Electricity Act, empower regulators with substantial scope and decision-making authority. However, several loopholes undermine their authority. Populist political interference (e.g. free power to farmers) is one problem. State ministries desire to protect and control the incumbent utilities adds a new dimension to capture possibilities by the government. Since, state-owned utilities provide several benefits to bureaucrats, the reality puts the regulator directly against the government in influencing management decisions of the utilities. State Governments have often encouraged utilities to defy regulator's rules and sometimes litigated against regulatory orders. Regulators are often reluctant to penalize state-owned enterprises for non-compliance. When they do, their effectiveness is limited, since financial penalties mean little to state-owned utilities. Although State Governments in recent years have ostensibly imposed hard budget constraints, mostly they make good utilities shortfalls. Capture by government also occurs through regulatory appointments. Third, all regulatory commissions are funded through a consolidated budget, which gives the government control in staffing and growth.

- **Independence of Regulators.** There should be clear delineation of responsibilities and understanding between the regulators and the government. The government should retain the authority to give policy directions to the regulator confirming to the objectives of the relevant regulatory legislation. They should relate to the policy matter and not to the technical and administrative matters. The power with the Central Government to issue directions to the Authority on questions of policy and power of suppression of the Authority should be used cautiously so that the autonomy and independence of the Authority is not compromised. In the administrative and technical matters they should enjoy a certain degree of freedom to effectively discharge duties under the statute. Autonomy of the regulator should be guaranteed under the statute. A regulator should enjoy sufficient degree of freedom to effectively discharge its duties under the statute along with financial autonomy and independence. The survival of the regulator should not be dependent on the pleasure of the executive.

- **Transparency and Public Accountability.** The regulatory system must operate transparently, so that, investors and consumers "know the terms of the deal". When regulators regulate in secret, consumers tend to assume the worst — that the regulator or government has been "bought out" by new private investors and that consumers will end up paying for this "secret deal." The long-term sustainability of any regulatory system requires transparency because transparency is the first step to trust. The independence of the regulator should be accompanied with appropriate measures of public accountability. For this the regulatory process should incorporate certain crucial steps like opportunity to the stakeholders to present their views; the regulatory decisions must be published and the reasons for such decisions clearly stated; and provision for the appeal against the decision of the regulator. This would ensure that all the stakeholders are aware about the regulator's decisions and give them an opportunity to present their free and frank opinion.

- **Relation with Other Regulators.** There is need to remove areas of conflict between the economic regulators for specific sectors as well as between economic regulators and the umbrella regulators such as anti-trust agency. The purpose of all these agencies is to promote competition, so their roles and relationships should be complementary to each other. Further, in sectors such as power, ports, roads etc. where the jurisdiction of the Centre and State overlap, the role of the regulators should be well defined and complementary. Overlapping areas of operation should be identified to the extent possible and spelt out in the regulation.

- The regulator should ensure level playing field for all the players and a fair return on the investments made by them. In areas where there are still natural monopolies, the regulator has to ensure that those in monopolistic position do not exploit this power.

- Legitimacy requires that consumers and investors believe that the regulatory system is producing value for them. If consumers and investors do not see any value coming out of the regulatory system, it will not have any allies when there is a political crisis. It will be an institution "without any friends". This is another way of saying that there must be a demand for the regulatory system, and the demand must come from groups to whom politicians will pay attention. Thus, the consumers should be ensured fair price of services and commensurate quality of service. It is thus the duty of the regulator to balance the interests of the consumers on one side and those of the regulated agencies on the other. The regulators should take initiatives to arrange mechanisms like periodic interactions etc. for the consumers to express their opinions in honest and free manner. This will provide useful feedback in discharge of duties and responsibilities by the regulators.

- **Adopting Explicit Standards for Regulatory Quality.** Regulators should identify the problem to be addressed and assess its significance, identify and assess alternatives to direct regulation, design regulation in the most cost-effective way, regulate only upon a reasoned determination that benefits justify costs, avoid regulations that are inconsistent or duplicative with other regulations, and draft regulations which are simple and easy to understand.

- **Assessing Regulatory Impacts.** Regulatory Impact Assessment of the proposed regulations should be carried out by the agencies requiring assessment of benefits and costs against several key threshold, cost-effectiveness, and benefit-cost principles. A separate assessment of small business impacts should also be required by law.

- **Promoting Regulatory Reform and Quality within the Administration.** There should be a system for centralized oversight and quality management located at the very centre of government which will perform the strong coordination, reviewing, and reporting role for regulatory reform.

- Finally, it may be emphasized that provision should be made for regular review of regulations at the operational level. For this, adequate fund allocation should be made as a part of the regulatory authority's budget.

6.3. Perspectives on Regulatory Reform

The market-oriented regulatory reforms that globalization processes encourage states to pursue can be conceptualized in different ways. A state's action or inaction in the face of changing economic forces is thus subject to many interpretations.[7]

One of the theoretical contention is that state welfare programmes, significant portions of which are privatized, as well as the use of federal corporations — especially those that avoid the state action doctrine — are all steps back to a nineteenth century *laissez faire* conception of the State. The overall direction of market-oriented regulatory reforms is that they take us "back to the future" — representing a return to a nineteenth century *laissez faire* conception of the proper relationship of the state to the market, that is to say, the State's role is expected to be minimal, especially at the federal level, and most problems are viewed as essentially private and amenable to market solutions or aid provided by institutions thought to be part of "civil society". The administrative law for such a conception of the state would consist largely of the common law doctrines and approaches that dominated the so-called 'traditional' model of administrative law. For legislative proponents of a back to the future view of regulatory reform, the state is like a rubber band that has been stretched too far. At a minimum, a procedural *laissez faire* approach resists any additional or new role for the State and, over time, the State must be allowed to snap or slip back to a minimalist starting position.

This kind of hard-edged, philosophical view of regulatory reform also drives a certain kind of domestic politics, a politics that sees government as a major contributor to a national problem characterized by declining competitiveness, fewer industrial jobs, high taxes and governmental institutions incapable of offering or implementing any constructive solutions. The public-private dichotomy is often emphasized to the point where almost any governmental attempt to rectify a problem is assumed to be doomed to failure, but the market consistently is seen as a major source of liberation. Such an approach, however, fails to create the kinds of domestic governmental structures and approaches necessary for the global level.

Closely related to a *laissez faire* approach to government is another version of the back to the future thesis, but one which is more optimistic in nature, and one which does not necessarily reject a role for government to play. This approach, called as the "economic growth model", posits as free a market economy as possible as the ultimate goal, with the explicit assumption that less regulation and less costly government will increase economic growth in a manner that will benefit everyone. But rather than emphasizing a pure philosophical belief in the value of individual freedom from government intrusion, this view places more emphasis on the consequences that can flow from markets and efficient government — namely economic prosperity for all. Though government will have a role to play, that role should be made to adhere to corporate organizational forms and structures whenever possible and be subject to the discipline and rigours of the market. If it is necessary to enlist the private sector to carry out certain governmental tasks, that may be necessary, if it is the most efficient way of proceeding.

Besides reliance on the market, either as a form of bureaucratic organization or as a substitute for government, another aspect of this perspective on regulatory reform involves some relatively new ways in which interest groups may interact with the government. Certain aspects of the theory assume a bargaining relationship between the government and selected representative interest groups and an outcome that is really a brokered policy in which government often plays more a role of mediator, than judge. The outcome of a bargaining process between the state agencies and those organized interests whose power in the political marketplace means that their cooperation is indispensable if agreed policies are to be implemented.

The need for increased bargaining on the part of the state to achieve goals that are realistically enforceable is indicative of a state that can no longer accomplish its objectives by direct command-control regulations. This is true for a number of reasons. First, the processes of globalization can weaken the State in various ways, not the least of which is that they make it relatively easy for some industries to move production around the globe, avoiding excess costs, but often affecting local employment opportunities as well. There is, thus, a greater premium on the part of the state to negotiate with potential regulatees, perhaps to convince them of the necessity of the regulation and that what it proposes is as cost-effective as possible. As the funding of agencies decreases, effective enforcement of the regulations promulgated increasingly requires the cooperation of the regulated. They need to be given the discretion to reach the desired results in ways that make sense for them. Industries also increasingly need to be part of the planning and regulatory process.

The increasing reliance on markets and market approaches as substitutes for more direct forms of regulation highlights efficiency concerns and it also suggests a regulatory discourse that is much closer to market concerns and modes of operation. This is likely generally to be more in tune with business interests, but a market discourse applies especially easily to companies doing business in multiple countries. They are freer to reject the political costs of doing business in any one jurisdiction if they can move production around the globe relatively easily. Thus, these market approaches and discourses also suggest new roles for the private sector to play when designing new rules or regulatory approaches, and new bureaucratic structures for government to use, structures that seek quite consciously to copy the form and disciplines of corporate structures.

Finally, since so many regulatory reforms are driven by cost considerations in both the industries to which they apply and in the agencies that promulgate them, localities in competition for foreign investment also wish to have these functions performed in the most efficient way possible and in a manner that is closest to the level of government actually affected. Thus, devolution of regulatory responsibilities to the states and even to localities within those states is increasingly common. But the farther one gets from the national level, the easier it is for forms of interest group-government negotiation to occur and the 'deals' that are ultimately struck often involve incentives for multinationals to locate in that area.

A third view of regulatory reform held by those who philosophically believe in an active government begins with the assumption that government regulation can be positive. It is not inconsistent, however, for such proponents of regulatory reform also to believe that regulation need not only be the traditional, so-called "command-control" type. New forms of regulation that seek to co-opt the market as a regulatory tool can be both effective and efficient. The market is a means, to an end, not an end in itself. It should also be remembered that markets as well as states both are not the creation of God. Using the market in this way represents the public uses of the private interest. Markets are used not just to maximize wealth, however, it might be distributed, but to structure incentives in such a way as to achieve public interest goals. The government itself also can function more efficiently and in less expensive ways. In an era of intense global competition and scarce resources, incorporating some of the accountability and the discipline of the market into government activities is, thus, also viewed as an important reform. The more efficient government becomes, better it can accomplish its public interest goals. However, such a view does not see use of privatized structures as essentially relieving the state of the responsibility for policy outcomes reached by these structures but simply a new hopefully more effective way of advancing public interest. In this perspective, use of market and market incentives as a mean to further public ends do, indeed, differ significantly from reforms designed to return to the market as an end in itself or from those that seek to have government approximate market structures and outcomes, as ends in themselves.

Different conceptions of the roles of the state, the private sector and the public interest are involved in each of the perspectives sketched above and each generates the need for somewhat different legal doctrines or, at least, different conceptual and interpretive approaches to these doctrines. For those who see the market as an end in itself, be they advocates of back to the future or economic growth advocates who see the federal corporate form as an end in itself, a clear distinction between the state and the private sector is necessary. It is, therefore, important that the line between public and private be a bright one. From a constitutional point of view, this means that what falls within the private realm is the domain of the market and private, individual decision-making. The role of law is to assure that such private activity can occur safely beyond the reach of the state. Given the assumption that such a public or governmental role will be relatively small compared to the private sector, there is also a presumption against state compared to the private sector, there is also a presumption against state intervention in economic matters and in favour of maximum private involvement. In such an analysis, the concept of private for profit and public not for profit may also be taken into consideration.

For those who wish to co-opt the market for public purposes, the public/private dividing line is problematic. Given that it may be sensible to have a more market-oriented state, the state must still be an independent public interest force. But if the state is to forge new alliances with the private sector to carry out public interest goals, a constitutional structure that too rigorously defines what is private in opposition to what is public can hamper the creativity of these new state/private partnerships or inappropriately shield activities and decisions that have broad public impact from the kinds of procedures that "public" law can provide. Moreover, for those who see the market as a means to achieve public interest ends and believe government agencies can carry out these programmes, the role of the state remains important in setting goals, standards and structuring incentives in new ways that can funnel private interests in public interest directions.

However, it would be a mistake, to assume that even with the more public interest emphasis of the third perspective, the role of the state continues to be the same or, arguable, as powerful or as extensive as in previous eras. Further, the more the market and market approaches are used to reach public interest results, important values that are not easily quantified may, in effect, be omitted entirely from consideration. Costs are usually easier to quantify than benefits. Similarly, while equating citizens with consumers may clarify the role or duties of the state in certain contexts, there is something lost from this translation as well. The concept of citizenship is a deep one that can both include and transcend the role of individuals as mere consumers of state services. Thus, the market metaphor has its limits; its rhetoric can and often does limit the roles the state may play.

The tensions these newer approaches to regulation produce raise important questions involving what is public and what is private and, more importantly, the extent to which the public interest retains any viability as a concept beyond efficiency. Regulatory reforms that rely on the private sector and market incentives do not represent a return to the past or simply more of the same, but the beginnings of a new model of administrative law in which the line between the public and the private is no longer distinct, and the lines between and among levels of government — international, federal, state and local — should not be so sharp as to prevent synergistic interplay among them and the creation of new combinations or partnerships between government and the private sector. Indeed, the future role the administrative law will be to incorporate and justify new mixes of private and public power as well as to try to ensure the opportunity for a broad based public interest discourse, one that resists the idea that narrow, technocratic, cost-benefit analyses are always determinative. Such, a role would be compatible with more cooperative approaches to governance at the global level.

6.4. Impact of Privatization and Globalization on Administrative Law

Deregulation, cost-benefit analysis, market-oriented regulatory approaches, declining regulatory budgets, devolution and the delegation of public tasks to the private sector are but some of the hallmarks of the global era of administrative law.[8] These deregulatory trends typify new approaches to public law in various countries around the world. These market oriented reforms either substitute markets and the private sector for regulatory regimes or have public agencies use market approaches, structures and incentives to achieve their regulatory goals. The end result is less institutionalized public involvement in decision-making processes that can and often do have widespread public effects. Decisions that were once subject to public law processes and values such as participation and transparency, are now governed primarily by market forces and market values. In globalization there are varieties of complex, dynamic legal and social processes in which states increasingly are "actors" only indirectly. In many instances, these processes significantly undercut a state's autonomy, though the state may not wish to see it that way. The processes like competition, new patterns of trade and corporate finance occur without direct agency of the state. They not only are changing the shape of and the ways in which the private sector does business, but these processes also challenge fundamental ideas of what the state is, what its relationship to the private sector should be, and what actions the state can realistically take to deal effectively with perceived social, economic and political problems.

A basic question on how globalization impacts governance is: what role can the state effectively play as a regulator, given the collapse of the distinction between domestic and global, as well as that between public and private? The impact of today's globalization processes on administrative law is transforming it in new ways. There are changing roles for the state to play based largely on new ways of incorporating market regulatory approaches (and the private sector generally) to public interest ends. Three broad regulatory innovations signal the beginning of new transformation of administrative law: (1) the delegation of public functions to the private sector; (2) the increasingly common recourse to market regulatory approaches as a substitute for command — control rules; and (3) the application of market organizational models such as federal corporations — the retention of governmental responsibility for implementation purposes, but the privatization of the procedures and structures used to implement these governmental programmes. The effect of such a transformation shifts the role of the legal system primarily from legitimating new extensions of public power and increased state intervention, to legitimating new mixes of public and private power, new uses of private power and increased reliance on market approaches to further public interest goals. The move from the public to the private is a common theme in legal systems throughout the world.[9]

The application of this new rhetoric in a global context augurs significant changes in administrative law that include: (1) new blends of public and private sectors at all levels of government; (2) a redefinition of what is public and what is private, or at least what kinds of public functions can be fulfilled in the private sector; (3) greater reliance on bargaining and negotiation models of decision-making when it comes to the exercise of agency discretion; (4) a diminution of public participation stemming from increased reliance on privatization and the delegation of public functions to private entities; and (5) a market discourse that arguably narrows the role of public interest values, and replaces them with the rhetoric of cost-benefit analysis.

The administrative law is viewed as "having its premise in the need to control the exercise of power in a welfare state with a largely regulated economy." With a sharp reduction in the degree of direct governmental involvement in the economy with corporatizing and privatizing of trading activities of the state, the question arises: Will the rolling back of the state result in a rolling back of judicial review? What part, if any, can administrative law play in a society where state trading enterprises are commanded to mimic the private sector and where privatization is in vogue?

What we see is not the total retreat of the state, but rather the substitution of one form of involvement by the state in the economy for another. There is a wide choice of regulatory tools. It is often overlooked that privatization is usually accompanied by regulation. In this scenario Sir Ivor Richardson raised the question: Should the philosophical approach underpinning administrative law and its doctrines now be modified to reflect the less expansive rule of government in the more market-oriented State?[10] Michael Taggart has answered this question in affirmative but not in the direction Sir Ivor apparently favours.[11] According to him the philosophical approach to administrative law should be broadened to include the exercise of significant market power by privatized enterprises and, ultimately by private corporations. Similar view has been expressed by a number of authors.[12] The courts, too, seem to be inclining in this direction, although it is hard to tell whether the holdings and dicta are straws in the wind or the stuff from which constitutional bricks are made. These strands may one day be drawn together to support judicial review of the exercise of significant market power by privatized and private bodies.

The common law has long been concerned with the control over persons and corporations enjoying a legal or *de facto* monopoly in the provision of services to the general public. For centuries the courts regulated such monopolies "in the public interest" and required them to serve the public at reasonable prices and without discrimination. In some countries and in some industries this role has fallen to regulatory agencies, but elsewhere the privatization of public utilities may inspire a revival of these common law doctrines. It has also been recognized by courts that a private sporting body may make a decision of such national importance as to be subject to judicial review.[13] Furthermore, self-regulatory bodies without visible means of legal support — be it prerogative, statute, common law or contract — have been held by the English Court of Appeal to be subject to judicial review.[14] Much of the reasoning in these cases can be used to support judicial review of powerful private bodies whether they perform regulatory functions or not. The ambit of administrative law may yet develop to include the exercise of power other than that derived from the legislature which adversely affects the interests of the public.

The process of privatization strips away most of the accountability mechanisms that operate in the public sector — Ombudsman review, freedom of information, scrutiny by the Auditor-General, Ministerial responsibility. There is an accountability vacuum which the courts may be drawn into. This, however, raises questions of legitimacy. The tasks of administrative law and the administrative lawyer extend beyond judicial review. The fundamental values of public law — openness, fairness, participation, impartiality and rationality — not only provide a yardstick against which to measure the activities of privatized enterprises with market power,[15] but should be embodied in the design of institutions and regulatory schemes at the outset.[16]

Before closing the chapter it would perhaps be appropriate to mention that the importance and value of administrative law in the future will not diminish. Rather in search of better mechanism to protect the rights and interests of individuals the process of restatement of values of administrative law by way of its restructuring will be accepted as appropriate answer.

NOTES

1. Levi-Faur, David (2005), "The Global Diffusion of Regulatory Capitalism", *Annuls of the American Academy of Political and Social Science*, 598, pp. 12-32.
2. See Ayres and Braithwaite (1992), *Responsive Regulation*, Oxford University Press, New York, pp. 7-12.
3. Jacobs, Scott (1999), "The Second Generation of Regulatory Reforms", paper presented at *IMF Conference on Second Generation Reforms*, November 8-9, Washington D.C.
4. See *OECD Regulatory Cooperation for an Independent World*, OECD, Paris, 1994.
5. See Jacobs, Scott, *et al.* (1997), "Regulatory Quality and Public Sector Reform", in the *OECD Report on Regulatory Reform: Sectoral and Thematic Studies*, OECD, Paris.
6. Majone, G., (ed.) (1989), *Deregulation or Re-regulation*, London, Pinter, q. in C. Hood (1994), *Explaining Economic Policy Reversals*, Open University Press, Buckingham, p.20.
7. Alfred, C. Aman Jr., "Administrative Law for a New Century", in Aseem Prakash and Jeffery A. Hart, (eds.), *Globalization and Governance*, Routledge, London and New York, pp. 277-85.
8. Alfred, C. Aman Jr., "Administrative Law for a New Century", in Aseem Prakash and Jeffery A. Hart, (eds.), *Globalization and Governance*, Routledge, London & New York, p. 267. See generally A.C. Aman (1992), *Administrative Law in a Global Era*, Cornell University Press, Ithaca, New York.
9. Alfred, C. Aman Jr., "Administrative Law for a New Century", in Aseem Prakash and Jeffery A. Hart, (eds.), *Globalization and Governance*, Routledge, London & New York, pp. 268-285.
10. Richardson, Sir Ivor (1991), "Changing Needs for Judicial Decision-Making", *Journal of Judicial Administration*, 1(1), p. 64.
11. Michael Taggart (1992), "The Impact of Corporatization and Privatization on Administrative Law", *Australian Journal of Public Administration*, Vol. 51, No. 3, September, pp. 370-71.
12. Craig, P.P. (1989), *Administrative Law*, Sweet & Maxwell, London, pp. 15-33, 156-71, 420-1; See also Woolf, Sir Harry (1986), "Public Law-Private Law: Why the Divide? A Personal View", *Public Law*, Autumn; Oliver, Dawn (1987), "Is the Ultra Vires Rule the Basis of Judicial Review", *Public Law*, Winter; Borrie, Sir Gordon (1989), "The Regulation of Public and Private Power", *Public Law*, Winter; Beloff, M. (1988), "The Boundaries of Judicial Review", in Jeffrey Jowell and Dawn Oliver (eds.), *New Directions in Judicial Review*, Stevens, London; Hutchinson Alan (1990), "Mice Under a Chair: Democracy, Courts and the Administrative State", *University of Toronto Law Journal*, 40(3).
13. *Finnigan* vs. *New Zealand Rugby Football Union Inc.* (1985) 2 NZLR 159 and 181.
14. *R* vs. *Panel on Take-Overs and Mergers, ex p Datatin Plc* (1987) 1 QB 815.
15. McAuslan, J.P.W.B (1988). "Public Law and Public Choice", *Modern Law Review*, 51(6), pp. 699-700; Bayne, P. (1988), "Administrative Law and the New Managerialism in Public Administration", *Australian Law Journal*, 62(10), p. 1045; Daintith, T. (1985), "The Executive Power Today: Bargaining and

Economic Control" , in Jeffrey Jowell and Dawn Oliver (eds.), *The Changing Constitution*, Oxford University Press, Oxford, p. 175.

16. See Prosser, Tony (1986), *Nationalized Industries and Public Control: Legal, Constitutional and Political Issues*, chs. 1-2; Prosser Tony, "Democratization, Accountability and Institutional Design: Reflections in Public Law", in P. McAuslan and J. McEldowney (eds.) (1985), *Law, Legitimacy and the Constitution*, Sweet & Maxwell, London.

BIBLIOGRAPHY

Original Sources

Statutes

Consumer Protection Act, 1986.
Deposit Insurance and Credit Guarantee Corporation Act, 1961.
Employee's State Insurance Act, 1948.
General Insurance Business (Nationalization) Act, 1972.
Indian Contract Act, 1872.
Industrial Disputes (Banking and Insurance Companies) Act, 1949.
Insurance Act, 1938.
Insurance Regulatory and Development Authority Act, 1999.
Life Insurance (Emergency Provisions) Act, 1956.
Life Insurance Corporation Act, 1956.
Marine Insurance Act, 1963.
Motor Vehicles Act, 1988.
Personal Injuries (Compensation Insurance) Act, 1963.
Public Liability Insurance Act, 1991.
Railways Act, 1989.
Workmen's Compensation Act, 1923.

Rules/Regulations

Banking Ombudsman Scheme, 2006.
IRDA (Acturial Report and Abstract) Regulations, 2000.
IRDA (Advertisements and Disclosure) Regulations, 2000.
IRDA (Appointed Actuary) Regulations, 2000.
IRDA (Appointment of Insurance Advisory Committee) Regulations, 2000.
IRDA (Assets, Liabilities and Solvency Margin of Insurers) Regulations, 2000.
IRDA (Conditions of Service of Officers and Other) Regulations, 2000.
IRDA (General Insurance — Reinsurance) Regulations, 2000.
IRDA (Insurance Surveyors and Loss Assessors) (Licensing, Professional Requirements and Code of Conduct) Regulations, 2000.

IRDA (Investment) (Amendment) Regulations, 2001.
IRDA (Investment) Regulations, 2000.
IRDA (Licensing of Insurance Agents) Regulations, 2000.
IRDA (Life Insurance — Reinsurance) Regulations, 2000.
IRDA (Meetings) Regulations, 2000.
IRDA (Member of Insurance Advisory Committee) Regulations, 2000.
IRDA (Preparation of Financial Statement and Auditors' Report of Insurance Companies) Regulations, 2000.
IRDA (Registration of Indian Insurance Companies) Regulations, 2000.
IRDA (Re-Insurance Advisory Committee) Regulations, 2001.
IRDA (Third Party Administrator — Health Services) Regulations, 2001.
IRDA (Distributions of Surplus) Regulations, 2002.
IRDA (Insurance Brokers) Regulations, 2002.
IRDA (Investment) (Amendment) Regulations, 2002.
IRDA (Licensing of Corporate Agents) Regulations, 2002.
IRDA (Licensing of Insurance Agents) (Amendments) Regulations, 2002.
IRDA (Manner of Receipt of Premium) Regulations, 2002.
IRDA (Obligations of Insurers to Rural or Social Sectors) (Amendment) Regulations, 2002.
IRDA (Obligations of Insurers to Rural or Social Sectors) Regulations, 2002.
IRDA (Preparation of Financial Statement and Auditors' Report of Insurance Companies) Regulations, 2002.
IRDA (Protection of Policy-holders' Interest) (Amendments) Regulations, 2002.
IRDA (Protection of Policy-holders' Interest) Regulations, 2002.
IRDA (Registration of Indian Insurance Companies) (Amendment) Regulations, 2003.
IRDA (Investment) (Amendment) Regulations, 2004.
IRDA (Obligations of Insurers to Rural or Social Sectors) (Amendment) Regulations, 2004.
IRDA (Qualification of Actuary) Regulations, 2004.
IRDA (Insurance Advisory Committee) Regulations, 2005.
IRDA (Micro-Insurance) Regulations, 2005.
IRDA (Obligation of Insurers to Rural or Social Sectors) (Amendment) Regulations, 2005.
IRDA (Insurance Brokers) (Amendment) Regulations, 2007.
IRDA (Licensing of Corporate Agents) (Amendment) Regulations, 2007.
IRDA (Licensing of Insurance Agents) (Amendment) Regulations, 2007.

IRDA (Conditions of Service of Officers and Other) (Second Amendment) Regulations, 2008.

IRDA (Investment) (Fourth Amendment) Regulations, 2008.

IRDA (Obligation of Insurers to Rural or Social Sectors) (Third Amendment) Regulations, 2008.

IRDA (Obligation of Insurers to Rural or Social Sectors) (Fourth Amendment) Regulations, 2008.

IRDA (Registration of Indian Insurance Companies) (Second Amendment) Regulations, 2008.

Redressal of Public Grievance Rules, 1998.

Reports

190th Law Commission of India Report on Revision of the Insurance Act, 1938 and the Insurance Regulatory & Development Authority Act, 1999, Law Commission of India, 2004.

Annual Report 2000-01, Insurance Regulatory and Development Authority, 2001.

Annual Report 2001-02, Insurance Regulatory and Development Authority, 2002.

Annual Report 2002-03, Insurance Regulatory and Development Authority, 2003.

Annual Report 2003-04, Insurance Regulatory and Development Authority, 2004.

Annual Report 2004-05, Insurance Regulatory and Development Authority, 2005.

Annual Report 2005-06, Insurance Regulatory and Development Authority, 2006.

Annual Report 2006-07, Insurance Regulatory and Development Authority, 2007.

Annual Report 2007-08, Insurance Regulatory and Development Authority, 2008.

Brownlow Commission Report of the President's Committee on Administrative Management, Washington, DC, Government Printing Office, 1937.

Hansand Commission Report, the Report of the Commission in the Regulation of Privatized Utilities, London, 1996.

Hoover Commission Report on the Organization of the Executive Branch of Government, McGraw-Hill, Inc. New York, 1949.

KPN Committee on Provisions of the Insurance Act, 1938, IRDA, 2005.

Regulation — Less is More, Reducing Burdens, Improving Outcomes, Better Regulation Task Force, UK, March 2005.

Report of Advisory Group on Insurance Regulation, Reserve Bank of India, September 2000.

Report of Advisory Group on Securities Market Regulation, Reserve Bank of India, 2001.

Report of the Committee on Reforms in the Insurance Sector (Malhotra Committee Report), Ministry of Finance, GoI, January 1994.

Report on Legal Services and Procedure, U.S. House of Representatives, Task Force on Legal Services and Procedure, Prepared by Commission on Organization of the Executive Branch, House Doc. No. 1128, 84th Cong., 1st Sess., 1955.

The OECD Report of Regulatory Reforms: Synthesis, OECD, Paris, 1997.

The OECD Review of Regulatory Reforms in United Kingdom, OECD, November 2002.

The OECD Review of Regulatory Reforms in United States of America, OECD, 1999.

U.S. Senate Report of the Attorney General Committee on Administrative Procedure, Administrative Procedure in Government Agencies, Sen. Dec. No. 8, 77th Congress, 1st Sess., 1941.

Secondary Sources

Books

Achinstein, Asher (1950), *The Welfare State: The Case for and Against, the Library of Congress*, Legislative Reference Services, Washington D.C.

Agarwal, U.C. (ed.) (2004), *Public Administration: Vision and Reality*, Indian Institute of Public Administration, IIPA Golden Jubilee Publication.

Alcock, P. (2003), *Social Policy in Britain*, MacMillan.

Aman, C. (1992), *Administrative Law in a Global Era*, Cornell University Press, Ithaca, New York.

Anderson, Thomas J. (1958), *Our Competitive System and Public Policy*, South Western.

Armstrong, Mark, Simon Cowan, and John Vickers (1999), *Regulatory Reform: Economic Analysis and British Experience*, Cambridge, MA: The MIT Press.

Ayres, I. and J. Braithwaite (1992), *Responsive Regulation: Transcending the Regulation Debate*, Oxford University Press, Oxford.

Bailey, Elizabeth E. and Janet Rothenberg Pack, (ed.) (1995), *The Political Economy of Privatization and Deregulation,* Edward Elgar, Aldershot.

Baldock, J., *et al.*, (ed.) (1999), *Social Policy*, Oxford University Press.

Baldwin, R. and C. Mccrudden (1987), *Regulation and Public Law*, Weidenfeld & Nicolson, London.

Baldwin, R., Scott, C. and Hood, C. (1998), *A Reader on Regulation,* Oxford University Press, New York.

Baldwin, Robert, and Martin Cave (1999), *Understanding Regulation: Theory, Strategy, and Practice*, Oxford University Press, Oxford.

Bartle, Ian, Markus M. Müller, Friedrich-Alexander, Stephen Wilks (2002), *The Regulatory State: Britain and Germany Compared,* Anglo-German Foundation for the Study of Industrial Society, September.

Berg, Sanford V., and John Tschirhart (1988), *Natural Monopoly Regulation: Principles and Practice*, Cambridge University Press, New York.

Bernstein, Marver H. (1955), *Regulating Business by Independent Commission,* Princeton University Press.

Bhargava, B.D. (2008), *Insurance Theory and Practice*, Pearl Books, New Delhi.

Bhujabal Gajendra (2006), *Insurance for the Poor: An Analytical Approach to Micro-Insurance in India*, 31st APPPA, IIPA.

Bodla, B.S., M.C. Garg and K.P. Singh (2004), *Insurance — Fundamentals, Environment and Procedures*, Deep & Deep Publications Pvt. Ltd., New Delhi.

Bonbright, James C., Albert L. Danielsen, and David R. Kamerschen (1988), *Principles of Public Utility Rates*, Arlington, VA: Public Utilities Reports.

Boyer, Robert and Yves Saillard (ed.) (1995), *Regulation Theory*, Routledge, London & New York.

Breyer S. (1982), *Regulation and Its Reform*, Cambridge, MA: Harvard University Press.

Brown, Jethro W. (2006), *The Underlying Principles of Modern Legislation,* the Law Book Exchange Ltd., New Jersey.

Brown, S.J., and D.S. Sibley (1986), *The Theory of Public Utility Pricing*, Cambridge, U.K.: Cambridge University Press.

Buscaglia, Edgardo and William Ratliff (2000), *Law and Economics in Developing Countries*, Hoover Institution Press, Stanford, California.

Cane, Peter (ed.) (2002), *Administration Law*, Ashgate, Dartmouth.

Cars, Sir C. (1921), *Delegated Legislation*, Cambridge.

Cassese, Sabino (1994), *Deregulation and Privatization in Italy*, Open University Press, Buckingham.

Chaudhary, R.N.P. (2005), *Consumer Protection Law*, Deep & Deep Publications Pvt. Ltd., New Delhi.

Chester, Sir Norman (1970), *The Nationalization of British Industry 1945-51,* HMSO.

Coen, David, Adrienne Heritier and Dominik Bollhoff (2002), *Regulating the Utilities: UK and Germany Compared*, Anglo-German Foundation for the Study of Industrial Society, October.

Commager, H.S. (ed.) (1963), *Documents of American History*, Vol. II, 7th edn., Appleton-Century-Crofts, New York.

Cooper, Phillip J. (2000), *Public Law and Public Administration*, 3rd edn., F.E. Peacock Publishers.

Cornish, W., G. de N. Clark. (1989), *Law and Society in England 1850-1950*, Sweet & Maxwell, London.

Corwin, E.S. (1934), *The Twilight of the Supreme Court*, Yale University Press.

Craig, P.P. (1989), *Administrative Law*, Sweet & Maxwell, London.

Davis, Kenneth Culp (1969), *Discretionary Justice: A Preliminary Inquiry*, Baton Rouge, Louisiana State University Press.

Derthick and Quirk (1985), *The Politics of Deregulation*, Brookings, Washington.

Dhameja, Nand and K.S. Sastry (1998), *Privatisation — Theory and Practice*, Wheeler Publishing, New Delhi.

Dicey, A.V. (1905), *Lectures on the Relation between Law and Opinion in England in the Nineteenth Century,* MacMillan, London & New York.

Doing Business in 2004: Understanding Regulation, World Bank, Washington, D.C., 2004.

Edley, Christopher F. Jr. (1990), *Administrative Law Rethinking Judicial Control of Bureaucracy*, Yale University Press, London.

Estache, Antonio and Gines de Rus (eds.) (2000), *Privatization and Regulation of Transport Infrastructure: Guidelines for Policymakers and Regulators*, World Bank, Washington, D.C.

Fainsod, Merle and Lincoln, Gordan (1948), *Government and the American Economy*, rev. edn., W.W. Norton & Co. Inc., New York.

Fitzpatrick, Tony (2001), *Welfare Theory: An Introduction*, Palgrave, New York.

Forder, Anthony (1974), *Concepts in Social Administration — A Framework for Analysis*, Routledge & Kegan Paul Ltd., London and Boston.

Freund, Ernst (1928), *Administrative Powers over Persons and Property: A Comparative Survey*, University of Chicago Press, Chicago.

Friedmann (1971), *The State and the Rule of Law in a Mixed Economy*, Stevens & Sons, London.

Fromm, G. (ed.) (1981), *Studies in Public Regulation*, Cambridge, MA: MIT Press.

Garg, A.; M. Kabra, and R. Kacker (2003), *Regulatory Reforms in India: Effectiveness, Efficiency and Impacts*, the Energy and Resources Institute, New Delhi, India.

Garg, S.C. (1993), *Deregulation of Telecom Sector — Experiences Abroad and their Relevance to Indian Telecom*, APPPA 1992-93, IIPA, New Delhi.

Garner, J.F. (1979), *Administrative Law*, 5th Edn., Butterworth, London.

Gart, Alan (1994), *Regulation, Deregulation, Re-regulation — The Future of the Banking, Insurance and Securities Industries*, John Wiley and Sons Inc.

Gellhorn, E. and R.J. Pierce Jr. (1982), *Regulated Industries*, West Publishing Co., St. Paul.

Gentle, Christopher J.S. (1996), *After Liberalization: A Vision of Europe in the Global Economy of the Twenty-first Century*, Macmillan Press, London.

Ginsburg, Tom and Robert A. Kangan (eds.) (2005), *Institutions and Public Law — Comparative Approaches*, Peter Lang, New York.

Glennerster, H. (1997), *Paying for Welfare Towards 2000*, Prentice Hall.

Goldman, Eric (1960), *The Crucial Decade and After: America, 1945-1960*, Vintage Books, New York.

Gómez-Ibáñez, José (2003), *Regulating Infrastructure: Monopoly, Contracts, and Discretion*, Cambridge, MA: Harvard University Press.

Graham, Cosmo (2000), *Regulation Public Utilities*, Hart Publishing, Oxford.

Guasch, J. Luis, and Pablo Spiller (1999), *Managing the Regulatory Process: Design, Concepts, Issues, and the Latin America and Caribbean Story*, Washington, D.C.: The World Bank Group.

Hall, M. Penelope (1953), *Social Services of Modern England*, 2nd edn., Routledge & Kegan Paul.

Hampton, Phillip (2005), *Reducing Administrative Burdens: Effective Inspection and Enforcement*, March.

Hancher, Leigh and Michael Moran (eds.) (1989), *Capitalism, Culture and Regulation*, Clarendon Press, Oxford.

Hawke, Neil (1989), *An Introduction to Administrative Law*, 1st Edn., Aditya Books, New Delhi.

Hayek, F.A. (1960), *The Constitution of Liberty,* Chicago: University of Chicago Press.

Hayek, F.A. (1973), *Law, Legislation and Liberty, Vol. 1: Rules and Order*, Chicago: University of Chicago Press.

Héritier, A. (ed.) (2002), *Common Goods: Reinventing European and International Governance,* Lanham, Rowman & Littlefield Publishers.

Héritier, A. (1998), *After Liberalisation: Public-Interest Services in the Utilities*, Bonn, Preprint, Max Planck Project Group Common Goods: Law, Politics, Economics.

Héritier, A.; Kerwer, D.; Knill, C.; Lehmkuhl, D.; Teutsch, M. and Douillet, A.C. (eds.) (2001), *Differential Europe: New Opportunities and Restrictions for Policy-Making in Member States,* Lanham: Rowman & Littlefield Publishers.

Hewart, Lord (1929), *New Despotism*, Cosmopolitan Book Corp., New York.

Hill, Michael and Glen Bramley (1986), *Analysing Social Policy*, Basil Blackwell Ltd.

Holdsworth, Sir William (1956), *History of English Law*, Vol. X, 7th edn., Methuen & Co. Ltd.

Hood, Christopher (1994), *Explaining Economic Policy Reversals*, Open University Press, Buckingham.

Hughes, C. (1957), The *British Statute Book*, Hutchinson University Library, London.

Hughes, G., G. Lewis (eds.) (1998), *Unsettling Welfare*, Routledge.

Hunt, Sally (2002), *Making Competition Work in Electricity,* New York: Wiley & Sons.

Intven, Hank (2000), *Telecommunications Regulation Handbook*, Washington, D.C.: World Bank.

Jackson, R.H. (1941), *The Struggle for Judicial Supremacy*, Knopf, New York.

Jacobs, Scott H. (1999), *Regulatory Reforms in the United States*, OECD.

Jain and Jain (2007), *Principles of Administrative Law*, Lexis Nexis, Butterworth & Wadhwa & Co., Nagpur, 5th edition.

Jamison, Mark A., Sanford V. Berg (2004), *Annotated Reading List for a Body of Knowledge on the Regulation of Utility Infrastructure and Services*, Public Utility Research Center, University of Florida.

Jamison, Mark A., Sanford V. Berg, Farid Gasmi and Jose I. Tavara (2004), *The Regulation of Utility, Infrastructure and Services*, WB & PPIAF.

Jowell, Jeffrey and Dawn Oliver (eds.) (1985), *The Changing Constitution*, Oxford University Press, Oxford.

Kagami, Mitsuhiro and Masatsugu Tsuji, (eds.) (2000), *Privatization, Deregulation and Economic Efficiency: A Comparative Analysis of Asia, Europe and the America*, Edward Elgar, Cheltenham.

Kahn, Alfred (1988), *The Economics of Regulation: Principles and Institutions*, MIT Press, Cambridge, MA.

Kaur, Simrit (2003), *Privatization and Public Regulation: The Indian Experience*, MacMillan, New Delhi.

Kaushal, Anoop K. (2006), *Practical Guide to Consumer Protection Law*, Universal Law Publishing Co. Pvt. Ltd., Delhi.

Kaushik, P.D. (2007), *Regulations Nurture Illegality — Counterproductive Regulations of Delhi*, Bookwell in collaboration with Friedrich Naumann Stiftung and Rajiv Gandhi Institute for Contemporary Studies.

Kay, J., *et al.* (1986), *Privatisation and Regulation — The U.K. Experience*, Oxford.

Keith, Hawkins (1992), *The Uses of Discretion*, Clarendon Press, Oxford.

Keller, Morton (ed.) (1963), *The New Deal: What was It?*, Holt, Rinehart & Winston, New York.

Kessides, Ioannis N. (2004), *Reforming Infrastructures: Privatization, Regulation and Competition*, World Bank, Washington, D.C.

Kettl, Donal F. (1993), *Sharing Power — Public Governance and Private Market*, Brooking Institute, Washington, D.C.

Khanna, Sri Ram, Savita Hanspal, Sheetal Kapoor and H.K. Awasthi (2007), *Consumer Affairs*, Universities Press Pvt. Ltd.

Klein, Michael U. and Bite Hadjimichael (2003), *The Private Sector in Development: Entrepreneurship, Regulation, and Competitive Disciplines*, World Bank, Washington, D.C.

Kolko, G. (1977), *The Triumph of Conservatism*, Free Press, New York.

Laffont, Jean-Jacques, and Jean Tirole (1993), *A Theory of Incentives in Procurement and Regulation*, Cambridge, Massachusetts: The MIT Press.

Laffont, Jean-Jacques (2005), *Regulation and Development*, Cambridge University Press.

Landis, James M. (1938), *The Administrative Process*, New Heaven, CT, Yale University Press.

Lee, Phill and Colin Raban (1988), *Welfare Theory and Social Policy: Reform or Revolution*, Sage, London.

Leiserson, Avery (1942), *Administrative Regulation — A Study in Representation of Interests*, The University of Chicago Press, Chicago, Illinois.

Leuchtenburg, William E. (ed.) (1968), *The New Deal*, Harper & Row, New York.

Longley, D., *et al.* (1996), *Administrative Justice: Central Issues in UK and European Administrative Law*, Cavendish Publishing Ltd., London.

MacAvoy, P.W. (1979), *The Regulated Industries and the Economy*, New York: Morton.

MacNeil, Neil and Harold W. Metz (1956), *The Hoover Commission Report, 1953-1955: What it Means to You as Citizens and Taxpayers*, Commission on Organisation of the Executive Branch of Government, MacMillan, New York.

Maitland, F.W. (1908), *Constitutional History of England*, Cambridge.

Majone, G. (ed.) (1989), *Deregulation or Re-regulation*, Pinter, London.

Majone, G. (1996), *Regulating Europe*, Routledge, London.

Major, John (1968), *The New Deal*, Longman, Green & Co. Ltd.

Majore, G. (1989), *Evidence, Argument and Persuasion in the Policy Process*, Yale University Press, New Haven, CT.

Malyarov, O.V. (1983), *The Role of the State in the Socio-Economic Structure in India*, Vikas Publishing House Pvt. Ltd.

Mashaw, Jerry L. (1976), *Due Process in the Administrative State*, Yale University Press, London.

Massey, I.P. (2005), *Administrative Law*, Eastern Book Co., Lucknow.

Mathur, Vipin (2008), *Consumer Behaviour: Challenges of New Millennium Markets*, Cyber Tech.

McCloskey, D.N. (1985), *The Rhetoric of Economics*, Madison, WI, Wisconsin University.

McCrudden, C. (ed.) (1990), *Regulation and Deregulation*, Oxford University Press, Oxford.

McEldowney, John F. (2002), *Public Law*, Sweet & Maxwell's Textbook Series, Sweet & Maxwell, London.

Meier, K.J. (1985), *Regulation: Politics, Bureaucracy, and Economy*, St. Martin's Press, New York.

Menon, N.R.M. and N.G. Mysore (1970), *Law Relating to Government Control over Private Enterprise*, Eastern Book Company, Lucknow & Delhi.

Mishra, Ramesh (1981), *Society and Social Policy*, MacMillan, London.

Mitchell, B., and I. Vogelsang (1991), *Telecommunications Pricing: Theory and Practice*, Cambridge University Press, Cambridge, U.K.

Mitnick, B.M. (1980), *The Political Economy of Regulation*, Colombia University Press, New York.

Moran, M. (2003), *The British Regulatory State: High Modernism and Hyper Innovation,* Oxford.

Moran, Michael and Tony Prosser (ed.) (1994), *Privatization and Regulatory Change in Europe*, Open University Press, Buckingham.

Morawetz, David (1977), *Twenty Five Years of Economic Development 1950-1975*, Washington.

Morgan, K.O. (1984), *Labour in Power 1945-51*, Larendon.

Mund, Vernon A. (1960), *Government and Business*, 3rd edn., Harper & Bros. Publishers, New York.

Nayak, R.K. (1991), *Consumer Protection Law in India*, Indian Law Institute, N.M. Tripathi Pvt. Ltd., Mumbai.

Newbery, David M. (2001), *Privatization, Restructuring, and Regulation of Network Utilities*, MIT Press, Cambridge, MA.

Noll, R. (ed.) (1985), *Regulatory Policy and Social Sciences*, Berkeley Calif.

OECD (2001), *Restructuring Public Utilities for Competition*, Washington, D.C.

Offe, Claus (1984), *Contradictions of the Welfare State*, Hutchinson & Co. Ltd., London.

Ogus, A. (2001), *Regulation, Economics and the Law*, Edward Elgar.

Ogus, A. (2005), *Regulation: Legal Form and Economic Theory*, Hart Publishing, Oxford.

Organization for Economic Cooperation and Development (1999), *Regulatory Reform in the United States,* OECD: Paris.

Osborne, David and Ted Gaebler (1992), *Reinventing Government: How the Entrepreneurial Spirit the Public Sector,* School House, Addison-Wesley.

Oyen, Else (ed.) (1986), *Comparing Welfare States and their Futures*, Gower Publishing Company Ltd., England.

Padhi, P.K. (2007), *Labour and Industrial Laws*, Prentice-Hall of India Pvt. Ltd., New Delhi.

Palast, Greg, Jerrold Oppenheim, and Theo MacGregor (2003), *Democracy and Regulation — How the Public can Govern Privatised Essential Services*, Pluto Press, London.

Pandey, J.N. (2003), *Constitutional Law of India*, Central Law Agency.

Pares, R. (1953), *George III and the Politicians*, Oxford.

Parris, H. (1965), *Government and the Railways in Nineteenth Century Britain*, Routledge & Kegan Paul.

Parris, Henry (1969), *Constitutional Bureaucracy — The Development of British Central Administration since the Eighteenth Century*, George Allen & Unwin Ltd., London.

Pfaller, Alfred Gough, Ian and Therboun Goran (1991), *Welfare Statism and International Competition: The Lesson of the Case Studies*, MacMillan, London.

Phillips, Charles F. Jr. (1993), *The Regulation of Public Utilities*, Arlington, VA: Public Utilities Reports.

Pierson, Christopher and Francis G. Castles (ed.) (2000), *The Welfare State: A Reader*, Polity Press, Cambridge, UK.

Prakash, Aseem and Jeffrey A. Hart (eds.) (1999), *Globalisation and Governance*, Routledge, London & New York.

Privatization Lessons Learned by State and Local Governments, GAO/GGD-97-48; US General Accounting Office, Washington, DC, 1997.

Prosser, T. (1997), *Law and the Regulators*, Clarendon Press, Oxford.

Prosser, T. (1986), *Nationalised Industries and Public Control: Legal Constitutional and Political Issues*, Basil Blackwell Inc., Oxford, U.K.

Rabin, Robert (1986), *Federal Regulation in Historical Perspective*, Leland Stanford Junior University.

Ramanathan, K. and Shahid Hasan (2005), *Privatisation of Electricity Distribution — The Orissa Experience*, Tata Energy Research Institute, TERI, New Delhi.

Rao, Rajyalakshmi (2008), *Consumer Is King!!*, Universal Law Publishing Co. Pvt. Ltd.

Rao, S.L. (2004), *Governing Power — A New Institution of Governance: The Experience with Independent Regulation of Electricity*, the Energy and Resources Institute, TERI.

Rauch Basil (1975), *The History of the New Deal 1933-1938*, Octagon Books.

Razdan, Dheeraj (2009), *A Treatise on the Law of Insurance*, Cyber Tech Publications, New Delhi.

Razdan, Dheeraj (2009), *Insurance: Principles, Applications and Practice*, Cyber Tech Publications, New Delhi.

Redford, E.S. (1952), *Administration of National Economic Control*, MacMillan Co., New York.

Redlich, J. and F. Hirst (1903), *Local Government in England*, MacMillan & Co., London.

Rhoads, Steven E. (1985), *The Economist's View of the World—Government, Markets and Public Policy*, Cambridge University Press, Cambridge.

Richardson and Genn (1994), *Reviewing Judicial Review: Administrative Law and Government Action*, Oxford: Oxford University Press.

Ripley, R. and G. Franklin (1986), *Policy Implementation and Bureaucracy*, 2nd ed., Dorsey Press, Chicago.

Roberts, D. (1960), *Victorian Origins of the British Welfare State*, New Haven.

Robinson, Edgar E. (1955), *The Roosevelt Leadership 1933-1945*, J.B. Lippincott Co., Philadelphia & New York.

Robson, W.A. (1951), *Justice and Administrative Law,* Stevens & Sons, London.

Sankhdher, M.M. (1985), *The Welfare State*, Deep & Deep Publications Pvt. Ltd., Delhi.

Sarkar, S.K. and Vivek Sharma (eds.), *Legal Aspects of Regulation in South Asia*, TERI, New Delhi, 2002.

Sarkar, S.K. and Kaushik, Deb (eds.), *Regulation in Infrastructure Services: Progress and the Way Forward,* Tata Energy Research Institute, TERI, New Delhi, 2001.

Sarkar, S.K. and Leena Srivastava (eds.) (2002), *Reforms in the Infrastructure Sectors: Next Steps*, Tata Energy Research Institute, TERI, New Delhi.

Sathe, S.P. (2004), *Administrative Law*, Seventh Edition, Lexis Nexis, Butterworths.

Savas, E.S. (1977), *Alternatives for Delivery Public Services toward Improved Performance*; Westview Press, Boulder.

Scharpf, F.W. and Schmidt, V.A. (2000), *Welfare and Work in the Open Economy: Diverse Responses to Common Challenges*, Oxford University Press, Oxford.

Schuck, Peter H. (1994), *Foundations of Administrative Law*, Oxford University Press, New York.

Schwartz, B. and Wade (1972), *Legal Control of Government: Administrative Law in Britain and the United States*, Clarendon Press, Oxford.

Schwartz, Bernard (1958), *An Introduction to American Administrative Law*, Oceana Publications Inc., New York, USA.

Self, P. (1985), *Political Theories of Modern Government*, Allen & Unwin, London.

Self, Peter (1993), *Government by the Market?*, London, U.K.: Westview Press.

Self, Peter (2000), *Rolling Back the Market — Economic Dogma and Political Choice*, MacMillan Press Ltd., London.

Shepherd, W.G. and C. Wilcox (1979), *Public Policies Toward Business*, 6th ed., Homewood, IL: Irwin.

Shukla, V.N. (1994), *Constitution of India*, Eastern Book Co., Lucknow.

Singh, Avatar (2002), *Law of Contract and Specific Relief*, 8th edn., Eastern Book Co., Lucknow.

Singh, Servendra (2004), *Licensing, Regulation and Monitoring or Telecommunication in India*, Indian Institute of Public Administration, New Delhi.

Sisson, C.H. (1959), *Spirit of British Administration*, Faber & Faber Ltd.

Skowronek, Stephen (1982), *Building a New American State: The Expansion of National Administrative Capacities 1877-1920*, Cambridge University Press.

Slack, Kathleen M. (1966), *Social Administration and the Citizen*, Michael Joseph, London.

Spulber, Daniel F. (1989), *Regulation and Markets*, The MIT Press, Cambridge, Massachusetts, London, UK.

Srinivasan, M.N. (2002), *Principles of Insurance Law*, 7th edn., Wadhwa and Co., Nagpur.

Srivastava, Leena and S.K. Sarkar (eds.) (1999), *Transition to a Liberalized Environment — Experiences and Issues in Regulation*, TERI, New Delhi.

Stainslaw, Joseph, Yergin (1999), *The Commanding Heights: The Battle between Government and Marketplace that is Remaking the Modern World*, Touchstone.

Stern, Jon and John Cubbin (2005), *Regulatory Effectiveness: The Impact of Regulation and Regulatory Governance Arrangements on Electricity Industry Outcomes*, World Bank, Washington, D.C.

Sundar, S. and S.K. Sarkar (2000), *Framework for Infrastructure Regulation*, Tata Energy Research Institute, New Delhi, India.

Sunder, S., M.P. Ram Mohan and Satnam Singh Kalra (eds.) (2005), *Regulatory Law in Practice — Compendium of Orders in Electricity and Telecom Sectors*, Tata Energy Research Institute, TERI, New Delhi.

Sunstein, Cass R. (1997), *Free Markets and Social Justice*, Oxford University Press, New York.

Taxmann's Insurance Law Manual (2009), 7th Edition, Taxmann Allied Services (P.) Ltd.

Taylor, A.J.P. (1965), *English History 1914-1945*, Oxford University Press, London.

The Changing Role of Government: Administrative Structure and Reforms (1992), Proceedings of a Commonwealth Roundtable, Sydney, Australia.

Thoenes, Piet (ed.) (1966), *The Elite in the Welfare State*, Faber & Faber, London, and Free Press, New York.

Titmuss, Richard M. (1968), *Commitment to Welfare State*, Allen & Unwin, London.

Titmuss, Richard M. (1963), *Essays on 'the Welfare State'*, Allen & Unwin, London.

Train, Kenneth E. (1991), *Optimal Regulation: The Economic Theory of Natural Monopoly*, Cambridge, Massachusetts: The MIT Press.

United Nations Conference on Trade and Development, Model Law: the Relationship between a Competition and Regulatory Bodies, Including Sectoral Regulators, TD/B/COM. 2/CPL/23 including Corr. 1,18 June, 2001.

Universal's Insurance Laws (2005), Universal Law Publishing Co. Pvt. Ltd.

Vecchino, Giorgio del (1953), *Justice*, Philosophical Library, New York.

Vijaykumar, A. (2009), *Indian Insurance Sector in Liberalised Era*, Mahamaya Publishing House, New Delhi.

Viscusi, W. Kip, John M. Vernon, and Joseph, E. Harrington, Jr. (2000), *Economics of Regulation and Antitrust*, MIT Press, Cambridge, MA.

Vittas, Dimitri (2004), *Insurance Regulation in Jordan: New Rules-Old System*, World Bank, Washington, D.C.

Vogel, D. (1986), *National Style of Regulation*, Cornell Press, London.

Wade and Forsyth (2005), *Administrative Law*, 9th edn., Oxford University Press.

Webb, Sidney and Beatrice (1922), *English Prisons under Local Government*, Longmans, Green & Co., London.

Webb, Sidney and Beatrice (1922), *Statutory Authorities for Special Purposes,* Longmans, Green & Co.

Whincop, Michael J. (2003), *From Bureaucracy to Business Enterprise: Legal and Policy Issues in the Transformation of Government Services*, Ashgate, Hampshire.

Williams, O.C. (1948), *Historical Development of Private Bill Procedure and Standing Orders in the House of Commons*, His Majesty's Stationery Office.

Williamson, Oliver E. (1985), *The Economic Institutions of Capitalism*, Free Press, New York.

Wilson, James Q. (1989), *Bureaucracy*, Basic Book Inc., Harper Collin Publishers.

Yardley, D.C.M. (1986), *Principles of Administrative Law*, 2nd edn., Butterworth, London.

Articles

"Address of the Prime Minister in Chief Ministers Conference on the Working of Electricity Regulatory Authority", *The Hindustan Times*, dated 29.05.2007, p. 1.

"Consultation Paper on Revision of the Insurance Act, 1938 and the Insurance Regulatory and Development Authority Act, 1999", Law Commission of India, 2003.

"M'rashtra to Set-up Housing Regulator", *Deccan Herald*, April 5, 2008, p. 13.

"Regulatory Body for TV: Minister", *The Hindustan Times*, July 28, 2009.

"Reinventing Clinton", *Wall Street Journal*, Eastern Edition, New York, December 2, 1992, p. 1.

"Umpire not Empire — Maharashtra is Set to Acquire a Housing Regulator", *The Times of India*, April 5, 2008, p. 20.

"What You Did Not Know About Your Insurance Company", *Consumer Voice*, May-June 2006, pp. 8-13.

Achamma, Samuel (2000), *"Insurance: The Indian Experience"*, Reserve Bank of India Occasional Papers, 21(2-3), Monsoon & Winter, pp. 349-73.

Agarwal, O.P. and S.P. Paul (2001), "Framework for Independent Regulation in India: An Overview" in S.K. Sarkar and Kaushik Deb (eds.) *Regulation in Infrastructure Services: Progress and Way Forward*, TERI, pp. 3-16.

Agarwala, C.B. (1959), "Administrative Regulation of Business in India", *Journal of the Indian Law Institute*, No. 1, 1959, pp. 139-49.

Ahluwalia, Harjeet (1999), "Insurance: Beyond 2001", *Pioneer*, June 1, p. 7.

Ahuja, Narender L. (2006), "Community Derivatives Market in India: Development, Regulation and Future Prospects", *International Research Journal of Finance and Economics*, Issue 2, pp. 153-162.

Ahuja, Rajeev (2004), "Insurance: Over the Transition", *Economic and Political Weekly*, 39(32), August 7, pp. 3569-3571.

Alagh, Yoginder K. (2009), "Regulating Regulators", *The Indian Express*, June 5, p. 10.

Aman, Alfred C. Jr., "Administrative Law for a New Century", in Aseem Prakash and Jeffery A. Hart (eds.), *Globalisation and Governance*, Routledge, London & New York, pp. 267-88.

Anonymous (1991), "Government *vs*. Business: The Endless Struggle", *Financial World*; June 25, 160, 13; pp. 48-54.

Ansari, H. (2006), "Insurance Reforms — A Journey without End", *IRDA Journal*, February, pp. 21-24.

Antonelli, Angela (1998), "Return to the Regs", *Orange County Business Journal*, Newport Beach, April 20, Vol. 21, Iss. 16, p. 34.

Arnold, Peri E. (2007), "The Brownlaw Committee, Regulation, and the Presidency", *Public Administration Review*, Vol. 67, No. 6, November/December, pp.1030-1040.

Asher, Mukul and Deepa Vasudevan, "The Role of Pension Regulators", *Margin*, Vol. 38, No. 1, pp. 1-12.

Baldwin, Robert and Black Julia (2007), "Really Responsive Regulation", *LSE Law, Society and Economic Working Papers*, 15, Department of Law, London, School of Economic and Political Science, London.

Bartle, Ian and Peter Vass (2007), "Self-Regulation within the Regulatory State: Towards a New Regulatory Paradigm", *Public Administration*, Vol. 85, No. 4, pp. 885-905.

Bartle, Ian (2006), "Political Participation and Market Citizenship in a Global Economy: The European Union in Comparative Perspective", *International Journal of Public Administration*, 29, pp. 415-436.

Baswan, B.S. (1993), "Economic Deregulation and Civil Service Training in India", *The Administration*, Vol. XXXVIII, July-September, pp. 41-44.

Bauer, Johannes M. (2005), "Regulation and State Ownership: Conflicts and Complementarities in EU Telecommunications" *Annals of Public and Cooperative Economics*, 76(2), June, pp.151-77.

Bautista, Lilia R. (2003), "Challenges to Effective Regulation", *Philippine Journal of Public Administration*, Vol. XLVII, No. 1-4, January-October, pp. 371-78.

Bayne, P. (1988), "Administrative Law and the New Managerialism in Public Administration", *Australian Law Journal*, 62(10), pp. 1040-45.

Beloff, M. (1988), "The Boundaries of Judicial Review", in Jeffrey Jowell and Dawn Oliver (eds.), *New Directions in Judicial Review*, Stevens, London, pp. 5-22.

Berg, Stanford (2006), "Institutional Requirements for Second Generation Infrastructure Reform: Processes and Performance in Developing Countries", *PURC Working Paper,* Department of Economics, University of Florida.

Bertelli, Anthony (2004), "Building the Administrative State", *Public Administrative Review*, 64(4), July/August, pp. 502-04.

Black, J. (2002), "*Critical Reflections on Regulation*", Discussion Paper No. 4, London: Centre for Analysis of Risk and Regulation, London School of Economics and Political Science.

Black, Julia (1999), "Using Rules Effectively" in C. McCrudden (ed.), *Regulation and Deregulation*, Oxford: Oxford University Press, pp. 95-122.

Böllhoff, D. (2002), "The New Regulatory Regime — The Institutional Design of Telecommunications Regulation at the National Level", in Héritier, A. (ed.), *Common Goods: Reinventing European and International Governance,* Lanham, Rowman & Littlefield Publishers, pp. 235-62.

Borrie, Sir Gordon (1989), "The Regulation of Public and Private Power", *Public Law,* Winter, p. 552.

Brady, David, Jason Beckfield and Martin Seeleib-kaiser (2005), "Globalization and the Welfare State", *American Sociological Review*, Vol. 70, No. 6, December, pp. 921-48.

Breyer, Stephen (1994), "Regulation and its Reforms", in Peter H. Schuck (ed.), *Foundations of Administrative Law*, Oxford University Press, New York, pp. 17-21.

Briggs, Asa (2000), "The Welfare State in Historical Perspective" in Christopher Pierson and Francis G. Castles (eds.), *The Welfare State,* Polity Press, Cambridge, UK, pp. 18-31.

Brownbridge, Martin and Kirkpatrick, Colin (2000), "Financial Regulation in Developing Countries", *Journal of Development Studies,* 37(1), October, pp.1-24.

Cameron, Wayne (2004), "Public Accountability: Effectiveness, Equity, Ethics", *Australian Journal of Public Administration*, 63(4), December, pp. 59-67.

Cananea, Giacinto della (2002), "The Regulation of Public Services in Italy", *International Review of Administrative Sciences,* Vol. 68, No. 1, March, pp. 73-93.

Chakraborty, Moloy Kr. (2006), "Indian Insurance Sector: A Post-Globalisation Scenario", *Journal of Economic and Social Development,* Vol. II, No. 1, January.-June 2006, pp. 20-29.

Chakravarthy, Nikhil (1993), "Globalisaion — Hazards of Mantra", *The Hindustan Times*, December 25.

Chatterjee, Anup (2006), "Looking Back, Looking Ahead — The Ushering of a Silent Revolution in Indian Insurance", *IRDA Journal*, February, pp. 25-28.

Chatterjee, Biswajeet and Ram Pratap Sinha (2006), "Regulatory Reforms and The Indian Capital Market", *Journal of Economic and Social Development*, Vol. II, No.1, January-June, pp. 1-9.

Chauhan, Chetan (2009), "Government to Regulate Fee Structure of Private Varsities", *The Hindustan Times*, February 9, pp. 1 and 14.

Chowdary, T.H. (2002), "Telecom Regulation and Consumer Welfare", *Economic and Political Weekly*, 37(43), 26 October, pp. 4354-356.

Chowdary, T.H. (2000), "Regulation of Telecom in India", *ASCI Journal of Management*, 29(2), March, pp. 64-73.

Christensen, Tom and Per Laegreid (2007), "The Whole-of-Government Approach to Public Sector Reform", *Public Administration Review*, Vol. 67, No. 6, pp. 1059-66.

Cohen, Stanley E. (1981), "The Ronald Reagan Era: Another New Beginning", *Journal of Advertising* (pre-1986); 10, 2, pp. 3-8.

Cook, P. and Minogue, M. (2002), "Privatization, Regulation and Competition in Developing Countries: Introduction", *Annals of Public and Cooperative Economics*, 73(4), December, pp. 485-92.

Cook, P. (2002), "Competition and its Regulation: Key Issues", *Annals of Public and Cooperative Economics*, 73(4), December, pp. 541-58.

Craig, P.P. (1993), "Privatisation and Economic Neutrality of the Constitution", *Public Law*, p. 465.

Crandall, Robert W. (1988.1989), "Regulatory Reform: Are We Ready for the Next Phase?", *The Brookings Review*, Winter, 7(1), pp. 18-19.

D'Souza, Errol (2000), "Prudential Regulation in Indian Banking", *Economic and Political Weekly*, 35(5), 29 January, pp. 287-98.

Dabas, J.C. (1999), "The Insurance Sector — Privatisation of", *CBT Bulletin*, 7(6), June, pp. 6-7.

Daintith, T. (1985), "The Executive Power Today: Bargaining and Economic Control" in Jeffrey Jowell and Dawn Oliver (eds.), *The Changing Constitution*, Oxford University Press, Oxford, pp. 174 *et seq*.

Das Gupta, Gurudas (1996), "Insurance Sector: Move in the Wrong Direction", *The Statesman*, November 7, p. 8.

Dash, Abani Kumar (1997), "Future of Capitalism", *The Hindustan Times*, February 28, p. 11.

Dave, B.B. (2008), "Policy Framework for Regulation of Courier Services", *Economic and Political Weekly*, January 19-25, Vol. XLIII, No. 3, pp. 24-27.

Davis, Kenneth Culp (1969), "A New Approach to Delegation", *U. Chicago L. Rev.*, 36, p. 713.

Davis, Peter (2007), "The Significance of Parliamentary Procedures in Control of the Executive: A Case Study: The Passage of Part 1 of the Legislative and Regulatory Reforms Act, 2006", *Public Law*, Winter, pp. 677-700.

Dawn, Oliver (1987), "Is the Ultra Vires Rule the Basis of Judicial Review", *Public Law,* Winter, p. 543.

Derham, David P. (1959), "Some Constitutional Problems arising under Part XIII of the Indian Constitution", *Journal of the Indian Law Institute*, Vol. 2, pp. 523-63.

Dhar, A.N. (1994), "Liberalisation — What is Wrong?", *The Hindustan Times,* December 29.

Diver, Colin S. (1981), "Policy-making Paradigms in Administrative Law" *Harvard Law Review,* Vol. 95, No. 2, December, pp. 393-434.

Document (2007), "Extracts of the Draft of the Proposed Broadcasting Service Regulation Bill, 2007", *Social Action — A Quarterly Review of Social Trends*, Vol. 57, No. 4, October–December, p. 426.

Dolowitz, David P. (2006), "Bring Back the States: Correcting for the Omissions of Globalisation", *International Journal of Public Administration*, 29, pp. 263-80.

Donlan, Thomas G. (2004), "Architect of Change", *Barron's*, 84, 24, June 14, p. 38.

Dowling, James H. (1990), "Balkanizing America", *Chief Executive,* 62, October, pp. 46-48 .

Drueker, Peter, F. (1995), "Really Reinventing Government", *SPAN*, December, pp. 11-15.

Eason, Henry (1984), "Deregulation: Dream Deferred", *Nation's Business* (pre-1986), February, 72, 2, pp. 24-26.

Espos, Edna A. (2003), "Institutions, Regulation and Performance: The Case of the Philippine Telecommunication", *Philippine Journal of Public Administration*, Vol. XLVII, Nos.1-4, January-October, pp. 38-61.

Fels, Allan A.O. (2004), "Regulating Markets: Marketing Regulation", *Australian Journal of Public Administration*, 63(4), December, pp. 29-36.

Frame, David E. (2001), "Insurance and Community Welfare", *Journal of Urban Economics,* 49(2), March, pp. 267-84.

Galal Ahmed and Bharat Nauriyal (1995), "Regulating Telecommunications in Developing Countries — Outcomes, Incentives, and Commitment", *Policy Research Working Paper 1520,* WB, October.

Garg, Manish Chandra (2001), "New Paradigms in Indian Insurance Industry", *Yojana*, Vol. 45, April, pp. 27-32.

Ghosh, Arun (1999), "Insurance, Privatisation and Public Interest", *Mainstream,* 37(50), December 4, pp. 3-4.

Ghosh, Shailendra Nath (1998), "Insurance Reform or De-reform?", *Mainstream,* Annual, pp. 125-26.

Ghosh, Shailendra Nath (1999), "Insurance Reforms", *Pioneer*, January 20, p. 9.

Gill, Peter (2002), "Policing and Regulation: What is the Difference?", *Social and Legal Studies*, 11(4), December, pp. 521-46.

Gilland, T., "The Regulatory Regime of the Electricity Industry in England and Wales", in Sturm, R. and Wilks, S. (eds.) (1996), *Wettbewerbspolitik und die Ordnung der Elektrizitätswirtschaft in Deutschland und Großbritannien,* Baden-Baden, Nomos, pp. 239-60.

Glaeser E.L. and A. Shleifer (2003), "The Rise of the Regulatory State", *Journal of Economic Literature*, Vol. XLI, pp. 401-25.

Gonzalez, Eduardo T. (2003), "Regulation Campaign Finance in Philippines: Limits and Challenges", *Philippine Journal of Public Administration*, Vol. XLVII, Nos. 1-4, January-October, pp. 276-301.

Gore, Albert Jr. (1987), "A Senator Surveys Some Utility Issues", *Public Utilities*, Fortnightly, 119(3), February 5, pp. 11-14.

Goyal, Ashima (2005), *"Regulation and De-regulation of the Stock Market in India"*, September 8, *www. igidr.ac.in/~ashima*

Green, Richard (1999), "Checks and Balances in Utility Regulation — The U.K. Experience", Note No. 185 in *Public Policy for the Private Sector*, Washington, D.C.: World Bank Group, May.

Guislain, Pierre (1992), "*Divestiture of State Enterprise*", World Bank Technical Paper, No. 186.

Gunningham, Neil (2009), "The New Collaborative Environmental Governance: The Localization of Regulation", *Journal of Law and Society*, Vol. 36, No. 1, March, pp. 145-66.

Guria, R.C. (2008), "Laws, Rules, Regulations Governing Marine Insurance", *IRDA Journal,* March, pp. 22-28.

Hayek, Friedrich Von (2000), "The Meaning of the Welfare State", in Christopher Pierson and Francis G. Castles, (eds.), *The Welfare State*, Polity Press, Cambridge, UK, pp. 90-95.

Held, David (2000), "Regulating Globalisation?: The Reinvention of Politics", *International Journal of Sociology,* 15(2), June, pp. 394-408.

Henisz, Witold J., Bennet A. Zelner and Mauro F. Guillen (2005), "The Worldwide Diffusion of Market-Oriented Infrastructure Reforms, 1977-1999", *American Sociological Review,* Vol. 70, No. 6, December, pp. 871-97.

Héritier, A. and Schmidt, S.K. (2000), "After Liberalisation: Public Interest Services and Employment", in Scharpf, F.W. and Schmidt, V.A., *Welfare and Work in the Open Economy: Diverse Responses to Common Challenges in Twelve Countries*, Oxford: Oxford University Press, pp. 554-97.

Hogwood, B.W. (1990), "Developments in Regulatory Agencies in Britain", *International Review of Administrative Sciences,* 56, pp. 595-612.

Hollander, Robyn (2006), "National Competition Policy, Regulatory Reform and Australian Federalism", *Australian Journal of Public Administration*, 65(2), June, pp. 33-47.

Hossain, Kamal (2001), "Review and Appeal of Regulators' Decisions in the South Asian Context," in S.K. Sarkar (ed.), *Proceedings of the SAFIR Workshop on Regulatory Strategy*, Tata Energy Research Institute, New Delhi, India, pp. 17-24.

Humphreys Peter (2006), "Globalisation, Regulatory Competition, and EU Policy Transfer in the Telecom and Broadcasting Sectors", *International Journal of Public Administration*, 29, pp. 305-34.

Hutchinson, Alan (1990), "Mice under a Chair: Democracy, Courts and the Administrative State", *University of Toronto Law Journal*, 40(3), pp. 374-404.

Hwang, Edward (1997), "Political Development, Political Conflict and Regulation Policies", *Chinese Public Administration Review,* 6(3), June, pp. 95-134.

Jacint, Jordana and David Levi-Faur (2006), "Toward a Latin American Regulatory State? The Diffusion of Autonomous Regulatory Agencies Across Countries and Sectors", *International Journal of Public Administration,* 29, pp. 335-66.

Jacob, Scott H. (2000), "The Golden Age of Regulation", *Organization of Economic Cooperation and Development*, Paris, November 13.

Jacob, Scott H. (1999), "The Second Generation of Regulatory Reforms", *Paper Presented at IMF Conference on Second Generation Reforms*, Nov. 8-9, Washington, D.C.

Jacobs, Scott (2004), "Governance of Asian Utilities: New Regulators Struggle in Difficult Environments", *The Governance Brief*, ADB, Issue 10.

Jain, Anil Kumar and Gupta Parul (2008), "Globalisation: The Indian Experience", *Mainstream*, 46(8), February 8, pp. 15-21.

James, Oliver (2000), "Regulation Inside Government: Public Interest Justifications and Regulatory Failures", *Public Administration,* 78(2), pp. 327-43.

Jampala, Rajesh C. and Bh. Venkateswara Rao (2005), "Investment Portfolio and Performance of the LIC", *The Journal of the Institute of Public Enterprise*, Vol. 28, Nos. 3 and 4, July-September, October-December, pp. 166-80.

Johnston, Van R. (2007), Paul Seidenstat, "Contracting Out Government Services: Privatisation at the Millennium", *International Journal of Public Administration*, 30, pp. 231-47.

Kapoor, Sheetal (2008), "Banking Ombudsman Scheme", *Yojana*, December, pp. 81-84.

Kessides, Ioannis, N. (2005), "Infrastructure Privatization and Regulation: Promises and Perils", *World Bank Research Observer,* 20(1), Spring, pp. 81-108.

Klein, Michael, and Neil Roger (1994), "Back to the Future: The Potential in Infrastructure Privatization", Note No. 30 in *Public Policy for the Private Sector,* Washington, D.C. World Bank, November.

Klein, Michael, and Philip Gray (1997), "Competition in Network Industries —Where and How to Introduce It", Note No. 104 in *Public Policy for the Private Sector*, Washington, D.C.: World Bank Group.

Knight-John, Malathy, Shantha Jayasinghe and Andren Perumal (2003), "Regulatory Impact Assessment in Sri Lanka: The Bridges that have to be Crossed", *Philippine Journal of Public Administration*, Vol. XLVII, Nos. 1-4, January-October, pp. 173-218.

Knill. C. (2001), "Reforming Transport Policy in Britain: Concurrence with Europe but Separate Development", in Héritier, A.; Kerwer, D.; Knill, C.; Lehmkuhl, D.; Teutsch, M. and Douillet, A.C. (eds.), *Differential Europe: New Opportunities and Restrictions for Policy-Making in Member States,* Lanham: Rowman & Littlefield Publishers, pp. 113-87.

Kodwani, Devendra G. (2000), "Economic Regulation of Utility Industries", *Economic and Political Weekly*, 35 (30), 22 July, pp. 2657-61.

Korosec, Ronnie LaCouurse (2002), "Non-Profit Contracting from 1982-1997: A Comparison of Sector Based Factors", *International Journal of Public Administration*, 25(4), pp. 423-39.

Krishnamurthy, Gnanasundaram (2006), "The Spirit of the Law-Read the Meaning, not the Words", *IRDA Journal*, February, p. 29.

Krisnamurthy, S. (2005), "Insurance Industry in India: Structure, Performance and Future Challenges", *Vikalpa*, 30(3), July-September, pp. 93-105.

Legaspi, Perla E. (2003), "Local Regulatory Governance in the Philippines Focus on Quezon City", *Philippine Journal of Public Administration*, Vol. XLVII, Nos.1-4, January-October, pp.1-37.

Levi Faur, David (2005), "The Global Diffusion of Regulatory Capitalism", *Annuls of the American Academy of Political and Social Science*, Vol. 598, pp. 12-32.

Levine, Richard (1989), "Unfinished Business: Reagan's Regulatory 'Relief'", *Management Review*, 78, 3, March, pp. 18-23.

Lewis, Norman (1994), *"Reviewing Change in Government, New Public Management and Next Steps", Public Law*, Spring, pp. 105-113.

Liou, Kuotsai Tom (2007), "Changes and Challenges in Regulatory Reform", *International Journal of Public Administration*, Vol. 30, No. 3, pp. 271-88.

Macmillan, Rory (2005), "Reflections on Regulation and Dispute Resolution in the Indian Telecommunication Sector", *Journal of the Indian Law Institute*, 47(1), January-March, pp. 29-52.

Majone, G. (1997), "From the Positive to The Regulatory State: Causes and Consequences of the Changes in Modes of Governance", *Journal of Public Policy*, 17(2), pp. 139-67.

Majone, G. (1999), "The Regulatory State and its Legitimacy Problems", *West European Politics*, 22(1), 1999, pp. 1-24.

Majone, Giandomenico (1996), "Regulation and its Modes: The European Experience", *International Journal of Public Administration*, 19(9), pp. 1597-1637.

Majone, Giandomenico (2003), "The Internationalization of Regulation: Implications for Developing Countries", *Philippine Journal of Public Administration*, Vol. XLVII, Nos. 1-4, January-October, pp. 329-54.

Markandeya, A. (1998), "The Cost of Environmental Regulation in Asia: Command and Control *versus* Market-based Instruments", *Asian Development Review,* 16(1), pp. 1-30.

Marshall, T.H. (1972), "Value Problems of Welfare-Capitalism", *Journal of Social Policy*, Vol. I, Issue 1, January, pp. 15-32.

McAuslan, J.P.W.B. (1988), "Public Law and Public Choice", *Modern Law Review,* 51(6), pp. 681-705.

McCraw, Thomas K. (1975), "Regulation in America: A Review", *Business History Review*, Vol. 49, No. 2, Summer, pp. 159-83.

McCubbins, M.D., R.G. Noll and B.R. Weingast (1987), "Administrative Procedures as Instruments of Political Control", *Journal of Law, Economics and Organisation,* 3, pp. 243-77.

McDowell, Moore (1997), "Amending the Competition Act: The Implications of Regulation and Public Ownership", *Administration,* 45(1), Spring, pp.72-90.

McGraw, Thomas K. (1975), "Regulation in America: A Review Article", *Business History Review,* Vol. 49, No. 2, Summer, pp. 159-83.

Meier, Henk Erik (2008), "Independent Regulatory Bodies and Impossible Jobs: The Failure of German Public Service Broadcasting Regulation", *Public Administration*, 86(1), pp. 133-48.

Mendoja, Villamejor Maria Fe (2003), "Electricity Rate Regulation and Public Interest: The Case of the Energy Regulatory Board and Manila Electric Company", *Philippine Journal of Public Administration,* 47(1-4), January-October, pp. 103-56.

Mendoza, Xavier and Alfred Vernis (2008), "The Changing Role of Governments and the Emergence of the Relational State", *Corporate Governance*, Vol. 8, No. 4, pp. 389-96.

Miller, William H. (1988), "What's Ahead in Regulation?", *Industry Week,* 237, 8, October 17, pp. 70-74.

Minocha, O.P. (2007), "Revamping the Role of Government as a Regulator", *Indian Journal of Public Administration*, Vol. LIII, No. 3, July-September, pp. 398-408.

Minogue, K. (1986), "Loquocentric Society and its Critics", *Government and Opposition*, 21, pp. 338- 61.

Minogue, M. (2002), "Governance-based Analysis of Regulation", *Annals of Public and Cooperative Economics,* 73 (4), December, pp.649-66.

Minogue, Martin and Ledivina Carino (2006), "Regulatory Governance in Developing Countries", in Minogue, Martin and Ledivina Carino, *Regulatory Governance in Developing Countries*, Edward Elgar Publishing Ltd., pp. 3-16.

Minogue, Martin (2003), "Regulatory Governance and the Improvement of Public Services", *Philippine Journal of Public Administration*, Vol. XLVII, Nos. 1-4, January-October, pp. 157-72.

Mishra, R.K. (1995), "The Market and Its Regulation in India: A Study in Operation of the Monopolies and Restrictive Trade Practices Act", *Indian Journal of Economics*, 75(299), April, pp. 505-525.

Moore, John A. (2002), "Regulatory Burden Won't Go Away", *World Refining*, 12, 10, December, p. 44.

Moran, M. (2001), "Not Steering but Drowning: Policy Catastrophe and the Regulatory State", *The Political Quarterly*, 72(4), pp. 414-27.

Moran, M. (2002), "Understanding the Regulatory State", *British Journal of Political Science*, 32, pp. 391-413.

Mulgan, Richard (2006), "Government Accountability for Outsourced Services", *Australian Journal of Public Administration*, 65(2), June, pp. 48-58.

Muller, Kobus and Frederick M. Uys (2003), "Regulatory Governance of the Water Sector in South Africa", *Philippine Journal of Public Administration*, Vol. XLVII, Nos. 1-4, January-October, pp. 219-50.

Muralidharan, Sukumar (2007), "Broadcast Regulation: Narrow Consultation, Indifferent Results", *Economic and Political Weekly*, 42(37), 15 September, pp. 3690-692.

Muralidharan, Sukumar (2007), "Broadcast Regulation and Public Right to Know", *Economic and Political Weekly*, 42(9), 3 March, pp. 743-51.

Muralidharan, Y.G. (2007), "Popularise Consumer Grievance Redressal Systems", *The Indian Express*, Bangalore, November 26, p. 2.

Murshed, S. Mansoob (2003), "Transaction Cost Politics Rent Seeking, Institutions for Commitment and Regulation", *Philippine Journal of Public Administration*, Vol. XLVII, Nos. 1-4, January-October, pp. 62-79.

Nagarajan, N. (2003), "Regulation as an Augmenter of Competition: The Indian Experience with the Banking Sector", *South Asian Economic Journal*, 4(2), July-December, pp. 205-20.

Nair, S.K.N. (2008), "Electricity Regulation in India: Recent Reforms and their Impact", *Margin — The Journal of Applied Economic Research*, Vol. 2, No.1, January-March, pp. 87-144.

Noll, R. (1987), "The Political Foundations of Regulatory Policy" in K. McCubbins and T. Sullivan (eds.), *Congress*, Cambridge: Cambridge University Press, pp. 479-82.

Ogus, A. (2002), "Regulatory Institutions and Structures", *Annals of Public and Cooperative Economics*, 73(4), pp. 627-48.

Ogus, A. (2004), "*The Importance of Legal Infrastructure for Regulation (and Deregulation) in Developing Countries*", Working Paper No. 66, CRC, University of Manchester, Manchester.

Ogus, Anthony (2003), "The Importance of legal Infrastructure for Regulation (and Deregulation) in Developing Countries", *Philippine Journal of Public Administration,* Vol. XLVII, Nos. 1-4, January-October, pp. 251-75.

Oliver, Daniel (1989), "The Market Doesn't have to Work Perfectly to Work Better than Government", *Executive Speeches*; November, 4, 4; pp. 6-9.

Oyen, Else (1986), "Identifying the Future of the Welfare State" in Else Oyen (ed.), *Comparing Welfare States and their Futures*, Gower Publishing Company Ltd., England, pp. 1-19.

Pant, Niranjan (2000), "Development Agenda for Insurance Regulation", *Economic and Political Weekly*, 35(10), 4 March, pp. 762-64.

Parker, D. (2002), "Economic Regulation: A Review of Issues", *Annals of Public and Cooperative Economics,* 73(4), December, pp. 439-519.

Parker, David (1999), "Regulating Public Utilities Lessons from The U.K. Experience", *International Review of Administrative Sciences*, 65(1), March, pp.117-31.

Parthasarathi, Ashok (2007), "Public Assets, Private Gain", *The Hindustan Times,* June 4, p. 10.

Patel, A.R. (2001), "Insurance: Untapped Rural Market", *Kurukshetra*, 49(10), July, pp. 25-26.

Pearson, Margaret M. (2007), "Governing the Chinese Economy: Regulatory Reform in the Service of the State", *Public Administration Review*, 67(4), July-August, pp. 718-30.

Pillai, Karunakaran G. (1999), "Insurance Regulatory Authority Bill and its Impact", *Yojana*, 43(3), March, pp. 10-13.

Piven, Frances Fox and Richard A. Cloward (1986), "The New Class War in the United States", in Else Oyen (ed.), *Comparing Welfare States and Their Futures*, Gower Publishing Company Ltd., England, pp. 47-63.

Prosser Tony (2001), "Regulating Public Enterprises", *Public Law,* Autumn, pp. 505-26.

Prosser, T. (2004), "Regulation, Markets, and Legitimacy" in J. Jowell and D. Oliver (eds.), *The Changing Constitution*, Oxford University Press, Oxford, pp. 2237-2256.

Prosser, Tony (1985), "Democratisation, Accountability and Institutional Design: Reflections in Public Law", in P. McAuslan and J. McEldowney (eds.), *Law, Legitimacy and the Constitution,* Sweet & Maxwell, London.

Prosser, Tony (1992), "Public Service Broadcasting and Deregulation in UK", *European Journal of Communication*, Vol. 7, pp. 173-93.

Rabin, Robert (1994), "Federal Regulation in Historical Perspective", Peter H. Schuck, *Foundations of Administrative Law*, New York: Oxford University Press, pp. 39-49.

Rajesh Kumar, Singh, Kulwant and Surinder Kumar (2005), "Regulation of Power Sector by Independent Regulator: Haryana Experience", *Journal of Institute of Public Enterprises*, 28(1-2), January-March and April-June, pp. 30-45.

Ralp, Bradburg and Ross R. David (1991), *"Regulation and Deregulation in Industrial Countries*", WPS 699, World Bank, June.

Ramaswami, V. (1959), "Rule of Law and a Planned Society", *Journal of the Indian Law Institute*, No. 2, pp. 31-38.

Ramaswamy M. (1959), "Indian Constitutional Provisions against Barriers to Trade and Commerce Examined in the Light of Australian and American Experience", *Journal of the Indian Law Institute*, No. 2, pp. 321-99.

Ranade, Ajit and Ahuja, Rajeev (2000), "Insurance Industry: Equal Terms for Entrants and Incumbents", *The Times of India*, September 28, p. 14.

Ranade, Ajit and Ahuja, Rajeev (2000), "Issues in Regulation of Insurance", *Economic and Political Weekly*, 35(5), 29 January, pp. 331-38.

Rao, Ch. Sambasiva (2007), "Universalisation of Telecom Services: The Way Forward", *Economic and Political Weekly*, Vol. XLII, No. 43, October 27-November 2, pp. 17-19.

Rao, D. Narasimha and Subhashish Gupta (2006), "Regulatory Framework for Infrastructure", *INRM Policy Brief No. 8*, ADB.

Rao, G.V. (2006), "Reforms in Insurance Sector — The Agenda for Next Decade", *IRDA Journal*, February, pp.18-20.

Rao, R. Nageswar (2005), "Deregulation of Banking and Life Insurance Sector in India — A Comparative Study of the Market Leaders' Challenge", *The Journal of the Institute of Public Enterprise*, Vol. 28, Nos. 3 and 4, July-September, October-December, pp. 181-87.

Rao, S.L. (2000), Electricity Reform and Regulation: Some Issues", *Economic and Political Weekly*, 35(26), 24 June, pp. 2231-234.

Rao, Srinivasan K. (1994), "Insurance Sector Reforms", *The Hindu (Business Law)*, April 20, p. 8.

Rauch, Basil (1963), "The First New Deal", in Morton Keller (ed.), *The New Deal — What Was It?*, Holt Rinehart and Winston Inc., pp. 23-35.

Reich, Charles A. (1965), "Individual Rights and Social Welfare: The Emerging Legal Issues", *Yale Law Journal,* 74, p. 1245.

Reich, Charles A. (1964), "The New Property", *Yale Law Journal,* 73, p. 733.

Reynolds, Larry (1987), "Deregulation with a Difference", *Management Review,* 76, 4, April, pp. 12-13.

Rhodes R.A.W. (1994), "The Hollowing Out of the State: The Changing Nature of Public Service in Britain", *The Political Quarterly*, Vol. 65, No. 2, April-June, pp. 138-54.

Rice, William G. (1959), "Division of Power to Control Commerce between Centre and States in India and in the United States", *Journal of the Indian Law Institute*, No. 1, pp. 151-70.

Richardson, J.E. (1962), "The Control of Monopolies and Restrictive Trade Practices in the United States of America, Canada and the United Kingdom", *Australian Law Journal*, 35, p. 332.

Richardson, Sir Ivor (1991), "Changing Needs for Judicial Decision-Making", *Journal of Judicial Administration*, 1(1), pp. 61-68.

Rimmer, Stephen (2006), "Best Practice Regulations and Licensing as a form of Regulation", *Australian Journal of Public Administration*, 65(2), June, pp. 3-15.

Ripley, Mary Louisa (1987), "Bank Regulatory Authority in China", *International Journal of Public Administration*, Vol. 10, No. 3, pp. 255-314.

Roy, Ash Narain (1996), "Wither Neo-liberalism", *The Hindustan Times*, February 20, p. 13.

Samarajiva, Rohan (2002), "Alternative Regulatory Practices and Alternative Dispute Resolution", in S.K. Sarkar and Vivek Sharma (eds.), *Legal Aspects of Regulation in South Asia*, New Delhi, India: Tata Energy Research Institute, pp. 36-44.

Sankar, T.L. and Ramachandra, Usha (2000), "Regulation of the Indian Power Sector", *ASCT Journal of Management*, 29(2), March, pp. 47-63.

Sarada, A. and Ila Singh (2004), "Regulatory Governance in Infrastructure Sector in India", *Indian Journal of Public Administration*, Vol. L, No. 1, January-March, pp. 236-45.

Sarkar, S.K. (2006), "Regulatory Process in Infrastructure Sectors: Consumer Interest", *Management in Government*, April-June, pp.1-13.

Sawant, P.B. (1998), "Print Media Regulation: In the Regime of the New Information Technology", *Press Council of India Review*, 19(2), April, pp.1-9.

Schiller, Reuel E. (2007), "The Era of Deference: The Courts, Expertise, and the Emergence of New Deal Administrative Law", *Michigan Law Review*, Vol. 106, December, pp. 399-441.

Schoenbrod, David (1999), "Putting the "Law" Back into Environmental Law", *Regulation*, 22(1), Winter, pp. 17-23.

Selznick, P. (1985), "Focusing Organizational Research on Regulation" in R. Noll (ed.), *Regulatory Policy and Social Sciences*, University of California Press, Berkeley, p. 363.

Shastri, C.N.S. (2006), "Men and Boys — How to Tell between the Two in Insurance Markets", *IRDA Journal*, February, pp. 30-31.

Singh, Rajeev (2007), "Power Sector", *Yojana*, Vol. 51, December, pp. 65-67.

Singh, S.N. (1971), "Antitrust Laws of the United States of America", *Journal of the Indian Law Institute*, Vol. 13(4), pp. 581-94.

Singh, S.S. and Suresh Misra (1994), "Public Law Issues in Privatisation Process", *Indian Journal of Public Administration*, Vol. XL, No. 2, pp. 396-410.

Sinha, Tapen (2005), "*An Analysis of the Evolution of Insurance in India*", CRIS Discussion Paper Series.

Skowronek, Stephen (1994), "Building A New Administrative State: The Expansion of National Administrative Capacities, 1877-1920", in Peter H. Schuck, *Foundations of Administrative Law*, New York: Oxford University Press, pp. 33-38.

Smith, Eve Darian and Colin Scott (2009), "Regulation and Human Rights in Socio-Legal Scholarship", *Law and Society,* Vol. 31, No. 3, July, pp. 271-81.

Sodhi, J.S. (2008), "An Analysis of India's Development: Before and After Globalization", *Indian Journal of Industrial Relations*, 49(3), January, pp. 317-54.

Solomon, Jason M. (2008), "Law and Governance in the Twenty-first Century Regulatory State", *Texas Law Review*, 86(4), March, pp. 819-55.

Somerville, R.A. (2004), "Insurance, Consumption and Saving: A Dynamic Analysis in Continuous Time", *American Economic Review*, 94(4), September, pp.1130-40.

Spiller, Pablo T. (1998), "Regulatory Agencies and the Courts" in Newman, P., *Palgrave Dictionary of Law and Economics*, Vol. 3, London: Macmillan.

Stewart, R. (1988), "Regulation and the Crisis of Legalism in the US", in Terence Daintith (ed.), *Law as an Instrument of Economic Policy*,

European University Institute, Series A, Law, No. 7, Firenze: Badia Fiesolana.

Stigler, G.J. (1971), "The Theory of Economic Regulation", *Bell Journal of Economics*, 2, Spring, pp. 3-21.

Stigler, G.J. (1981), "Comments on Joskow and Noll", in G. Fromm (ed.), *Studies in Public Regulation*, Cambridge, MA: MIT Press, pp. 73-77.

Sundar, S. and Sarkar, S.K. (1999), "Privatization and Regulation", *The Economic Times,* 6 May, p. 6.

Sundar, S. and Sarkar, S.K. (2000), "Quality of Services: The Ultimate Objective of Regulation", *ASCT Journal of Management*, 29(2), March, pp. 14-24.

Sundar, S., S.K. Sarkar, and Prerna Kohli (2002), "Regulatory Interface with the Judiciary: The Indian Experience," in S.K. Sarkar and Vivek Sharma (eds.), *Legal Aspects of Regulation in South Asia*, Tata Energy Research Institute, New Delhi, India, pp. 95-112.

Taggart, Michael (1992), "The Impact of Corporatisation and Privatisation on Administrative Law", *Australian Journal of Public Administration*, Vol. 51, No. 3, September, pp. 368-73.

Thatcher, M. (1998), "Institutions, Regulation, and Change: New Regulatory Agencies in the British Privatised Utilities", *West European Politics,* 21(1), pp. 120-47.

Thatcher, Mark (1998), "Regulating the Regulators: The Regulatory Regime of British Privatised Utilities", *Parliamentary Affairs*, 51(2), April, pp. 209-22.

The Editors of the New Republic, "The New Deal in Review 1936-1940", in Morton Keller (ed.) (1963), *The New Deal — What Was It?*, Holt Rinehart and Winston Inc., pp. 59-73.

Tikku, Alok (2007), "PM flays Cancer of Power Theft", *The Hindustan Times,* May 29, p. 1.

Tripathi, Vishwa Nath (2008), "Welfare: The Pension Scheme", *Yojana*, 52, March, pp. 76-77.

Tugwell, Rexford G. (1963), "The New Deal in Retrospect", Morton Keller (ed.), *The New Deal — What Was It?*, Holt Rinehart and Winston Inc., pp. 74-82.

Turnbull, P. (1999), "*Regulation or Re-regulation of Transport?*" Discussion Paper, International Labour Organization, Geneva.

Vadlamannati, Krishna Chaitanya (2008), "Do Insurance Sector Growth and Reform affect Economic Development? Empirical Evidence from India", *Margin — The Journal of Applied Economic Research*, Vol. 2, No. 1, January-March, pp. 43-86.

Venkatramani, S.H. (1996), "The State cannot Wither", *The Hindustan Times*, September 6, p. 13.

Vidushi (2007), "Media Regulation: Strengthening Democracy for an Equitable and Just Society", *Social Action — A Quarterly Review of Social Trends*, Vol. 57, No. 4, October-December, pp. 337-48.

Virmani, Arvind (2006), "India's Economic Growth History: Fluctuations, Trends, Break Points, and Phases", *Indian Economic Review*, Vol. XXXXI, Number 1, January-June, pp. 81-103.

Vittal, N. (1997), "Government Initiatives, Regulation, and Financing of the Telecommunications Sector", *Vikalpa*, 22(1), January-March, pp. 3-9.

Warrick, Smith (1997), "Utility Regulators — Decision-making, Structures, Resources, and Start-up Strategy", Note No. 129 in *Public Policy for the Private Sector*, Washington, D.C.: World Bank Group.

Warrick, Smith (1997), "Utility Regulators: Roles and Responsibilities", Note No. 128 in *Public Policy for the Private Sector*, Washington, D.C.: World Bank Group.

Warrick, Smith (1997), "Utility Regulators: The Independence Debate", Note No. 127 in *Public Policy for the Private Sector*, Washington, D.C.: World Bank Group.

Weidenbaum, Murray (1981), "Regulation: How Washington will Switch", *Nation's Business* (pre-1986), 69, 2, February, pp. 26-29.

Weimer, David L. (2006), "The Puzzle of Private Rulemaking: Expertise, Flexibility, and Blame Avoidance in US Regulation", *Public Administration Review*, 66(4), July-August, pp. 569-82.

Wilks, S. (1996), "Regulatory Compliance and Capitalist Diversity in Europe", *Journal of European Public Policy*, 3, pp. 536-59.

Williams, Robert (2002), "Conduct Unbecoming: The Regulation of Legislative Ethics in Britain and the United States", *Parliamentary Affairs*, 55(4), October, pp. 611-25.

Wilson, James Q. (1975), "The Rise in Bureaucratic State", *The Pubic Interest*, No. 41, Fall, pp. 77-103.

Woolf, Sir Harry (1986), "Public Law-Private Law: Why the Divide? A Personal View", *Public Law, Autumn*, p. 220.

INDEX